W9-DDK-722

Ethnicity and Nationalism

Ethnicity and Nationalism

Theory and Comparison

PAUL R. BRASS

SAGE PUBLICATIONS
New Delhi/Newbury Park/London

Copyright © Paul R. Brass, 1991

All rights reserved. No part of this book may be reproduced or utilised in any form or by any means, electronic or mechanical, including photo-copying, recording or by any information storage or retrieval system, without permission in writing from the publisher.

First Published in 1991 by

Sage Publications India Pvt Ltd
M 32 Greater Kailash Market I
New Delhi 110 048

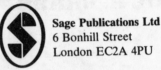

Sage Publications Inc
2455 Teller Road
Newbury Park, California 91320

Sage Publications Ltd
6 Bonhill Street
London EC2A 4PU

Published by Tejeshwar Singh for Sage Publications India Pvt Ltd, photo-typeset by Pagewell Photosetters, Pondicherry, and printed at Chaman Enterprises, Delhi.

Library of Congress Cataloging-in-Publication Data

Brass, Paul R.
    Ethnicity and nationalism : theory and comparison / Paul R. Brass.
        p.   cm.
    Includes bibliographical references and index.
    1. Nationalism. 2. Ethnicity. 3. Ethnic groups—Political activity.
I. Title.
JC311.B73   1991   320.5′4—dc20   91-15766

ISBN: 81–7036–238–5 (India-hb) 0–8039–9694–2 (US-hb)
            81–7036–239–3 (India-pb) 0–8039–9695–0 (US-pb)

Contents

List of Figures and Tables

FIGURES

TABLES

Preface

The nine essays included in this volume were written between 1978 and 1990. All constitute extensions from my earlier work on *Language, Religion, and Politics in North India* published by Cambridge University Press in 1974. They are extensions both theoretically and comparatively. Chapters 1, 2, 8, and 9 are theoretical essays which draw illustrations from multiethnic societies around the world and systematically present the basic theoretical arguments of the volume as a whole.

Two central arguments run through the volume. The first is that ethnicity and nationalism are not 'givens,' but are social and political constructions. They are creations of elites, who draw upon, distort, and sometimes fabricate materials from the cultures of the groups they wish to represent in order to protect their well-being or existence or to gain political and economic advantage for their groups as well as for themselves. The second argument is that ethnicity and nationalism are modern phenomena inseparably connected with the activities of the modern centralizing state.

These arguments separate my position from writers in the field who consider ethnicity and nationalism to be reflections of primordial identities and who have searched the past to find evidence of the existence of ethnic identities and nationalism throughout recorded history.* My position, on the contrary, is that ethnic identity and modern nationalism arise out of specific types of interactions between the leaderships of centralizing states and elites from non-dominant ethnic groups, especially but not

---

* See especially Anthony D. Smith, *The Ethnic Origins of Nations* (Oxford: Basil Blackwell, 1986) and John A. Armstrong, *Nations before Nationalism* (Chapel Hill: University of North Carolina Press, 1982).

exclusively on the peripheries of those states. The occurrence of ethnic mobilization and nationality-formation in centralizing multiethnic states and the particular forms they take when they do occur depend upon the kinds of alliances made between centralizing and regional or other non-dominant elites. Moreover, the alliances are often not two-way, but multiple: many regions in large multi-ethnic states such as India themselves contain a multiplicity of ethnic groups whose elites engage in conflict or cooperation with each other. In such situations, state leaders may either choose neutrality or identification with elites from one ethnic group rather than another or may seek to divide one or both ethnic groups in order to assure the stability of their own power and support within particular regions. I have tried to specify the various possible patterns of conflict, cooperation, and state action and the consequences of the several types in chapter 1 and most systematically in chapter 8.

Although I have drawn examples to illustrate the theoretical arguments from situations around the world, Indian examples and case studies comprise the heart of the volume. Chapter 4 presents a general interpretation of the problems of the centralizing state in India and contrasts the relationships between the center and the states during the Nehru and post-Nehru periods. Chapters 3, 5, and 6 focus specifically on two minority groups in India: north Indian Muslims and the Sikhs of Punjab. The chapter on Muslims focuses particularly on the theoretical question of whether ethnic identity is best explained in primordial or instrumental ways. In it, I show how the central symbols of ethnic identity for Muslims have been influenced by the perspectives and political goals of different elite groups within the Muslim community. The chapters on Punjab focus on the second issue of the relationships between the policies of centralizing state leaders and local ethnic group elites.

A second substantial source of illustrations for the theoretical arguments presented in the book is Eastern Europe and the Soviet Union. It has always seemed to me that Eastern Europe in the nineteenth century, especially in the Habsburg Empire, and the Soviet Union in the twentieth century have provided the closest parallels to India with regard to the multiplicity of cultural groups living side by side, often in conflict with each other and with the authorities in centralizing states. Examples from nineteenth and twentieth century Eastern Europe are used extensively to illustrate the arguments in chapters 1, 2 and 7 especially. Chapter 8 presents a direct comparison of language-based ethnic problems in India and the Soviet Union.

The concluding chapter 9 discusses the issue of conflict resolution in contemporary multiethnic states. Here I argue against the influential consociational perspective, whose proponents see the solutions to ethnic conflicts in the creation of systems of group representation based on the plural cultural segments of these societies. Since my arguments assumes that there are no such things as fixed plural segments in multiethnic societies, but that ethnic identities are always in flux, this 'solution' constitutes to my mind nothing but the freezing of a particular system of elite collaboration and elite advantage. The logic of my position therefore is towards keeping such systems open and in flux while attempting to decentralize the over-centralized states of the contemporary world and de-center ethnic group relations in the process.

I have grouped the essays in three parts. Part I opens with two theoretical chapters and concludes with the case study of Muslim identity in pre-Independence India. Part II focuses on the strains in center–state relations in contemporary Indian politics which have developed especially since the death of Nehru. Chapter 4 in this part provides an overview of center–state relations in India since independence, while chapters 5 and 6 focus on the Punjab crisis and its implications for the future of Indian unity. Part III brings together the arguments on the relationship between ethnic groups and the state in a theoretical chapter 7, a comparative analysis of India and the Soviet Union in chapter 8, and a critique of the consociational solution in chapter 9.

All the previously published essays have been edited and revised specifically for this volume. In some cases, only minor editorial changes were required to correct errors, update footnotes, alter verb tenses, and take note of recent political changes. In other cases, more extensive revisions have been done to introduce new examples and to update tables and text. Chapter 9 has never been published before.

Seattle, Washington   PAUL R. BRASS
August 1990

——————————————————————— I

Ethnic Groups and Nationalities: The Formation, Persistence, and Transformation of Ethnic Identities Over Time

Introduction

The first two chapters of this book originated as a theoretical extension of my work on ethnicity and nationalism in India, first published in *Language, Religion, and Politics in North India* in 1974. A very concise statement of the theoretical arguments was first published in the September 1976 issue of the journal, *Ethnicity*, a longer version with examples drawn mainly from Eastern Europe as the introductory chapter in Peter F. Sugar (ed.), *Ethnic Diversity and Conflict in Eastern Europe*, published in 1980. For purposes of this volume, further illustrative material mainly from South Asia has been incorporated, some minor editorial changes have been made, and the essay has been divided into two chapters.

The principal arguments have remained unaltered. They may be summarized in a few main points. The first relates to the variability of ethnic identities. The point of view taken in them is that there is nothing inevitable about the rise of ethnic identity and its trans- formation into nationalism among the diverse peoples of the contemporary world. Rather, the conversion of cultural differences into bases for political differentiation between peoples arises only under specific circumstances which need to be identified clearly.

The circumstances in which this conversion occurs constitute the theoretical focus of these chapters and of the book as a whole. The theoretical argument comprises two central ideas. The first is the theory of elite competition as the basic dynamic which precipitates ethnic conflict under specific conditions, which arise from the broader political and economic environments rather than from the cultural values of the ethnic groups in question. The theory is consistent with the assumption that ethnic identity is itself a vari- able, rather than a fixed or 'given' disposition. It is also consistent with some important works published in history and the social sciences during the past decade, which point to the ways in which traditions are invented[1] and social realities constructed.

The second theoretical argument emphasizes the critical role of the relationships established between elites and the state, particularly the roles of collaborators with and opponents of state authority and state intrusion into regions inhabited by distinctive ethnic groups. The term elite used in this book refers to influential subgroups within ethnic groups and classes. Lasswell defined elites as 'those who get the most of what there is to get,' the latter being defined in turn in relation to 'deference, income, and safety.'[2] In some circumstances, particularly when referring to subgroups within ethnic groups, the terms elite and class may coincide. For example, in pre-modern societies, where land is the most valued resource, the aristocracy is likely to be the most influential group, the primary elite group within its ethnic group. On the other hand, religious elites in such societies—the clerics, the learned and holy men—may come from different class backgrounds. Similarly, in modernizing societies, senior administrative and military officers may come from both the landed and the urban middle classes. They constitute privileged multiclass elites within their societies, though in some cases the bulk of the senior civil servants and military officers may come from one or another dominant class in the broader society.

Within social classes, it is also possible to distinguish those who are more or less influential. Within the middle classes, rich and famous attorneys are often particularly influential. Educated elites also often constitute an influential group within the middle classes and very frequently take the lead in ethnic movements demanding recognition for particular languages. Finally, following Michels, the leaders of most political organizations tend also to constitute elites in relation to the rank and file and the mass of voters who follow their lead.

The argument concerning the critical importance of the relationships established between particular elite groups and state authorities is sketched in chapter 1 of this volume and elaborated further in the concluding chapter of the volume as a whole. Since the writing of the two essays in which this argument was first developed, an important new book which takes up the same theme was published by John Breuilly, *Nationalism and the State* (Chicago: University of Chicago Press, 1982).

There is a third theoretical theme in these two chapters from which I have moved away somewhat in my later writing on this topic. When I wrote *Language, Religion, and Politics in North India*, the only systematic theory of nationalism available was Deutsch's theory of social communications, whose central argument was that the existence of a socially mobilized population within a distinctive ethnic group was a precondition for the development of nationalism among its members. I used Deutsch's theory centrally in *Language, Religion, and Politics*, though I became aware of the importance of political leadership as an independent force in the process of writing that book. While I am still not prepared to entirely discard the relevance of Deutsch's arguments, my emphasis on political factors and upon the role of state authorities in influencing the development of ethnic communities and nationalities has increased and is more marked in the concluding chapter of this volume. It also appears clearer to me now that political mobilization of traditional rural communities can occur in modernizing societies in the absence of fully developed systems of mass communication, especially through traditional networks of religious communication.

It follows from the assumption of ethnic variability and from the nature of the dynamics out of which ethnic identities are produced that the process of ethnic identity formation has consequences for the very definition of the ethnic group in question and for its persistence. The cultural forms, values, and practices of ethnic groups become political resources for elites in competition for political power and economic advantage. They become symbols and referents for the identification of members of the group, which are called up in order to create a political identity more easily. The symbols used to create a political identity also can be shifted to adjust to political circumstances and the limitations imposed by state authorities. If the authorities impose a ban on the use of religious symbols for political purposes, elites may turn to the distinctive language of the religious group, if it has one, or may emphasize slight differences of dialect which will serve the same purpose of differentiating the group from others.

In the process of transforming cultural forms, values, and practices into political symbols, elites in competition with each other for control over the allegiance or territory of the ethnic group in question strive to enhance or break the solidarity of the group. Elites seeking to mobilize the ethnic group against its rivals or against the centralizing state strive to promote a congruence of a multiplicity of the group's symbols, to argue that members of the group are different not in one respect only, but in many and that all its cultural elements are reinforcing. All members of the group, it is said, either do or ought to practice the same religion, speak the same language, wear the same kind of clothes, eat the same foods, and sing the same songs. Elites seeking to challenge the authenticity of an ethnic group's claim for individuality will do the opposite and argue that the members of the group in question are, in fact, divided by one or more of these several criteria and that they share some of them with other ethnic groups.

It follows, finally, from all these points that the process of ethnic identity formation and its transformation into nationalism is reversible. It is reversible because of both the dynamics of external competition and the internal divisions and contradictions which exist within all groups of people, however defined. Political and economic circumstances may cause elites to downplay or discard the symbolic manipulation of cultural forms, values, and practices and to instead seek cooperation with other groups or collaboration with the state authorities. Elites and others within the group also may resist both the political distortions of the group's culture and the attempts to impose arbitrary cultural congruities where they do not in fact exist.

The arguments just outlined, which are elaborated in the rest of this volume, fall clearly into the 'instrumentalist' rather than the 'primordialist' view of ethnic identity formation. Ethnic identity formation is seen in this volume as a process created in the dynamics of elite competition within the boundaries determined by political and economic realities. My arguments, however, fall short of the most extreme instrumentalist views associated with some proponents of rational choice theory, who transform all choices, including cultural ones, into economic choices. My aim is in no way to disregard or discard the cultural forms, values, and practices of distinctive ethnic groups as unimportant. On the contrary, my purpose is to show that political and economic elites who make use of ethnic group attributes are constrained by the beliefs and values which exist within the group and which limit the kinds of appeals which can be made. At the same time, the process by which elites mobilize ethnic identities simplifies those beliefs and values, distorts them, and selects those which are politically useful rather than central to the belief systems of the people in question. Insofar as political elites succeed in mobilizing an ethnic group by such means, the ethnic community or nation created in this way does not necessarily constitute an entirely new entity but one that has been transformed, whose boundaries have in some ways been widened, in other ways confined.

All these arguments are illustrated in the case study of aspects of ethnic identity among South Asian Muslims in chapter 3 of this part. It is argued that instrumentalist rather than primordialist explanations serve to explain better the rise of Muslim separatism in South Asia. It is shown how Muslim ethnic identity evolved out of elite competition between Hindus and Muslims. Also demonstrated is how different definitions of the Muslim community were articulated by distinct elites within the group. Finally, it is also shown how political mobilization among the Muslims involved selective attention to particular symbols of identity and efforts to bring a multiplicity of such symbols into congruence with each other.

NOTES

1. Eric Hobsbawm and Terence Ranger (eds.), *The Invention of Tradition* (Cambridge: Cambridge University Press, 1983).
2. Harold D. Lasswell, *Politics: Who Gets What, When, How* (New York: Meridian Books, 1958), p. 13.

Ethnic Groups and Ethnic Identity Formation

There are three ways of defining ethnic groups—in terms of objective attributes, with reference to subjective feelings, and in relation to behavior. An objective definition assumes that though no specific attribute is invariably associated with all ethnic categories, there must be some distinguishing cultural feature that clearly separates one group of people from another, whether that feature or features be language, territory, religion, color, diet, dress, or any of them. The problem with objective definitions is that it is usually extremely difficult to determine the boundaries of ethnic categories in this way.[1] The difficulty with subjective definitions is that they make it impossible to answer the basic question of how a group of people arrives at subjective self-consciousness in the first place. Behavioral definitions are really a form of objective definition since they assume that there are specific, concrete ways in which ethnic groups behave or do not behave, particularly in relation to and in interaction with other groups. Behavioral definitions merely suggest that there are cultural differences between ethnic groups, but that the critical distinctions reveal themselves only in interaction with other groups.[2] But, the existence of explicit codes of behavior and interaction is rather more characteristic, more all-pervasive, and more evident in simple than in complex societies in which people may establish their separateness with reference to specific attributes without adopting an entirely distinct code of behavior.

Subjective definitions will not, therefore, serve the analytical purposes of this book, which is to specify the conditions for the formation, persistence, and transformation of ethnic identities over time, whereas interactive definitions lack the universality required. The most appropriate definition for the aims of this book is one that begins with objective cultural markers but which also recognizes that they are susceptible to change and variation. Any group of people dissimilar from other peoples in terms of objective cultural criteria and containing within its membership, either in principle or in practice, the elements for a complete division of labor and for reproduction forms an ethnic category. The objective cultural markers may be a language or dialect, distinctive dress or diet or customs, religion or race. The inclusion in the definition of the phrase 'contains within its membership, either in principle or in practice, the elements for a complete division of labor and for reproduction' is designed to emphasize the cultural basis of ethnicity and to distinguish ethnic categories from other social categories based on class or gender or age grades.

Ethnicity is a sense of ethnic identity, which has been defined by De Vos as consisting of the 'subjective, symbolic or emblematic use' by 'a group of people . . . of any aspect of culture, in order to differentiate themselves from other groups.'[3] This definition can be used for the analytic purposes required here by altering the last phrase to read 'in order to create internal cohesion and differentiate themselves from other groups.' An ethnic group that uses cultural symbols in this way is a subjectively self-conscious *community* that establishes criteria for inclusion into and exclusion from the group. At this point, matters of descent, birth, and a sense of kinship may become important to ethnic group members, for the methods of inclusion and exclusion into the group often involve the explicit or tacit adoption of rules of endogamy and exogamy. Ethnicity or ethnic identity also involves, in addition to subjective self-consciousness, a claim to status and recognition, either as a superior group or as a group at least equal to other groups. Ethnicity is to ethnic category what class consciousness is to class.

Ethnicity is an alternative form of social organization and identification to class, but it is a contingent and changeable status that, like class, may or may not be articulated in particular contexts or at particular times.[4] Ethnic groups that use ethnicity to make demands in the political arena for alteration in their status, in their economic well-being, in their civil rights, or in their educational opportunities are engaged in a form of interest group politics which became prominent in the United States during the 1960s and 1970s and which sought to improve the well-being of group members as individuals.[5] However, some ethnic groups in other contexts go further and demand that corporate rights be conceded to the group as a whole, that they be given not just individual educational opportunities on the same basis as others, but that they be given control over the public system of education in their areas of concentration so that they can teach the history, language, and culture of their group to their own children. They demand a major say for the group in the political system as a whole or control over a piece of territory within the country, or they demand a country of their own with full sovereignty. In the latter case, the ethnic group aspires to national status and recognition. Insofar as it succeeds by its own efforts in achieving any one of these goals either within an existing state or in a state of its own, it has become a nationality or a nation.[6] A nation, therefore, may be seen as a particular type of ethnic community[7] or, rather, as an ethnic community politicized, with recognized group rights in the political system.[8]

Nations may be created by the transformation of an ethnic group in a multiethnic state into a selfconscious political entity or by the amalgamation of diverse groups and the formation of an inter-ethnic, composite or homogeneous national culture through the agency of the modern state. Although the two processes of nation-formation have different starting points and raise quite different kinds of analytical and theoretical questions, the end result historically has been sometimes the same, and the two processes have much in common.[9] In both cases, the effort is made to give subjective and symbolic meanings to merely objective distinctions between peoples and to increase the number of attributes and symbolic referents that they have in common with each other and that distinguish them from other groups. Ethnic nationalism and state-centered nationalism may be seen, therefore, as subtypes of a more general process of identity formation, defined as the process of intensifying the subjective meanings of a multiplicity of symbols and of striving to achieve multisymbol congruence among a group of people defined initially by one or more central symbols, whether those symbols are ethnic attributes or loyalty to a particular state.[10] More often than not, ethnic demands center initially around a single central symbol, such as language, religion, territory, or color. In the movement to create greater internal cohesion and to press more effectively ethnic demands against rival groups, ethnic and nationalist elites increasingly stress the variety of ways in which the members of the group are similar to each other and collectively different from others. This effort, however, creates its own problems because the selection of additional symbols inevitably involves either the loss of potential adherents or the need to persuade or coerce group members to change their language, religion, behavior, or dress. It also may lead nationalist leaders into expansionist military adventures and conflicts with other states when the drive to achieve multisymbol congruence involves irredentist claims. It is important to recognize that this striving for multisymbol congruence is pursued by ethnic group leaders as much as by state-builders. If the process is more or less successful, the nationality created out of an ethnic group is sure to be quite a different social formation from the initial group.

The process of nationality-formation may or may not be pursued to the point where political structures are made congruent with the nationality by creating an autonomous or independent selfgoverning entity. Similarly, the process of nation-building by state authorities may or may not succeed in creating relatively homogeneous national groups congruent with the territorial boundaries of the state. More often than not, ethnic groups that come into conflict in multiethnic societies reach accommodations with each other. State authorities also usually find that it is politically wiser to recognize and tolerate some forms of cultural diversity rather than impose a total uniformity by forcible means. Tolerance of diversity may take the form of recognition of the corporate rights of ethnic groups within the state or the removal of specific symbols from the concept of the nation and their relegation to the private sphere as, for example, happened with religion in the United States. However, both processes of nationality-formation and state-building may be pushed beyond pluralist accommodations to extreme, even pathological limits, to expulsions, counter-expulsions, the exchange of population groups and even to genocide.

Although the processes of forming nationalities out of ethnic groups and of building national cultures to conform with state boundaries are similar in many respects, the principal interest here centers on outlining more precisely the process of nationality-formation rather than the process of state-building, and on developing a theory to account for the reasons why some ethnic groups become communities or nationalities and pursue successfully their social, economic, and political goals while others do not. The process of nationality-formation is one in which objective differences between ethnic groups acquire increasingly subjective and symbolic significance, are translated into a consciousness of, and a desire for, group solidarity, and become the basis for successful political demands. There are two stages in the development of a nationality. The first is the movement from ethnic category to community. Depending on the context, this stage may involve such changes as the creation of a selfconscious language community out of a group of related speakers,[11] the formation of a caste association from a caste category, or a community of believers from the followers of a particular religious leader. The subjective meanings of symbols of identity are intensified and become more relational (interpersonal) than personal or instrumental. Language becomes not merely a means of communication, but a priceless heritage of group culture; religion becomes not only a matter of personal belief and of a relationship between a person and a deity, but a collective experience that unites believers to each other; familiar places and historical sites become sacred shrines and 'freedom trails'.[12] At this stage also the effort to bring multiple symbols in congruence begins. The leaders of the movement to create a language community may, at the same time, stake a claim to the dominance of that language in a particular territory; the supporters of the demands for a religious community may also seek protection for the language or script in which their religious texts are written and may promote the identification of the language with the religion and encourage its increasing use by all believers.

This process of development of communities from ethnic categories is particularly associated with the early stages of modernization in multiethnic societies where languages have not yet become standardized, where religious groups have not become highly structured and compartmentalized, and where social fragmentation is prevalent. However, the transition may occur even in postindustrial societies such as the United States, where Negroes have become Blacks, Mexican-Americans Chicanos, and many other ethnic groups have rediscovered their origins and identities.

The second stage in the transformation of ethnic groups involves the articulation and acquisition of social, economic, and political rights for the members of the group or for the group as a whole. Depending upon the perceived needs and demands of the group, its size and distribution, its relations with other groups, and the political context, demands may aim at relatively modest civil, educational, and political rights and opportunities for the individual members of the group or for recognition of the group's corporate existence as a political body or nationality. Insofar as an ethnic group succeeds by its own efforts in achieving and maintaining group rights through political action and political mobilization, it has gone beyond ethnicity to establish itself as a nationality.

The delineation of the process of nationality-formation in this manner suggests several problems that require explanation. First, what are the conditions under which ethnic groups become communities and under which ethnic demands, ethnic competition, and ethnic conflict take place? Second, what are the conditions under which an ethnic community is likely to make the major demand for status as a nationality and what are the requirements for success? Third, how does one explain the transformations that take place in the culture, behavior, and boundaries of a people as it undergoes the movement from ethnic group to nationality? Fourth, since it is also evident that ethnic and nationality movements frequently ebb and flow over time within the same group, how can one explain the resurgence of ethnicity and nationalism among diverse groups of people at different times and in different places? The focus of the remainder of this chapter will be on the first two questions, but the analysis will also touch, at several places, on the last two.

ETHNIC DIFFERENTIATION: FROM ETHNIC GROUPS TO COMMUNITIES

The movement from ethnic group to community is a transition that some groups never make, that others make initially in modern times, and that still others undergo repeatedly at different points in time. In the first category are the various 'lost' peoples and speakers of diverse dialects who have merged into or are merging into other peoples—the Cornish in the United Kingdom, the Frisians in Holland, the Sorbs and Wends of Eastern and Central Europe, the Maithili-speaking people and numerous other dialect-speakers in north India. In the second category are the newly-formed ethnic groups and nationalities of the nineteenth and twentieth centuries— the Welsh and the Irish, the nationalities in Austria-Hungary, the Ibos in Nigeria, the Naga tribes in northeastern India and most of the language communities of contemporary India, the Malays in Malaysia. In the last category are the ancient peoples of the world, Jews, Han Chinese, Egyptians, and the major nationalities of Western Europe.

What are the conditions that determine whether or not one group will merge into another group, or will establish or reestablish and redefine its identity? The richness of a group's cultural heritage, the stage of development of its language, and the distinctiveness of its religious beliefs do not by themselves predetermine that one group of people will be more internally solidary than another and will be more likely to perpetuate itself through time. Absence of or loss of a distinctive language has not prevented Blacks in the United States or Celtic groups in the United Kingdom, or non-Hebrew, non-Yiddish speaking Jews in the United States from acquiring or maintaining a sense of ethnic identity. By the same token, over the centuries in Europe, old, fully standardized, written languages—Latin, Anglo-Saxon, Provencal, Low German, Church Slavonic—some of them spoken by peoples occupying compact geographical areas, have been 'submerged' while other languages have replaced or absorbed them.[13] Moreover, despite the fact that European culture, civilization, and science have for centuries been dominated increasingly by the three great languages, English, French, and German, this has not prevented 'the growth of linguistic diversity in Europe from 16 [standard] languages in 1800 to 30 in 1900 and to 53 in 1937'[14] and the attendant development of language communities among many of them.

Distinctive minority religious groups in modern times have often developed into ethnically selfconscious communities, but it has also often happened, particularly in Eastern Europe and in South Asia, that religious differences have been used or even created to establish or emphasize between peoples barriers that have nonreligious origins. The attempt to establish a Uniate Church in Bulgaria, which culminated in the development of a separate hierarchy of Eastern Orthodoxy, has over time served to reinforce the ethnic separateness of Bulgarians from Greeks, but it was not religious distinctiveness that intially inspired the rise of Bulgarian ethnic consciousness. Islam in non-Muslim states has often provided a strong basis for Muslim separatism, but again it is not the distinctiveness of Islam as such in relation to other religions that is decisive, for the degree of Muslim communal selfconsciousness varies in different contexts. For example, in Eastern Europe, Islam has served more effectively as a basis for ethnic separatism in Yugoslavia than in Albania.[15] Nor can Jewish religious distinctiveness explain Jewish ethnic separatism that culminated in Zionism, for often enough Jews chose to assimilate in Eastern Europe when conditions were favorable. In South Asia, Sikhism as a distinctive religion has its origins in the early sixteenth century, but it was not until the late nineteenth and early twentieth centuries that a militant body of believers began the process that continues up to the present day, i.e., of shaping and defining the boundaries of the Sikh community to conform to a particular view of Sikh orthodoxy and instilling in large segments of the Sikh population a sense of communal solidarity and separateness from Hindus.[16]

The process of creating communities from ethnic groups involves the selection of particular dialects or religious practices or styles of dress or historical symbols from a variety of available alternatives. It will be shown below that it is always the case that particular social groups, leaders, or elites stand to benefit and others to lose from the choices that are made.

Ethnicity and Elite Competition

Ethnic communities are created and transformed by particular elites in modernizing and in postindustrial societies undergoing dramatic social change. This process invariably involves competition and conflict for political power, economic benefits, and social status between competing elite, class, and leadership groups both within and among different ethnic categories. Several scholars of ethnicity and nationality have pointed out that modernization and industrialization in large, multiethnic societies tend to proceed unevenly and often, if not always, benefit some ethnic groups or some regions of a country more than others.[17] However, inequality between different ethnic groups or culturally distinct regions does

not by itself spur the development of communal or national consciousness. Speakers of an unstandardized local dialect in a
backward rural region of a modernizing country may very well go
on speaking their language and cultivating their fields without
becoming concerned that their language is being neglected and
without developing any sense of solidarity.[18] They may do so either
because they are completely in the backwash of modernization,
remote from urban lifestyles and only marginally affected by new
educational opportunities and new means of mass communication
and transportation, or because the locally powerful economic,
religious, and political elites find it to their advantage to cooperate
with external authorities and adopt the language and culture of the
dominant ethnic group in order to maintain or enhance their own
power. Relevant examples here are the Anglicized Welsh aristocracy in Wales in the nineteenth century, the Polonized Lithuanian
nobility in Lithuania, and the Magyarized Romanian nobility in
Transylvania. This kind of cooperation between internal elites and
external authorities usually leads to a situation of persistent ethnic
differences among the mass of the people, but without the articulation of ethnic demands.

Ethnic selfconsciousness, ethnically-based demands, and ethnic
conflict can occur only if there is some conflict either between
indigenous and external elites and authorities or between indigenous
elites. Four sources of elite conflict that may spur the development
of ethnic communalism or separatism in preindustrial or early
modernizing societies are those (a) between a local aristocracy
attempting to maintain its privileges against an alien conqueror;
(b) between competing religious elites from different ethnic
groups; (c) between religious elites and the native aristocracy
within an ethnic group; and (d) between native religious elites and
an alien aristocracy.

Local aristocracy versus alien conqueror

Most alien conquerors in preindustrial societies strive to gain
control over the land and landholders by either imposing a new
aristocracy or gaining the collaboration of the old aristocracy or by
establishing a direct relationship between the state and the peasantry.

Where any such effort is successful, as with the imposition by the Habsburgs of a predominantly non-Czech, Catholic landlord class in the Czech lands in the seventeenth century, the development of ethnic consciousness among the conquered people may be delayed until industrial development leads to the formation of new social classes.[19] Where the conqueror lacks the degree of control necessary to achieve one of these goals and the native aristocracy lacks the military strength to establish its independence though retaining its control over the land, the nobility may promote an indigenous ethnic separatism to support its local dominance. A leading example of this type of development in Eastern Europe is what Barany has called the 'aristocratic nationalism' promoted by the Magyar nobility in the nineteenth century.[20] The Romanian boyars in Moldavia and Wallachia in the eighteenth and early nineteenth centuries also used symbols of Romanian nationalism as a basis for preserving and extending their own privileges under Ottoman rule.[21] The success of a native aristocracy in this regard will depend on its relations with the tenantry and on its ability to prevent alliances forming between its tenants and the state authorities to undermine its local control. The Polish aristocracy was far less successful than its Magyar counterpart and found in both the 1830 and 1863 rebellions that it could not carry with it most of the Polish-speaking and, even less, the non-Polish speaking peasantry of the former eastern territories of the Polish commonwealth.[22]

Interethnic competition between religious elites

A second type of interethnic elite conflict may occur when the dominant external group attempts to impose its religion or permits proselytizing activities among an indigenous population. In that case, the local religious elites will naturally move quickly to defend their interests in promoting ethnic consciousness by attempting to arouse their followers in defense of the native religious system. Such competitive proselytization has, of course, been endemic for centuries in the East European countries in the conflicts among Catholic, Orthodox, and Islamic groups and in South Asia among Hindu, Muslim, Sikh, and Christian elements especially since British rule.

Intraethnic competition between native aristocracies and religious elites

The third type of elite competition is intraethnic. When a native aristocracy collaborates with an external or colonial authority, it may or may not adopt the religion of the external group, but it almost always adopts and promotes the alien culture in a way that threatens the authority of indigenous religious leaders. This kind of division between traditional religious elites and native landlords is a common early cleavage that has spurred movements of ethnic communalism. In Wales, the Nonconformist ministers emerged to lead the Nonconformist tenantry in struggles against the Anglican, Anglicized Welsh landlord class.[23] In north India, the *ulema* parted company with the local collaborationist Muslim aristocracy when the latter promoted the establishment of a modern, English-medium college that would take the education of the sons of the elite out of their hands.[24] In Ceylon (Sri Lanka), the establishment of Christian missionary schools and the Europeanization of the lifestyles of the collaborationist elite threatened the hold Buddhist monks had over the people. These monks worked within a competitive network of Sinhalese vernacular schools and Buddhist colleges.[25]

Competition between indigenous religious elites and alien aristocracies

In Eastern Europe, the fourth type of competition, i.e., between indigenous religious elites and local, but alien aristocracies was more common than intraethnic rivalries. Thus, in non-Magyar areas of Austria-Hungary under ⸱e control of the Magyar nobility, such as Slovakia and Transylvania, and in the Balkans under Ottoman rule where the Turks controlled the land, as in Serbia and Bulgaria, ethnic identities and the early stages of nationalism were promoted by parish priests and 'the native lower clergy.'[26] Sometimes interethnic and intraethnic conflicts of this sort merge in complex ways, as in Transylvania in the eighteenth century where the Orthodox and Uniate clergy sustained a sense of Romanian ethnic identity among a peasantry dominated by an oppressive Magyar and Magyarized Romanian aristocracy. Many of the Orthodox clergy themselves were hardly distinguishable from the peasants whom they served and they resented the privileged position which the Protestant and Catholic churches and clergy were accorded in the area. Their desire to enhance their own status and their identification with the interests of the peasantry suffering at the hands of the Calvinist and Catholic Magyar nobility led some of them into a union with the Roman Catholic Church (the Uniate Church) and to an effort to gain support from the Habsburg Court for improvements in the status of the Romanian peasantry.[27]

Elite competition and ethnic transformation

It is with such conflicts either between competing landholders and alien conquerors, between competing religious elites, or between religious leaders and local aristocracies that the first stages of ethnic transformation often begin. In the latter two cases, the conflicts spur movements of religious revivalism which seek two objectives that are critical for the shaping of ethnic boundaries, namely, the removal from indigenous religious practices and beliefs of alien forms derived from interaction with other religions along with the promotion of education in either the vernacular language or the language of the scriptures. If the dominant indigenous elite is collaborationist and there is only one external alien authority or group, the local counterelite will be in a position exclusively to manipulate ethnic particularist symbols to challenge the leadership of its rivals and it will appeal to alternative social classes in doing so. Thus, the religious counterelite will have the edge in capturing the allegiance of the masses as modernization proceeds and it will promote the education of new classes in the vernacular language, whose support will ultimately be brought to bear in overthrowing the old elite.

However, in external colonial situations where a multiplicity of ethnic groups are often in competition with each other, the native collaborationist aristocracy may itself manipulate ethnic symbols in order to mobilize group support to maintain its lead over counterelites from another ethnic group. For example, in north India, the Muslim aristocracy, whose leading figures collaborated with the British authorities, sought to protect their privileges against rising Hindu elites and manipulated the symbols of language and religion in order to do so. The result was that there were two elite groups in the Muslim community, the native aristocracy and the *ulema*, competing with each other and with the Hindus in the mobilization of the Muslim masses on the basis of ethnic appeals.[28]

Language, religion, and ethnic group differentiation. Where both religious and linguistic symbols are potential bases for differentiating one ethnic group from another, it is easy to understand how the process of promoting multisymbol congruence begins. In early modernizing societies it is often, however, a mistake to assume either that such symbols are likely to be congruent to begin with or that it is a pre-existing congruence that predisposes ethnic groups towards differentiation and conflict. Rather, it is more often the case that the choice of the leading symbol of differentiation depends upon the interests of the elite group that takes up the ethnic cause.[29] Religious elites will usually select the group's religion as the leading symbol and language will be used, insofar as possible, as a secondary reinforcing symbol of unity. Moreover, the religious elites will attempt to promote the congruence of language with religion by promoting education and by publishing religious pamphlets in the vernacular. Thus, in Transylvania at the end of the seventeenth century, Orthodox Romanians established the Romanian Uniate Church. In the middle of the eighteenth century, the monks at a monastery in Blaj established a printing press for the publication of books in Romanian. They also proceeded to emphasize the Latin origin of the Romanian language, 'two of the seminarians composed a Romanian grammar' in 1780, and the Latin alphabet was adopted to replace the Cyrillic script. In this way, Romanian ethnic consciousness came to be based upon the dual symbols of religion and language.[30]

However, where the clergy itself is ethnically stratified, the lower clerics may adopt language—the 'language of the people' versus the liturgical language—as its central symbol and demand that a separate church be established congruent with the language of the ethnic community. Thus, in the eighteenth century Bulgarian monks resisted the dominance of the Greek Orthodox clerics and the Greek liturgy by promoting the development of the Bulgarian popular language and a separate Bulgarian church.[31] In Yugoslavia, the religious difference between Croatian Catholics and Orthodox Serbs has been reinforced linguistically by the use of the Latin alphabet by Croats and the Cyrillic script by Serbs to write the common Serbo-Croatian language.

In some cases it is easier to promote such a congruence of linguistic and religious symbols than in others. The strength of modern Polish nationalism, based primarily on language,[32] has been reinforced by the fact that nearly all Poles are also Catholics and are to be distinguished, therefore, on both linguistic and religious grounds from other Slav peoples.[33] However, such a congruence was never achieved in Albania where ethnic consciousness has been based upon language in the face of continued religious diversities.[34] In Slovakia, the existence of a significant Protestant minority less receptive to Slovak ethnic appeals than the majority Roman Catholic population constituted a political obstacle to the achievement of Slovak demands during the interwar period when many Slovak Protestants supported the idea of 'Czechoslovakism'[35] instead.

In Sri Lanka during British rule and after independence, the Buddhist monks supported the cause of the Sinhalese language and promoted the reestablishment of a Buddhist–Sinhalese identity relatively easily because the collaborationist elite on the island became both Anglicized in language and Christianized in style of life if not always in religion, and because the principal competing ethnic group on the island was Hindu and spoke Tamil. Yet, even in the case of Sri Lanka, what has occurred has not been the emergence of a 'given' identity, but the transformation of an old one. Where previously to be Sinhalese implied being Buddhist, now to be Buddhist implies being Sinhalese. Although the same two symbols are being used, the implications of the reversal of priorities are different. Because of the Westernization of some local elite groups it could no longer be assumed that all Sinhalese-speakers were Buddhists. The new identity changes the boundaries of the group by making religion the central symbol and language secondary.[36]

The promotion of religious–linguistic congruence is often more difficult than in the Buddhist–Sinhalese case. Sometimes, as in the case of the Muslims of India, the religious community appealed to may be too diverse linguistically for such a strategy to be effective. There, the attempt was made to promote the Urdu language as a secondary symbol of Muslim identity, but the effort had meaning only in the north and failed miserably among Bengali Muslims.[37]

Moreover, in the course of development of a people from an

ethnic category to a community or to a nation, communal and
nationalist leaders may emphasize different symbols and promote
alternative conceptions of the group's boundaries. For example, in
the development of the Greek nation from the nineteenth century
up to the present time, competing ideas of the boundaries of the
nation have appeared, depending upon how Greek leaders have
chosen to combine the three symbols of Greek Orthodoxy, the
Greek language, and Greek descent from the Hellenic peoples of
antiquity.[38] Some Greek leaders confined their nationalist aspirations to the creation of a political unit congruent with that group
of people who were both Orthodox and spoke Greek. However,
from 1830 until 1922, a larger vision prevailed among Greek
nationalists that impelled them to strive for the expansion of the
Greek state to conform more with the classical boundaries of
Hellenic civilization. Such an expanded Greek state would have
included peoples who followed Greek Orthodox rites but did not
speak Greek, Greek-speakers who were not Orthodox, and many
peoples of presumed Hellenic stock who were neither Greek
Orthodox nor spoke Greek. This irredentist and expansionist
vision of a Greek state was given its death blow in the war with
Turkey during 1921–22, which led not to territorial expansion but
to the exchange of Greek and Turkish populations. Contemporary
Greek nationalism is based on the narrower conception of the
Greek nation consisting of only those who are both Orthodox and
speak Greek. Inclusion of the island of Cyprus within the Greek
nation rests on these grounds rather than on the recreating of a
pan-Hellenic civilization.

Elite competition in modernizing societies. In other instances
religious differences are not a factor in the inevitable competition
for new opportunities in multiethnic modernizing societies and the
principal ethnic differences are based on caste, tribe, or language.
In these cases, if the native aristocracy is not collaborationist, its
leading members may promote the language and culture of the
group, but if it is collaborationist or has been imposed or is
ineffectual, then the development of ethnic consciousness will
depend upon the creation of new elites and social classes emerging
out of the modernization process itself as literacy spreads, urbanization takes place, industrialization begins, and government
employment opportunities open up. The development of ethnic

consciousness among Czech middle class leaders in the industrial centers of Bohemia in the early eighteenth century belongs to this type.[39]

In early modernizing colonial and ex-colonial societies, government employment is often the critical factor in the growth of ethnic rivalries because it provides the authorities with a means both to reward the sons of the collaborationist aristocracy and to create new collaborationist groups by distributing opportunities unevenly, whether intentionally or unintentionally. If government employment expands rapidly enough and other employment opportunities keep pace, while literacy and urbanization are kept relatively low, then such a system of authority may perpetuate itself for some time without severe ethnic conflict. However, usually fairly soon, the social mobilization of backward ethnic groups begins to move more rapidly than the creation of new job opportunities. At this point, the classic problem of the developing or modernizing society occurs: that of the discontent of the educated unemployed.

Where caste, tribal, or linguistic differences exist to separate ethnically the relatively disadvantaged aspirant elite groups from their competitors in the dominant group, these differences will be the basis for a special claim for jobs and other advantages. Such demands are usually associated with efforts to mobilize the disadvantaged ethnic group and to create a new sense of identity among its members. At this point also, the process of intensifying and multiplying the points of difference between the disadvantaged group and the dominant group may begin. A disadvantaged caste group may claim that the dominant group is really culturally different and descends from alien intruders and that it alone represents the true and indigenous culture.[40] A tribe or linguistic group may do the same, and those aspirant elites who manage to find employment in schools and colleges may strive to assert the distinctiveness of their mother tongue, may seek to standardize it, and may uncover lost or neglected treasures written in their language to demonstrate its greatness. If the speakers of the language are geographically concentrated, then a claim will be made for the dominance of the language as the medium of education in the schools and the administration in the relevant territory.

Although elite conflict and job competition are common in modernizing societies, they do not always impel distinctive cultural groups towards ethnic differentiation. The process of modernization may produce so great an imbalance between one group and another that many ethnic groups may become assimilated to another language and culture. This can happen, however, only if government policy also works to favor one group over another, particularly with regard to the medium of education in the schools. Such a situation may arise when speakers of an unstandardized local dialect or of an old, but non-modernized language are concentrated in a backward region of a modernizing country. Urbanization and industrialization in the region are minimal, but educational opportunities are available in the official language of the state, which is different from the local language. Where there are no local religious elites and relatively few socially mobilized people are produced from the local language group, a gradual process of assimilation to the language and culture of the dominant group will take place. When modernization and industrialization begin to significantly affect this area, new elite groups may arise to mobilize the remnants of the group more or less successfully, but the size and shape of the group will have been affected permanently by the earlier period of assimilation. Areas that conform to this pattern of development include Macedonia in relation to Bulgaria and Serbia and Montenegro in relation to Serbia in Eastern Europe, Byelorussia in relation to Russia in the Soviet Union, and speakers of various languages in several regions of north India in relation to the dominant Hindi-speaking culture group.

An alternative situation also favorable to assimilation and decline in ethnic identity occurs when differential modernization so favors a minority ethnic group that it chooses to assimilate to the language and culture of the ruling ethnic group. Such a development occurred among the Jews of Hungary during the middle nineteenth century, many of whom collaborated with the Magyar ruling political elite and aristocracy and played a critical role in the development of commerce and industry in Hungary. Their success was such, Barany reports, that

before World War I, the majority of Hungarian Jews . . . managed to achieve economic success, social satisfaction, and Magyar nationality even without conversion. Among the assimilated Jews, many knew no Yiddish at all and took no particular pride in developing a special Jewish ethos: the Jewishness of the more traditional-minded consisted chiefly of a stricter observance of religious practices, and this was is no way incompatible with loyalty to Magyardom during the liberal era.[41]

However, such a process of assimilation may not save an ethnic group from being the target of the next to rise as education and industrialization penetrate more deeply into the society. The assimilated group may remain distinguishable enough by cultural or religious markers—even when its members do not choose to use such markers to build communal consciousness—for it to be singled out as a scapegoat for the next group to rise and thereby serve as an instrument for building communal solidarity in the newly aspirant group. Such was the case in Hungary when 'a new intelligentsia' arose 'from the ranks of the peasantry and Christian small bourgeoisie' to compete for a shrinking number of government jobs and for economic opportunities with the Jewish middle classes.[42] Anti-Semitism has been, of course, a common form in which the ethnic and nationalist aspirations of the peoples of Eastern Europe have been manifested at different times and under different regimes. In contemporary Eastern Europe, as well as in the Soviet Union, anti-Semitism has again recurred and has in part reflected this pattern of upwardly mobilizing ethnic majorities seeking to exploit cultural differences against a minority in order to displace the minority from privileged positions. In several of the East European Communist states, this device was used in the 1950s and 1960s to eliminate Jews from prominent positions in the state and Communist Party bureaucracies.[43]

Thus, differential social mobilization in modernizing, multiethnic societies may favor the differentiation or assimilation of particular groups and the transformation of ethnic boundaries, but it nearly always leads at some stage to some forms and degrees of ethnic conflict and competition, arising out of elite competition for control over the local society or for new opportunities in the modern segments of a developing society. It affects only groups that either contain threatened traditional elites or those that benefit by modernization and industrialization sufficiently to produce an educated intelligentsia or an entrepreneurial class in a position to compete for prestige positions and economic advantages. Most of the members of such ethnic groups in societies at early stages of modernization may, however, remain for decades a relatively unmobilized rural peasantry or occupy lower class positions in the cities and towns. They are mobilized over time, manipulated by contending elite groups, and taught the language and culture that the predominant elites determine they should learn.

NOTES

1. Even where it is possible to do so, argues Barth, the use of cultural attributes to identify ethnic boundaries may be superficial, confusing form with content: Fredrik Barth, 'Introduction' and 'Pathan Identity and its Maintenance,' in Fredrik Barth (ed.), *Ethnic Groups and Boundaries: The Social Organization of Cultural Difference* (Boston: Little, Brown, 1969), pp. 15, 131–32.
2. Barth, 'Introduction,' op. cit., and Harald Eidheim, 'When Ethnic Identity is a Social Stigma,' in Barth, *Ethnic Groups and Boundaries*, op. cit., pp. 15 and 39–57.
3. George de Vos, 'Ethnic Pluralism' in George de Vos and Lola Romanucci-Ross (eds.), *Ethnic Identity: Cultural Continuities and Change* (Palo Alto, Calif.: Mayfield Publishing Co., 1975), p. 16.
4. Cf. Joan Vincent, 'The Structuring of Ethnicity,' *Human Organization*, XXXIII, No. 4 (Winter, 1974), pp. 376–77. The same remarks apply to the concept of nationality or nation as used here; cf. Benjamin Akzin, *State and Nation* (London: Hutchinson University Library, 1964), p. 36 and Karl M. Deutsch, *Nationalism and Social Communication: An Inquiry into the Foundations of Nationality*, 2nd ed. (Cambridge, Mass: M.I.T. Press, 1966), p. 23.
5. This point has been made by Nathan Glazer and Daniel P. Moynihan, 'Introduction,' in Nathan Glazer and Daniel P. Moynihan (eds.), *Ethnicity: Theory and Experience* (Cambridge, Mass.: Harvard University Press, 1975), pp. 7–10, but they overgeneralize their argument to other societies where ethnicity is more than merely interest, and may be a stage on the way to a claim to national status.
6. Cf. Akzin, *State and Nation*, op. cit., pp. 10, 12, 29, 31–34, 46, 81, 133, 143.
7. Since the nation is defined here as a type of ethnic group and ethnic groups have been defined without reference to any specific attributes or set of attributes, it follows that the nation (or nationality) also is not to be defined by any particular attributes such as language, religion, territory, or any others. Cf. Anthony D. Smith, *Theories of Nationalism* (New York: Harper & Row, 1971), pp. 18, 147–50, 181–85; Dankwart A. Rustow, *A World of Nations: Problems of Political Modernization* (Washington, D.C.: The Brookings Institution, 1967), pp. 47–48; Rupert Emerson, *From Empire to Nation: The Rise to Self-Assertion of Asian and African Peoples* (Boston: Beacon Press, 1960), pp. 102–87. For contrary views that see a close connection between language and nation or nationality, see Munro Chadwick, *The Nationalities of Europe and the Growth of National Ideologies* (New York: Cooper Square Publishers, 1973; reprint of 1945 edition); Carl J. Friedrich, 'Corporate Federalism and

Linguistic Politics,' unpublished paper presented at the International Political Science Association Congress, Montreal, 1973, pp. 3–5; and Ernest Gellner, *Thought and Change* (Chicago: University of Chicago Press, 1964), pp. 163–65. The predominant European tradition has been to distinguish the terms 'nationality' and 'nation,' using the former term for language groups and the latter to define the attachment of people of one or more language groups to a single state. Cf. Peter F. Sugar, 'External and Domestic Roots of Eastern European Nationalism,' in Peter F. Sugar and Ivo J. Lederer (eds.), *Nationalism in Eastern Europe* (Seattle: University of Washington Press, 1969), pp. 3–6. Emerson, who considers most other objective criteria unhelpful in defining the nation, insists, however, upon an inseparable relation between a nation and a 'national territory,' however loosely defined; *From Empire to Nation*, op. cit., pp. 105–9.

8. This definition follows Akzin, *State and Nation*, in not including independence, statehood, or sovereignty in the definition of the nation. Many definitions do insist on this latter criterion; for example, see Friedrich, 'Corporate Federalism,' p. 4; another statement of Friedrich's definition in Karl W. Deutsch and William J. Foltz (eds.), *Nation-Building* (New York: Atherton Press, 1966), pp. 11–12; and Oscar Jaszi, *The Dissolution of the Habsburg Monarchy* (Chicago: University of Chicago Press, 1961), p. 26. However, such definitions prepare the way for the confusion of the concept of the nation with that of the state from which much of the existing literature on nationalism suffers. Some leading scholars of nationalism have, however, avoided this confusion; for example, Emerson, *From Empire to Nation*, pp. 95–102 and Deutsch, *Nationalism and Social Communication*, pp. 104–5, who reserve the term nation-state for nations that have acquired sovereignty.

The most troublesome issues arise when the nation is defined in terms of group solidarity without reference to the state, but nationalism is defined as the striving for statehood. Then, any demands made by nations short of that for statehood cannot be analyzed in a study of nationalism! See Rustow, *A World of Nations*, p. 21.

9. However, the creation of relatively homogeneous national cultures out of diverse ethnic groups by the state usually takes centuries and even then leaves ethnically distinct enclaves, as in modern France and Spain. Tabouret-Keller has pointed out, for example, that it required four hundred years for French to become the national language of France after its adoption as the official language of the country in 1539; A. Tabouret-Keller, 'Sociological Factors of Language Maintenance and Language Shift: A Methodological Approach Based on European and African Examples,' in Joshua P. Fishman, *et al.* (eds.), *Language Problems of Developing Nations* (New York: John Wiley & Sons, 1968), p. 109. And, even today, language and dialect differences remain important in the country in such regions as Breton and Languedoc. Moreover, it has been argued that the process of nation-building through the agency of the state was historically less effective in Eastern than in Western Europe because, whereas political centralization preceded the development of nationalism in Western Europe, the two processes occurred simultaneously in Eastern Europe in the nineteenth century. Oscar J. Janowsky, *Nationalities and National Minorities (With Special Reference to East-Central Europe)* (New York:

Macmillan, 1945), pp. 19–20, cited in Sugar, 'Roots of Eastern European Nationalism,' p. 11.

10. It is preferable to treat ethnic nationalism and state-centered nationalism as subtypes rather than either insisting that only one type of nationalism is the true type or making the analytically hopeless error that Smith makes in attempting to define the nation in ethnic terms and nationalism in statist terms, rendering it impossible to discuss analytically the nationalism of ethnic groups until a claim for statehood is made explicitly. Actually, Smith's definition of the nation itself is not as 'ethnicist' as he claims since it contains the notion of 'common citizenship rights' which rarely exist outside the framework of the state; Smith, *Theories of Nationalism*, pp. 171, 175–76. Fishman makes an analytically more sensible (but typographically impossible) attempt to use different terms to describe the two processes of nationality-formation and state-formation, reserving the term 'nationalism' for the former and 'nationism' for the latter; Joshua A. Fishman, 'Nationality-Nationalism and Nation-Nationism,' in Fishman, *Language Problems*, pp. 39–51. See also Walker Connor, 'Nation-Building or Nation-Destroying?' *World Politics*, XXIV, No. 3 (April, 1972), 332–36, who argues rather dramatically that, because 'ethnic identity' is the only 'true nationalism' and because the process of building state loyalties often involves overcoming ethnic identities, the appropriate terms for the development of state loyalties is 'nation-destroying.'

11. Deutsch, *Nationalism and Social Communication*, op. cit., pp. 41–44.

12. Cf. Fishman, 'Nationality-Nationalism and Nation-Nationism,' op. cit., pp. 40–41.

13. Karl W. Deutsch, 'The Trend of European Nationalism—The Language Aspect,' in Joshua A. Fishman (ed.), *Readings in the Sociology of Language* (The Hague: Mouton, 1968), p. 599.

14. Deutsch, 'The Trend of European Nationalism,' op. cit., p. 606.

15. For example, compare T. Zavalani, 'Albanian Nationalism,' in Sugar and Lederer, *Nationalism in Eastern Europe*, op. cit., p. 68; and Paul Shoup, *Communism and the Yugoslav National Question* (New York: Columbia University Press, 1968), pp. 107–9. Of course, the distinctiveness of Islam itself varies in different contexts, but this does not seem to be a significant factor as between Albanian and Yugoslav Muslims.

16. Paul R. Brass, *Language, Religion and Politics in North India* (New York: Cambridge University Press, 1974), pp. 277–86.

17. See, for example, Robert H. Bates, 'Ethnic Competition and Modernization in Contemporary Africa,' *Comparative Political Studies*, Vol. VI, No. 4 (January, 1974), pp. 457–84; Gellner, *Thought and Change*, op. cit., esp. pp. 166 and 171–72; Chong-do Hah and Jeffrey Martin, 'Toward a Synthesis of Conflict and Integration Theories of Nationalism,' *World Politics*, Vol. XXVII, No. 3 (April, 1975), 373–79; Michael Hechter, 'Towards a Theory of Ethnic Change,' *Politics and Society*, Vol. II, No. 1 (Fall, 1971), esp. pp. 42–43 and 'The Persistence of Regionalism in the British Isles, 1885–1966,' *The American Journal of Sociology*, Vol. LXXIX, No. 2 (September, 1973), pp. 319–42; Robert Melson and Howard Wolpe, 'Modernization and the Politics of Communalism: A Theoretical Perspective,' *American Political Science Review*, Vol. LXIV, No. 4 (December, 1970), pp. 1112–18; and Smith, *Theories of Nationalism*, op. cit., esp. pp. 116–18, 132.

18. Consider, for example, the case of rural Slovaks even as late as the turn of the twentieth century who, upon emigrating to the United States 'were unaware of their specific national identity,' knowing 'only that they were from a certain village in what was called Hungary, they were sternly ruled by people who spoke a different tongue, and they were very poor.' David W. Paul, *The Cultural Limits of Revolutionary Politics: Change and Continuity in Socialist Czechoslovakia* (Boulder, Colo.: East European Quarterly, 1979), p. 195.
19. Peter Sugar, 'The Nature of the Non-Germanic Societies Under Habsburg Rule,' *Slavic Review*, Vol. XXII, No. 1 (March, 1963), pp. 2–3.
20. George Barany, 'Hungary: From Aristocratic to Proletarian Nationalism,' in Sugar and Lederer, *Nationalism in Eastern Europe*, op. cit., pp. 259 ff.
21. Stephen Fischer-Galati, 'Romanian Nationalism,' in ibid., pp. 375 ff.
22. Peter Brock, 'Polish Nationalism,' in ibid., pp. 325–28.
23. Kevin R. Cox, 'Geography, Social Contexts, and Voting Behavior in Wales, 1861–1951,' in Erik Allardt and Stein Rokkan (eds.), *Mass Politics: Studies in Political Sociology* (New York: The Free Press, 1970), pp. 127–33.
24. Brass, *Language, Religion, and Politics in North India*, op. cit., pp. 133 ff.
25. Gananath Obeyesekere, 'Sinhalese-Buddhist Identity in Ceylon,' in De Vos and Romanucci-Ross, *Ethnic Identity*, op. cit.
26. Sugar, 'Roots of Eastern European Nationalism,' op. cit., p. 53.
27. Keith Hitchins, *The Rumanian National Movement in Transylvania, 1780–1849* (Cambridge, Mass.: Harvard University Press, 1969), ch. 1.
28. Brass, *Language, Religion, and Politics in North India*, op. cit., pp. 159–61 and 163–65.
29. Brass, *Language, Religion, and Politics in North India*, op. cit., pp. 31–32.
30. Stavro Skendi, 'Language as a Factor of National Identity in the Balkans of the Nineteenth Century,' *Proceedings of the American Philosophical Society*, Vol. CXIX, No. 2 (April, 1975), p. 188.
31. Ibid., pp. 186–87; see also Marin V. Pundeff, 'Bulgarian Nationalism,' in Peter F. Sugar and Ivo J. Lederer (eds.), *Nationalism in Eastern Europe* (Seattle: University of Washington Press, 1969), pp. 93–115.
32. Brock, 'Polish Nationalism,' op. cit., pp. 315–16.
33. Sugar, 'Roots of Eastern European Nationalism,' op. cit., emphasizes the inseparability of Catholicism and Polish nationality, p. 34.
34. Skendi, 'Language as a Factor in National Identity in the Balkans,' p. 188; T. Zavalani, 'Albanian Nationalism,' op. cit., pp. 56, 66–68; and Chadwick, *The Nationalities of Europe*, op. cit., pp. 32–33.
35. Paul, *Continuity and Change in Socialist Czechoslovakia*, op. cit., ch. vii.
36. Obeyesekere, 'Sinhalese Buddhist Identity in Ceylon,' op. cit.
37. On the growth of Urdu as a symbol of Muslim identity in north India, see Brass, *Language, Religion, and Politics in North India*, op. cit., pp. 127–38 and 182–217. However, the attempt to impose Urdu as the official language of Pakistan was an early cause of Bengali resentment there; see, for example, Rounaq Jahan, *Pakistan: Failure in National Integration* (New York: Columbia University Press, 1972), pp. 37 ff.
38. This account of Greek nationalism is derived from Stephen G. Xydis, 'Modern Greek Nationalism,' in Sugar and Lederer, *Nationalism in Eastern Europe*, op. cit., pp. 207–58.
39. Sugar, 'Non-Germanic Societies Under Habsburg Rule,' op. cit., p. 12.

40. In Madras, during British rule, non-Brahman caste leaders who resented Brahman dominance in the public sphere and in other aspects of life developed a myth that the Brahmans were alien intruders from north India, 'descendants of Aryan invaders who had conquered the indigenous Dravidian people'; Marguerite R. Barnett, *The Politics of Cultural Nationalism in South India* (Princeton, NJ: Princeton University Press, 1976). See also Eugene Irschick, *Politics and Social Conflict in South India: The Non-Brahman Movement and Tamil Separatism, 1916–1929* (Berkeley: University of California Press, 1969).

41. George Barany, ' "Magyar Jew or: Jewish Magyar"? (To the Question of Jewish Assimilation in Hungary),' *Canadian-American Slavic Studies*, Vol. VIII, No. 1 (Spring, 1974), p. 39.

42. Barany, ' "Magyar Jew or: Jewish Magyar"?,' op. cit., p. 36.

43. Andrew Janos, 'Ethnicity, Communism, and Political Change in Eastern Europe,' *World Politics*, Vol. XXIII, No. 3 (April, 1971), pp. 501–8.

2

Nationality-Formation: From Communities to Nationalities

Whether or not an ethnic group, mobilized by its disgruntled elites to a growing sense of communal solidarity, goes on to make major political demands and how far it succeeds depend principally on four factors—the persistence or the perception of the persistence of an unequal distribution of resources either against the advantage or to the advantage of the group, the degree to which the process of building communal consciousness has involved the creation of the organizational resources necessary to build a political movement, the response of the government to the demands and grievances of the group, and the general political context.

INEQUALITY, RELATIVE DEPRIVATION AND ETHNIC DIFFERENCES IN THE DIVISION OF LABOR AND RESOURCES

Many theories of the politicization of ethnicity or of the development of nationalism in ethnic groups stress the importance of inequality in the distribution of available resources, social benefits, and opportunities between distinct ethnic groups. In its simplest form, the argument contends that nationalism arises in response to objective exploitation of an indigenous group by an alien group, or of one social class by another.[1] However, the realization by many contemporary scholars of ethnicity and nationalism that the mere existence of inequality, on the one hand, is not sufficient to produce a nationalist movement and, on the other hand, that nationalist movements sometimes arise among dominant groups has led to somewhat more elaborate statements of this point of view

One elaboration is the relative deprivation theory, which argues that is not objective inequality as such that precipitates nationalism but a feeling of frustration or relative deprivation defined as 'the balance between the goods and conditions of life to which people believe they are rightfully entitled and the goods and conditions they think they are capable of attaining or maintaining, given the social means available to them.'[2] For example, the rise in Croatian nationalism in contemporary Yugoslavia in the face of genuine economic advancement by the Croats is to be explained, so the argument goes, not in terms of the persistence of real inequalities between Croats and Serbs, but because Croats came to expect the attainment of economic well-being comparable to that achieved in West European nations and they felt this result was not possible within Yugoslavia.[3]

There are several problems with this type of explanation. One is that there is no way of measuring or even describing adequately the levels of relative deprivation experienced by different ethnic groups in different societies to test the basic theory that 'those groups which experience the highest levels of relative deprivation may be expected to be most nationalistic.'[4] A second problem is that the theory accepts the arguments and myths of nationalists as data to demonstrate relative deprivation rather than as myths themselves in need of explanation. Third, the deprivation theory cannot explain the nationalism of privileged groups such as that of Afrikaaners in South Africa.

Another elaboration of the theory of inequality has been presented by Glazer and Moynihan to explain the politicization of ethnicity. Their argument is that the salience of ethnicity is influenced by the extent to which non-dominant groups fail to achieve success according to the norms established by the dominant group, which may lead to the persistence of status inequalities even in the face of economic successes. Where there is no single dominant group, ethnic conflict is even more likely because there will be competition between different norms.[5] It is difficult to see how such an argument can be meaningfully applied to many situations of national or ethnic conflict. For example, Glazer and Moynihan cite the case of Indian traders expelled from Kenya because they were better traders than the African. But, what does this show?

Presumably, that African traders or Africans generally suffered a loss of status because they were not as good traders as the Indians and they expressed this feeling in ethnic antagonism and expulsion. The trouble with this fragment of a theory is that it is too elaborate to explain a situation readily understandable in simpler terms, namely, that Indians controlled a segment of the economy and attendant resources to which Africans wanted greater access. When Africans took power in Kenya, they had the political means to adopt the easy solution of depriving a culturally distinct minority group of its economic control rather than pursuing political and economic policies that would mediate ethnic conflict while long-range economic development plans were pursued to create new opportunities for Africans. In other words, it is a case not of status discrepancies but of competition for resources valued equally by two groups. In Eastern Europe, the comparable case to that of the Indian traders in Africa is clearly that of the Jewish commercial, business, and financial groups in the late nineteenth and early twentieth centuries who controlled resources and jobs that rising classes from the dominant nationalities wished to control.

What place, then, does inequality occupy in a theory of nationalism? The objective existence or subjective perception of inequality is indispensable to justify nationalism, but it is not in itself an explanation for it. The only certainty is that every nationalist movement has always justified itself in terms of existing oppression or anticipated oppression by a rival group. Black nationalists in the United States have been able to point to objective economic and status inequalities to justify their demands. On the other side, Afrikaaner nationalists will argue that their inequality of numbers would lead to their suppression by a black African majority in a system in which blacks were given equal political rights with Whites and they mobilize nationalist sentiment to ward off the perceived threat of inequality and to justify their dominance.

Most situations of ethnic group conflict that lead to competing nationalisms fall somewhere in between these two opposite examples of disadvantaged and privileged groups. Sometimes rival ethnic groups face each other directly in ethnically heterogeneous urban areas, but conflict situations may also arise between ethnic groups unevenly distributed between urban and rural areas or between different regions of a country. Nationalism is most likely to develop when new elites arise to challenge a system of ethnic stratification in the cities or an existing pattern of distribution of economic resources and political power between ethnically distinct urban and rural groups or ethnically distinctive regions. One moment at which such challenges tend to arise most forcefully is when industrial development and political centralization have led to concentrations of job opportunities in key urban centers and to the need for trained personnel to fill the new positions. It is at this point also in pluralistic societies that the issue of language becomes critical because the choice of the official language and the medium of education determines which groups have favored access to the best jobs.[6] Ethnic competition in multinational states may focus directly on specific job opportunities or on the allocation of the investment capital and other resources required to create jobs. Such conflicts may also arise in relation to other kinds of economic scarcities, such as, housing, which precipitated interethnic conflict in urban areas in several parts of the Soviet Union in 1989 and 1990.

To return now to the example of the reassertion of Croatian nationalism in contemporary Yugoslavia, the Croatian case—and the whole question of relations between the nationalities in contemporary Yugoslavia—can be explained satisfactorily in terms of competition for economic and political opportunities and resources without reference to Croatian feelings of 'relative deprivation'. In fact, what appears to be at issue in Yugoslavia—as in many developing societies—is competition for economic resources, particularly for the investment funds needed to promote economic development and technological change and to provide employment, and for political power that crystallized in the issue of constitutional changes in the direction of centralization and decentralization.[7] At the same time, the demand was also made for recognition of Croatian as an official language of Yugoslavia distinct from Serbo-Croatian.[8] The explanation for the reassertion of Croatian nationalism in this form is not that Croatians are actually deprived, but that there is advantage to be gained, economically and politically, by emphasizing Croatian distinctiveness. In the contemporary political context of Yugoslavia, regional decentralization of both political power and economic resources serves the interests of the Croat managerial and professional strata, who prefer to control opportunities in Croatia rather than to move to less developed regions of Yugoslavia. Croatian nationalism, therefore, has been articulated in terms of a demand for regional

autonomy.[9] Serbian interests in Yugoslavia, in contrast, have been
identified more with centralizing policies and practices because the
Serbian elites are in a position, as the numerically dominant
nationality, to control more of the political and economic resources
of a centralized Yugoslavian state than any other nationality.

Nationalism may also arise when there is a sectoral division of
ethnic groups with one dominant in the countryside and another in
the cities. In Deutsch's formulation, one of the typical cases of
national conflict occurs when rural groups move into urban sectors
dominated by linguistically and culturally distinct urban ethnic
groups.[10] In that case, either the newly mobile groups must be
assimilated and taught the language of the ruling group or the
dominant group itself will be replaced in power by the newly
mobilized and culturally different elements or some sort of complex
pluralist solution will have to be devised to make multilingualism
compatible with the technological and administrative requirements of the modern state.

The kind of elite competition that precipitates a major nationalist
movement bears a family resemblance to, but is different both in
degree and in quality from, the communal job competition
engendered in the early stages of modernization. It now becomes a
case not merely of competition for a few privileged positions, but
of a challenge by one group to the entire distribution of resources
or to the division of power between two whole societies or potential
societies. It is no longer a question simply of who shall have certain
jobs, but who shall determine how jobs and other resources are
distributed.

The critical contact points in ethnic nationalist confrontations
are the educational and political arenas—the schools and colleges,
on the one hand, and the institutions of power and governance, on
the other. A disadvantaged minority will demand control over the
schools first if it is dispersed or will contest for the schools and for
local political power in a particular region if it is geographically
concentrated. The schools and colleges are critical contact points
for two reasons. They provide a source of high status employment
for new elites and they are also an instrument of control over the
ethnic group. Whoever controls the schools determines whether or
not the ethnic group will maintain its cultural distinctiveness and
thereby be available for ready political mobilization on ethnic
grounds.

Such conflicts for control over the schools are endemic in nearly all multilingual developing societies where they focus specifically on the question of medium of education. Examples abound in the history of Eastern Europe and in South Asia. In the former region, struggles such as the Magyar resistance in the eighteenth century to Joseph II's efforts to introduce German language instruction in the schools[11] or the conflicts between Germans and Poles in Upper Silesia in the nineteenth century over the teaching of German and Polish in the schools there[12] illustrate the point. In South Asia, resistance to the introduction of Hindi in the curriculum of primary and secondary schools in Tamil Nadu or the conflicts between Hindi-speakers and speakers of other north Indian languages and dialects over the medium of instruction as well as over languages of education in the schools there provide further examples of this type of conflict.

If the disadvantaged ethnic group is a minority concentrated in a geographical area, its elites will also demand the use of the regional language as the principal language of administration in the area. They will also call for some form of political–administrative devolution or decentralization of political power, or, in some cases, for outright secession. A disadvantaged majority will, of course, demand the democratic right of power in the political system as a whole.

Thus, ethnic nationalism and conflict are most likely to develop when the educational, technological, and administrative requirements of an industrializing, centralizing state and the democratic demands of previously disadvantaged mobilizing groups make it increasingly difficult to sustain a system of ethnic stratification or a particular regional or urban-rural distribution of economic resources and political power. New elites arise from culturally distinct, disadvantaged groups to compete for economic and political opportunities controlled by the dominant group. The more widespread the competition and the more intransigent the dominant elite, the more likely it is that disgruntled elements from the disadvantaged group will turn to nationalism. How far such a nationalist movement will be taken and how successful it will be depend upon both the character of internal social and political communication and organization within the group and upon the political relations with other ethnic groups. For an ethnic nationalist movement to succeed, it is necessary for the elites who begin the process to be able to pursue, or at least to appear to pursue, effectively the interests of other social classes within the ethnic group.

A potential nationalist movement may peter out if the immediate demands of its elites are satisfied in the political and economic systems. It may also peter out or remain of marginal importance if the mass of the people, whether they are rural peasants or urban proletariat, find their economic needs satisfied through the existing system. Peasants may find that they and their leaders can be elected to positions of power in the system and that agrarian policy and rural patronage can be influenced to their advantage. In such cases, the rural masses may not find the appeals of their urban intelligentsia for the protection of their language and culture of great interest. Similarly, if the labor market is expanding in the industrial sector, the urban proletariat and the landless in search of urban jobs will not be moved by ethnic appeals. They may be influenced, however, if employment opportunities are not expanding sufficiently rapidly to accommodate new entrants and if the better positions are held by persons from different ethnic groups.

In summary, then, it is not inequality as such or relative deprivation or status discrepancies that are the critical precipitants of nationalism in ethnic groups, but the relative distribution of ethnic groups in the competition for valued resources and opportunities and in the division of labor in societies undergoing social mobilization, industrialization, and bureaucratization. The potential for ethnic nationalism exists when there is a system of ethnic stratification in which one ethnic group is dominant over another, but it is not usually realized until some members from one ethnic group attempt to move into the economic niches occupied by the rival ethnic groups.[13] To the extent that they fail to do so or have bitter experiences in doing so, they will protest against the system of ethnic stratification as a whole and attempt to mobilize the ethnic group. Such mobilization may either lead to communalism involving no more than the mobilization of one's community for more effective competition, or to nationalism and a more fundamental challenge to the whole division of labor, resources, and power in the society. On the other side, the privileged group may mobilize to defend its interests and may also use ethnic sentiments in doing so. The second type of situation that may precipitate competing ethnic nationalisms is one in which one ethnic group dominates rural society and another the urban economy. A third type is that of the multinational state in which distinct ethnic groups occupy compact geographical regions that are at different levels of economic development. In either of the latter two situations there may be

intense competition over the sectoral distribution of resources by
the state, over political power in the system, and over the languages
of education and administration.

POLITICAL FACTORS

Nationalism is a political movement by definition. It requires
political organization, skilled political leadership, and resources to
gain support to make successful demands in the political system.
Moreover, the movement must be able to compete effectively
against alternative political groups and must be strong enough to
withstand government efforts to suppress it or to undercut its
political support. Effective political organization and political
leadership and the resource base to maintain them are independent variables that profoundly influence the outcomes.

Political organizations that can command some community
resources are likely to be more effective and successful than those
that cannot. Some of the most successful nationalist organizations
have been able to build and draw upon resources created during a
previous period of communal mobilization. For example, in the
1940s and 1950s the NCNC (National Council of Nigeria and the
Cameroons) in Nigeria based its organization on the tribal unions
created during the previous decades of Ibo ethnic consolidation and
advancement;[14] the Akali Dal in Punjab built an unshakeable base of
nationalist support through its ability to call upon the resources of the
Shiromani Gurudwara Prabhandak Committee (SGPC), a body that
manages all the Sikh temples in the province and that was itself
created in an earlier period of Sikh communal mobilization;[15] the
Zionist movement in Europe and America was able to call upon, if
not command, the financial resources of its bourgeoisie.

A political organization that succeeds in identifying itself with
the community rather than merely representing the community or
pursuing its interests is also likely to be more effective against
external political competition and potential internal rivals. For
many Sikhs the Akali Dal in Punjab became equivalent to the
Panth or the Sikh community.[16] The Zionist movement has so
effectively identified itself with the Jewish community that to
attack Zionism is considered by many Jews as well as by many

non-Jewish supporters of Israel as equivalent to anti-Semitism. The important goal for nationalist movements in this regard is exclusivity, the drive to become the sole political representative of the community so that the community may act cohesively and unitedly. This is especially important if the group is a minority, for a cohesive minority may be able to achieve its goals against a larger, but more fragmented group, whereas organizational division in a minority ethnic group may be fatal to its interests.

A third feature of the more effective ethnic nationalist movements is their ability to shape the identity of the groups they lead. Again, the Akali Dal has not only identified itself with the Sikh community, but has played an increasingly important role in defining what it means to be a Sikh.[17] The Zionist movement has also succeeded in redefining for many Jews what it means to be a Jew; namely, not merely to be descended from a Jewish mother or be a follower of certain rituals, but to believe in the right and duty of Jews to emigrate to Israel or at least to support the cause of Israel if one does not or cannot emigrate.

Fourth, a political organization, to be effective in the pursuit of nationalist goals, must be able to provide continuity and must be able to withstand changes in leadership. Most successful nationalist movements are led by strong, dynamic, and sometimes charismatic leaders, but such leadership may not be sufficient to sustain a movement to the end. Prominent leaders may die or be killed or may turn away from nationalism before the group's goals are attained. There must, therefore, be a clear successor or a second rung of leaders who can effect a succession without dividing the movement. The more successful nationalist movements, such as those of the Sikhs and Jews, have provided leadership continuity and have coped with succession problems, but Welsh nationalism ebbed after Lloyd George became Prime Minister and the black community in the United States lost much of its unity and the momentum of the movement after the death of Martin Luther King.

Finally, it is of critical importance in the success of nationalist movements that one political organization be dominant in representing the demands of the ethnic group against its rivals. The Muslim League in preindependence India always insisted, in all its dealings with non-Muslim political groups, in being recognized as the sole spokesman of Muslim political interests. Its leaders knew that to do otherwise would make it possible for its opponents to divide and undercut its support.

Political organization, then, is both an instrument of an ethnic group in achieving, and evidence of the achievement of, multi-symbol congruence. The most successful nationalist political organizations have succeeded in shaping the boundaries of their groups to conform to the political goals they set for them. In this way, a group becomes defined not only by its language and/or its religion and/or its claimed territory, but by the political organization that pursues its interests.

Government Policies

Government policies and institutional mechanisms may be critical factors in influencing a group's capacity or desire to survive as a separate entity, its self-definition, and its ultimate goals. The policies available to governments to prevent the maintenance of separate ethnic identities or to limit the influence of ethnic groups range from the most extreme forms of repression, including geno-cide and deportation, to policies designed to undercut potential bases for ethnic group mobilization through assimilation in the schools or through the integration or cooperation of ethnic group leaders into the structures of power and wealth in the society. Alternatively, governments may choose to follow explicitly pluralist policies and solutions to state–nation relations[18] by establishing political structures such as federalism or by conceding to different ethnic groups the right to receive education through the medium of their mother tongue and to protect, preserve, and promote their culture in a variety of ways. Governments may also indirectly influence the development of ethnic conflict through policies that distribute state resources and opportunities for government employment.

The whole range of government policies towards ethnic groups has found expression at different times in Eastern Europe. At the most extreme end, several of the East European states cooperated with the Nazis in the extermination and deportation of the Jews. In the post-World War II period, some of these same states, then under Communist regimes, cooperated with (or submitted to) the Soviet Union in the deportation of German minorities.[19] Population transfers have also been used to resolve ethnic minority problems involving neighbouring states, as in the Greek–Turkish, Greek–Bulgarian exchanges at the end of World War I.[20] Alternatively restrictions on the movement of ethnic minorities have been used as a mechanism of confining ethnic groups to particular areas, as in the confinement of Jews to the Polish Pale by Catherine II of Russia.[21] Another variant on this theme of population movement or restriction is the policy of colonization, as in the efforts by the German government to support German movement to and purchase of lands owned and occupied by Poles in Posen in the nineteenth century.[22] Less extreme efforts to deny ethnic minority groups recognition of separate cultural or political status through forced assimilation to a dominant language or culture have also been common in Eastern Europe, such as the Magyarization policies of the Hungarian monarchy or the Russification policies of the Russian monarchy in the nineteenth century[23] and the similar attempts of the Soviet Union under Stalin. Such policies, of course, often have the contrary effect to that desired, thus frequently leading to the stimulation of ethnic feelings among the articulate segments of the minorities denied the right to use their own language or express their own cultural values in the public sphere.

Examples of institutional mechanisms that may influence the development of separatist movements are the demarcation of administrative areas to conform to presumed ethnic boundaries, the establishment of systems of separate confessional autonomy, and the creation of a federal system of government based upon cultural–linguistic–territorial groups. It is well known that, in Africa, the imperial powers often established local administrative areas that conformed to tribal boundaries.[24] The Ottoman millet system, in contrast, recognized the autonomy of religious groups without reference to ethnic or territorial boundaries. In India, in 1909 the British established, on the request of Muslim leaders, the famous system of separate electorates for Muslims and later for other minorities. In the United States, the Bureau of Indian Affairs accepts, enforces, and has sometimes encouraged racially-defined criteria for membership in particular Indian tribes.

Among the institutional mechanisms available to multiethnic or multinational states for satisfying national demands within a common political framework is federalism. Federalist solutions to nationality conflicts are usually viewed with trepidation by the central authorities in such states who see their primary purpose as the maintenance of the unity and territorial integrity of their states because they fear that federalization is but a step away from secession and disintegration. On the other side, however, it is often argued that the failure to grant some form of political auto- nomy in a federal state to aspirant national groups may itself promote secessionist and disintegrative tendencies that federalism might resolve. One of the great recurring questions in this regard, insofar as Eastern Europe is concerned, is whether or not Austria– Hungary might have developed into a viable modern multinational state had it established a federal system in 1849.[25]

In contemporary Eastern Europe, only Yugoslavia and Czecho- slovakia have sought federal solutions to satisfy the national aspir- ations of their constituent peoples within a common political framework.[26] In the Czech case, however, a highly centralized party structure was superimposed upon a federal administrative arrangement. Moreover, in the Yugoslav case, the devolution of real political and economic power to the federal units and the decentralization of the party structure in the 1960s was followed by a revival of nationalist sentiments and demands and by a consequent reimposition of centralized controls. However, in the post-Tito era of the 1980s, the centralized system of author- ity collapsed and a new central executive council was established with a rotating president from each of the eight republic provinces.

State–nation relations are often viewed as a zero-sum game in which state concessions to ethnic nationalist demands are con- ceived as invitations or steps on the road to secession and the disintegration of the state. In fact, however, there is a very large range of policy choices that are available both in federal and in unitary states for states and nations to reach accommodations short of secession. Nowhere is this more clear than in the area of language policies. Governments may adopt one, two or many official languages. They may adopt one or more languages for administrative use at the federal level and others at the provincial level. They may adopt special language requirements for entry into government service or they may permit the use of several languages as media of examination and require on-the-job language training in other languages after admission. In the schools, governments may recognize some languages and not others either as media of education or as languages of instruction. For example, the two components of the Austro-Hungarian empire followed different policies in this regard, with the Hungarian government pursuing Magyarization to the extent of denying national minorities education in the medium of the mother tongue whereas, in Austria, the medium of education was the mother tongue and German was taught as a second language.[27] In contemporary Slovenia, an extremely liberal policy of providing bilingual primary education, using both German and Slovenian as media of education as well as languages of instruction, has been developed.[28] Governments may recognize the right of a group to control the public schools in a particular area and to use its own language as medium of education or it may permit only an individual choice option, in which the local mother tongue will be used only if it is requested by a specified number of parents. Governments may choose to follow a policy of equality with respect to the claims of competing language groups, enforcing a state-wide policy of bilingualism for all, or it may recognize only minority rights where one language is spoken only in a particular area or by a dispersed group and may be used legally only in the area in question or only for certain purposes.

The kinds of language policies chosen may be very important in influencing whether or not an ethnic group becomes assimilated or demands recognition as a nationality. Insofar as language and employment, particularly government employment, are closely interconnected, groups whose languages are recognized earlier than others as languages of administration and media of education will derive a competitive advantage. Groups whose languages are not recognized then have two broad choices. They may give up their mother tongue or use it only at home and choose education through the medium of the language that provides access to employment or, if the community has the resources, it may develop its own network of private schools to maintain its language and culture and simultaneously work to change government policies towards its language.

In this interaction between the variety of government language policies and community choices, there are many points at which either conflict or accommodation may occur. Moreover, the interaction may lead to the disappearance of some languages, the decrease in numbers of language speakers over time in the case of others, and the standardization, modernization, and consolidation of new speech communities with recognized cultural and political rights in the political system for still other groups. Although government language policies may influence the course of development of ethnolinguistic movements and their strength and weakness, mere recognition of an otherwise undeveloped language spoken by a non-modernizing people will not provide the motive force for linguistic nationalism nor will any but the most extreme discriminatory or genocidal policies destroy the language and culture of a group that has reached a point of communal solidarity and determination to maintain and perpetuate itself.

Another type of government policy that may influence the development of nationalities from communities is the way in which the state distributes the economic resources and public service jobs at its command. Here, as in the previous two sets of examples, government policies may or may not succeed and cannot be considered in a vacuum separate from other motive forces promoting national differentiation. For example, two regimes in Czechoslovakia of vastly different political orientation—the parliamentary regime of the interwar period and the communist regime of the post-World War II period—pursued the similar policy of diverting economic resources into the less developed region of Slovakia in order to rectify the historical imbalance in industrialization and general prosperity between the Czech and Slovak regions of the country.[29] However, neither regime made sufficient concessions to Slovak desires for political autonomy,[30] with the result that Slovak nationalism reemerged forcefully when political opportunities became available. However, the form taken by Slovak nationalism in these two periods also differed significantly according to the different political contexts in which it operated. In the interwar period, Slovak resistance to the centralizing tendencies of the Czechoslovakian parliamentary regime took the form of a reactionary, clericalist, authoritarian movement—the Slovak People's Party—and culminated in the establishment of the Slovak Republic, a puppet regime of the Nazis.[31] When Slovak nationalism reasserted itself under the Communist regime in 1968, it took the form of a political alliance with Czech reformists.[32] Common to both situations is the fact that economic policies favorable to the Slovaks failed to prevent the resurgence of Slovak nationalism in the absence of political policies to satisfy the desires of Slovak political elites for regional autonomy and federalism rather than a centralized state.

In South Asia, a persistent complaint of East Bengalis in Pakistan was that they were being treated like colonial subjects of West Pakistan and that there was an imbalance in the development of the two wings of the country and in resource allocation against the East, that West Pakistanis dominated elite positions in the public service and in the army, and that East Bengalis had been deprived of their promised political autonomy and even their political rights by the dominant forces in West Pakistan. Under the presidential autocracy of Ayub Khan, efforts were made to rectify the imbalance in economic development by putting more resources into the East. Efforts were also made to recruit more Bengalis into elite public service positions. However, the very emphasis on efforts to redress the regional imbalance at a time when the government continued to deny democratic rights to the Bengali political classes gave the latter the incentive to continue to draw attention to the problem and intensified rather than alleviated Bengali discontent.[33]

Nationalist movements make both economic and political demands. Experience in both Eastern Europe and South Asia demonstrates that they cannot be mollified by policies that deal with only one set of demands.

Political Context

The movement from community to nationality involves an inevitable struggle for power between competing ethnic groups. The ebb and flow of nationalism in an ethnic community, the intensity of its drive for power, and the particular form that its demands take are influenced by the political context. Three aspects of the political context are especially important: the possibilities for realignment of political and social forces and organizations, the willingness of elites from dominant ethnic groups to share power with aspirant ethnic group leaders, and the potential availability of alternative political arenas.

In an early modernizing society where the first groups to organize politically are ethnic groups, or where the leading organizations articulate local nationalisms, the question of political realignment may not arise. It becomes important when an ethnic group has made the transition to a community but has not developed its own political organizations. A community may choose not to do so because existing non-ethnic political organizations are so well-entrenched that the only sensible course lies in acting as a pressure group through them, or, as in the East European Communist states, because the formal organization of ethnic movements was simply prohibited.

Through pressure group activity, concessions may be extracted that fall short of achieving national recognition for the group, but are sufficiently attractive to ward off further political mobilization by ethnic group leaders. Alternatively, new class organizations may arise that compete more effectively on economic grounds for the allegiance of members of the ethnic group than its own embryonic nationalist political organizations. Both these developments, for example, have historically limited the appeal, the intensity, and the demands of Welsh nationalism. In the nineteenth century, the Liberals captured national sentiment effectively by making major concessions to the developing sense of Welsh nationality.[34] Later, in the post-World War I period, the class appeal of the Labour Party swamped an incipient revival of Welsh nationalism under the banner of Plaid Cymru. The post-World War I period constituted an era of general political realignment in both Wales and the United Kingdom generally. It is in such periods of political realignment that new organizations are formed based on class and/or ethnic appeals. In Wales the stronger force proved to be that of class and the unionization of the coalfield.

In the 1960s, 1970s, and 1980s, however, the United Kingdom once again went through the throes of a potential political re-alignment, evidenced by the electoral decline of the Conservative and Labour parties and the corresponding rise of the Liberal Party, the Welsh and Scottish Nationalist parties, and the Social Democratic Party. In Wales the force behind the attempted political realignment was the decline of the coalfield and the social-political structure based on it and the rise to prominence in Welsh public life of a new class of academic, professional, and business-industrial personnel. An hypothesis consistent with the analysis presented so far is that this shift in the elite and occupational structure of Welsh society engendered both internal competition within the old Labour political leadership for political power in Wales and new forms of competition with Englishmen for jobs in the United Kingdom, and that these changes were the precipitants of the new force of national differentiation and political realignment in modern Wales.

Possibilities for political realignment occur when existing political organizations fail to keep in tune with social changes that erode their support bases or in times of revolutionary upheaval. A general political realignment presents new opportunities for nationalist political organizations to arise and to present an effective blend of cultural and economic appeals. The outcome in a situation of this sort cannot be predicted on the basis of cultural differences between rival ethnic groups, but depends upon the patterns of elite competition for power in local party and government structures, upon the ability of competing elites to communicate effectively across class lines and to new social classes, and upon the relative skills and effectiveness of competing leaders and organizations.

Once a society has reached a stage of political development in which large-scale political organizations have become entrenched, even dramatic social and economic changes, which in the early stages of modernization would precipitate national conflict, may not be sufficient to provide a basis for an effective nationalist movement unless these social changes also precipitate a general political realignment. These remarks apply especially to single party states, where nationalist demands can be articulated effectively only within the single party and only at moments of dramatic change in the structure or leadership of the party. Such contextual changes have occurred occasionally even in single party states, however, as for example in Czechoslovakia in 1968 when the replacement of the Novotny regime by that of the reformist group led by Dubcek, presented an opportunity for Slovak nationalist demands to be articulated. It is hardly surprising, therefore, that the fundamental political changes which began in the Soviet Union under Gorbachev have been associated with widespread manifestations of interethnic conflict and nationalist demands or that Croatian and Slovakian demands for regional autonomy in the post-Tito era in Yugoslavia have shifted to demands for independence.

The second political context variable that may affect the movement of an ethnic group from communal consciousness to national status concerns the willingness of elites from dominant ethnic groups to share political power. Where that willingness does not exist, the society in question is headed for conflict, even civil war and secessionism. However, where such willingness does exist, the prospects for pluralist solutions to ethnic group conflicts are good.

No regime, even the most authoritarian, can avoid confronting the issues of power-sharing and pluralism in modernizing multi-ethnic societies. The former Communist regimes of Eastern Europe, like the Soviet Union, had to confront these issues without much guidance from Marxist ideology which, in principle, does not regard ethnic differences as desirable bases for social differentiation in modern societies. In fact, however, Burks has shown that Communist Party support in Eastern Europe in the interwar period relied more on its appeal to ethnicity than to class aspirations.[35] The success of the Yugoslav Partisan movement during World War II also depended upon an extremely skillful handling of ethnic and nationality protests and conflicts.[36] However, once in power, none of the Eastern European regimes, anymore than the Soviet Union, has been able to avoid the recurrence of ethnic and nationality questions, nor have the Eastern European regimes followed consistent policies toward ethnic minorities and distinctive nationalities.

Yugoslavia, like the Soviet Union, in principle recognized the right of selfdetermination for its nationalities, although in practice it was assumed that the right was exercised when the several nations agreed to the establishment of the Yugoslav Federal Republic in the 1946 Constitution.[37] In the years immediately following World War II, Yugoslavia, again like the Soviet Union, adopted a federal system in form, but a centralized system in practice.[38] The regime also permitted the different ethnic groups and nationalities in Yugoslavia to retain their distinctive languages and cultures and tried assiduously to ensure that all the major nationalities were represented on most party and government organs—though not the critical decisionmaking bodies—in proportions close to their actual distribution in the total population.[39] However, from the point of view of power-sharing, the Yugoslav policy towards the nationality question constituted, even in the early postwar years, a significant shift away from the Serbian domination that characterized the interwar political system. Nevertheless, Serbian-Croatian political conflict persisted and reemerged forcefully in the 1980s and 1990s along previous lines. The Serbian Communist leadership sought to retain a semblance of centralized political authority in Yugoslavia against the demands of the non

Communist Croation (and other) nationality leaders for either regional autonomy or secession.

Czechoslovakia also, particularly after the events of 1968, moved toward a federal system which, though it did not provide for full sharing of power between Czechs and Slovaks, provided a good deal more genuine participation in power by the Slovak minority than was then permitted to minority groups in the Soviet Union.[40] Although such limited policies in the direction of increased minority participation in power clearly have not prevented a new rise in national consciousness in Communist multinational states in recent years,[41] the willingness of Communist leaders to provide ethnic minorities access to positions of power at both the federal and regional levels was an important factor in moderating such movements in the past. The persistence of demands from ethnic elites in several Soviet republics to increase their representation in local decisionmaking structures[42] and the reassertion of Croatian national sentiments in Yugoslavia in 1971–72 were, however, evidence of continuing problems in both states, which have burst forth with intensity as the old regimes of Eastern Europe and the Soviet Union have crumbled.

In sharp contrast to the Yugoslav and Czech efforts to move towards pluralist solutions to ethnic and nationality policies was the increasingly repressive and assimilationist attitude of the Romanian Communist regime toward its minorities. In pursuing a policy of 'Romania for the ethnic Romanians' the Romanian government in the 1950s and 1960s gradually withdrew the rights of the Hungarian minority in Transylvania, permitted the emigration of Germans and Jews, and sought to increase the proportions of Romanians and decrease the proportions of minorities in leading positions in the government and in the Communist Party.[43] However, the assimilationist and discriminatory policies of the Romanian government[44] also have failed to reduce the degree of ethnic and national consciousness among the minority groups in Romania.[45]

The third political context variable concerns the availability of, and the relative costs to be borne by, an ethnic group in shifting to an alternative political arena. In unitary and centralized states that contain geographically concentrated minorities, it is certain that, at some point, when the political demands of a minority are not being satisfied adequately by the state authorities, the demand will be made for administrative and/or political decentralization of power. In the United Kingdom in the 1970s, it appeared for a time that such demands were to be granted in the form of legislative assemblies or regional parliaments for Wales and Scotland. In multiethnic federal systems, where local ethnic groups are concentrated regionally, and compete for power in provincial units, demands often arise for the reorganization of provincial boundaries to conform more closely to the boundaries of ethnic groups. However, it also sometimes occurs that local minorities, particularly dispersed minorities, may demand protection from the central or federal government against provincial governments dominated by rival ethnic groups and may orient their own political activities to an extra-provincial arena. In premodern colonial or imperial systems, it may also happen that an ethnic majority in a region dominated by ethnic minorities will appeal to the central government for justice, as did the Romanian leadership in Transylvania in the eighteenth century, who appealed to the Habsburg Emperor to grant the Romanian nation political and religious equality with the three dominant 'nations' of the principality he ruled.[46]

Federal solutions to the conflicts of multiethnic societies provide considerable political flexibility and present minority ethnic groups with both the possibilities of demanding the construction of new or the reorganization of old political arenas. Simultaneously they also provide alternative arenas in which minority groups may operate. In India, Pakistan, and Nigeria, such demands for internal reorganizations of boundaries and the availability of more than one level in which minority groups may operate have been persistent features of ethnic conflict and bargaining. The United States also, though it does not provide realistic federal solutions to Black–White power struggles, has provided multilevel political arenas. In the 1950s and 1960s, Blacks were able to use the federal arena to influence their power position in the states. In the 1960s, 1970s, and 1980s, Black political leaders found that they could use Black communal solidarity to gain control over many cities.

The use of strategies of political arena reorganization and multilevel conflict adjustment work best under the following conditions: where a relatively open system of political competition and bargaining exist; where there is a system in which the federal and provincial or local units all have or are granted significant powers such that the capture of power at one level by one ethnic group does not close all significant avenues to power; where there is a multiplicity of ethnic groups rather than only two or three; where ethnic conflicts do not run afoul of ideological disagreements between unitarists and federalists; and where external powers are not willing to intervene. Where any of these conditions are lacking, federalist and multilevel strategies may fail and civil war or secession may result. Most of these conditions have, in fact, been absent in the Eastern European states where, with the exception of contemporary Yugoslavia, federalist solutions to ethnic pluralism have either not been adopted (as in Austria–Hungary) or have involved little real decentralization of power. Partly for these reasons, secessionist and irredentist movements have been recurring and persistent in Eastern Europe for the past century.

In contrast, all these conditions have been present in India since independence where these strategies have been used with some success. However, most of the conditions were lacking in Pakistan before the secession of Bangladesh. There, a bargaining system was replaced by a military-dominated authoritarian regime, the powers of the provinces were reduced, a deliberate policy of reducing the political importance of ethnic multiplicity was followed by uniting all ethnic groups in the West against the Bengalis in the East, an ideology of unitarism was propagated by the military elite, and India ultimately proved willing to intervene on the side of the Bengalis.

In general, however, the secessionist strategy is a high-cost strategy that most political elites will not adopt unless the significant roads to power in the existing system appear to be blocked and unless there is a reasonable prospect of external intervention in their favor. Otherwise, maximalist programs of national minorities tend to take the form of demands for 'autonomy,' 'selfgovernment,' or 'confederation' within existing multinational states. Even in Eastern Europe, the leaders of many national movements have chosen these goals rather than outright secession.[47] Under Gorbachev in the Soviet Union, several of the nationalities have one by one confronted this dilemma of whether or not to press for secession or for an enhanced status within a reorganized Soviet state. By 1991, 6 of 15 Soviet republics were pressing for outright secession.

The most favorable period in modern times for secessionist strategies was, of course, the pre-World War I period in the Balkans when the major powers in Central and Eastern Europe and in Russia had direct interests in each other's internal ethnic

conflicts. The consequences of this period of interethnic international conflict have produced the term 'Balkanization,' which
has now become a part of the language of proponents of national
integration everywhere, using it as a bad example to be avoided at
all costs. Whatever the moral merits of this attitude, the free use of
the term has tended to draw attention away from the great variety
of political solutions that are available in multiethnic societies in
between a forced 'national integration' and 'Balkanization'.

CONCLUSION

These first two chapters have been used to develop an approach to
the study of ethnicity that focuses on processes of identity formation
and identity change. The approach is designed to be comparative
and universalistic, oriented to questions concerning the conditions
under which ethnic groups, at different times and in different
places, undergo the processes of transformation leading to subjective selfconsciousness as ethnic communities and/or political
significance as nationalities. Consequently, a set of definitions is
needed that can be used to analyze groups and processes of change
that have occurred everywhere in the world and at different historical times. The definition used here of the term ethnic *category*
is an objective one that implies that one can, in principle, at any
point in time, divide the peoples of the world or of a particular
society into categories distinguished by cultural characteristics and
symbolic referents. However, in early modernizing societies where
the process of ethnic transformation has just begun and in postindustrial societies where considerable linguistic and cultural
assimilation have taken place among ethnic groups, the division
between peoples may not be of such nature as to divide them into
clearly compartmentalized groups with sharp boundaries. Rather,
linguistic and other cultural distinctions may overlap and are often
not congruent with each other, though there will be differences
between some ethnic groups and others in this regard at any point
in time.

Whether or not a particular ethnic group's boundaries are sharply
defined or not in its pre-mobilization stage, it is of the essence of
the process of ethnic transformation that boundaries are made

sharper, that old symbols acquire new subjective significance, and that attempts are made to bring a multiplicity of symbols and attributes into congruence with each other. In this process of ethnic transformation, which is to be distinguished from the mere persistence of ethnic differences in a population, cultural markers are selected and used as a basis for differentiating the group from other groups, as a focus for enhancing the internal solidarity of the group, as a claim for a particular social status, and, if the ethnic community becomes politicized, as justification for a demand for either group rights in an existing political system or for recognition as a separate sovereign nation. Although the definition of ethnic category emphasizes objective rather than subjective differences and cultural markers, the argument presented above has been that such differences are only necessary, but not sufficient conditions for the process of ethnic transformation to begin.

Also necessary, but still not sufficient conditions for communal mobilization are either elite competition for control over a local society or intraclass competition between competing elites from different ethnic groups for control over new opportunities in the modern segments of a developing society or over prestige and high-paying positions in an industrial society. Four characteristic forms of elite competition for local control are those between local land controllers and alien authorities, between competing religious elites, between local religious elites and collaborationist native aristocracies, and between native religious elites and alien aristocracies. The second general type of elite conflict that may precipitate communal mobilization arises out of the inevitably differential character of the processes of modernization and social mobilization that in developing societies typically takes the form of competition for government jobs and in industrial societies for jobs in government, industry, and in the universities.

However, the kinds of elite competition noted above provide only the catalyst for the symbol manipulation that is involved in communal mobilization. The sufficient conditions for successful communal mobilization are the existence of the means to communicate the selected symbols of identity to other social classes within the ethnic group, the existence of a socially mobilized population to whom the symbols may be communicated, and the absence of intense class cleavage or other difficulties in communication between elites and other social groups and classes. The means necessary to promote such interclass communication are growth in literacy rates, the development of media of mass communication, particularly newspapers, the standardization of the local language, the existence of texts and other books in the local language, and the availability of schools or classes in which the native language and culture can be taught. The corollary to this condition concerning means is that, to use Deutsch's terms, there must be in the local society new groups of people who are becoming 'available' for more intensive communication,[48] who are demanding education and new jobs in the modern sectors of the economy.

Once the means and the demand for new opportunities and new forms of communication have been created, the question arises concerning which elites can more effectively capture the newly mobilizing social groups. A native aristocracy may manipulate ethnic symbols in order to provide a justification for its own privileges, but if it oppresses the peasantry, the peasant classes and the sons of the peasantry who move into new occupations will oppose the continued dominance of the local landlords, may reject the cultural appeals made by them, and may look to the state authorities for support against their local oppressors. It may also happen that there is no strong native elite group to promote the local language and culture, but only a limited intelligentsia working through literary societies to standardize the language and create a new literature in it. Such a group may transform the native language, but unless its leaders can ensure that the employment opportunities of newly mobilizing social groups will be enhanced by the learning of it, their efforts will not lead to significant communal mobilization. In early modernizing societies, a high degree of communal mobilization will be achieved most easily in two types of situations: (*a*) where there is a local religious elite in command of temples, shrines, or churches and the lands and trusts attached to them and a network of religious schools; or (*b*) where the local language has been recognized by the state authorities as *both* a legitimate medium of education and administration, thereby providing the native intelligentsia with both material and cultural rewards to offer to new social groups aspiring to education and new opportunities.

The necessary and sufficient conditions for communal mobilization are also the preconditions for the development of a successful nationalist movement. Nationalism as an elite phenomenon may arise at any time, even in the early stages of communal mobilization. However, for nationalism to acquire a mass base, it must go beyond mere elite competition for local control or a narrow range of privileges. The mass base for nationalism may be created when widespread intraclass competition occurs brought about by the movement of large numbers of people from either a previously overwhelmingly rural group or from a disadvantaged group into economic sectors occupied predominantly by other ethnic groups. If such movement is resisted by the dominant group, supported openly or tacitly by the state authorities, then the aspirant group will be easily mobilized by nationalist appeals that challenge the existing economic structure and the cultural values associated with it. If the aspirations of the mobilizing group are perceived as a major threat to the status and economic opportunities of the dominant group, then the groups threatened by such displacement may become available for a nationalist movement. (Sometimes, however, the situation of the group threatened with displacement may be too untenable for nationalism to have any meaning, as in the case of Indians in East Africa.) The mass base for competing nationalism also may be provided by the uneven distribution of ethnic groups in urban and rural areas or in different regions of a country in such a manner that there is competition for control over the state structure and the distribution of resources for the entire society.

While intraclass ethnic competition for economic opportunities or sectorally-based competition for control over state power provides the mass basis for nationalism, the demands that are articulated and the success of a nationalist moveme.t in achieving them depend on political factors. Three sets of such factors were identified above: the existence of and the strategies pursued by nationalist political organizations, the nature of government response to ethnic group demands, and the general political context. Even when an ethnic group has achieved a high degree of communal or political mobilization, it is far from inevitable that it must then move to create complete political congruence with its cultural identity by acquiring a separate sovereign state. There are a variety of political goals to be attained short of sovereignty and a wide variety of government policies that may be pursued to undercut, sidestep, or accommodate within an existing state the demands of an aspirant ethnic group. Among those goals, and in the face of the political means and the power of the modern state as well as the contemporary aspect of the international system, secessionism had been the least likely outcome of conflicts between states and nations in the post-world war II bipolar order.[49]

NOTES

1. Chong-do Hah and Jeffrey Martin, 'Toward a Synthesis of Conflict and Integration Theories of Nationalism,' *World Politics*, Vol. XXVII, No. 3 (April, 1975), pp. 372–74.
2. Hah and Martin, 'Toward a Synthesis,' op. cit., p. 380.
3. Gary K. Bertsch, 'Relative Deprivation and Yugoslav Nationalisms: The Rationalization of Frustrations,' paper presented at the 1973 meeting of the American Political Science Association, p. 18.
4. Hah and Martin, 'Toward a Synthesis,' op. cit., p. 381.
5. Nathan Glazer and Daniel P. Moynihan, 'Introduction,' in Nathan Glazer and Daniel P. Moynihan (eds.), *Ethnicity: Theory and Experience* (Cambridge, Mass.: Harvard University Press, 1975), pp. 12–24.
6. The formulation of my argument here has been influenced in part by comments made by Ernest Gellner on the original draft of this chapter.
7. Nicholas R. Lang, 'The Dialectics of Decentralization: Economic Reform and Regional Inequality in Yugoslavia,' *World Politics*, Vol. XXVII, No. 3 (April, 1975), pp. 309–35.
8. Frits W. Hondius, *The Yugoslav Community of Nations* (The Hague: Mouton, 1968), pp. 326–28.
9. George Klein, 'The Role of Ethnic Politics in the Czechoslovak Crisis of 1968 and the Yugoslav Crisis of 1971,' *Studies in Comparative Communism*, Vol. VIII, No. 4 (Winter, 1975), pp. 350–51.
10. See especially Karl M. Deutsch's use of the example of Swedes and Finns in Finland in *Nationalism and Social Communication: An Inquiry into the Foundations of Nationality*, 2nd ed. (Cambridge, Mass.: M.I.T. Press, 1966), pp. 196–208.
11. Keith Hitchins, *The Rumanian National Movement in Transylvania, 1780–1849* (Cambridge, Mass.: Harvard University Press, 1969), pp. 46–48.
12. Leon Dominian, *The Frontiers of Language and Nationality in Europe* (New York: Henry Holt, 1917), pp. 127, 129.
13. For an analysis of the rise of 'nativist' movements in different parts of India, explained precisely in this way, see Myron Weiner, *Sons of the Soil: Migration, Ethnicity, and Nativism in India* (Cambridge, Mass.: Center for International Studies, 1975).
14. James S. Coleman, *Nigeria: Background to Nationalism* (Berkeley: University of California Press, 1963), p. 347 and *passim*.
15. Paul R. Brass, *Language, Religion, and Politics in North India* (New York: Cambridge University Press, 1974), pp. 311–18.

16. Brass, *Language, Religion, and Politics in North India*, op. cit., pp. 352–55.

17. Brass, *Language, Religion, and Politics in North India*, op. cit., p. 408.

18. See Benjanin Akzin, *State and Nation* (London: Hutchinson University Library, 1964), chaps. vi and vii for a comprehensive survey of pluralist state policies.

19. See, for example, the account of the deportation of Romanian Germans to the Soviet Union in Georges Castellan, 'The Germans of Rumania,' *Journal of Contemporary History*, Vol. VI, No. 1 (1971), pp. 67 *ff.*

20. Marin V. Pundeff, 'Bulgarian Nationalism,' in Sugar and Lederer, *Nationalism in Eastern Europe*, op. cit., p. 142.

21. Leon Dominian, *The Frontiers of Language and Nationality in Europe* (New York: Henry Holt, 1917), p. 124.

22. Dominian, *Frontiers of Language and Nationality*, op. cit., pp. 127–28.

23. Munro Chadwick, *The Nationalities of Europe and the Growth of National Ideologies* (New York: Cooper Square Publishers, 1973; reprint of 1945 edition), pp. 37, 39–42.

24. See, for example, on this point, Robert H. Bates, 'Ethnic Competition and Modernization in Contemporary Africa,' *Comparative Political Studies*, Vol. VI, No. 4 (January, 1974), p. 465.

25. See, for example, Hans Kohn, 'The Viability of the Habsburg Monarchy,' and the 'Reply' by Peter F. Sugar in *Slavic Review*. Vol. XXII, No. 1 (March, 1963), pp. 37–46.

26. For some discussions of federalism in Yugoslavia and Czechoslovakia, see Paul Shoup, *Communism and the Yugoslav National Question* (New York: Columbia University Press, 1968), pp. 113–19; David W. Paul, *The Cultural Limits of Revolutionary Politics: Change and Continuity in Socialist Czechoslovakia* (Boulder, Colo.: East European Quarterly, 1979), ch. vii; and Stanislav J. Kirschbaum, 'Nationalisme et Féderalisme en Théorie Communiste: Le Cas de la Tchécoslovaquie,' *Etudes Intèrnationales*, Vol. VI, No. 1 (Mars, 1975), pp. 3–29.

27. Oscar Jaszi, *The Dissolution of the Habsburg Monarchy* (Chicago: University of Chicago Press, 1961), p. 346.

28. Ela Ulrik-Atena, 'National Linguistic Minorities: Bilingual Basic Education in Slovenia,' *Prospects*, Vol. VI, No. 3 (1976), pp. 430–38.

29. George Klein, 'The Role of Ethnic Politics in the Czechoslovak Crisis of 1968 and the Yugoslav Crisis of 1971,' *Studies in Comparative Communism*, Vol. VIII, No. 4 (Winter, 1975), pp. 343 and 350.

30. Joseph F. Zacek, 'Nationalism in Czechoslovakia,' in Sugar and Lederer, *Nationalism in Eastern Europe*, op. cit., pp. 194 and 202 and Klein, 'The Role of Ethnic Politics, op. cit., pp. 341, 368.

31. Zacek, 'Nationalism in Czechoslovakia,' op. cit., pp. 195 and 198; see also Paul, *Cultural Limits*, op. cit., ch. vi.

32. Klein, 'The Role of Ethnic Politics,' op. cit., pp. 353–54.

33. Rounaq Jahan, *Pakistan: Failure in National Integration* (New York: Columbia University Press, 1972), p. 180.

34. Kenneth O. Morgan, *Wales in British Politics, 1868–1922* (Cardiff: University of Wales Press, 1963).

35. Richard V. Burks, *The Dynamics of Communism in Eastern Europe*, 2nd ed. (Princeton, N.J.: Princeton University Press, 1965).

36. Shoup, *Communism and the Yugoslav National Question*, op. cit., ch. ii.

37. Shoup, *Communism and the Yugoslav National Question*, op. cit., p. 115.

38. Shoup, *Communism and the Yugoslav National Question*, op. cit., pp. 115–19.

39. Shoup, *Communism and the Yugoslav National Question*, op. cit., pp. 120 *ff*.

40. Kirschbaum, 'Nationalisme et Federalisme,' op. cit.

41. See, for example, Gary K. Bertsch, 'Currents in Yugoslavia: The Revival of Nationalisms,' *Problems of Communism*, Vol. XXII (November-December, 1973), pp. 1–15 and Teresa Rakowska-Harmstone, 'The Dialectics of Nationalism in the USSR,' *Problems of Communism*, Vol. XXIII (May-June, 1974), pp. 1–22.

42. Rakowska-Harmstone, 'The Dialectics of Nationalism,' op. cit., p. 12.

43. Burks, *Dynamics of Communism*, op. cit., pp. xxii-xxv.

44. For a different perspective on Romanian nationality policy, see Marilyn McArthur, 'The Saxon Germans: Political Fate of an Ethnic Identity,' *Dialectical Anthropology*, Vol. I (1976), pp. 349–64.

45. See Trond Gilberg, 'Influence of State Policy on Ethnic Persistence and Nationality Formation: The Case of Eastern Europe,' in Peter F. Sugar, *Ethnic Diversity and Conflict in Eastern Europe* (Santa Barbara, CA: ABC-Clio, 1980).

46. Hitchins, *The Rumanian National Movement*, op. cit., esp. ch. iv.

47. For example, compare the demands of the leaders of the Romanian and Albanian nationalist movements in the nineteenth century and those of the Croats and Slovaks in the interwar period in the twentieth century. Cf. Hitchins, *The Rumanian National Movement* op. cit., p. x; T. Zavalani, 'Albanian Nationalism,' in Sugar and Lederer, *Nationalism in Eastern Europe*, op. cit., p. 65; Shoup, *Communism and the Yugoslav National Question*, op. cit., pp. 10–11; and Paul, *Cultural Limits*, op. cit., ch. vii.

48. Deutsch, *Nationalism and Social Communication*, op. cit., pp. 126 *ff*.

49. Even in 1991, in the face of increasingly intense pressures for secession from several republics in both the Soviet Union and Yugoslavia, the US and the European Community have refrained from encouraging the break-up of the USSR and have opposed the disintegration of Yugoslavia.

Elite Groups, Symbol Manipulation and Ethnic Identity among the Muslims of South Asia

PRIMORDIALIST AND INSTRUMENTALIST INTERPRETATIONS OF ETHNIC IDENTITY

The study of the processes by which ethnic groups and nations are formed has been beset by a persistent and fundamental conceptual difference among scholars concerning the very nature of the groups involved, namely, whether they are 'natural,' 'primordial,' 'given' communities or whether they are creations of interested leaders, of elite groups, or of the political system in which they are included.[1] The primordialist argues that every person carries with him through life 'attachments' derived from place of birth, kinship relationships, religion, language, and social practices that are 'natural' for him, 'spiritual' in character, and that provide a basis for an easy 'affinity' with other peoples from the same background. These 'attachments' constitute the 'givens' of the human condition and are 'rooted in the non-rational foundations of personality.'[2] Some go so far as to argue that such attachments that form the

Acknowledgments Several friends and colleagues were kind enough to read two earlier drafts of this chapter and to provide detailed criticisms and suggestions. I am very grateful to Charles F. Keyes, Daniel S. Lev, Francis Robinson, David Taylor, Muna Vakil, and Malcolm Yapp, whose comments have aided me substantially in revising those earlier drafts. I absolve my colleagues from responsibility for any remaining errors or deficiencies and for the arguments presented.

core of ethnicity are biological and genetic in nature.[3] Whatever
differences in detail exist among the spokesmen for the primordialist
point of view, they tend to unite upon the explicit or implicit
argument that ethnicity, properly defined, is based upon descent.[4]
Since, however, it is quite obvious that there are very few groups
in the world today whose members can lay any serious claim to a
known common origin, it is not actual descent that is considered
essential to the definition of an ethnic group but a belief in a
common descent.

There are some aspects of the primordialist formulation with
which it is not difficult to agree. Even in modern industrial society,
let alone in premodern or modernizing societies, most people
develop attachments in childhood and youth that have deeply
emotive significance, that remain with them through life either
consciously, in the actual persistence of such attachments in the
routines of daily life, or embedded in the unconscious realms of
the adult personality. Such attachments also often provide a basis
for the formation of social and political groupings in adult life for
those for whom they have a continuing conscious meaning in their
daily lives. Even for those persons, particularly in modern societies,
who have been removed from their origins or have rejected their
childhood identifications, such attachments may remain available
in the unconscious to be revived by some appeal that strikes a
sympathetic psychic chord.

It is difficult, however, to travel much further than this with the
primordialists. First of all, it is clear that some primordial attachments are variable. In multilingual developing societies, many
people command more than one language, dialect, or code.[5] Many
illiterate rural persons, far from being attached emotionally to
their mother tongue, do not even know its proper name. In some
situations, members of linguistically diverse ethnic communities
have chosen to change their language in order to provide an
additional element in common with their group members. In other
situations, ethnic group members have deliberately shifted their
own language and educated their children in a different language
than their mother tongue in order to differentiate themselves
further from another ethnic group.[6] Finally, many people, if not
most people, never think about their language at all and never
attach any emotional significance to it.

Religious identification too is subject to change—and not only by modern cosmopolitan man engaged in enlightened spiritual quests. Shifts in religious practices brought about under the influence of religious reformers are common occurrences in premodern, modernizing, and even in postindustrial societies. Sometimes such shifts are clearly designed to promote internal solidarity and external differentiation from other groups.[7]

Even one's place of birth and kinship connections may lose their emotional significance for people or be viewed negatively. A psychoanalyst might argue that these attachments at least pursue men through life and must always remain as potential sources of affective involvement with others. Yet, millions of persons have migrated by choice from their native places in both modern and traditional societies and, while many have retained an emotional attachment to their place of origin, many others have chosen to assimilate to their new society and have lost any sense of emotional identification with their homelands.

For those who do not migrate, one's place of birth identifies a person, but a sense of identity based on attachment to one's region or homeland usually does not become a politically significant matter for those who remain there unless there is some perceived discrimination against the region and its people in the larger society. Moreover, even the 'fact' of one's place of birth is subject to variation. A person is born in a particular village or town, but one is not born in a 'region,' for a region is itself an artificial construct. A person may be born in Savannah, Georgia, and not consider himself a 'Southerner'. It is also possible obviously for 'Southerners' to be born out of their region.

Insofar as kinship connections are concerned, the range of genuine kin relationships is usually too small to be of political significance. Fictive kinship relationships may extend the range of some ethnic groups rather broadly, but their fictive character presumes their variability by definition. Consequently, even 'the facts of birth' are either inherently of no political significance or are subject to variation.[8]

As for the argument that it is not place of birth or kinship or mother tongue or native religion that defines ethnicity but a belief in a common descent that draws on one or more of these attachments, it must be conceded that the argument stated in this general form is not without force. Many ethnic communities do explicitly proclaim or implicitly assume that the underlying basis of their unity is shared descent. It is not at all difficult to find a broad spectrum of such communities. However, broad as the spectrum may be, it will still not suffice to encompass all the culturally-defined collectivities whose members lay claim to special privileges because of some shared cultural features and who are united internally by their attachment to them, unless we define common descent so broadly as to include shared historical, linguistic, or religious experiences. In the latter case, however, we do nothing more than redefine descent to equal shared cultural features.

There are two more serious objections to the primordialist point of view on ethnicity. One is the assumption that sometimes accompanies it that the recognition of distinct primordial groups in a society is sufficient to predict the future development of ethnic communities or nations. This assumption, which is associated principally with the early European ideologists of nationalism, is no longer widely held even by their primordialist descendants, for it is clearly an untenable proposition.

A second point of view is more widely held, namely, that ethnic attachments belong to the non-rational part of the human personality and, as such, are potentially destructive of civil society.[9] This notion suffers from two defects. One is that it ignores the possibility that an ethnic identity may be felt or adopted for rational as well as affective reasons to preserve one's existence or to pursue advantage through communal action. The second is the assumption that primordial attachments are more dangerous to civil order than other kinds of potential conflicts, presumably because of their highly emotive character. However, there is no empirical evidence to warrant the view either that primordial conflicts have produced more disruption in civil societies than economic, class conflicts or that the former conflicts are less amenable to compromise than the latter.

While many primordialists will concede that some aspects of culture are changeable and that the boundaries of ethnic groups may be shifted in the course of social and political movements that promote their interests, they stand firm on one point, namely, that ethnic groups properly so-called are groups based on distinctive cultures or origin myths or patterns of exchange with other groups that have core features that persist through time.[10] Even this bedrock position of the primordialists poses problems for the student of comparative ethnic movements. For one thing, while some ethnic groups do draw upon old and rich cultural heritages with a persisting core, many movements create their cultures after-the-fact, as it were. If, on the one hand, there are groups such as the Jewish people whose social and political identities have undergone innumerable transformations while a core culture has been retained and transmitted over the millennia by the rabbinate steeped in the Talmudic tradition and by ordinary believers following their daily 'self-defining routines,'[11] there are sufficient examples of other groups whose core cultures are less easy to identify, but that have nevertheless formed a basis for cohesive and sometimes successful ethnic and nationalist movements. The mushroom growth of ethnic political movements in the United States in recent times provides at least a few examples of the latter sort that are more than ephemeral in nature.[12]

A second difficulty with the bedrock primordialist position is that, even where there is a persisting core culture, knowledge of its substance may not be of much use in predicting either the development or the form of ethnic movements on behalf of the cultural groups in question. Certainly a knowledge of the core religious cultures of orthodox Judaism or of traditional Islam in India would have suggested that the least likely possibilities would have been the rise of a Zionist movement or of the movement for the creation of Pakistan for the traditional keepers of those cultures, the rabbinate and the *ulema*, have consistently argued that a secular national state is incompatible with either religion. Of course, both the rabbinate and the *ulema* have been largely responsible for the persistence of Jewish and Islamic communities wherever they have persisted, but they are communities differently defined and bounded than are Israel and Pakistan.

Do these criticisms of the primordialist perspective then mean that any cultural content should be removed entirely from the concept of ethnicity? Is ethnicity to be seen from the extreme instrumentalist point of view as the pursuit of interest and advantage for members of groups whose cultures are infinitely malleable and manipulable by elites? Are 'ethnic conflicts' merely 'one form in which interest conflicts between and within states are pursued'[13] and ethnicity 'a communal organization that is manipulated by an interest group in its struggle to develop and maintain its power'?[14] And is culture change part of 'a bargaining process' that can be understood best in terms of a market model by which ethnic group leaders and members agree to give up aspects of their culture or modify their prejudices for the right price?[15] The statements just cited come from a literature that tends to treat cultural factors in ethnic movements as ephiphenomenal. Abner Cohen in fact has written about groups that create cultural markers for purposes of internal communication with each other in secret societies and dominant cliques.[16]

The fact that new cultural groups can be created for purposes of economic and political domination, however, does not mean that the primordialist perspective is not relevant to our understanding of ethnic groups with long and rich cultural heritages. In other words, one possible route towards reconciling the perspectives of primordialists and instrumentalists may lie in simply recognizing that cultural groups differ in the strength and richness of their cultural traditions and even more importantly in the strength of traditional institutions and social structure. For example, the persistence over time of religiously-based communal institutions among Jews and Muslims wherever they are found means that these cultural groups always form potential bases for ethnic movements. However, the mere persistence of the core religious traditions of such groups as these offers no prospect for predicting whether or when ethnic movements will arise among them and whether or not such movements will be effective in mobilizing their members. Such cultural persistence suggests only that it is likely that the groups can be mobilized on the basis of specific appeals and not others and that, when ethnic appeals are made, the pre-existing communal and educational institutions of the groups will, if made available for the purpose, provide an effective means of political mobilization.

In short, the values and institutions of a persisting cultural group will suggest what appeals and symbols will be effective and what will not be and may also provide traditional avenues for the mobilization and organization of the group in new directions. Nevertheless, the leaders of ethnic movements invariably select from traditional cultures only those aspects that they think will serve to unite the group and which will be useful in promoting the interests of the group as they define them. When they do so, moreover, they affect the selfdefinition of the group and its boundaries, often to such an extent that the ethnic community or nationality created out of a pre-existing ethnic group may be a very different social formation from its progenitor. Or, in the case of groups that have had a sense of identity and community even before ethnic mobilization takes place and that contain elites whose traditional right to define the group and its boundaries are well-established, ethnic mobilization led by others than the traditional elites will introduce into the group conflicting definitions of its essence and extent.

Consequently, whether or not the culture of the group is ancient or is newly-fashioned, the study of ethnicity and nationality is in large part the study of politically-induced cultural change. More precisely, it is the study of the process by which elites and counter-elites within ethnic groups select aspects of the group's culture, attach new value and meaning to them, and use them as symbols to mobilize the group, to defend its interests, and to compete with other groups. In this process, those elites have an advantage whose leaders can operate most skillfully in relation both to the deeply-felt primordial attachments of group members and the shifting relationships of politics.

SYMBOLS OF HINDU AND MUSLIM IDENTITY IN SOUTH ASIA

The differences of viewpoint between primordialists and instrumentalists have also found expression among South Asia specialists in their efforts to interpret and explain ethnic and nationality movements there. The differences have been most pronounced in discussions of the origins and development of Muslim separatism and the Pakistan movement. From the primordialist point of view, which was also the view of the leaders of Muslim separatism, Hindus and Muslims constituted in premodern times distinct civilizations destined to develop into separate nations once political mobilization took place. The differences between the two cultures were so great that it was not conceivable that assimilation of the two could take place and that a single national culture could be created to which both would contribute. The contrary view is that the cultural and religious differences between Hindus and Muslims were not so great as to rule out the creation of either a composite national culture or at least a secular political union in which those aspects of group culture that could not be shared would be relegated to the private sphere. From this point of view, Muslim separatism was not pre-ordained, but resulted from the conscious manipulation of selected symbols of Muslim identity by Muslim elite groups in economic and political competition with each other and with elite groups among Hindus.[17]

This issue has recently been joined again in an exchange between Francis Robinson and me.[18] Although Robinson and I agree on many aspects of the Muslim separatist movement, an apparent difference persists concerning the relative weight to be assigned to the pervasiveness of Islamic values, to the strength of Muslim religious institutions, and to the extent to which a Muslim identity existed in the nineteenth century as constraining factors on the possibilities for Hindu–Muslim cooperation and on the freedom of Muslim elite groups to manipulate symbols of Muslim culture in the political process. Robinson argues that 'the religious differences' between Muslims and Hindus in the nineteenth century, before social mobilization began, 'were fundamental' and that some of those differences, such as on idol worship, on monotheism, and on attitudes towards the cow 'created a basic antipathy' between the two communities 'which helped to set them apart as modern politics and self-governing institutions developed in town, district and province.' The Muslims of Uttar Pradesh (UP), primed by these fundamental religious differences, already conscious of themselves as a separate community, and aware that they were a minority, 'feared that the Hindu majority would not only interfere with their religious practices such as cow-sacrifice, but also . . . would discriminate against them' on such matters 'as education and employment'.[19] In short, Hindus and Muslims in nineteenth-century India were separate religious communities predisposed towards, if not necessarily pre-ordained as, separate national groups. If it was not a foregone conclusion that Hindus and Muslims would go separate ways politically, it was unthinkable that the separate identities of either group could be subordinated or assimilated to the other.

Robinson's argument is not entirely inconsistent with the model developed in *Language, Religion and Politics in North India* which, although it emphasized the roles played by elite groups in manipulating cultural symbols to create political identities, did not ignore either pre-existing cultural values or intergroup attitudes as factors influencing the ability of elites to manipulate particular symbols. In fact, the model developed in *Language, Religion and Politics* did not take off from an extreme instrumentalist perspective or from the assumption that either elites or the groups whose interests they claim to represent are cultural blank slates. Rather, it began with the following question: Given the existence in a multi-ethnic society of an array of cultural distinctions among peoples and of actual and potential cultural conflicts among them, what factors are critical in determining which of those distinctions, if any, will be used to build political identities? In *Language, Religion and Politics*, the factors emphasized were the roles played by particular elite groups, the balance between rates of social mobilization and assimilation between ethnic groups, the building of political organizations to promote group identities and interests, and the influence of government policies. However, it was not assumed that the pre-existing cultures or religious practices of ethnic groups are infinitely malleable by elites.

Nevertheless, it is an important and not well-explored question to consider to what extent and in what ways the pre-existing values, institutions, and practices of cultural groups with long and rich heritages constitute primordial attachments that constrain elites who manipulate symbols of group identity for political purposes. In the remainder of this essay, this question will be explored with specific reference to three elements involving Hindu and Muslim traditional cultural values, institutions, and communication in South Asia during the last century—attitudes toward cow protection and cow sacrifice, the role of the personal and family law components of the Sharia in Muslim life, and the attitudes of Hindus and Muslims towards the Hindi and Urdu languages. In this section, the issue will be taken up by considering separately each element of traditional culture and its use by elites in politics. In the following section, the extent to which elites are able to alter the definition of a group's boundaries by manipulating sets of symbols will be analyzed.

Cow Protection and Cow Sacrifice

Consider first the different attitudes of Hindus and Muslims towards the cow. As Robinson points out, 'Hindus revered the cow, the Muslims ate it.'[20] Moreover, Muslims sacrificed cows at certain religious festivals such as Bakr-Id.[21] The cow, therefore, was always a potential symbol of group identity for Hindus and of group conflict between Hindus and Muslims. However, it is also important to recognize that the symbol of the cow has had differential import for Hindus and Muslims. For orthodox Hindus, it is simply mandatory to avoid the killing of kine. It is not, however, mandatory for Muslims to eat kine. It is a disputed matter whether or not cow sacrifice is essential to Muslim religious ritual.[22] These 'objective' cultural parameters clearly limited and constrained the freedom of movement of Hindu and Muslim elites in the late nineteenth and twentieth centuries in South Asia, but they did not confine them completely. Hindus might have ignored the fact that Muslims slaughtered cows for both dietary and ritual purposes—except insofar as cow slaughter was flaunted before them—but in the 1880s and 1890s many chose to form cow protection societies and to demand passage of laws to prevent cow slaughter.[23] Muslims might have avoided cow slaughter and, thereby, made a grand concession to Hindu sentiment without violating their own religious susceptibilities. In fact, Abd al-Bari, the fiery *alim* of Firangi Mahal offered to stop cow slaughter by Muslims during the early days of the Khilafat and non-cooperation movements[24] and the Muslim League, in its 1919 meeting, passed a resolution recommending the substitution of 'the sacrifice of other animals in place of cows.'[25] The predominant leaders of the Indian National Congress attempted to restrain the leaders of the cow protection movement and tried to prevent them from demanding laws to prevent cow slaughter, even though the cow protection movement had considerable support among Congressmen in the northern provinces.[26] Moreover, even the most militant cow protectors used an economic argument for the prevention of cow slaughter which, however transparent a cover it may seem for religious sentiment, always kept open the possibility that Hindus and Muslims could reach an agreement on secular grounds concerning an issue of profound religious import.[27] That the issue was not settled on terms such as these was not because of its primordial character, but because several elite groups among both Hindus and Muslims found it useful as a convenient symbol in their efforts to build internal unity and in their conflicts with each other. The cow was a symbol that could be used equally by orthodox Hindus defending traditional religious practices, by revivalist Hindu leaders who wished to promote a specifically Hindu form of Indian national-ism,[28] and by Muslim religious and political elites who feared Hindu dominance and found anti-cow slaughter movements useful as an example of how Muslims would be oppressed under a representative system in which Hindus would be in a majority.

John McLane has suggested that the political significance of the cow in Indian politics should not be overemphasized and that it is not possible to separate controversy over the cow slaughter issue from other issues of elite conflict over access to education, government employment opportunities, and political representation with which it was 'intertwined'.[29] Moreover, he has argued that, although the cow protection movement of the 1880s and 1890s had a great impact on Hindu–Muslim relations and precipitated a chain of riots in 1893, the disappearance of the cow protection move-ment thereafter 'suggests that popular sentiment was not broad or adamant and that Hindu leaders regarded the alienation of Muslims and the government as too heavy a price to pay for any possible benefits' for its continuance. He suggests further that 'the issue of cow slaughter was more symbolic than substantive,' that it 'was not central' to the persisting substantive issues of Indian politics, which concerned 'the distribution of political power' under the constitutional structures devised under British rule in India.[30]

It would be more precise to say that the cow protection issue was not central to the political elites who dominated the leading poli-tical organizations of Indian nationalism and Muslim separatism. It was central to the Hindu religious leaders, revivalist and orthodox, and it later became a useful symbol for Hindu communal organ-izations committed to a Hindu definition of Indian nationalism, such as the Hindu Mahasabha and the Jan Sangh. It was also a persistent irritant in Hindu–Muslim relations in municipal politics in the towns of the United Provinces in the late nineteenth and early twentieth centuries.[31] After independence, the Constituent Assembly of India acknowledged Hindu sentiment on the matter by including in the directive principles of state policy an article containing a mandate for the state to prohibit cow slaughter. This mandate has since been implemented by most state governments in India. Morevoer, as late as 1966, a movement was launched by Hindu revivalist groups, supported by the most prestigious orthodox gurus associated with the holiest sanctuaries of Hinduism, in support of the demand that the Government of India impose a ban on cow slaughter throughout the country. The movement culminated in the largest mass demonstration ever witnessed in the postindependence period on the streets of Delhi. However, the government refused to accept the demand.

The cow, therefore, may be seen as a primordial attachment for Hindus, to which religious reformers and Hindu nationalists in the late nineteenth century attached new meaning as a symbol of Hindu communal identity, and which secular political leaders of the time either avoided because they could not control its use or used provocatively in constructing catalogues of grievances against their opponents from the rival community. Differences in Hindu and Muslim attitudes toward the cow, therefore, provide an example of the intrusion into politics of a symbol that had primordial meaning for Hindus and that served to threaten the religious and political position of Muslims in India. The cow protection movement brought Hindu and Muslim religious sentiments into direct conflict, even though the issue was of less religious significance for Muslims than for Hindus. Moreover, Hindu sentiment toward the cow was such that it limited the freedom of action even of the secular leaders of the Congress. Elites were therefore constrained on this highly emotive issue, although a few Hindu leaders took independent action on it in opposition to the primordial feelings of Hindus in hopes of political cooperation with Muslims, and Muslim religious and political elites offered to defer to Hindu sentiment on the matter.

Muslim Personal Law

The issue of Muslim personal law provides a somewhat different example of a symbol of great religious significance to Muslims and with no religious significance to Hindus, but which has brought Muslims in India into conflict with secular nationalists, both Hindu and Muslim. It is a religious obligation for Muslims to adhere to the body of laws that make up the Sharia and that includes the 'personal law' relating to marriage, divorce, and inheritance. However, the application of the law is often a complex matter that may involve the intervention of clerical authority. Muslims must be taught some of the most important laws of Islam from an early age, but ordinary Muslims can hardly be expected to know more than a fraction of the body of prescriptions and proscriptions contained in the Sharia. The interpretation and application of the Sharia is one of the principal mechanisms by which the *ulema* maintain their control over Islamic society. While an orthodox Muslim would not think of violating the more evident and established principles of the Sharia and while he would revere the law, the Sharia means most to the Muslim clerics.

In Muslim-majority societies undergoing secularization, the Sharia invariably emerges as a symbol of conflict between the *ulema* and the secular political elites, who wish to establish a centralized state for which they consider a modern legal system essential. In former colonial societies with large Muslim populations and in societies such as contemporary India where Muslims are in a minority, the issue naturally acquires a different significance, for the modernizing elite will then be predominantly non-Muslim and will, therefore, be attacked for interfering with the religious rights of Muslims. This, of course, has been the case in India both under British rule and since independence where any attempt to discuss the formulation of a uniform civil code has been sure to call forth the nearly unanimous opposition of the *ulema*.

The British did impose a secular system of criminal and procedural law in India and they abolished the *qazi* courts that had previously enforced Muslim law, but they did not develop a uniform civil code for personal and family law.[32] On the contrary, both Hindu and Muslim personal law were formally recognized and were applied in the government courts.[33] Although the constitution of independent India established the passage of a uniform civil code as one of the directive principles of state policy, that directive has been carried out only with respect to non-Muslims under the Hindu Code Acts of 1955–56.

Neither the British nor the leaders of postindependence India were willing to antagonize the *ulema* on the matter of reform of Muslim personal law, for it is believed that the *ulema* have succeeded in imparting to most Muslims the feeling that any tampering with the personal law would amount to an attack on Islam. The fear that the *ulema* would be able to mobilize the mass of Muslims in India in opposition to any efforts to reform their personal law has enabled them to hold hostage both the secular Hindu political elites and all Muslim political leaders who seek to represent

Muslim interests. During the nationalist period in India, when the Congress and the Muslim League vied for the support of the Muslim public, Congress leaders succeeded in forming a political alliance with the Jami'yat-al-ulama-i-Hind, founded in 1919 for 'the exclusive purpose of safeguarding the "Shari'ah".[34] For its part, the Muslim League, many of whose leaders were secular politicians opposed both to the rigid application of the Sharia and to the continued hold of the *ulema* over the Muslim masses, nevertheless felt obliged to include in its demands protection for Muslim personal law.

In this case, therefore, the issue, however much the Sharia is seen as essential to Islam, does not involve conflict with Hindus as such. It is a symbol that Muslim religious elites use to constrain Muslim political elites who, in turn, have often found it useful as a symbol in their conflicts with Hindu elites for political influence in the Muslim community. Since Muslim adherence to the Sharia does not impinge upon the religious feelings of Hindus and does not endanger Hindu–Muslim relations, the secular political elites in modern India have been able to avoid a confrontation on this issue with Muslims. Whereas on the issue of cow protection, many otherwise secular-minded Hindu elites felt constrained to support cow protection legislation in the Constitution of India and in state legislation after independence, they have been negatively constrained on the question of a uniform civil code.

The strategy followed in India since independence has been to use secular Muslims to speak on behalf of modernization of the Muslim personal law, but to avoid any action on the issue that would endanger Hindu–Muslim relations. In effect, a tacit bargain has been struck in modern India whose terms are that Muslims will not be permitted to violate Hindu feelings by slaughtering cows, while the Muslims retain the right to have a separate system of civil laws.[35] This bargain could have been struck at any time before independence had it not served the interests of Hindu religious elites and Muslim political elites to keep the issues alive. It was not struck because Hindu revivalists found the symbol of the cow invaluable in uniting Hindus, because the Muslim political elites found the cow protection issue useful to demonstrate the dangers of Hindu majority rule, and because both Hindu and Muslim political elites found the issue of the Sharia valuable in recruiting the support of the *ulema* in their conflicts with each other for political influence.

The Urdu Language and Muslim Identity

A third major symbol of Muslim identity and Hindu–Muslim conflict, particularly in the north Indian states of UP and Bihar, is the Urdu language. The adoption of Urdu as a symbol of Muslim identity by Muslim political elites in north India fro..1 the late nineteenth century onwards illustrates several points concerning the uses made of cultural symbols by political elites.[36] One is the way in which elites attach new value to symbols for purposes of promoting identity and differentiating one group from another. In the nineteenth century in north India, before the extension of the British system of government schools, Urdu was not used in its written form as a medium of instruction in traditional Islamic schools, where Muslim children were taught Persian and Arabic, the traditional languages of Islam and Muslim culture.[37] It was only when the Muslim elites of north India and the British decided that Muslims were backward in education in relation to Hindus and should be encouraged to attend government schools that it was felt necessary to offer Urdu in the Persian–Arabic script as an inducement to Muslims to attend the schools. And it was only after the Hindi–Urdu controversy developed that Urdu, once disdained by Muslim elites in north India and not even taught in the Muslim religious schools in the early nineteenth century, became a symbol of Muslim identity second only to Islam itself.[38]

A second point revealed by the Hindi–Urdu controversy in north India is how symbols may be used to separate peoples who, in fact, share aspects of culture. It is well known that ordinary Muslims and Hindus alike spoke the same language in the United Provinces in the nineteenth century, namely Hindustani, whether called by that name or whether called Hindi, Urdu, or one of the regional dialects such as Braj or Awadhi. Although a variety of styles of Hindi–Urdu were in use in the nineteenth century among different social classes and status groups, the legal and administrative elites in courts and government offices, Hindus and Muslims alike, used Urdu in the Persian–Arabic script. When the Urdu-speaking elite divided politically on the question of script, however, that division was communicated and transmitted to the mass of the people. As more and more government schools were set up, it became a critical question, therefore, for Urdu and Hindi spokesmen to insist that Hindus had the right to be taught through the medium of Hindi in Devanagari script and that Muslims had the

right to be taught through the medium of Urdu in Persian script
because their languages and cultures were inseparable. Moreover,
leaders of the Hindi movement and of the Urdu movement set out
to separate the two languages through Sanskritization and Persian-
ization of its two forms.[39] In this way, the literary elites of the
United Provinces deliberately chose to emphasize and even to
create linguistic differences rather than to emphasize and enhance
the linguistic elements held in common by Hindus and Muslims
alike by such devices, for example, as developing a common
vocabulary and teaching both scripts.

A third point is that the choice of a symbol often has a material
basis, arising out of elite competition for economic advantage.
Urdu became a symbol of Muslim identity in north India when the
British, partly because of the demands of Hindi supporters, moved
to either replace Urdu with Hindi as the language of administration in the northern provinces or to admit Hindi on an equal basis
with Urdu. The Muslim elites in north India rose to defend Urdu
because the replacement of Urdu by Hindi or even its admission to
equality threatened the advantage that Muslims traditionally held
in government employment, particularly in the United Provinces.
It should be especially emphasized in this regard that the adoption
of the Devanagari script presented only a slight difficulty for
Muslims, whereas the maintenance of Urdu in Persian–Arabic
script raised much greater difficulties for Hindus. It is a relatively
small matter for a Hindustani-speaker to learn to read and write
the language in Devanagari, which is a quite simple script, but it
requires a much greater educational investment to learn and
maintain the Persian–Arabic script. The defence of Urdu, therefore, could not have arisen out of a fear that Muslims would
acquire an undue burden by the need to learn the Devanagari
script but out of a desire to maintain the rather heavier burden on
Hindus of acquiring proficiency in the Persian–Arabic script to
qualify for government jobs.

A fourth point is that the same symbol may be used at different
times for contrary objectives. When the demand was made to
admit Hindi in Devanagari script as an official language in the
North-Western Provinces and Oudh, along with Urdu in Persian–
Arabic script, Muslims argued that Urdu was not their language
only, but the common possession of Hindus and Muslims alike and
that it should be retained as the sole official language for this

reason and for its alleged technical advantages over Hindi. The argument that Urdu is the language of both Hindus and Muslims continues to be made up to the present by its defenders. Moreover, the argument has some historical validity. However, Urdu has also often been used as a symbol by Muslim elites to separate themselves from the Hindus. When Hindu leaders refused to withdraw their demands for official recognition of Hindi and for its use in the educational system and when its use threatened the material interests of Muslim elites, many Muslims began to argue that Urdu was the special language of Muslims, that its cultural heritage was expressed through it, and that it was nearly as much a part of Muslim identity as Islam itself.

The final point illustrated by the Muslim adoption of Urdu in Persian–Arabic script is the tendency for ethnic groups in conflict to separate themselves from each other by multiple symbols and to seek to make those symbols congruent. In the early nineteenth century, Muslims and Hindus had different religious traditions and practices and, insofar as they were educated at all, they were taught Persian or Arabic, if they were Muslims, Hindi or Sanskrit, if they were Hindus. In the different dialect or language regions of north India, however, Muslims and Hindus alike spoke the language of the region in which they lived. In other words, they may have used different languages to communicate with their deity, but they used a common language to communicate with each other. In the course of the Hindi–Urdu controversy, however, as Hindi and Urdu were developed as alternative regional standard languages taught in all government schools in the different dialect regions of the north, Hindi in Devanagari script became the language of Hindus and Urdu in Persian script the language of Muslims. The functions of language in the north thereby became transformed from their traditional uses for ritual communication with a deity or for ordinary discourse into symbolic links among members of the same ethnic group, barriers to communication between members of different religious groups, and additional marks of identity and separateness for such groups.

The changes over the past century in both Muslim and Hindu attitudes towards the Urdu language and the several different symbolic uses to which it has been put by Muslim elites in their competition with Hindus demonstrate that 'primordial' attachments may be subject to substantial variation for the sake of political and

economic interests. Hindus and Muslims in north India had the
same 'given' mother tongues. The religious and political elites of
north India and the British authorities, however, made decisions
about official languages and scripts and about media of instruction
in the schools that, over time, have affected the ways in which
ordinary Hindus and Muslims feel about their language and how it
should be used. In fact, the two languages, Hindi and Urdu, have
also diverged in the past century. Initially, however, the language
controversy was principally a struggle over scripts. The Persian–
Arabic and Devanagari scripts, however, are not 'givens'. They
are cultural transmissions, with religious significance because they
are the scripts used to decipher the religious texts. But they did not
have to become symbols of group identity. They became symbols
of identity because elite groups, with the aid of government,
promoted them as such in their conflicts with each other.

ELITE COMPETITION, SYMBOL MANIPULATION, AND COMPETING DEFINITIONS OF THE MUSLIM COMMUNITY

The three examples given above illustrate the interrelationship
among a group's cultural symbols, the interests of specific elite
groups in relation to particular symbols, and the freedom of action
that elites have or do not have to manipulate such symbols in the
political process. However, in order to fully perceive the nature of
the relationship between the ethnic identity of a cultural group and
the actions of its elites, it is necessary to consider how sets of
symbols are used to define the boundaries of a group. It is important
to recognize beforehand, however, that at no time in the history of
any cultural group is there likely to be anything like unanimous
agreement on defining what it means to be a member of a particular cultural group. Moreover, any definition that acquires a high
degree of consensus within a community at a particular point in its
history is likely at some time to be subject to redefinition as a
consequence of either internal conflicts of interest or ideology
within the group or as a consequence of external changes that
affect segments of the group differentially.
  Insofar as the Muslims of India are concerned, two features of

their historical development as a community are particularly relevant here. One is that, when the British arrived, the Muslim community of India or of any part of India was much less of a social fact that it is today. Second, in the course of the social and political development of the Muslim community in the nineteenth and twentieth centuries, the symbols used to define its boundaries have varied depending upon the elites who have done the defining. With regard to the social reality of the Muslim community in India before the arrival of the British, Hardy has described it as 'unified at best by a few common rituals and by the beliefs and aspirations of a majority—not the totality—of its scholars.'[40] Titus has pointed out that Muslims in India have always been divided along sectarian lines, some of them sharply antagonistic, and has described in detail several Muslim groups whose religious practices were quite similar to those of Hindus.[41] Seal has remarked that the Muslim community in the nineteenth century 'was not homogeneous. Language, caste and economic standing worked together to divide Muslim from Muslim no less than Hindu from Hindu.'[42]

In what sense, then, was there a Muslim community at all in India in the nineteenth century? There was certainly a community of Muslim believers, united by a common relationship to a deity, by a belief in the prophethood of Muhammad, by a recognition that the Quran was the ultimate source of religious authority, and by participation in common worship. Many, but not all, Muslims were guided by the Sharia, there was a considerable diversity of religious practices, rituals, and beliefs at the mass level not recognized or condemned outright by the orthodox *ulema*, Muslims spoke different languages, and they did not have a common origin, some being descendants of invaders from the Middle East, others being indigenous converts. In the early nineteenth century, then, there was at most a Muslim community of believers, with only a limited set of beliefs and religious practices held in common, but not a Muslim political or speech community.

During the late nineteenth and twentieth centuries, however, elites within the Muslim religious community, in their efforts to adjust to the extension of the British imperial system in India and to new sets of relationships with other religious groups, began to define the Muslim community in different ways. The British authorities materially assisted this process for all elite groups involved in it by treating the Muslims of India as an official

category for purposes of census enumeration, distribution of
government appointments, political representation, and education.

The View of the *Ulema*: Muslims as a Religious and Legal Community

One such elite group, itself internally diverse in some ways, was
the *ulema*. Through movements of religious revivalism, through
the establishment of networks of educational institutions, and
through political action they set about to unify the Muslim
community, to educate the Muslim masses in Islamic beliefs and
rituals and to persuade them to avoid non-Islamic religious practices,
and to seek government recognition for a legal definition of the
Muslim community in India as well.[43]

Muslim revivalism arose initially out of the need felt by the
ulema to combat the threats of Christian missionaries to convert
Muslims, of western education to subvert them, and of the imperial
state to loosen their control over the faithful by introducing a
modern legal system. Although Muslim revivalism was directed
initially against the alien rulers, it brought Muslims into conflict
with Hindu revivalists who were engaged in a similar enterprise
and who resented Muslim proselytization as much as Christian
missionary activity. The conflict between the two revivalisms led
to a sharpening of the religious boundaries between Hindus and
Muslims to the extent—which to this day is far from complete—
that each side succeeded in convincing its followers to relinquish
ritual practices and forms of worship held in common.

Thus, the *ulema* did not accept Muslim religious identity in the
form that they found it in the nineteenth century, but worked to
impart to the Muslim masses an understanding and a practice of
Islam more in line with what the *ulema* considered to be proper for
the faithful. In doing so, the *ulema* who led the 'traditionalist
revival' were also concerned with defending their definitions of
Islamic propriety from the reformist interpretations of the mod-
ernists in Islam, particularly of Sayyid Ahmad Khan and the
Aligarh movement, who had by the end of the nineteenth century
also become a threat to the control of the *ulema* over the Muslim
community.[44] Religious revivalism had a dual impact on the
Muslims as a religious community in that it both solidified the

relationship between the clerics and the masses[45] and separated the faithful more clearly from non-Muslims. The *ulema* also set about to extend the enforcement of the Sharia among Muslims who had not been fully subject to it.[46] For the *ulema*, then, the Muslims of India constituted both a religious and a legal community. Such a definition of the Muslim community is, of course, exactly in conformity with orthodox Islam,[47] but it did not exist in nineteenth-century India as fully as the *ulema* wished and it had, therefore, to be enforced.

It is important to recognize that the conception of the Muslim community held by the *ulema* in the nineteenth century did not include a definition of the Muslims of India as a political community in the modern sense of the term, that is, as a selfdetermining entity with the right to have a state of its own and the authority to make its own laws. Such a definition would have then been considered contrary both to the orthodox teachings of Islam concerning the universality of the Muslim community and concerning the duty of Muslims to follow the Sharia rather than man-made law. It was not until the second decade of the twentieth century that some of the *ulema* began to articulate a different conception of the 'Muslims as forming a political community . . . capable of combining in common enterprises because its members share the values of Islam.'[48] However, that conception did not include the idea that the Sharia could be applied or interpreted 'by popular decision and collective will.'[49] That task was to remain the prerogative of the *ulema*. Moreover, insofar as any of the *ulema* in India articulated a modern conception of 'territorial nationhood,' it was not to apply to the Muslims as a separate people but to India as a whole,[50] in which the Muslims after independence were, it was hoped, to constitute a 'largely self-governing' religious community.[51]

Although the elimination of non-Islamic religious practices prevalent among Indian Muslims and the protection of the Sharia were the more prominent goals of the *ulema* who became active in politics and social movements, particularly in the Jami'yat-al-ulama formed in 1919,[52] they also played a part through the Jami'yat and through their educational network in promoting the spread of the Urdu language among Muslims and its use as an additional symbol of Muslim identity. An Urdu strongly infused with Arabic and Persian words was the medium of instruction at the leading *ulema*-dominated school at Deoband in UP and at its affiliated *madrasahs* spread throughout north India.[53] Although Arabic, not Urdu, was the language used by *ulema* in Kerala, in the north and in Hyderabad, the *ulema* found that a Persianized-Arabicized Urdu was the most useful vehicle both to provide access to traditional Islamic literature and to communicate with ordinary Muslims. In its 1926 conference, the Jami'yat-al-ulama passed a resolution demanding that the 'Urdu language and Urdu script be declared as the accepted National Language and the accepted National Script' of India.[54] In the postindependence period, as Urdu lost some of its hold in the government schools in the north, the *ulema* rushed to the defence of Urdu, which came to be seen as part and parcel of Muslim 'social and cultural identity and their spiritual inheritance.'[55]

For the *ulema*, then, the Muslim community of India has been defined primarily in religious and legal terms. The primary symbol of Muslim identity for the *ulema*, however, is Islam itself, in which adherence to the Sharia is an indispensable aspect. Urdu has also been included in the *ulema*'s definition of the Muslim community but as a secondary symbol only, used defensively in conflict with Hindus. However, while the *ulema* would exclude from the Muslim community those persons who blatantly violate the Sharia, they would clearly not exclude non-Urdu speakers.

Muslim Aristocratic Elites and the Definition of the Muslims as an Historical–Political Community

For the Muslim political elites who founded the Aligarh movement and the Muslim League and who successfully led the movement for the creation of Pakistan, the values attached to the several potential symbols of Muslim identity in India were quite different. Moreover, from the beginning, the definition of the Muslim community articulated by the modernizing Muslim elites associated with Sayyid Ahmad Khan and the Aligarh movement was a political one. In contrast to the *ulema*, who attached most value to symbols of Muslim identity that not only separated Muslims from non-Muslims but isolated Muslims from contamination by alien religious and legal influences and preserved the influence of the *ulema* within the Muslim community, the modernist elites were initially interested in using the community as a base for the exercise of influence in the wider society. The Muslim aristocrats and

government servants who founded the various institutions associated with the Aligarh movement moved in the same spheres as,
and had similar interests to those of, their Hindu counterparts. As
landlords, they wanted to retain control over their tenants, who
were both Hindu and Muslim. As government servants, they
wanted to ensure that they and their children could continue to
have favored access to the best jobs in government.

Whereas the interests of the *ulema* required only the striking of
a bargain whose terms were that the personal law provisions of the
Sharia would not be tampered with or replaced by secular laws in
return for which the *ulema* would not resist the authority of the
imperial state in other respects, the interests of the Muslim aristocrats and government servants required active collaboration with
the British authorities. The terms of the bargain worked out in the
last decades of the nineteenth century and the first two decades of
the twentieth between the modernist Muslim elites and the British
were that the British would recognize the existence of a Muslim
community in India, with the Muslim aristocrats and government
servants as its spokesmen, would concede to those spokesmen a
separate political arena in which they would not have to compete
with non-Muslims, would grant extra representation to those
spokesmen in a proportion beyond the actual population of the
community they were to represent, and would help the Muslims to
maintain their advantage in government employment. In return,
the Muslim landlords and government servants were expected not
only to avoid opposing the government but to provide positive
support for it and opposition to its detractors.[56]

The primary symbols of Muslim identity used by the privileged
Muslim classes in the late nine', enth century were political and
historical. They argued that the Muslims of India had been the
rulers of the country until the British arrived,[57] that their previous
tradition of rule gave them an historical and political importance
far beyond the mere numbers of the Muslim population of the
country, and that they were, therefore, entitled to a continued and
more than proportionate share in political power under British
rule. The Muslim elites and their historiographical and literary
apologists looked back to the great days of Muslim expansion and
political power not only in India but in the Middle East, Africa,
and Europe for inspiration. For these Muslim elites, as for the
ulema, the Urdu language became a secondary symbol of Muslim

identity only when it came under attack by Hindu revialists, with
the support of the British government. Since, however, it was
through the Urdu language that the Muslim elites in the nineteenth century preserved their priviledged access to government
jobs, recognition of Hindi by the provincial governments in north
India, particularly in the North-Western Provinces and Oudh,
threatened the special political position of the Muslim minority in
the Hindu majority areas and upset the Muslim–British bargain.

It is noteworthy that the Sharia does not appear as a prominent
symbol of Muslim identity for the Muslim landlords and government
servants. Although the landed Muslim classes had a specific
interest in the application of the Muslim law of *wakf* in such a way
that they could put their properties into a trust for the use of their
descendants, they did not like those aspects of Sharia that restricted
their abilities to dispose of their properties to persons of their
choice.[58] Islam itself was but a secondary symbol for the Muslim
political elites of the nineteenth century. Although Sayyid Ahmad
Khan did, on occasion, defend Islam from the attacks of Christian
missionaries, he was not interested in launching an Islamic counter-
offensive, but rather in 'demonstrating the basic similarity
between Islam and Christianity,'[59] which fitted well with his persistent design for a collaborative alliance between the British and the
Muslims of India. Nor were the nineteenth-century political elites
even seriously engaged in defining the boundaries of the Muslim
community. Rather, they accepted the British official recognition
of the existence of a Muslim community, which involved their
enumeration in the decennial censuses and frequent reports and
inquiries into the conditions of this community and its alleged
backwardness in relation to Hindus. The Muslim elites of the
nineteenth century were concerned principally to use the data
provided by the British concerning the backwardness of the mass
of Muslims, with whom the leaders had little contact, as an argument for preserving their own privileges.

Although Sayyid Ahmad Khan was concerned to promote
Western education among the Muslims so that they would be in a
better position to qualify for high government office, he did not
feel that education alone qualified a man for a position of importance in the realm. Such distinctions were to be reserved for persons
'of high social position' and 'of good breeding,' not for men 'of low
caste or insignificant origin.'[60] Nor did he favor competition with

the Hindus, particularly with the despised Bengalis, but he urged
the Muslims to educate themselves so that they might be eligible to
be selected to serve the Raj. He proposed, in effect, a collaboration between the former ruling nations and classes of Hindustan,
among whom he sometimes included the Rajputs, with the then
ruling nation, the British.

Elite, Diversification, Secular Political Elites, and the Definition of the Muslims as a Nation

After World War I, however, the secular Muslim elites became
more diversified and middle class professionals and professional
politicians became more prominent in Muslim politics. At the
same time, as the franchise was extended to larger numbers of
people under the Montagu–Chelmsford reforms and later the
Government of India Act, 1935, it became necessary, if Muslim
leaders were to substantiate their claim to represent their community, for them to engage in political mobilization of the people
in whose abstract name elite benefits had been previously sought.
Moreover, the diversification of elites within the Muslim community
itself led to intracommunal elite competition for the right to speak
for the community.

Robinson has described the initial impact on Muslim politics of
elite diversification and increasing pressures for political mobilization during the Khilafat movement of 1919–20. During this
movement, the newer groups of middle class professionals and
full-time politicians joined in an alliance with the *ulema* in a
campaign whose central symbol was a pan-Islamic one.[61] Most
members of the traditional Muslim elite groups and the secular-
oriented Muslim leaders such as Jinnah refused to have anything
to do with this movement, the former because it involved a challenge
to the government and their collaborative relationship with it, the
latter because it involved an emotional merging of religion and
politics.

In the decades after the Khilafat movement, however, the secular
political leadership of the Muslim League dominated Muslim politics
and sought to achieve for the Muslim community in India the kinds
of goals that had been set by the Aligarh movement leaders, most
of which concerned satisfactory political representation. The

famous Fourteen Points drafted by Jinnah in 1929 contained twelve points that focused on matters of political representation, including such questions as the proportion of seats to be allotted to Muslims in legislatures and cabinets, maintaining or extending the number of Muslim-majority provinces, and the retention of separate electorates. Only two of the fourteen points specifically mentioned religious or cultural matters. Point seven demanded full religious liberty and point twelve demanded constitutional 'safeguards for the protection of Muslim culture and for the protection and promotion of Muslim education, language, religion, personal laws and Muslim charitable institutions.'[62] The issue of the Sharia, of such central and overwhelming importance to the *ulema* and considered by many others than the *ulema* to be essential to any definition of the Muslim community, is relegated to two words in a long sentence without any specific mention of the nature of the 'safeguards' to be sought. It is also noteworthy that Urdu is not mentioned specifically in the Fourteen Points. In Jinnah's later statements and in various resolutions and manifestoes of the Muslim League, protection of Urdu was sometimes mentioned. However, it is clear enough from the infrequent attention given to the Urdu issue in his own speeches and writings that the language issue was not his primary concern.[63] As for the Sharia and the *ulema*, Jinnah hardly ever referred to the former and occasionally criticized the latter, some of whom he described as 'that undesirable element of Maulvis and Maulanas' from whose political clutches the Muslim League had freed the Muslim masses.[64]

Jinnah's definition of the Muslim community was a political one, rather than a religious–legal or linguistic one. Although, therefore, it was entirely different from the definition used by the *ulema*, it also moved away from the historical–political definition of the early leaders of the Aligarh movement. The Muslim community for Jinnah was not an abstract historical–political entity but a contemporary political force. Safeguards and weightage in representation for Muslims were now sought not because of the historical importance of the Muslim community in India but because, though they were a minority, they were also a separate people with distinct interests. They could not, therefore, be treated like the shifting minorities in a representative system who could be voted down on one issue, but would have a chance to prevail on other issues. On the contrary, the Muslims of India represented a permanent and persisting political interest and could not be treated only as a minority.

Jinnah's political methods were also entirely different from those of the Muslim political elites of the nineteenth century. Collaboration with the British authorities could not provide the necessary safeguards for Muslims, especially as India moved closer to selfgovernment. What was required was unity, solidarity, and organization. After the formation of Congress governments in six provinces in India in 1937 and the unwillingness of the Congress to cooperate with the Muslim League on its terms in those provinces, Jinnah's call for Muslim unity and solidarity became his principal theme. The Muslims, Jinnah insisted, should follow the Muslim League as its 'only authoritative and representative organization'[65] and should pursue 'one single definite uniform policy.'[66] Only by organization and unity could the Muslim minority protect its 'rights and interests' against what Jinnah saw as 'a permanent Hindu majority.'[67]

It was a short step from this position ideologically, but rather a larger one rhetorically, to the position articulated by Jinnah after the failure of the Muslim League to achieve its political goals in India in the 1930s and the passage of the Pakistan resolution of 1940, namely, the idea that the Muslims of India constituted a selfdetermining political community, a nation in the modern sense of the term. The differences between Hindus and Muslims in India were now seen as not merely religious differences, but as entirely different ways of life and thought. Hindus and Muslims in India were distinct peoples, with 'different religious philosophies, social customs, literatures,' and histories.[68] As such, it was unthinkable that they could live as a mere minority in a Hindu-dominated country. Rather, they must have a state of their own in which they would establish their own constitution and make their own laws.

Once the state of Pakistan was founded, however, Jinnah reverted to a position much more consistent with his secular political orientation, namely, that the differences between Hindus and Muslims were matters of personal religion only, which did not prevent their cooperating together as citizens of the same state.[69] His death in 1948, however, meant that others in Pakistan had to face up to the fundamental contradiction between the secular political conception of a modern Muslim state and the religious–legal conception of it held by the *ulema*. Others too had to face the contradictions posed by the fact that north Indian Muslims who had taken the lead in Muslim separatism had for decades been promoting the view that Urdu was the language of the Muslims, a position vehemently denied by the Bengali majority in the new state. These contradictions have so far proved to be irresolvable. The first contributed to the prolonged difficulties in reaching a consensus on a constitution for Pakistan, the second to its disintegration. The persistent problems of maintaining national unity in Pakistan in the face of linguistic and cultural diversities suggest that a satisfactory definition of the boundaries of the Muslim nation is yet a long way off.

ELITE INTERESTS, CULTURAL SYMBOLS, AND PRIMORDIAL ATTACHMENTS

In the preceding pages, the relationship between elite interests and three Hindu and Muslim cultural symbols in South Asia in the nineteenth and twentieth centuries have been discussed. It remains to consider what the discussion suggests about the relationships between these 'givens' of Hindu and Muslim existence in north India and the symbols used by religious and political elites.

In some senses, all three of the symbols discussed can be considered primordial attachments: the cow, the Sharia, and the Urdu language. For the orthodox Hindu, the prohibition against killing and eating beef is inseparable from his religion and his whole moral outlook on life. It is, therefore, inconceivable that any Hindu politician could expect to be effective in mobilizing support by proposing that the prohibitions against cow slaughter be discarded as superstitious.[70] It is also evident that the cow is always potentially a symbol that can be called up by Hindu religious or political elites to mobilize large numbers of Hindus either to build internal unity or to engage in action directed against Muslims. To say that the cow is always potentially available as a mobilizing symbol, however, does not mean that any Hindu politician or religious leader who uses it at any time is bound to succeed. It does mean, though, that if the government or the Muslims flaunt Hindu sentiment by permitting open or too evident slaughtering of cows, Hindu religious leaders are likely to rise and mobilize Hindus in protest. Does this mean that Hindu–Muslim conflict was inevitable in Hindu-majority India and that Muslims must submit to Hindu sentiment on the issue? The strength of Hindu feeling on cow protection and the relatively much smaller significance of cow slaughter for Muslims surely dictated that the terms of any political accommodation between Hindus and Muslims would involve limitations on Muslim freedom to slaughter cows. In the preindependence period, the symbol of the cow was also available to those Muslim leaders who wished to provoke Hindu–Muslim conflict by using it to protest against Hindu oppression of Muslims. It would be nothing but folly for any Muslim politician in India to so use it in postindependence, post-partition India.

The Sharia has been used as a symbol of Muslim identity in a manner similar to the use of the cow by Hindus. It has been a central symbol for the Muslim religious elites, the *ulema*, but only a secondary symbol for the secular Mulsim political elites. The *ulema* have fought to protect the personal law portions of the Sharia and their right to interpret those provisions against the inroads of the state and the desires of other Muslims who are not *ulema* to reform the personal law. The success of the *ulema* in using the Sharia as a symbol of Islam has meant that the state and secular Muslim leaders are constrained from attempting to reform the Muslim personal law by a mass public opinion that has been socialized to believe that it will be un-Islamic to do so.

Unlike the symbol of the cow for the Hindus, however, the Sharia is a divisive symbol within the Muslim community itself. One would be hard put to find many Hindus who think it important to slaughter cows,[71] but many secular Muslims consider it essential to modernize the Sharia and to adopt a uniform civil law administered by the state. This division within the Muslim community and the fact that the Sharia is not a divisive symbol in Hindu–Muslim relations made possible political bargains before independence between Hindu and Muslim elites, that is, between the secular Hindu political elites and the *ulema*, to undercut the hold of secular Muslim elites over Muslim public opinion. After independence, however, in the changed political contexts of India and Pakistan, the Sharia has become a potential symbol of conflict between the *ulema* and the secular political elites in both states. The hold of the Sharia over Muslim public opinion in South Asia then has become a 'given' of religious belief, but the use of the

Sharia as a symbol of conflict or cooperation between elites never-theless varies according to political circumstance. In other words, political contexts and elite interests determine the political signi-ficance of this religious symbol.

The most variable symbol discussed here is also the most 'pri-mordial' of the three. Surely, one's mother tongue is second only to one's family relationships as a 'given' and surely it is acquired sooner and more instinctively than feelings of reverence for a religious symbol such as the cow or than respect for a complex body of laws such as the Sharia. Yet, despite the high degree of shared features in the spoken languages of Hindus and Muslims in north India, both sides have claimed as their true language one of the two regional conflicting standard languages, Hindi or Urdu, and alternately argued either that one is merely a version of the other or that the two are entirely different languages. In the late nineteenth century, the predominantly Muslim Urdu-speaking elite argued that Hindi was but a dialect of Urdu less effectively written in the Devanagari script than in the Persian–Arabic script and that therefore, Urdu in the latter script should be retained as the sole official language of the North-Western Provinces and Oudh. After independence, the predominantly Hindu elites in the same province have argued that Urdu is but a variant of Hindi and that therefore there is no need to grant official recognition and status to it, that only Hindi should be recognized as the official language of the state. Yet, throughout the long history of the Hindi–Urdu controversy, many of the spokesmen for both sides have taken the quite different view that the two languages are entirely distinct, that Hindi is the proper language of Hindus and Urdu the proper language of Muslims, and that a threat to either language is equivalent to a threat to the religion of the respective community. Sometimes, in fact, the argument that one language is but a variant of the other has been made for political purposes only by people whose true feelings are that each language is identified with one of the two communities.

The three examples suggest the following generalizations con-cerning the relationships among elites, symbols, and primordial attachments. First, although the 'givens' of human existence and of long-persisting cultural communities may constrain the free manipulation of cultural symbols by elites, they do not entirely prevent their manipulation or even alteration of their meaning. It is after all a different proposition to say, 'Hindus revere the cow,' than it is to say, 'Those who revere the cow are Hindus'.

Second, when primordial symbols are brought forth into the political arena, it is likely that a particular elite stands to gain from their use. Far be it for any non-Muslim to deny the religious significance of the Sharia for Muslims. Yet, when the Sharia is brought forth as a political symbol, it is certain either that the *ulema* are concerned about a threat to their authority in Muslim society or that secular Muslim elites are using it for advantage against perceived threats from a rival elite to their control over the Muslim community.

Third, the cultural 'givens' may make their appearance in the political arena in a dramatic way at one time or another and then may disappear for long periods because it is in no one's interest to bring them forth as central symbols. Such has been the case with the cow protection issue, which has occupied the center of the stage only twice in modern Indian history: once in the late 1880s and early 1890s, and then again in 1966. In between, there was no loss of Hindu reverence for the cow, and its symbolic uses did not cease, but no great movements were launched in its defence.

Finally, the existence of primordial attachments, even of contradictory attachments held by rival communities, does not mean that bargains cannot be struck over them based on agreements to respect each others' feelings and to keep them out of politics. Hindus revere the cow and Muslims are brought up to eat it, but dietary habits are changed more easily than religious beliefs. Consequently, Muslims may change their primordial attachment to eating beef for the sake of the Hindu primordial attachment to the sanctity of the cow, particularly if Hindus agree not to tamper with those attachments that Muslims value more than the Hindus, such as the Sharia. Now, this particular bargain, though not an explicit one, surely exists tacitly in contemporary India. It is at least certain that the *ulema* will not rise up in a body to defend cow sacrifice as long as there is no interference with Muslim personal law.

An examination, one by one, of the use of specific cultural symbols and the attachment of new value to them by religious and political elites does not take us to the heart of the process of identity formation, which involves the manipulation of a multiplicity of symbols and attempts to define a group in terms of sets of

symbols. It is in the ways in which symbols are combined and the
emphasis given to particular symbols in relation to others that the
boundaries of communities are established or break down. It has
been shown previously how, in the history of Muslim separatism,
three different elite groups used the same sets of symbols, but
emphasized and combined them in different ways, thereby arriving
at different definitions of the Muslim community in India. Muslim
landlords and government servants in nineteenth-century north
India were interested in establishing the historical importance of
the Muslim community in India and the right of its elites to occupy
ruling positions in public life. Therefore, for the nineteenth-
century Muslim political elites, the central symbols were historical
ones, with religion and language secondary.

For the *ulema*, religion and law, with the two defined as inseparable, were the primary symbols, with Urdu again being
secondary. The Muslim community was defined in terms of religious
beliefs, ritual practices, and adherence to the Sharia. Muslims
need not seek political sovereignty or domination in multicom-
munal India. It was sufficient, if not ideal, that they constitute a
religiously and legally autonomous community guided by the
ulema.

For the secular political elite of middle class professionals and
politicians who dominated the Muslim League in the 1930s and
1940s, however, it was not law that mattered but political power.
For this elite, the Muslim community was defined in political
terms, that is, as a selfdetermining nation, distinctive in religion,
history, philosophy of life, literature, and language from the
Hindus, but unfortunately a minority. During the drive for Pakistan,
Jinnah went nearly to the point of defining the Muslims of India as
those who followed the Muslim League. No one else, he insisted,
had the right to speak, politically at least, for the Muslims of India.
Those who remained outside the League were classed into two
categories: those yet to be organized and those who were 'careerists'
and betrayers of the cause of Muslim unity.

For all three elite groups in the north and even for Jinnah, the
Urdu language at some point also became an important symbol,
but always a secondary one. Nevertheless, it proved to be the
proverbial double-edged sword. For, while Urdu was a convenient
symbol to reinforce the sense of separateness of north Indian
Muslims, it was resisted vehemently by the Bengali political elites,

by Sindhi-speakers, and by other language-group leaders in post-independence Pakistan.

The game of symbol selection and symbol manipulation, therefore, is clearly one that requires considerable skill and that is not always played successfully. Elites are indeed limited and constrained by the cultures of the groups they hope to represent. Some symbols are emotionally powerful, but may be dangerous to use—not only because their use threatens civil disorder, but because their use will benefit one elite group rather than another. Other symbols may be useful for conflict with a rival community, but potentially divisive internally. The great dilemma constantly faced by political elites who manipulate symbols of identity among peoples with rich cultures is that political mobilization of the community against its rivals requires unity and solidarity, which in turn requires that sets of symbols be made as congruent as possible. However, since most cultures are internally diverse, the search for additional symbols of unity often leads to internal discord rather than to the desired solidarity and cohesion.

Where in all this does the idea of ethnic groups as descent groups fit? It is simply irrelevant to the case of Muslim separatism in north India, unless the notion of descent is defined so broadly as to include a sense of a separate history. Unless one is willing to stretch the notion of descent to this extent, the only option for those who insist upon including descent in the idea of ethnicity is to exclude from its scope cases such as that of the Muslims of India. However, we will then be placed in an analytically difficult position for there is no *prima facie* case to be made for the idea that processes of identity-formation among groups for whom an origin myth is a central symbol are any different from those among groups for whom it is not.

A final point remains to be taken up, namely, the notion that, whatever changes take place in the boundaries of ethnic groups, there remains a cultural core that persists through time. If this argument is applied to the Muslim case, it has an evident, but superficial relevance. For, while it is certainly true that Islamic symbols have been important to all groups who have sought to establish the existence of a Muslim community or nation in India and while it is also true that some of those symbols remain relatively constant—in form, if not always in meaning—the ethnic community or nation for whom they are a constant has not yet been established. The Quran, the prophet Muhammad, the Sharia are constants for Muslims everywhere, at least wherever Islam and the *ulema* have a strong hold, but the Muslims of the world are neither an ethnic community nor a nation.

Muslim political elites in India in the nineteenth and twentieth centuries attempted to argue that the Muslims of the subcontinent formed a distinct nation and they had a grand, but ephemeral success. It proved to be ephemeral because beyond the core of Islamic symbols, all other symbols proved to be divisive and could not be made congruent with the religious ones. In fact, Islamic symbols, whose 'unifying power'[72] has indeed often been demonstrated, have been repeatedly used by political elites in different contexts in South Asia in pursuit of competitive advantage against rivals from other communities and as a base for achieving political power, but their repeated use has not yet established a firm basis for a Muslim nation anywhere in South Asia. Rather, there exists on the Indian subcontinent a multiplicity of Muslim ethnic groups, communities, and potential nationalities, congruent in both religion and language, but nowhere defined by descent.

NOTES

1. Malcolm Yapp has contrasted the arguments of those theorists of nationalism who see it as a 'natural' phenomenon with those who see it as 'unnatural' in 'Language, Religion and Political Identity: A General Framework,' in David Taylor and Malcolm Yapp (eds.), *Political Identity in South Asia* (London: Curzon Press, 1979). Judith A. Nagata has made a similar comparison between two groups of scholars of ethnicity whom she labels 'primordialists' and 'circumstantialists' in 'Defence of Ethnic Boundaries: The Changing Myths and Charters of Malay Identity,' in Charles F. Keyes (ed.), *Ethnic Change* (Seattle: University of Washington Press, 1981). Joshua A. Fishman contrasts the work of those who approach the study of ethnicity from the subjective, internal point of view of the actors themselves with what he calls the 'objectivist, externalist' school in 'Social Theory and Ethnography: Neglected Perspectives on Language and Ethnicity in Eastern Europe,' in Peter F. Sugar (ed.), *Ethnic Diversity and Conflict in Eastern Europe* (Santa Barbara, CA: ABC-Clio, 1980). In this chapter, the two perspectives will be referred to as 'primordialist' and 'instrumentalist'. The latter term refers to a perspective that emphasizes the uses to which cultural symbols are put by elites seeking instrumental advantage for themselves or the groups they claim to represent.

2. The quotations are, of course, from Clifford Geertz, 'The Integrative Revolution: Primordial Sentiments and Civil Politics in the New States,' in Clifford Geertz (ed.), *Old Societies and New States: The Quest for Modernity in Asia and Africa* (New York: Free Press, 1967), pp. 108–10 and 128.
3. Fishman, 'Social Theory and Ethnography,' op. cit., takes this view. An extreme statement of the position may be found in Pierre L. van den Berghe, 'Race and Ethnicity: A Sociobiological Look,' *Ethnic and Racial Studies*, Vol. I, No. 4 (October, 1978).
4. See especially Fishman, 'Social Theory and Ethnography,' op. cit., Charles F. Keyes, 'Towards a New Formulation of the Concept of Ethnic Group,' *Ethnicity*, Vol. III, No. 3 (September, 1976), pp. 202–13; and E.K. Francis, *Interethnic Relations: An Essay in Sociological Theory* (New York: Elsevier, 1976), pp. 6–7.
5. See, for example, Joshua A. Fishman, 'Sociolinguistics and the Language Problems of the Developing Countries,' in Joshua A. Fishman, et al. (eds.), *Language Problems of Developing Nations* (New York: John Wiley, 1968), p. 3, and John J. Gumperz, 'Some Remarks on Regional and Social Language Differences in India' and 'Language Problems in the Rural Development of North India,' in University of Chicago, The College, *Introduction to the Civilization of India: Changing Dimensions of Indian Society and Culture* (Chicago: University of Chicago Press, 1957), pp. 31–47.
6. All the situations mentioned in this paragraph have occurred among different language groups in north India. For details, see Paul R. Brass, *Language, Religion and Politics in North India* (London: Cambridge University Press, 1974).
7. The conversion of untouchable Hindu castes in India to Buddhism is a case in point. See Owen M. Lynch, *The Politics of Untouchablility: Social Mobility and Social Change in a City of India* (New York: Columbia University Press, 1969), ch. v. Another well-known example is the Black Muslim movement in the United States.
8. Keyes, 'Towards A New Formulation,' op. cit., pp. 204–5, takes a rather different view on 'the facts of birth' than the one presented here.
9. See esp. Geertz, 'The Integrative Revolution,' op. cit.
10. Fishman, 'Social theory and Ethnography,' op. cit., is especially insistent on this point. See also Keyes, 'Towards a New Formulation,' op. cit., p. 210.
11. Fishman, 'Social theory and Ethnography,' op. cit. Even for the Jews, however, there have been important internal divisions of attitude and feeling towards some aspects of the core culture. For an interesting analysis of the ways in which the meanings of persistent Jewish cultural symbols have been reinterpreted at different times and in different cultural contexts, see Pearl Katz and Fred E. Katz, 'Symbols as Charters in Culture Change: The Jewish Case,' *Anthropos*, Vol. LXXII (1977), pp. 486–96.
12. Even if, for example, one accepts Martin Kilson's view that 'black ethnicity' in the United States has 'lacked until recently the quality of authenticity—that is, a true and viable heritage, unquestionable in its capacity to shape and sustain a cohesive identity or awareness,' Blacks have, in fact, adopted or created new cultural symbols and used them to build a political cohesiveness and identity of greater strength than that of other groups with more 'authentic' cultural

    traditions. 'Blacks and Neo-Ethnicity in American Political Life,' in Nathan
    Glazer and Daniel P. Moynihan (eds.), *Ethnicity: Theory and Experience*
    (Cambridge: Harvard University Press, 1975), p. 243.
13. Nathan Glazer and Daniel P. Moynihan, 'Introduction,' in Glazer and
    Moynihan, *Ethnicity*, op. cit., p. 8.
14. Abner Cohen, 'Variables in Ethnicity,' in Keyes, *Ethnic Change*, op. cit.,
    p. 325.
15. Michael Banton, 'The Direction and Speed of Ethnic Change,' in Keyes,
    Ethnic Change, op. cit.
16. Abner Cohen, *Two-Dimensional Man: An Essay on the Anthropology of
    Power and Symbolism in Complex Society* (Berkeley: University of California
    Press, 1974), pp. 98–102 'and 106–10.
17. I have contrasted these opposing points of view and presented my own in
    Brass, *Language, Religion, and Politics*, op. cit., ch. iii.
18. Francis Robinson, 'Nation Formation: The Brass Thesis and Muslim Separatism'
    and Paul R. Brass, 'A Reply to Francis Robinson,' *Journal of Commonwealth
    and Comparative Politics*, Vol. XV. No 3 (November, 1977), pp. 215–34.
19. Francis Robinson, *Separatism Among Indian Muslims: The Politics of the
    United Provinces' Muslims, 1860–1923* (Delhi: Vikas Publishing, 1975), p. 13.
20. Robinson, *Separatism Among Indian Muslims*, op. cit. p. 13.
21. Robinson, *Separatism Among Indian Muslims*, op. cit., pp. 77–78.
22. Robinson, *Separatism Among Indian Muslims*, op. cit., pp. 285 and 299 and
    John R. McLane, *Indian Nationalism and the Early Congress* (Princeton, NJ:
    Princeton University Press, 1977), p. 279.
23. Since this article was written, Sandria B. Freitag has shown how the symbol of
    the cow was used by Hindu organizations—both revivalist and traditionalist in
    orientation—and in the Cow Protection movement of the 1890s in eastern UP
    as part of the broader process of defining a Hindu community which would
    transcend traditional divisions of caste and village, town and countryside; see
    her 'Sacred Symbol as Mobilizing Ideology: The North Indian Search for a
    "Hindu" Community,' *Comparative Studies in Society and History*, Vol. XXII,
    No. 4 (October, 1980), pp. 597–625.
24. Robinson, *Separatism Among Indian Muslims*, op. cit., p. 299. Abd al-Bari's
    offer was not without precedent in Indian Muslim history. Akbar, whose
    memory admittedly is not revered by pious Muslims, prohibited cow slaughter
    during his reign. Emperor Bahadur Shah also prohibited cow slaughter during
    the Mutiny of 1857. Vincent A. Smith, *Akbar the Great Mogul, 1524-1605*, 2nd
    ed. (Oxford, 1919), p. 220, cited in McLane, *Indian Nationalism*, op. cit.,
    pp. 277–78.
25. A. M. Zaidi (ed.), *Evolution of Muslim Political Thought in India*, Vol. II:
    Sectarian Nationalism and Khilafat (New Delhi: Michiko & Panjathan, 1975),
    p. 217.
26. McLane, *Indian Nationalism*, op. cit., pp. 280, 304–5. However, McLane
    argues that officially the Congress kept silent on the cow protection issue and
    on the participation of Congressmen in Hindu communal activities, when a
    more forthright and outspoken stand against both was called for 'to allay
    Muslim fears'; p. 330.
27. McLane, *Indian Nationalism*, op. cit., pp. 285–88. The merging of religious

and economic arguments for cow protection has been a persistent feature in the cow protection movement. See, for example, the detailed economic arguments for cow protection presented i.1 Thakur Das Bhargava, *Cow in Agony* (Bombay: Bombay Humanitarian League, 1958). The author, who also supports cow protection for cultural and religious reasons, reaches the conclusion on economic grounds 'that there are no useless cattle in India which cannot justify their existence and sufferance to reach full physical age,' p. 16.

28. McLane, *Indian Nationalism*, op. cit., pp. 275, 280, 282–84.

29. McLane, *Indian Nationalism*, op. cit., pp. 272–73 and chs. ix and x, *passim*.

30. McLane, *Indian Nationalism*, op. cit., p. 326.

31. See, for example, Robinson, *Separatism Among Indian Muslims*, op. cit., pp. 56, 81–82. However, even in the municipalities, Robinson's work suggests that where Hindu–Muslim political alliances existed, as among the landlords in eastern UP, the cow slaughter issue was not permitted to intrude into politics, p. 79.

32. Tahir Mahmood, *Muslim Personal Law: Role of the State in the Sub-continent* (New Delhi: Vikas Publishing House, 1977), pp. 3–4, 62–63.

33. Mahmood, *Muslim Personal Law*, op. cit., chs. i & ii.

34. Ziya-Ul-Hasan Faruqi, *The Deoband School and the Demand for Pakistan* (Bombay: Asia Publishing House, 1963), p. 68.

35. Muhammad Ismail, the Kerala Muslim League leader, suggested a formal and explicit bargain of this sort in the Constitutent Assembly of India in December, 1948; Mahmood, *Muslim Personal Law*, op. cit., p. 95.

   The bargain was nearly upset in the Shah Bano case of 1987 when alimony was granted to a Muslim divorced woman by the civil courts against the provisions of the Sharia. However, after agitations on the matter led by orthodox and conservative Muslim leaders and organizations took place, then Prime Minister Rajiv Gandhi demonstrated the continued adherence of the Government of India to the tacit bargain by obtaining passage of the Muslim Women (Protection of Rights on Divorce) Bill, which introduced into the secular law the exact provisions of the Sharia.

36. See Brass, *Language, Religion, and Politics*, op. cit., pp. 127–38 for the background of the Hindi–Urdu controversy in UP and for further illustration of some of these points.

37. William Adam, *Reports on the State of Education in Bengal (1835 and 1838), Including Some Account of the State of Education in Bihar and a Consideration of the Means Adopted to the Improvement and Extension of Public Instruction in Both Provinces*, edited by Anathnath Basu (Calcutta: Calcutta University Press, 1941), pp. 290–91.

38. Robinson also notes the shift of Muslim attitudes from dislike for Urdu to the identification of Urdu as 'a symbol of Muslim power and influence' and the attachment to it of 'an almost religious significance'. He suggests that this shift occurred 'in the second half of the nineteenth century' but that it predated the Hindi–Urdu controversy. If so, the latter controversy certainly intensified the new feelings of attachment of Muslims to the Urdu language. The dimensions of the shift, however, can hardly be doubted. Sayyid Ahmad Khan who later became a great proponent of Urdu criticized the British education policy in 1858 for its neglect of Arabic and Persian and its attention to Urdu and English

which, he wrote, had 'tended to strengthen the idea that Government wished
to wipe out the religions which it found in Hindustan.' [*sic*!] *Separatism Among
Indian Muslims*, op. cit., pp. 70, 91, 98.

39. These remarks are based on the work of Jyotirindra Das Gupta and John
J. Gumperz, 'Language Communication and Control in North India,' in
Fishman, *Language Problems of Developing Nations*, op. cit., esp. p. 157.
Francis Robinson has, however, suggested in a personal communication to me
that Urdu was already Persianized in the nineteenth century. Even so, the
commonalities between Hindi and Urdu were sufficient to make it a matter of
choice what kind of Hindi–Urdu—or Hindi and Urdu—was to be taught in the
schools and used at the elite level for administrative and literary purposes.
Robinson argues further that, in fact, a de-Persianization of Urdu took place in
the nineteenth century. I do not have the competence or knowledge to judge
whether Robinson's or Das Gupta and Gumperz's observations are more
accurate, but the point is that Hindi and Urdu can be used as one common
language or as two separate languages, as vehicles of common communication
or as separate expressions of the distinctive cultures of Hindus and Muslims.
Some elites among both Hindus and Muslims in the nineteenth century chose
the latter course.

40. P. Hardy, *The Muslims of British India* (Cambridge: University Press, 1972),
p. 2.

41. Murray T. Titus, *Islam in India and Pakistan: A Religious History of Islam in
India and Pakistan* (Calcutta: Y.M.C.A. Publishing House, 1959), ch. v and
pp. 170 *ff*. Cf. Bernard S. Cohn who has remarked that 'at the folk level,' there
has been 'little functional difference between Hindus and Muslims,' *India: The
Social Anthropology of a Civilization* (Englewood Cliffs, NJ: Prentice-Hall,
1971), pp. 66–67. See also David M. Mandelbaum, *Society in India*, Vol. II:
Change and Continuity (Berkeley: University of California Press, 1970),
pp. 413, 527, 546–49 for a survey of the anthropological literature on Hindu–
Muslim similarities and differences in Indian villages with respect to social and
religious practices. Hardy too has noted the observance of common festivals,
celebrations, and worship by Hindus and Muslims in town and country in
Mughal times in *The Muslims of British India*, op. cit., pp. 19, 27.

42. Anil Seal, *The Emergence of Indian Nationalism: Competition and Collaboration in the Later Nineteenth Century* (Cambridge: University Press, 1971),
p. 300

43. Most of the religious societies formed to defend Islam in the late nineteenth
century against perceived Christian missionary and Hindu attacks adopted
explicit goals of unifying the Muslim community. The Anjuman-i-Himayat-i-
Islam, founded in Lahore in 1885, for example, established as one of its goals
'the creation and preservation of friendly feelings and concord between the
different sects of Islam.' The goals of educating the masses to a common
understanding of proper Islamic beliefs and practices were also clear in the
missionary activities of some of the societies which were designed to reach
'ignorant Muslims' as much as or more than non-Muslims; Seal, *The Emergence
of Indian Nationalism*, op. cit., p. 351. The Jami'yat-al-ulama was quite explicit
in its goals of persuading 'all the Muslims of India to give up the unnecessary,
useless and wasteful practises and ceremonies which are against the commands

of God and His Prophet.' A.M. Zaidi (ed.), *Evolution of Muslim Political Thought in India*, Vol. III: *Parting of the Ways* (New Delhi: S. Chand, 1977), p. 686. The Jami'yat also, of course, took the lead in demanding governmental enforcement of Muslim personal laws and in opposing any legislation on matters of personal and family law perceived not to be in conformity with the Sharia; Mahmood, *Muslim Personal Law*, op. cit., pp. 27–31, 52–55, 83–85, and *passim*.

44. Aziz Ahmad, *Islamic Modernism in India and Pakistan, 1857–1964* (London: Oxford University Press, 1967), ch. v.

45. Aziz Ahmad has remarked that one of the objectives of the Deoband seminary was 'to re-establish contact between the *alim* and the average Muslim'; Ahmad, *Islamic Modernism in India and Pakistan*, op. cit., p. 104.

46. Mahmood, *Muslim Personal Law*, op. cit., p. 21.

47. See Peter Hardy, *Partners in Freedom—and True Muslims: The Political Thought of Some Muslim Scholars in British India, 1912–1947* (Lund: Student-litteratur, 1971), p. 15.

48. Hardy, *Partners in Freedom*, op. cit., p. 23.

49. Hardy, *Partners in Freedom*, op. cit., p. 31.

50. Hardy, *Partners in Freedom*, op. cit., pp. 37–38.

51. Hardy, *Partners in Freedom*, op. cit., p. 41.

52. See, for example, the statement of the goals of the Jami'yat, given in Faruqi, *The Deoband School*, op. cit., p. 68.

53. Faruqi, *The Deoband School*, op. cit., p. 36.

54. A.M. Zaidi, *Evolution of Muslim Political Thought*, Vol. III, op. cit., p. 692.

55. S. Abul Hasan Ali Nadwi, *Muslims in India*, translated by Mohammad Asif Kidwai (Lucknow: Academy of Islamic Research and Publications, n.d.), p. 133.

56. It was not only with Muslims and Muslim landlords that such a bargain existed, but with other collaborators with the British authorities as well, including Hindu landlords. Reeves has described how the government of the United Provinces instigated the collaborating landlords there in 1920–21 to join in an 'anti-non-cooperation movement' by forming *aman sabhas* to provide 'vocal support for the government and open denunciation of the non-cooperators.' Peter D. Reeves, 'The Politics of Order: "Anti-Non-Cooperation" in the United Provinces, 1921,' *Journal of Asian Studies*, Vol. XXV, No. 2 (February, 1966), p. 266.

57. 'What is this nation of ours?' asked Sayyid Ahmad Khan in 1887. 'We are those who have ruled India for six or seven hundred years.' Speech delivered at Lucknow on 28 December 1887, reprinted in A.M. Zaidi (ed.), *Evolution of Muslim Political Thought in India*, Vol. I: *From Syed to the Emergence of Jinnah* (New Delhi: Michiko & Panjathan, 1975), p. 42.

58. In the 1890s, the Privy Council restricted the rights of Muslims to establish *wakfs* that were clearly meant principally for the benefit of descendants rather than as charity for the poor. See Asaf A.A. Fyzee, *Outlines of Muhammadan Law*, 2nd ed. (London: Oxford University Press, 1955), pp. 254–66 and A.M. Zaidi, *Evolution of Muslim Political Thought*, I, op. cit., pp. 300–20. In 1913, Jinnah sponsored the successful passage in the Imperial Legislative Council of the Wakf Act, which restored the right of Muslims to place their

properties into trusts, the income from which would go to descendants. Zaidi, *Evolution of Muslim Political Thought*, I, op. cit., p. 429 and Hector Bolitho, *Jinnah: Creator of Pakistan* (London: John Murray, 1954), p. 53. Mahmood, however, claims that the Muslim landlords opposed the more general application of Sharia inheritance provisions that would have prevented them from excluding women from inheritance or bequeathing their properties to adopted sons, in *Muslim Personal Law*, op. cit., pp. 26 and 30–31.

59. Rafiq Zakaria, *Rise of Muslims in Indian Politics: An Analysis of Developments from 1885 to 1906* (Bombay: Somaiya Publications, 1970), p. 236.

60. Sayyid Ahmad Khan, speech of 28 December 1887, cited in Zaidi, *Evolution of Muslim Political Thought*, I, op. cit., p. 34.

61. Robinson, *Separatism Among Indian Muslims*, op. cit., chs. viii and ix.

62. Cited in Khalid B. Sayeed, *Pakistan: The Formative Phase, 1857–1948* (London: Oxford University Press, 1968), p. 73.

63. *Some Recent Speeches and Writings of Mr. Jinnah*, edited by Jamil-ud-Din Ahmad (Lahore: Sh. Muhammad Ashraf, 1942), *passim*.

64. *Some Recent Speeches and Writings of Mr. Jinnah*, op. cit., p. 42.

65. *Some Recent Speeches and Writings of Mr. Jinnah*, op. cit., pp. 87, 104.

66. *Some Recent Speeches and Writings of Mr. Jinnah*, op. cit., p. 30.

67. *Some Recent Speeches and Writings of Mr. Jinnah*, op. cit., p. 41.

68. Muhammad Ali Jinnah, Presidential Address at the All-India Muslim League, Lahore Session, March. 1940, in *Some Recent Speeches and Writings of Mr. Jinnah*, op. cit., p. 153.

69. Jinnah's inaugural address in the Pakistan Constituent Assembly, August 1947, cited in Mahmood, *Muslim Personal Law*, op. cit., p. 174.

70. Such suggestions are reserved only for the most ignorant Western journalists commenting sanctimoniously on the Indian scene. The most sanctimonious such advice ever seen by this author appeared in an article by Oriana Fallaci, 'Indira's Coup,' *New York Review of Books*, Vol. XXII, No. 14 (18 September 1975), pp. 14–21, which is so noteworthy for its total lack of understanding of Indian society, its cultures and peoples that it deserves to be exposed and condemned. Fallaci comments ignorantly, on p. 15, on the issue of cow slaughter as follows: 'There exists no politician in India daring enough to attempt to explain to the masses that cows can be eaten.' The especial stupidity of the comment, of course, lies not only in the fact that Fallaci thinks a politician who proposed such a thing would be 'daring' rather than insane, but in her belief that the masses are not aware that cows can be eaten.

71. Some Hindus do, of course, eat beef, but there is no serious movement among Hindus to legalize cow slaughter.

72. Robinson, *Separatism Among Indian Muslims*, op. cit., p. 356.

———————————————————————————————— II

Regionalism, Pluralism, and National Unity in India

Introduction

The theoretical chapters and the case study in Part I focused on the process of ethnic identity formation, looking at the issue from the point of view primarily of elites within ethnic groups. The three chapters in this part reverse the process and focus more on the consequences of the policies of the modernizing state—here India—for ethnic mobilization and for conflict between ethnic groups and the state.

Chapter 4 of this part examines the language policies of post-independence Indian governments and the framework of center-state relations. It is argued in this chapter that the Indian state has been a centralizing state since independence, but that the drives towards increasing central power and control over the states of the Union increased dramatically during the struggle for power at the center which brought Mrs. Gandhi to power. In the process, the balance in center–state relations was transformed and the boundaries between state and central politics were eroded The central government adopted increasingly interventionist practices in the states which, however, had the contrary effect of reducing effective central control, exacerbating inter-ethnic conflicts within the states, and increasing the dependence of the center upon shifts in state politics. These ineffective centralizing policies also precipitated increasing demands for a restructuring of center–state relations to give more autonomy to the states. The principal conclusion of this essay, written originally at the height of Mrs. Gandhi's centralizing drives in the late 1970s, was that the natural tendencies in Indian society and politics were towards pluralism, regionalism, and decentralization, and that the forces favoring such tendencies

either must ultimately prevail or leave the Indian state in a perpetual crisis of center–state relations.

I have revised the essay somewhat for this volume while retaining
the original argument and the original focus on the contrast
between central policies in the Nehru period and in the period of
Mrs. Gandhi's dominance. The revisions include some editorial
changes of tense as well as bringing up to date the discussion of
center–state finances and bringing up to 1985 the analysis of
electoral results and the uses of President's Rule. These revisions
were made during the first year in power of the National Front
government, whose policies on ethnic separatism, regional political
autonomy, and economic decentralization were constrained sharply
by the very types of strains discussed in the essay between centralizing and decentralizing and militant nationalist and tolerant
pluralist policies towards minorities. However, no attempt has
been made to analyze those strains at such an early stage in the
functioning of the new government.

Chapters 5 and 6 focus on the Punjab crisis of the 1980s. In
chapter 5, as in chapter 4, the essay is structured in the form of a
comparison between the policies of the Indian state in the Nehru
and post-Nehru periods. Two themes in particular link these two
chapters with chapter 4 and with part one. The first is the argument that the changes in the character of center–state relations
analyzed in chapter 4 provide the indispensable context for understanding why Punjab politics became transformed into a crisis of
Indian unity.

The second linkage is in the political emphasis in my analysis of
the Punjab crisis. While I believe that the internal dynamics of
politics in Punjab cannot be understood without a full appreciation
of Sikh religious, cultural and political values, I do not consider
that those values constitute an explanation for the rise of Sikh
separatism, including the making of explicit secessionist demands
by the most militant groups. As discussed in chapter 6, I recognize
also the importance in routine politics in Punjab of the great
economic changes which have occurred as a consequence of the
Green Revolution. At the same time, I reject the argument that
economic factors played a major role in the origins of the current
crisis.

On the contrary, I have tried to show how the interventionist

policies of the central government in Punjab have interacted with
the internal dynamics of politics within the Sikh community to
produce the Punjab crisis of the 1980s. I have also argued that the
Punjab crisis must be seen as a manifestation in extreme form of
the broader crisis in center–state relations in India and that it
cannot be resolved permanently in isolation from the broader
issue.

4

Pluralism, Regionalism, and Decentralizing Tendencies in Contemporary Indian Politics

Opinions on the nature of the balance between the center and the states in India's federal system have varied considerably over time since independence. They have also varied at particular points in time depending upon the institutions and processes the observer is examining. Moreover, there have also been problems in how to interpret types of evidence in terms of whether or not they reflect tendencies towards centralization, decentralization, or disintegration. Unfortunately, though the subject is one that attracts persistent interest, political scientists have not responded substantially to Marcus Franda's call a decade ago to begin to collect data on center–state relations in India and to examine the decisionmaking processes of such critical institutions in those relations as the Planning Commission and the Finance Commission.[1] Consequently, differing opinions on the nature of center–state relations remain opinions, based on limited evidence or on an examination only of particular institutions or processes in the Indian federal system. Still lacking is an overall view of the Indian federal system that encompasses all relevant aspects, institutions, and processes and that is grounded solidly in evidence. It goes without saying that it is hardly possible to arrive at definitive conclusions about the general

Acknowledgments: I am indebted to Myron Weiner, James Manor, and John Wood for their careful, detailed criticisms and suggestions for revision of the first draft of this chapter. Many of their suggestions were incorporated into the original published version. I am solely responsible for all opinions expressed and any errors of fact that remain.

direction of center–state relations in India until such an overall view is constructed.

Consider, for example, the difference between Morris-Jones' description of center–state relations in India in 1964 as a form of cooperative federalism that he characterized as 'bargaining federalism'[2] and a description published in 1977 by Haqqi and Sharma that characterized center–state relations in India as a system of 'centralized federalism.'[3] The term 'bargaining federalism,' Morris-Jones argued, described 'the character of Indian federalism throughout.' It referred to a pattern of center–state relations in which 'neither center nor states can impose decisions on the other' and in which 'hard competitive bargaining' takes place in such institutions as the Planning Commission, the Finance Commission, and the Zonal Councils.[4] In these institutions, bargaining occurs between the center and the states and among the several states for the allocation of resources and patronage and for the solution of such divisive problems as the rights of linguistic minorities in the linguistically reorganized states. In contrast to this description, Haqqi and Sharma argued that, with the exception of the brief period between 1967 and 1971 when different parties ruled at the center and in many of the Indian states, the Indian 'constitutional form' has been 'centralized federalism'. Moreover, they argue that the long-term tendency has been towards increasing centralization of power, manifested particularly in concentration of authority at the center as power has shifted upward in the Congress party organization and in concentration of authority in the executive as power has moved laterally at the center from the Congress party organization to the central government. Although Haqqi and Sharma argued that the Indian federal system had always been highly centralized, they were also arguing that it was becoming even more so.

Looked at from the point of view of the states, the issue is usually phrased as one of the relative autonomy of the states in relation to the center. In 1968, Weiner argued that state autonomy was considerable and that it was safe from central encroachment. He remarked that 'it is most unlikely that the center will be able to take power away from the states. Indeed the trend has been just the reverse: the states have tended to become politically more autonomous and to accept central advice reluctantly.'[5] Eleven years later, in an article on 'Presidential Rule in India,' Dua

commented that the 'increasing use' of President's Rule over the
past twentyfive years had reduced the autonomy of the states 'to a
farce'.[6] Unlike Haqqi and Sharma, however, who take the view
that the system has always been centralized, Dua argues that the
change in center–state relations has been accompanied by a
change in the character of Indian democracy as well that amounts
to 'a fundamental transformation of the system' such that it is
'useless' to 'search for continuity in political styles and traditions'
between the pre- and post-1969 periods.[7]

Differences concerning the nature of the Indian federal system
often arise out of differences in the institutions examined. Scholars
who look primarily at the Planning Commission and the Finance
Commission or at the use of President's Rule have tended to argue
that state autonomy has declined and central control over the
states has increased. Those who look at the Congress organization
have been more divided, some seeing a highly centralized organization, some seeing a highly decentralized one, others seeing
changes from time to time in the structure and decisionmaking
processes of the Congress from centralization to decentralization.
Those who look at state party systems or at language policy tend to
see regionalism and state autonomy predominant in center–state
relations.

It is, of course, hardly surprising, in a federal system of India's
size and diversity, that there should be contrary tendencies over
time and among different institutions and policy areas. Problems
of interpretation, however, become more serious when observers
look at the same institution at the same point in time and reach
different conclusions or feel incapable of deciding what are the
implications of the evidence. For example, Venkatarangaiya and
Shiviah argue that 'the Congress as a party has been a highly
centralized organization' in which 'state units have had little
freedom to take decisions on their own.'[8] Bombwall, in contrast,
argues that the centralization of the Congress was a temporary and
fortuitous phenomenon, a mere 'legacy from pre-independence
days' and that the Congress high command after independence
rapidly became 'a shaky colossus whose writ ran in state capitals in
inverse ratio to the cohesion and stability of the state party units,
the degree of rapport between the organizational and governmental
wings of the party and the strength of the state-level leadership.'[9]

Since, as I have already suggested, most of the evidence that is required to come to an overall assessment of the character of the Indian federal system is lacking, it will not be possible in this brief chapter to do more than offer another opinion based on fragmentary evidence about the long-term tendencies in center–state relations and about the dynamic character of the system. I do attempt, however, to present a coherent point of view concerning the overall character of the system and to offer some new evidence as well as suggest ways of reinterpreting the existing evidence in support of that point of view. The general argument of the paper is as follows. Insofar as long-term tendencies or underlying persistent patterns can be discerned across institutions and policy areas in India, the directions or the underlying patterns are towards pluralism, regionalism, and decentralization.[10] These tendencies run counter to the efforts of leaders of particular groups, such as the Hindi speech community, to impose their will over other groups; to the attempts by Mrs. Gandhi during her tenure in power to nationalize the electoral process; and to her persistent efforts to centralize political power and decisionmaking.

The tendencies towards pluralism are, however, clearer than those towards regionalism and decentralization, which are qualified by a high degree of interdependence of the center on the states and the states on the center. Moreover, there is also a fundamental tension in the system which arises because the constitutional structure has many strong unitary features and because there are historical tendencies in India, favored by several leaders and parties, towards aggregation and consolidation of power. In the 1970s, the aggregative and consolidating tendencies were set in motion particularly by Mrs. Gandhi. However, it is my contention that the process of consolidating power in India is inherently tenuous and that power begins to disintegrate immediately at the maximal point of concentration. At that point, regional political forces and decentralizing tendencies inevitably reassert themselves unless the national leadership chooses to attempt a more definitive consolidation by bringing into play the full range of unitary powers provided in the Constitution of India. However, it is also my contention that such an effort is doomed to failure in the long run[11] and that pluralist, regionalist, and decentralizing tendencies will inevitably reassert themselves against any centralizing, authoritarian regime. Evidence in support of the general argument will be provided below with respect to language policy, transfer of

resources from the center to the states, patterns and trends in
party support and inter-party relations, and the use of President's Rule.[12]

PLURALISM AND INDIAN LANGUAGE POLICY

For the first two decades after independence, the most salient,
divisive, and persistent set of issues centered around the various
language problems of India, including especially the controversies
over the linguistic reorganization of states, over the official language
of India, and over the status of Urdu and other minority languages
within the several states. In the minds of many observers and
participants, these issues seemed to threaten the very basis of
Indian unity and even to pose the prospect of a 'balkanization' or
disintegration of India into a number of separate linguistic nations.
For some time, the benchmark study that presented the issue of
the unity of India and the possibility of its disintegration most
starkly was Selig Harrison's *India: The Most Dangerous Decades*.[13]
Harrison saw the threats to Indian unity arising both from conflicts
between the central government and regions asserting their separate cultural identities and from interregional conflicts, particularly
between the Hindi-speaking region of north India and the non-
Hindi-speaking regions of the country. He argued that, although
Hindi-speakers constituted a large enough group in relation to all
others 'to assert a dominant position,' he thought also that they
were 'not quite large enough to achieve it'.[14] His prediction proved
accurate as the Hindi movement failed in the 1960s to impose
Hindi upon the rest of the country as the sole official language of
India. During the 1970s, moreover, several studies of various
aspects of India's language problems were published, arriving at a
consensus that the major linguistic issues were resolved in a
manner that preserved the cultural integrity of the major linguistic
groups in India and the unity of India, though leaving still unresolved
several matters pertaining to the rights of linguistic minorities and
the status of migrants in the linguistically reorganized states.[15]

That the resolution of the major linguistic conflicts has been a
pluralistic one can hardly be doubted. It is reflected both in official
policy and its implementation and in the actual use of the major
languages of India for various functional purposes. Insofar as the

official language issue is concerned, the Government of India has settled upon what amounts to an indefinite policy of bilingualism, with English and Hindi being alternative official languages at the center and alternative link languages for communication between the center and the states. Although the ideal of transforming Hindi into the sole official language of the country exists in the Official Language Act, 1963, and in the hearts of many Hindi-speakers and although plans have been partly implemented for increasing the use of Hindi by the central government, it has been made clear time and time again that the use of Hindi will not be imposed on non-Hindi speakers for official purposes in India.

Moreover, progress in implementing the increased use of Hindi by central government departments has been slow. Rules for implementing the Official Language Act were not even framed until 1976 and the state of Tamil Nadu has been excluded from their purview.[16] In fact, one observer has argued that English continues to be dominant in practice as the official language of the Government of India, as the link language of the country, and as the medium of higher education.[17] The continued preeminence of English is a mark of India's pluralism, for it distributes the burdens of learning the principal language of official communication at the central and intergovernmental levels equally between Hindi-speakers and non-Hindi-speakers.

Insofar as bilingualism has been modified in practice in relation to the non-Hindi-speaking states, it has been in the direction of even greater pluralism. For example, all languages listed in the Eighth Schedule of the Constitution of India are acceptable media of examination for entry into the Indian Administrative Service for the Essay and General Knowledge papers. In fact, however, English continues to be the overwhelmingly preferred language of applicants for both papers. In 1974, the latest year for which figures are available, 82 per cent of the Essay examinations and 91 per cent of the General Knowledge papers were written in English. The figures for Hindi were 14 per cent and 6 per cent for the two papers, respectively, for the two examinations. On this most politically sensitive aspect of official language policy, therefore, it is clear that the policy of the government is one of multilingual pluralism in which English remains dominant. English is even more dominant in the results of the examinations, for less than 5 per cent of the successful candidates choose a medium other than English.[18]

At the state level, in the linguistically reorganized states, the regional languages are becoming increasingly dominant as the official administrative languages, as the media of education in the schools, and as the languages of communication in the printed media. Even in the linguistically reorganized states, however, there remain significant pluralistic aspects of language policy and usage. English continues to be an important medium of higher education and of elite communication in the printed media, especially in the major metropolitan cities of the country. Various constitutional and other safeguards are supposed to be implemented in the states for the use of minority languages as media of education in the primary schools, for some official purposes, and for recruitment to the state services. However, the development of policies and procedures for the implementation of these safeguards is a recurring issue in center–state relations.

In fact, the major linguistic and ethnic problems of India up to the 1980s—before the rise of separatist movements in Punjab and Kashmir—concerned the status of minority languages, religions, and ethnic groups within the linguistically reorganized states. The status of Urdu continues to be a controversial issue in several of the Hindi-speaking states. Problems persist in implementing the established safeguards for other linguistic minorities in the states as well. Conflict between migrant and non-migrant populations has emerged as an increasingly important problem in some states, notably Assam.

In relation to the internal linguistic and ethnic conflicts of the states, the central government until the late 1970s usually played the role of protector of the rights of the minority populations. In fact, as I have argued elsewhere, the central government until then consistently pursued policies of pluralism in relation to the rights of linguistic and ·religious minorities in India in the face of the assimilationist and discriminatory policies of several states in relation to their minorities.[19] Although the role of the central government is indispensable to the preservation of minority rights in India, one has only to read the annual reports of the Commissioner of Linguistic Minorities to appreciate how much the implementation even of agreed safeguards depends upon the voluntary cooperation of the state governments. The central government has never been able to impose upon recalcitrant states specific procedures and mechanisms to ensure that minorities receive instruction in schools through the medium of their mother tongue or that they are not barred from entry into state employment because of lack of proficiency in the regional language.[20]

Finally, India's pluralism in relation to language policy is evident also in the failure of Hindi to gain ground as the principal link language of the country. Hindi has been virtually excluded as a language of education in Tamil Nadu and is hardly used as a medium of printed communication anywhere outside the Hindi-speaking states. In fact, in the country as a whole, English newspapers continue to hold a substantial position after Hindi in number and in circulation. The bulk of the literate newspaper-reading public, however, reads newspapers in the predominant regional languages of their province (Tables 4.1 and 4.2).

TABLE 4.1: Concentration of Newspapers by Language

Language	1983		1980		1970		1960	
	No.	*%*	*No.*	*%*	*No.*	*%*	*No.*	*%*
English	3,840	18.50	3,440	18.96	2,247	20.36	1,647	20.52
Hindi	5,936	28.60	4,946	27.27	2,694	24.41	1,532	19.09
Urdu	1,378	6.64	1,234	6.80	898	8.14	680	8.47
Regional languages	7,278	35.06	6,493	35.79	3,974	36.01	2,718	33.86
Others	2,326	11.21	2,027	11.17	1,223	11.08	1,449	18.05
Total	20,758	100.01	18,140	99.99	11,036	100.00	8,026	99.99

Source: Compiled from Government of India, Ministry of Information and Broad-casting, *Press in India, 1984*, I (Delhi: Controller of Publications, 1986), p. 21; *Press in India, 1981*, I (Delhi: Controller of Publications, 1978), p. 27; *Press in India, 1971*, I (Delhi: Manager of Publications, 1971), p. 19; *Annual Report of the Registrar of Newspapers for India 1961*, I (Delhi: Manager of Publications, 1961), p. 19.

From the point of view of Indian language policy and usage, therefore, there are several evident pluralistic features. The official language problem has been resolved in a partly bilingual, partly multilingual manner. English, rather than Hindi, continues to be the principal link language of the country. The regional languages are dominant in each of the states. Pluralism is qualified in practice at the state level by the discriminatory policies of some state governments towards their linguistic minorities. Effective protection of the rights of linguistic minorities by the central government

TABLE 4.2: Circulation of Newspapers by Language (x 1,000)

Language	1983		1980		1970		1960	
	No.	%	No.	%	No.	%	No.	%
English	10,627	19.19	10,532	20.68	7,173	24.48	4,147	22.76
Hindi	15,458	27.91	13,709	26.92	5,852	19.97	3,583	19.67
Urdu	2,536	4.58	2,076	4.08	1,455	4.97	1.055	5.79
Regional languages	25,030	45.19	22,911	44.99	13,639	46.54	8,297	45.54
Others	1,740	3.14	1,693	3.32	1,184	4.04	1,137	6.24
Total	55,391	100.01	50,921	99.99	29,303	100.00	18,219	100.00

Source: As for Table 4.4: *Press in India, 1984*, p. 31; *Press in India, 1981*, I, p. 44; *Press in India, 1971*, I, p. 44; *Annual Report of the Registrar of Newspapers for India, 1961*, I, p. 43.

cannot be implemented without the cooperation of the state governments. Here, cultural pluralism is countered by the relative autonomy of the states in practice in relation to the central government in educational and language policy and in recuitment to state services.

THE INCREASING ROLE OF THE STATES IN EMPLOYMENT AND EXPENDITURE

In 1956, in his book on *American State Politics*, V.O. Key dissented from the popular view that the American states had declined in political importance as a consequence of the increased role of the federal government under the New Deal. He argued to the contrary that 'state governments were expanding their staffs, enlarging the scope of their activities [and] spending more and more money.'[21] It was not, however, their own money they were spending, but moneys raised by the federal government and then distributed to the states through federal grants. Insofar as the states raised money through taxes, they did not spend it, but distributed their tax proceeds to local governments. Thus, the states had been converted 'into governments that spend money they do not raise and raise money they do not spend.'[22] Yet, in this curious manner, the states had become more pivotal in the American political system in the previous two decades.

If we apply V.O. Key's standards to the position of the states in the Indian federal system, we would have to conclude that the importance of the states has increased vastly since independence for their administrative staffs have expanded enormously, the scope of their activities also has enlarged dramatically, and they have been spending 'more and more money'. Not only have they been spending more, but they have been spending both 'money that they do not raise' and money that they do raise. Moreover, the control of the central government over state expenditures has decreased.

Consider first the size of the administrative staffs of the state governments in comparison with other units of government and the private sector in India. At the end of 1977, the state governments employed 5.2 million persons compared to 3.1 million employed by the central government, 2.0 million by local governments, and 6.2 million in large-scale industry. State and local employment constituted 50 per cent of the total public employment in India. Moreover, state government employment was the largest growth sector among these employing agencies between 1961 and 1977. In that period, the number of state government employees increased by 71 per cent, local bodies employees by 61 per cent, central government employees by 42 per cent, and large-scale industry workers by 23 per cent.[23] Ten years later, at the end of 1987, the state government employment figures had risen to 6.7 million whereas central government employment had increased only to 3.4 million and local government only to 2.2 million. Employment in large-scale industry remained at 6.5 million. In other words, state government employment expanded by 29 per cent in the previous decade compared to a rate of increase of 10 per cent for the center, 15 per cent for local bodies, and zero per cent for large-scale industry.[24]

There has also been an enormous increase in the development expenditures of the state governments, which grew from Rs. 1,702 crores to Rs. 9,155 crores between 1967 to 1977–78, that is by 450 per cent. The tax and non-tax revenues of the states also increased considerably between 1967–68 and 1977–78 by over four times in the case of tax revenue (from Rs. 1,065 to 4,384 crores) and by nearly five times in the case of non-tax revenue (from Rs. 399 to 1,969 crores). Although between 40 to 50 per cent of state revenues come from transfers of revenue from the central government, the states collect between 50 to 60 per cent of their revenues themselves.[25]

Nevertheless, it is a fact that the increase in state revenues has not kept pace with the increases in state expenditures and that the deficit has had to be made up by resource transfers from the central government to the states.[26] The constantly increasing needs of the states for resource transfers from the center has contributed in recent years to the developing controversy over the present status of center–state relations. Critics of the state governments argue that the states have been financially irresponsible, that they have used too many of their resources for non-productive purposes, and that they have failed to mobilize enough resources of their own, particularly from the agricultural sector. Consequently, it is argued, revenues raised by the center that could be used by the central government to create new productive assets for the nation are being squandered in filling budgetary deficits created by the fiscal mismanagement of state governments. Supporters of increased state autonomy and other critics of the central government argue, in contrast, that the constitution explicitly provides for transfers of many taxes collected by the center, that the center controls many of the most elastic sources of revenue, and that it is properly up to the states to decide how these resources should be expended.

Whatever the merits of the argument on both sides, which is not the subject of this chapter, there is no doubt that the proportion of central resources transferred to the states has increased substantially since independence. For example, the percentage of the gross revenue receipts of the central government transferred to the states increased from 14.4 per cent under the award of the First Finance Commission (1952–57) to 22.1 per cent under the award of the Sixth Finance Commission (1974–79).[27] However, the proportion of resources transferred in relation to both the total expenditures of the states and union territories and the total expenditures of the central government have not increased dramatically. Both the states and the central governments are raising new resources and spending more and more, but the states have not become significantly more dependent on the center for resource transfers than they were in the 1950s with smaller expenditures. The proportion of resources transferred to the total expenditures of the state governments increased from 38 per cent in the First Five Year Plan (1951 to 1956) to 47 per cent in Fourth Plan (1961 to 1974), but declined in the Sixth Plan (1979 to 1984) to less than 42 per cent.[28] Moreover, the contribution of the states to the total receipts of all governments, center and states, in India, remained above half, though it declined from 56 per cent in the First Plan period to 52 per cent in the Sixth.[29]

Neither the total amount nor the proportion of resources transferred from the center to the states indicates anything concerning whether control over and use of the resources transferred has been associated with a trend toward centralization and state dependence on the center or decentralization and increased state autonomy. In order to approach that issue, it is necessary to consider to what extent the Finance Commission, as a central agency, and the central government have been able to achieve their declared goals through the mechanism of resource transfers or whether the states or some group of powerful states have had their way in contradistinction to central policy goals. A related issue concerns control and use of central resources as an instrument of patronage. The relevant question in this regard is whether or not the central government has used the mechanism of resource transfers to reward states which have provided strong political support to the party in power and to punish those that have supported or been controlled by opposition parties.

With regard to the first issue, it has been the repeatedly declared policy of the several Finance Commissions to use the mechanism of resource transfers as a device for interstate equalization or, in other words, 'as a means of redressing regional imbalances'.[30] Such a policy means that the central government engages in redistributive transfers 'to help the poorer areas of the country' by transferring 'resources from relatively better-off states to the poorer ones.'[31] However, such redistributive transfers have been resisted effectively, for the most part, by the better-off states in the controversies that have surrounded the deliberations of the successive Finance Commissions. In fact, the more advanced states have tended to receive a higher per capita tax devolution than the less advanced states,[32] with the result that 'tax devolution' may have 'accentuated the disparities among the states'.[33] Other observers concur with this view. Venu, for example, has argued that, despite the weightage for backwardness in various Finance Commission formulas, 'the general redistributive results have been regressive'.[34]

These regressive results have occurred despite the fact that each successive Finance Commission from the Second through to the Eighth has increasingly favored the backward states in its resource transfers.[35] The chief reasons appear to be the following. First, the weightage in favor of the backward states did not become fairly uniform and substantial until after the Fifth Finance Commission (1969–74). Throughout the first four Finance Commissions, for example, Punjab received a higher per capita devolution of resources than Bihar. Second, even though the weightage has increasingly favored the backward states in the sense that Bihar or UP has usually ranked higher in per capita devolution than Punjab in the last fifteen years,[36] the per capita devolution of resources to the most populous backward states has not been significantly above their percentage in the country's population. In fact, in the case of UP, though it is ranked third from the bottom in per capita income and it received the fifth highest per capita resource transfer (among the major states) under the Eighth Finance Commission award,[37] its percentage share in the total amount of resources transferred was only 15.47, though the population of UP is 16.31 per cent of the whole country! The apparent weightage in favor of the backward states and against the advanced states is distorted as a consequence of the fact that the smaller states, such as Assam and Orissa on the backward side, and Punjab and Haryana on the advanced side, are heavily favored or disfavored while the allocations for the huge backward states such as Bihar, Madhya Pradesh, and UP are usually less than a percentage point, more or less, different from their percentage share in the population.

Similar issues have recurred concerning the deliberations of the Planning Commission which also has repeatedly declared one of its major goals to be balanced regional development in allocating central assistance to the states. However, the equalizing impact of the Planning Commission's distribution of central resources also has been very limited.[38] The prevailing method used by the Planning Commission beginning with the Fourth Five Year Plan was the so-called Gadgil Formula, which provided for only 10 per cent of 'central assistance to the states' in the plans to be distributed according to 'backwardness'.[39] The allocation of central assistance to the states under the plan adopted by the Janata government (1977–79), however, gave greater weight to backwardness. The backward states of UP, Bihar, Orissa, and Madhya Pradesh gained more central assistance, as did Tamil Nadu and West Bengal, whereas the more advanced states of Maharashtra, Punjab, Haryana, and Gujarat, along with Andhra and Rajasthan, received less, proportionately, than in the past.[40]

However, an examination of plan expenditures over the first six Five Year Plans (including the Annual Plans) and of the relative contributions of the states from their own resources and from central assistance to plan expenditures shows that recent efforts by the Planning Commission to favor the backward states have been no more significant or successful than the efforts undertaken by the Finance Commission. Overall plan expenditures for most of the relatively more advanced states have been consistently higher than those for the more backward states on a per capita basis even when central assistance to the more advanced states has been proportionately lower. The reasons are twofold: (*a*) the more advanced states have been able to raise more resources on their own than the more backward states; (*b*) the weightage in central assistance to the more backward states has not been sufficient to overcome their deficiencies in internal resource mobilization.

Whatever the reasons, there is virtual unanimity among scholars who have analyzed interregional disparities in India on two points: the disparities have increased and central policies on resource transfers have not only been unable to prevent the increasing gap between the rich and poor states, but may have contributed to accentuating the disparities.[41] In consequence, therefore, it can only be concluded with respect to the repeatedly reaffirmed goals of the Five Year Plans to achieve 'balanced regional development' and reduction of interstate disparities that 'the results of planned development' have not been 'in consonance with this national objective.'[42] Rather, inequalities between the advanced and poorer states have increased over time.[43]

The fact that most of the backward states that gained under the Janata government plan were also the principal states that supported Janata opens up the question whether or not there has been a general pattern of association between the distributing of central assistance and political support for the ruling party. In fact, however, there is no strong evidence for such an association. There is no strong association, for example, between the ranking of states in terms of per capita resource transfers during the periods of the Fifth and Sixth Finance Commissions[44]—whose recommendations were made during Mrs. Gandhi's tenure at the center in 1969 for the period 1969 to 1974 and in 1973 for the period 1974 to 1979— and support for or opposition to the Congress in this period. The only assertion for which there is consistent support in the record of the distribution of central assistance in the plans and of resource

transfers by the Finance Commissions is that the major Hindi-
speaking states of UP, Bihar, and MP, which had for long been
areas of disaffection from the Congress and provided the principal
bases of support for the Janata opposition, also consistently
received less per capita support than most other states until the
Janata regime, despite the fact that they have always ranked
among the most backward states in the country. Therefore, it is
possible that the failure of the center under Congress dominance
to pursue more rigorously a policy of redistributive transfers had
an underlying political basis.

Overall, however, it cannot be said that the central government
has adopted either a clear or persistent policy of interstate equalization or of rewarding friendly states and punishing recalcitrant
ones. The Planning Commission and the Finance Commission
have been arenas in which interstate disputes over the allocation of
resources have been resolved by the use of formulas that have not
significantly redistributed resources in any particular direction.
Consequently, there is not much support in the methods used to
transfer central resources to the states for the view that there has
been a significant increase in the willingness of the center to
exercise stronger centralized authority over the manner of their
distribution.

Nor has the central government had much success in persuading
the states to increase their own sources of revenue through additional taxes, particularly on the agricultural sector. It has been
pointed out that, although agriculture contributes 45 per cent of
India's GNP, the agricultural sector 'contributes less than 1 per
cent of the GNP' in taxes.[45] The reason for this situation is that the
state governments have been reluctant to tax the rural groups
upon whom their support is based or even to secure 'reasonable
returns on investments in irrigation and power projects,'[46] which
directly benefit those same groups. In fact, although the land
revenue still comprises the major direct tax on rural landholders, it
constitutes a steadily decreasing proportion of the total tax revenue
of the states.[47]

Despite the fact that the central government has been unable to
persuade the states to mobilize additional resources from the
agricultural sector, the deliberations of the Seventh Finance
Commission, which occurred during the Janata regime and in the
context of increased pressure from the states for revision of

previous patterns of resource transfers, resulted in major changes in favor of the states. The share of the states in central taxes, excise duties, and statutory grants was increased significantly, leading to an estimated overall devolution of resources from the Finance Commission award in the Sixth Five Year Plan of Rs. 23,063 crores, up from Rs. 11,168 crores in the previous plan.[48] Consequently, under the Janata regime, there was a noticeable shift in direction both towards increased devolution of resources to the states by the Finance Commission and towards increasing the share of the backward north Indian states in resources transferred by the Planning Commission.

These shifts in resource distribution have also been accompanied by a decline of central control over the way the states spend the resources transferred. It is well known that the Planning Commission in Nehru's time had considerably more power and authority than it does today and that the role of the states in plan formulation was 'quite limited'.[49] It is not clear that the role of the states in plan formulation has increased for most states have never developed adequate planning agencies comparable to the central Planning Commission.[50] It is clear, however, that the control of the Planning Commission and of the central ministries over state expenditure of central plan assistance has been reduced.[51] For a time, 'the number of centrally sponsored schemes' went down from 147 in 1966 to 90 in 1968 and to 52 in the Fourth Five Year Plan[52] and the expenditures for such schemes also went down accordingly. During the 1970s, however, the funding for various new centrally-sponsored programs, such as the Drought Prone Areas program, the Small Farmers Development Agency, and the Marginal Farmers and Agricultural Laborers program, rose dramatically. Nevertheless, despite the increase in central funding for such centrally-sponsored programs, the distribution of funding to the states for them has been made increasingly on the basis of formulas that severely limit the discretion of the Planning Commission and prevent the old pattern of 'secret negotiations between the Planning Commission and individual states.'[53]

Moreover, there has been a long-term shift in the sources of funds transferred from the center to the states to the Finance Commission rather than the Planning Commission and away from discretionary loans and grants. The trends are brought out in Table 4.3, which shows that the proportion of total resources

TABLE 4.3: Transfer of Resources from the Center to the States by the Finance Commission, the Planning Commission, and the Central Government (Rs. crores)

Plan	Years	Finance Commission		Planning Commission		Other Transfers		Total	
		Amount	%	Amount	%	Amount	%	Amount	%
First	1951–56	447	31	880	61	104	7	1,431	99
Second	1956–61	918	32	1,344	47	606	21	2,868	100
Third	1961–66	1,590	28	2,738	49	1,272	23	5,600	100
Annual	1966–69	1,782	33	1,917	36	1,648	31	5,347	100
Fourth	1969–74	5,421	36	4,731	31	4,949	33	15,101	100
Fifth	1974–79*	11,048	44	10,353	41	3,761	15	25,162	100
Sixth	1979–84	(22,757)	43	NA	NA	NA	NA	(52,768)	—
Total	1951–79	21,206	38	21,963	40	12,340	22	55,509	100

Source: India, *Report of the Finance Commission, 1973*, p. 6; India, *Report of the Finance Commission, 1984*, pp. 156–57; *Reserve Bank of India Bulletin*, September–October, 1979, p. 568; R.K. Bhargava, 'Rationalising Allocation of Resources,' *Mainstream*, 30 July 1983, cited in J.L. Bajaj, *et al.*, *Finance Commission and Backward States* (Lucknow: Print House, 1985), p. 166; I.S. Gulati and K.K. George, *Essays in Federal Financial Relations* (New Delhi: Oxford & IBH Publishing, 1988), p. 14. The latter source, from which the Sixth plan period figures were derived, makes an entirely different division of Plan and other (discretionary) transfers, in which the figures for the latter are much higher than for the former though the totals for the two headings are the same in all cases. I have not cited their figures under these heads for the Sixth plan period because of these differences.

* The Fifth Plan actually terminated in 1978, but specialists in Indian government finance prefer to show the figures for 1974 to 1979 to make them comparable with the resource distribution periods of the Sixth and Seventh Finance Commissions.

transferred by the Finance Commission went up from less than one-third in the 1950s and 1960s to 44 per cent in the 1974–79 period. In contrast, the proportion of total resources transferred by the Planning Commission decreased from 61 per cent in the period 1951–56 and somewhat less than 50 per cent during the next decade to around one-third in the period from 1966 to 1974 and back up again to 41 per cent in the most recent period. The most dramatic shifts have taken place in the category of 'other transfers,' mostly discretionary loans and grants, which showed a huge jump in the 1950s and 1960s, but were cut back again very substantially in the late 1970s. The use of discretionary transfers reached its peak during the period from 1969 to 1974, which coincides roughly with the period during which Mrs. Gandhi was consolidating her power in the country. The overall significance of these trends, however, is that they represent a tendency for more transfers to be made through the Finance Commission, which has exercised the least discretionary power and has operated with formulas that do not involve major redistributive or politically motivated transfers. At the same time, as already indicated, central control over the resources transferred by the Planning Commission has declined. Overall, therefore, while the center still has the potential ability to channel considerable financial resources in a discretionary manner, the long-term trend has been away from transfers of that sort to more automatic, formula-based transfers and to decreasing control over the use of the transfers awarded to the states.[54]

On all these matters of resource transfers and central control of state expenditures, the last Congress government of Mrs. Gandhi held diffferent views from its predecessor. Mrs. Gandhi continued to favor rapid industrialization, including growth of capital-intensive industries, which requires centralized planning and central control over resources. She did not support the massive shift of resources to agriculture favored by some elements in the previous Janata government and by the Lok Dal. On the contrary, she and her advisers favored additional resource mobilization by the states from the agricultural sector. She clearly did not favor the demands for increased financial autonomy proposed by states such as West Bengal and Tamil Nadu.

After her return to power in 1980, the Sixth Five Year Plan draft prepared by the Janata government was revised in favor of capital-intensive programs and away from the previous emphasis on

welfare programs for the benefit of the poor. The role of the
Planning Commission in revising the plan was considerably reduced.
Formulation of the new draft was carried out by the central
government, largely in secret, with the Planning Commission
taking the view that its role was simply to allocate funds made
available by the Union Finance Ministry 'as Central plan assistance
under established arrangements.'[55] Clearly, Mrs. Gandhi on these
issues, as in her political behavior, favored centralization and
central control over resource allocation, distribution, and expenditure. However, for the Congress or any other government to
attempt to restore the power of the center over revenues and
expenditures and the planning process that existed during Nehru's
days would be to struggle against a secular trend towards and a
widely shared demand for decentralization and increased state
autonomy.

THE PERSISTENCE OF REGIONALISM AND THE
ABSENCE OF A NATIONAL PARTY SYSTEM

The Congress

The Congress organization clearly has been the leading political
institution in postindependence India. Despite several splits and
the existence of competing Congress organizations from time to
time, it has, nevertheless, been a central fact of postindependence
Indian political history that there has always been one predominant
Congress organization in the country which has always been either
in power or has been the largest opposition party in Parliament
and which has also always had broader support in most states of
the Indian Union than any other party, even though it has never
won a clear majority of the popular votes in the country.

It has for some time been fairly well agreed among most observers of contemporary Indian politics that the Congress organization
has disintegrated in the districts in large parts of the country,
especially in the north.[56] The party's popular vote total in the
country also declined somewhat in the era of Mrs. Gandhi's
dominance from its level in the Nehru era. In the first three
postindependence elections, the Congress popular vote share in

the country as a whole ranged between 45.0 and 47.8 per cent, whereas the range in the 1967, 1971, and 1980 elections was between 40.7 and 43.7 per cent. In the 1977 elections, the party's vote share was reduced to 34.5 per cent.

The relative stability of the Congress vote in the country as a whole masks some very dramatic changes and fluctuations that have occurred in the states that bear on the question of national-ization versus regionalism. Figure 4.1, which graphs the per cent of the parliamentary vote polled by the Congress in the fifteen major states in each of the eight elections, brings out one of those changes, namely, the sharply increased dispersion of the vote for the Congress in the states in the last four elections compared to the first four.[57] The dispersion was greatest in the 1971 elections which, for the first time, delinked the parliamentary from the state assembly elections. Instead of having the hoped-for nationalizing effect, however, delinking initially had a strongly regionalizing effect. In fact, delinking was not complete in 1971 because simul-taneous legislative assembly elections were held in Orissa, Tamil Nadu, and West Bengal. Although, by delinking, Mrs. Gandhi hoped to free herself from dependence on the state Congress organizations and from locally powerful Congress leaders for success in the parliamentary elections, the Congress (I) became dependent in some states upon adjustments and alliances with other parties, which involved not contesting a large number of seats in states such as Kerala (delinked in 1971) and Tamil Nadu (linked in 1971). The very severe decline of the Congress vote in those states and in West Bengal was counterbalanced by the very sharp increases in the Congress vote shares in Andhra, Maharashtra, and Assam. Paradoxically, the high vote in the former two states of Andhra and Maharashtra had much to do with the fact that the Congress organization still remained strong in those states and still under the control of locally powerful leaders.

Although the dispersion of the vote was less in the last three elections of 1977, 1980, and 1984 than in 1971, it remained con-siderably above that in the first three elections, which is evident both from the graph and from a comparison of the standard deviations from the mean Congress vote by state in each of those elections. Moreover, the size of the mean swing away from and back to the Congress in these last three elections was much greater, often two or three times greater, than in the earlier elections. The

FIGURE 4.1: Vote for Indian National Congress for Parliament, 1952-1984

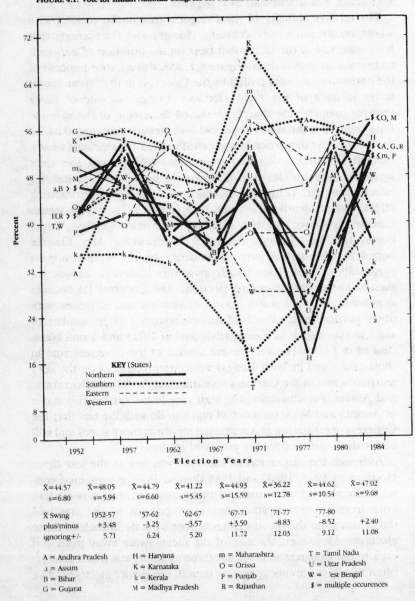

$\bar{X}$=44.57	$\bar{X}$=48.05	$\bar{X}$=44.79	$\bar{X}$=41.22	$\bar{X}$=44.93	$\bar{X}$=36.22	$\bar{X}$=44.62	$\bar{X}$=47.02
s=6.80	s=5.94	s=6.60	s=5.45	s=15.59	s=12.78	s=10.54	s=9.68

$\bar{X}$ Swing	1952-57	'57-62	'62-67	'67-71	'71-77	'77-80	
plus/minus	+3.48	−3.25	−3.57	+3.50	−8.83	−8.52	+2.40
ignoring+/-	5.71	6.24	5.20	11.72	12.03	9.12	11.08

A = Andhra Pradesh	H = Haryana	m = Maharashtra	T = Tamil Nadu
a = Assam	K = Karnataka	O = Orissa	U = Uttar Pradesh
B = Bihar	k = Kerala	P = Punjab	W = 'est Bengal
G = Gujarat	M = Madhya Pradesh	R = Rajasthan	$ = multiple occurences

relatively low mean swings in the Congress votes from 1967 to 1971
and from 1980 to 1984 mask the high volatility of the vote in both
cases. The fact that there was so much dispersion of the vote on
both sides of the mean led to an artificial evening-out of the mean
swing to a relatively low +3.50 from 1967 to 1971 and an even
lower+2.40 from 1980 to 1984. However, if the mean swing is
calculated ignoring plus and minus signs, it comes to the much
larger figures of 11.72 and 11.08, respectively. Further evidence of
the extreme volatility of the vote in these elections is provided by
the figures on the range in the swing which was close to the
extraordinarily high figure of 50 per cent in both.[58]

On the other hand, it should also be noted that the swing of the
Congress vote in the states from 1977 to 1980 was much more
uniform than in any election since that of 1967. In fact, the swings
in elections held after Mrs. Gandhi first became Prime Minister
until 1980 were fairly uniform in the sense that no less than two-
thirds of the states moved in one direction from one election to
another with the vote for the Congress having gone down in ten
out of fifteen states in 1967, up in eleven in 1971, down in ten in
1977, and up in twelve in 1980. In 1984, however, the uniformity in
the direction of the swing was reduced, with nine states increasing
their vote for Congress and six reducing it. The big difference after
Mrs. Gandhi came to power and particularly after the delinking of
parliamentary and state assembly elections was the increased
dispersion of the total vote in each state and the increased size of
the mean swing.

Delinking, nevertheless, clearly has had the intended effect of
separating voting patterns in national parliamentary and state
legislative assembly elections. The closeness of the linkage before
1971 is apparent from Figure 4.2, which plots the vote for the
Congress for Parliament against its vote in the legislative assembly
elections in 1967, the last year in which linked elections were held
in all states. In contrast to the famous 'coattails' effect in the
United States, which normally means dependence of the votes for
state candidates on the popularity of presidential candidates, the
dependence in the Indian states in the linked elections was of
parliamentary candidates upon the legislative assembly candidates.
Figure 4.3 illustrates how delinking has led to considerable differences between the Congress vote for parliament and its vote in the
nearest legislative assembly elections. Although the results in

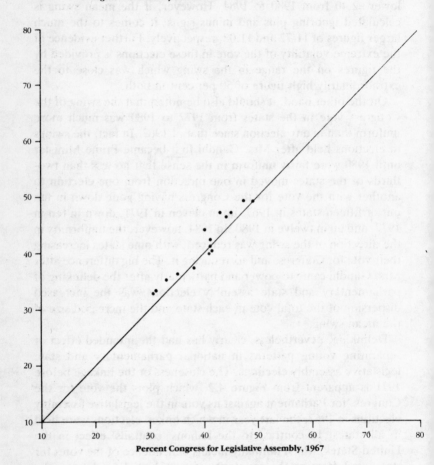

FIGURE 4.2: Vote for the Indian National Congress by State in the 1967 Parliamentary and Legislative Assembly Elections.

Percent Congress for Legislative Assembly, 1967

FIGURE 4.3: Vote for the Indian National Congress by State in the 1977 Parliamentary Elections and in Legislative Assembly Elections held between 1975 and 1978.

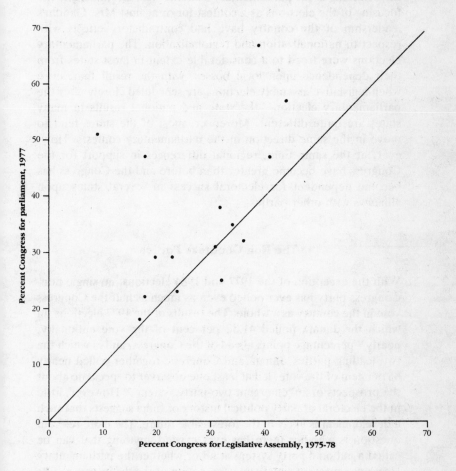

many states have not been substantially different as between the parliamentary and legislative assembly results, the clusterings around the dividing line on the graphs for the delinked elections clearly have been much less than that for 1967.

In effect, then, the disintegration of the Congress organization, the delinking of the parliamentary from the state elections, and the focusing of the elections as a contest for or against Mrs. Gandhi's leadership of the country have had contradictory effects with respect to nationalization and regionalization. The parliamentary elections were freed to a considerable extent in most states from their dependence upon local bosses, with the result that, even when legislative assembly elections are scheduled closely after the parliamentary elections, the state and national results in many states are quite different. Moreover, most of the states tend to move in the same direction in the parliamentary contests. However, at the same time, regional differences in support for the Congress have become greater than before and the Congress has become dependent for electoral success in several states upon alliances with other parties.

The Non-Congress Parties

With the exception of the 1977 and 1984 elections, no single non-Congress party has ever polled even as much as half the Congress vote in the country as a whole. The results of the 1977 elections, in which the Janata polled 41.32 per cent of the vote nationally, nearly 7 percentage points ahead of the Congress, and in which the two leading parties, Janata and Congress, together polled nearly 85 per cent of the vote, led at least one observer to speculate about the prospects of an 'emergent two-party system'.[59] However, little in the electoral or party political history of India suggests that such a development is likely in the foreseeable future. The more relevant question is whether there has ever existed anything that can be called a national party system at all or whether the parliamentary elections represent simply an aggregation of the distinctive results in each of the Indian states, the only common feature being the existence of the Congress as the largest or second largest party in every one of them.

The Election Commission has always made a distinction in the published figures for parliamentary elections between 'national' parties and other parties, variously characterized as state parties, registered parties, 'recognized' or 'unrecognized' parties. The results for the 'national' parties are listed individually, whereas the results for other parties are often lumped together in the official reports. Some of the separately listed 'national' parties have failed to win even 1 per cent of the vote nationally whereas some regional parties, such as the Dravida Munnetra Kazhagam (DMK) and the Akali Dal, have won a larger percentage of the national vote, but concentrated only in a particular state.

Leaving aside for a moment the obvious inadequacies in the distinction between 'national' and other parties, it does at least serve to distinguish strictly single state parties and independents from parties that contest in more than one state. Table 4.4 breaks up the results of the eight parliamentary elections into three categories—the vote shares for the dominant Congress, the non-Congress (including other Congress) 'national' parties, and 'other parties and independents'. The Table does indicate a trend toward 'nationalization' over the decades, with the vote for the 'national' non-Congress parties having gone up from the 20 to 30 per cent range in the 1950s to the 30 to 40 per cent range between 1962 and 1971 to the 40 to 50 per cent range in 1977 and 1980, with a corresponding decline in the relative vote shares of the category of 'other parties and independents'.

TABLE 4.4: Vote Shares for the Congress, 'National' Opposition Parties, and Others in Parliamentary Elections, 1952–84

Years	Congress	'National' Opposition	Other Parties and Independents	Total
1952	45.0	22.8	32.3	100
1957	47.8	25.2	27.0	100
1962	44.7	33.7	21.5	100
1967	40.8	35.5	23.8	100
1971	43.7	34.1	22.2	100
1977	34.7	50.1	15.3	100
1980	42.7	42.4	14.9	100
1984	48.1	29.7	22.2	100

Source: V.B. Singh and Shankar Bose, *Elections in India: Data Handbook on Lok Sabha Elections, 1952–85*, 2nd ed. (New Delhi: Sage, 1985), pp. 25 and 650.

The trend, however, was partly illusory and appeared especially chimerical in the face of the 1984 election results. It does not at all indicate the existence in any meaningful sense of a national party system, for the following reasons. First, the number of 'national' non-Congress parties has been large and their existence unstable. Twentythree parties have received such recognition as 'national' parties in the eight parliamentary elections.[60] However, beyond the Congress and the Communist parties and the Jan Sangh resurrected as the BJP, none of the other 'national' parties have persisted through time. Moreover, the second-place party has changed in every election since 1952, when the Socialist Party came in second with 10.6 per cent of the vote. The second-place parties in subsequent elections and their percentages of the total popular vote were as follows: 1957, PSP (10.4 per cent); 1962, CPI (9.9 per cent); 1967, Jan Sangh (9.4 per cent); 1971, Congress (O), (10.4 per cent); 1977; Congress, (34.5 per cent); 1980, Janata (18.9 per cent); 1984, BJP (7.4 per cent). It is also important to note that in any single parliamentary election the second-place party is likely to be different in different states. For example, in 1980, in the fifteen major states, Janata was the second-place party in seven, the Lok Dal in three, the CPM in two, the Akali Dal in one, and the AIADMK in one. In state legislative assembly elections, this kind of diversity is always even greater than in the parliamentary contests.

Second, many of the so-called national parties did not have a genuine national spread at all. For example, in 1980, in addition to the Congress, there were five 'national' parties, of which only the Janata and the INC (U), with 5.29 per cent of the vote share, had a fairly even spread in most states in the country. As for the other three, however, the Janata (S) or Lok Dal of Charan Singh polled 82.77 per cent of its 9.42 per cent national vote share in the five states of Rajasthan, Haryana, UP, Bihar, and Orissa. The CPM polled 67.45 per cent of its national vote share (6.16 per cent) in West Bengal alone and 80 per cent in the two states of Kerala and West Bengal. The distribution of the vote for most of the 'national' parties in all other elections is similarly skewed. In effect, therefore, most of the 'national' parties are regional parties or parties that have representation in two or more states, but not in all or most states in the country.[61]

A third reason for considering the trends in Table 4.4 to be

spurious is the fact that the fragmentation of the national vote for
political parties has been very high and relatively constant over the
seven elections. Rae's index of electoral fragmentation[62] for the
eight elections gives the following figures: 1952, .78; 1957, .75;
1962, .77; 1967, .80; 1971, .79; 1977, .71; 1980, .76; 1984, .75.
These figures are what one might expect from a 'system' which, to
the extent that it exists at all, could be characterized only as an
unstable, fragmented multiparty system in which one party has
always emerged dominant only because of the fact that the electoral
system is based upon the single-member plurality district in which
the candidate with the largest number of votes wins.

'Deviant' State Party Systems

The most important reason for doubting the existence in India of
anything that can be called a national party system is the fact that
all the Indian states have distinctive party systems. Although the
Congress has had strength in all states and has been the strongest
party in most, the configuration of the party system varies considerably from state to state. Some states have had multiparty
systems in which the Congress has been dominant, others have had
dualistic systems in which there have been two leading political
parties, some have had multiparty systems with several strong
parties, and still others have had fragmented multiparty systems
with no strongly institutionalized parties. In some states, the
parliamentary elections, even with delinking, are predominantly
projections onto the national scene of distinctive regional patterns
of competition and control or they primarily involve alliances and
adjustments between national and regional parties.

Moreover, despite the tendency since delinking for most of the
states to move in the same direction for or against the Congress in
parliamentary elections, strong regional tendencies persist even in
relation to the Congress vote. Figure 4.4 compares the deviation of
the Congress vote from the nationwide Congress percentage in all
elections from 1952 to 1980 in Gujarat and Kerala. These two
states were at opposite ends of the continuum of support for and
opposition to the Congress in 1952. In that year, the Congress
polled 56 per cent of the vote in the Gujarat districts of the old
Bombay province, but only 35 per cent in the present-day Kerala

FIGURE 4.4: Persistence of Regionalism: Deviation of Congress Percentages of Total
             Parliamentary Vote in Gujarat and Kerala from Congress Percentages of Total
             National Vote, 1952-1984

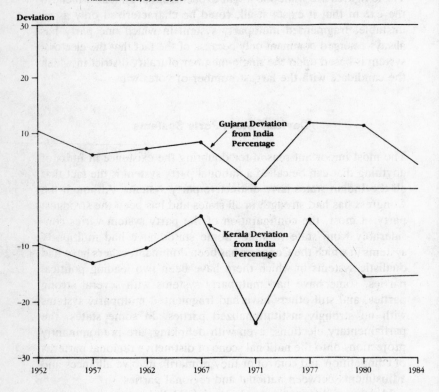

districts, a difference of 31 percentage points. Figure 4.4 shows that regional tendencies have persisted in both states, which have remained far from each other in voting patterns and often far from the mean vote for the Congress in the country.[63] Most important, although at times both states have moved towards conformity with national patterns, particularly in the period between 1957 and 1967 for Kerala and between 1957 and 1971 in Gujarat, the trajectory for both states overall has been highly individual and has generally moved away from the national norms.

Even those states which have generally been close to the national norm in relation to the vote for the Congress have differed considerably in one or more respects. For example, the distinctiveness of the Punjab party system has centered around the entrenchment of the Akali Dal as the major rival of the Congress and the persistent inability of other non-Congress parties to acquire broad bases of support in the state as a whole. In this state, support for the Congress has not deviated markedly from national trends, but support for national non-Congress parties has been relatively weak.

Tamil Nadu has deviated even more strongly from national trends than Punjab, for here the Congress itself has been markedly weak except during the period of its dominance by Kamaraj Nadar. In four elections—1952, 1971, 1977, and 1980—the Congress vote deviated markedly and negatively from the mean Congress vote in the country as a whole. Moreover, except in 1971, when the Congress (O) led by Kamaraj polled a large share of the vote, the vote for the non-Congress 'national' parties has also deviated markedly and negatively from their mean vote in the country as a whole. The principal non-Congress parties in this state, of course, have been the DMK and the ADMK.

The effect of Mrs. Gandhi's involvement in Tamil Nadu politics and her destruction of a strong Congress organization there has been to solidify the regional aspects of state politics. In 1971, Mrs. Gandhi pronounced the death knell of the Congress in Tamil Nadu by forming an alliance with the DMK in which the Congress was given nine seats for Parliament in exchange for giving the DMK a free hand in the rest of the parliamentary seats and in the state assembly elections. In contrast to the Punjab, where the main dynamic has been between the Congress and the Akali Dal, the principal dynamic in Tamil Nadu since 1971 has been provided by the competition between the DMK and the ADMK. In this competition, the Congress has had to ally with one side or the other in order to win representation to Parliament.

It would be possible to take up each of the remaining Indian states one-by-one and demonstrate significant regional differences in each. Moreover, the regional differences would be magnified even further if one were to examine the party systems in relation to the state legislative assemblies rather than Parliament. However, enough evidence has been provided to assert confidently that the nationalizing tendencies induced by Mrs. Gandhi's delinking of parliamentary and legislative assembly elections and by her controversial policies did not succeed in eroding significantly the distinctiveness of regional political patterns in India nor in establishing a truly national party system.

PRESIDENT'S RULE AND THE CYCLE OF CONSOLIDATION AND DISINTEGRATION OF CENTRAL POWER

The increasing use and abuse of the emergency provisions in the Constitution of India providing for the establishment of President's Rule (PR) in the Indian states has been cited frequently as an unequivocal demonstration of tendencies toward centralization in the Indian political system. In fact, however, a close examination of the history of the use of PR in postindependence India and of the reasons for its use suggests another interpretation. The point of view that is being suggested here is that, although PR does represent an extraordinary device, not available in most other federal systems, by which the central government takes over governmental functions in the Indian states and by which it can intervene in state politics, its frequent use is more appropriately to be seen as a failure of the Government of India to exercise effective central control over state affairs than as an index of centralization.

Consider first the basic facts concerning the frequency, the duration in particular states, and the trends over time in the use of PR. Counting only impositions of PR in the states and not the union territories, it was used sixtyeight times between 1951 and the end of 1985. It has been used for as short a period as eighteen days (in UP in 1970) and for as long as 712 days (in Kerala between

1965 and 1967). The average duration between 1951 and 1976 was 237 days, which means that most impositions have been extended beyond the initial six-months' period. Several states have undergone PR six to nine times since independence and one, Kerala, for a total duration, at different times, of over five years. Since 1967, there has never been a time when no state has been under PR. Moreover, the average annual frequency of use of PR rose with each prime minister until 1980.[64] The frequency of use of PR went up steadily after 1960 and dramatically after 1966, when Mrs. Gandhi became Prime Minister (see Figure 4.5).

Although it is reasonable to conclude from the increased frequency of use of PR that there has been, as a consequence of it, a 'reduction in the degree of state autonomy,'[65] this reduction has not meant effective central control over state politics or effective centralization of power. In fact, it is arguable that effective central control has declined. When the Congress was dominant in most of the country and when Nehru's leadership was unchallenged, central control over and intervention in state politics took place more frequently, though not exclusively, through the Congress organization rather than through the use of PR. It is no doubt true that there were many states which remained under the political dominance of powerful state leaders in the Nehru era, in which central intervention was not necessary, and that the number of such states was reduced significantly after Mrs. Gandhi began to interfere more frequently in state politics and began to use the government machinery more than the party machinery to control the states. Through her frequent interventions in state politics and because of her tendency to select as chief ministers of the states persons without strong independent support, Mrs. Gandhi contributed to political instability in the states rather than to the creation of conditions for the exercise of stable and effective control by the center over state politics. Her interventions also failed to create the conditions for the development of state leaders such as existed in Nehru's day, at once loyal to the Prime Minister and locally powerful. Moreover, the increasing use of PR as a control device rather than the central parliamentary board of the Congress or the working committee or respected arbitrators, as in the past, also reduced the amount of 'discussion, consent, and bargaining' that used to take place before a state chief minister was replaced in Nehru's time.[66]

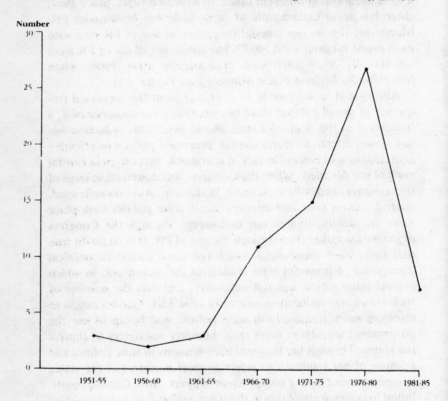

FIGURE 4.5: Increasing Number of Incidents of Imposition of President's Rule by the Central Government on the Indian States (Excluding Union Territories), 1951-1985.

It is useful in this context also to consider the differences between the most dramatic and impressive display of central control over the provinces exercised during the Nehru era without resort to PR: on the one hand, under the Kamaraj Plan of 1963, under which all Congress chief ministers in all the states of India submitted their resignations at the request of Pandit Nehru and several were replaced, and on the other, Mrs. Gandhi's replacements of chief ministers. The exercise of central control under the Kamaraj Plan involved extensive consultations with powerful regional leaders. It was an effort to consolidate power in the Congress by building a national coalition, which remained relatively stable through two successions, after the deaths of Nehru and Shastri. Mrs. Gandhi, in contrast, often imposed her will, replacing Congress chief ministers when she considered it desirable, but there was no coalition of forces nor any organization to make such changes persist after her death. Instead, she relied at the national level on cliques of political advisers, on senior bureaucrats, and on her sons to create an illusion of power through money and fear.

A final point to note with regard to the increased frequency of use of PR in the period 1967–1980 is that it has been inflated by the simultaneous impositions of PR in nine states by the Janata government to force state assembly elections in 1977 and in ten states in 1980 by Mrs. Gandhi's government for the same purpose. Such use of the PR provisions of the constitution clearly was no part of the intention of the framers. It also reflects the recent attempts to nationalize the state assembly elections, turning them into aspects of the continuing struggle for power at the center and making the outcome of the struggle for power in the states subsidiary to and dependent upon the former.[67]

The use of PR in this way as a device to force state legislative assembly elections seems again, on the face of it, to confirm the centralizing and nationalizing tendencies in Indian politics. Yet, even here, the implications are not so clear, for there is an interdependence of the center on the states and the states on the center. If power in the states depends upon the outcome at the center, it remains the case, as always, that power at the center depends upon control over the states. Moreover, that control continues to be ever-insecure and precarious. In fact, it became more insecure and precarious under Mrs. Gandhi than it was in the Nehru era because of the decay of the Congress organization[68] and because of the increased importance of non-Congress parties in several states, particularly West Bengal and Tamil Nadu, in addition to Kerala, where non-Congress parties often held power even in the 1950s and 1960s. The center came to use PR increasingly as an instrument of control both because the Congress monopoly of power in most of the states was broken and because, even when the Congress captured control at both the center and in nearly all the states, its hold on power was tenuous since it was not based on organizational strength in the states and districts. The same holds true for the non-Congress parties whose leaders, when in power at the center, must confront their own internal lack of unity, their absence of grassroots organization, and the fact that the Congress has never been ousted from power in all or nearly all the states.

The insecurity and precariousness of central control over state politics, whether the Congress or non-Congress parties are in power at the center, are easily demonstrated by examining the types of situations that have led to the imposition of PR. Dua, in his excellent work on *Presidential Rule in India*, has examined all the cases of the use of PR in India as 'crisis episodes' that reveal the true nature of center–state relations and what he calls the 'pathology of federalism'. He argues persuasively that PR has been used and abused as an instrument of central control and of Congress control over state politics and as a method of removing 'undesirable' state leaders and that its frequent misuse in this way has fundamentally transformed center–state relations.[69] He demonstrates convincingly that PR has been used repeatedly for both partisan and personal reasons, by Nehru and Shastri to solve intraparty disputes and to weaken opposition parties, by Mrs. Gandhi as 'an instrument to liquidate dissent of any kind,' and by both the Janata government and Mrs. Gandhi to precipitate state legislative assembly elections.

Dua also points out that Mrs. Gandhi surpassed all other Prime Ministers of India in her abuse of PR by using it to resolve crises in state politics deliberately created by her.[70] Specifically, both Dua and Maheshwari Prasad have shown that PR has been imposed primarily in situations of cabinet instability in the states, but not always or even usually in a clearly impartial manner. Rather PR has been imposed in such situations 'in some cases' when 'it was not strictly necessary' and, 'in a large number of instances the return of popular government was postponed more for political reasons than administrative ones.'[71] In other cases, even stable governments were dismissed on grounds that there were mass public protests against it or, in one of the clearest cases of misuse of the power of declaring PR, on grounds of corruption and that the state government 'held out "veiled threats" of secession' in Tamil Nadu in 1976.[72]

It is clear, therefore, that the use of PR has become a regular, normal feature of politics in India, rather than the exception, and that it is used at the most critical moments in state politics, namely, during ministerial crises. It is also used for the purpose of influencing the future course of politics in a state in such a way as to benefit the ruling party or parties at the center. The increased frequency of its use represents less an increase in centralizing tendencies than a shift in the instruments of central intervention and the arenas of center–state relations. The principal instrument of central intervention has become the central government administration rather than the Congress organization. The arenas of center–state relations have also shifted from the Congress organization to the state legislatures and the electoral process.

In the 1960s, when the Congress monopolized power in both the center and the states, the principal path to power in the states was through the Congress organization by mobilizing support in the districts. In the late 1960s and 1970s, as the Congress lost its monopoly of power and as the Congress organization itself disintegrated, the principal path to power became the electoral process and the legislature itself. In a sense, therefore, central control over provincial politics has declined while the political contest has become more nationalized.[73]

In the Nehru era, a Congress faction leader who wanted to capture control over a state government began by forming alliances in and gaining control over a majority in the state parliamentary board to ensure that a majority of the party tickets in the next election would go to candidates from his faction and allied factions. The next stage of the process occurred in the electoral arena where the main electoral contests were between rival factions in the Congress rather than between the Congress and opposition parties. A further stage occurred in the legislature after the election when it would be determined which factional coalition controlled a majority in the Congress legislature party. The process could be stopped or accelerated at any stage through central intervention, which occurred frequently. However, the process was selfcontained in each state and involved only district, state, and central Congress actors, but did not overlap into other states. Finally, at all stages in the process, the locality (district) and the state were the focal points because power was built up from the localities to the state level. The Congress leadership represented a power that could always intervene and stop the process, but not change its character.

In the late 1960s and 1970s, the stakes and the stages in the process and the importance of particular arenas all changed. First, after the death of Nehru, the stakes expanded to include control of the prime ministership and the central government. For a while, this change meant only the addition of a fifth and sixth step in the struggle for power, namely, the aggregation of factional coalitions to the central level and a contest for control over the national Congress organization followed by a determination of the balance of forces in the Parliament. However, after the split in the Congress in 1969 followed by Mrs. Gandhi's systematic elimination of most independent sources of power in the Congress and the consequent disintegration of the Congress organization, most of the main parties in Indian politics became shadow organizations dependent for their success and persistence upon the popularity of their leaders and their abilities to build electoral coalitions based upon broad social forces that cut across district lines and even state boundaries.

In the post-1969 process of struggle for power, the first stage occurs in the electoral arena as rival leaders in control of political parties, rather than factions, contest elections for control of the Parliament. Because the parliamentary elections have been held separately from the legislative assembly elections since 1971, success in these elections depends much less than in the past on powerful local leaders who control vote banks and much more on control over large blocs of voters—minorities, particularly Muslims, low castes and the poor, particular caste categories, and the middle peasantry especially. The second stage in the process, the selection of the Prime Minister, is similar to the situation that existed under Nehru if the Congress wins the election. If the Congress was successful, its leader, Mrs. Gandhi or Rajiv, automatically became the Prime Minister. If an opposition coalition is successful, the selection is made through consultation among top leaders of the party. Parliament plays no effective role in the process,[74] nor do the chief ministers of states as they did once in the selection of Lal Bahadur Shastri.

The third stage in the process is the precipitation of state legislative assembly elections in those states where parties in power are different from the victorious party at the center. At this stage, PR may be used either state-by-state or in a large number of states. The purpose of forcing elections, it is important to note, is not only to control the states—and not really mainly to control the states—but to consolidate power at the center by ensuring that elections to the Rajya Sabha and for President of the country, for which the state legislative assemblies constitute the electoral colleges, result in an upper house controlled by the ruling party and a President who can be counted upon to carry out its will.

The fourth stage, assuming the victory in the states of the party or coalition that controls the center, is the selection of the chief ministers of the states who are either chosen by the Prime Minister or are known allies of a powerful coalition leader at the center. The fifth stage is the disintegration of power in the states. If the Congress is in power in the states, the legislative party disintegrates into competing factions struggling to retain or replace the chief minister. If non-Congress coalitions are in power at the center and in the states, the various constituent parties and groups maneuver in the state legislature for the same purpose. During this stage, the central leadership will become involved in the struggles at the state level that focus on the office of chief minister, sometimes intervening to halt conflict, at other times to replace a chief minister. Ultimately, however, such *ad hoc* interventions cannot sustain stable governments in the states. As power disintegrates further in the states, and in an increasing number of them, there remain then two options before the leadership of the ruling group at the center: either move to prevent further disintegration by imposing Emergency rule and by using PR ruthlessly to remove any opposition in the states or permit the process of disintegration to continue until it causes the break-up of the ruling party or coalition at the center, when the process begins again.

Now, there are three principal differences between the processes outlined above in the Nehru era and in the 1970s and 1980s that relate to the issue of centralization. The first is the disintegration of the Congress organization, which has had the following consequences: the considerable decline in importance of a non-governmental mechanism of central intervention in state politics, of powerful state party bosses with bases of power independent of the center, and of the district as a critical political arena in which struggles for power at higher levels are fought and from which power is aggregated to the state level.[75] The second difference is the enlargement of the political arena to include interparty electoral competition as a critical factor, which in turn has involved some nationalization of politics or at least the transcendence of district and state boundaries in electoral contests, and the turning of parliamentary elections into contests between alternative Prime Ministers somewhat like the British pattern. However, nationalization is not the same as centralization.

The third difference is the increased interdependence of the center and the states in the outcome of political struggles for power. The last point is the most significant one, for it summarizes the basic change in the politics of center–state relations between the Nehru and post-Nehru eras. The center is not stronger than it was under Nehru. It is weaker. The central leaders are more dependent than ever on the outcomes of the struggles for power in the states, which is why Mrs. Gandhi and Rajiv tried ever harder to control state politics. The paradox is that the states too are weaker in relation to the center.

The explanation for the paradox is as follows. The center was stronger politically *in relation to the states* under Mrs. Gandhi than it was under Nehru, but its strength was illusory. Mrs. Gandhi and her inner circle of advisers at the center exercised more direct control more frequently over the selection and dismissal of chief ministers than was the case under Nehru, with the notable exception of the Kamaraj Plan. The selection of Congress candidates to contest legislative assembly elections also came under greater control by the party center. However, the state chief ministers selected or approved by the center were often politically weak in their states. Factionalism persisted in the state legislature Congress parties, with the struggle focusing on persuading the center of the incompetence and corruption of the incumbent chief minister as much as or more than on building an alternative coalition in the state party organization and in the legislature party.

At the same time, the central leaders had to remain concerned about the struggles for power in the states because their own power was more dependent upon the outcomes than in Nehru's time. The center could not afford to permit state politics to follow their own course because there were fewer leaders left in the states with independent bases of power who could be counted upon to maintain control over their legislature parties and to organize successful electoral campaigns. The immediate consequence of relaxation of central control in many states at any point in time would have been fragmentation of the Congress legislature party. Tenure of power in most states continued to be precarious, more dependent than in Nehru's time upon both central intervention and increasingly uncertain electoral outcomes. Paradoxically, therefore, although the center appeared stronger in relation to the states under Mrs. Gandhi than in Nehru's time, it was weaker and less effective in aggregating *and* maintaining a stable base of power, by conventional electoral and parliamentary methods, in the country as a whole than before.[76] Moreover, despite its greater willingness and capacity to replace chief ministers and select candidates for both parliamentary and legislative assembly elections, the center is no more effective, and may even be less effective, than in the past in ensuring that central policies and directives are implemented at the state level, particularly in the states farthest from Delhi and north India.[77]

The massive parliamentary majorities achieved by the Congress in 1971, the Janata in 1977 and the Congress again in 1980 and especially in 1984, like the great majorities achieved by the Awami League in Bangladesh, are facades that indicate not the power of the competing parties and certainly not the emergence of a two-party system, but the disintegration of party organizations with stable regional bases of support, the decline of the significance of district and state boundaries as selfcontained political segments, and the corresponding rise in the importance of waves of sentiment that affect large blocs of voters, and the increasing importance of a politics based on the appeals of popular leaders and mass movements. It is a politics of unstable interdependence between the center and the states. It is this underlying instability that impels a strong and impatient leader, such as Mrs. Gandhi, to attempt to stop the process at the point of consolidation and not permit the disintegrative process to begin a new cycle.

It is also clear why the prospect of a presidential system might have appealed to Mrs. Gandhi and even to some opposition leaders.

For, the principal advantage of a presidential system in this regard is that it would provide a fixed period of time during which power, so laboriously consolidated in Indian politics, could be maintained and exercised both at the center and, if a gubernatorial pattern were set up, in the states as well. However, the adoption of both the American presidential and gubernatorial systems would most likely foster state autonomy by protecting the states from perpetual intervention by the center and was not, therefore, acceptable either to Mrs. Gandhi or to non-Congress leaders who favor a strong center. A presidential system with governors appointed by the center would, of course, move India quite in the opposite direction. It is likely that Mrs. Gandhi and some opposition leaders as well would have been more comfortable with the French type of presidential system with a strong executive and a weaker parliament and judiciary than the American, but the French system provides no model for a federal polity.

Insofar as the recent Indian context is concerned, however, the frequent use of PR by the center has been a consequence of the requirements necessary for aggregating power at the center in a highly regionalized federal parliamentary system in which the aggregative and integrative capacities of the dominant political party have declined. It does not, however, necessarily represent a trend toward the reduction of provincial autonomy. If there is a pathological element in the frequent use of PR in India, it is less a 'pathology of federalism' than a pathology of constitutional procedure that arises from the fact that no consistent conventions have been developed to enable the public to judge when PR is being used properly or improperly. Although the frequent use of PR threatens both the parliamentary system and state autonomy, it at least keeps state politics in the forefront. The greater danger, however, arises from the prospect that a leader may attempt once again to stop the inevitable cycle of consolidation–disintegration at the peak point by making full use of both the Emergency and PR provisions of the constitution to impose an authoritarian regime.

CONCLUSION: CENTRALIZATION, DECENTRALIZATION, OR DISINTEGRATION IN INDIA'S FEDERAL SYSTEM

Although I have argued that the predominant tendencies in the development of India's federal system have been towards pluralism, regionalism, decentralization, and interdependence, strong forces also favor centralization. At present, those forces include, among other political parties, especially the Congress and the BJP. Many of Mrs. Gandhi's most decisive political actions were taken with a view toward decreasing the power and independence of state politicians and the salience of issues specific to the states while centralizing authority and power in the Congress organization at the national level and in the central government in her own hands and those of her closest advisers and while emphasizing national issues. The specific measures that Mrs. Gandhi took to centralize power and authority in her own hands and to nationalize political issues are well known and have been discussed above. They include the political destruction of the state political bosses, the consequent disintegration of the Congress organization in the districts, and the selection by her and her closest advisers of chief ministers in the states who lacked independent bases of power and who could, therefore, be counted upon to follow the directions of the central government. They include also the delinking of parliamentary and state legislative assembly elections and the emphasis in parliamentary elections on programs, appeals, and issues that are national in scope.

For example, Mrs. Gandhi attempted, with some success, to build a national following among categories and groups of voters whose needs were not adequately satisfied by the state governments or who had identifications that crossed state boundaries. Clearly included in such groups were the Muslims and other minorities, the scheduled castes, the tribal peoples, the poor and the landless, and the north Indian Brahman castes. The Brahman castes were tied to Mrs. Gandhi and the Congress for a combination of emotional and practical reasons, including caste solidarity with Mrs. Gandhi in an organization that is Brahman-dominated in many areas and opposition to the aspirations of non-elite castes who threaten Brahman preponderance in elite educational, administrative, and political positions. It should be noted that the main threats to the continued importance of Brahmans in public life come not from the scheduled castes but from other elite castes and from the 'backward' or middle castes. Measures that have been taken in the past or promised in the future to promote the interests of minorities and disadvantaged groups include strengthening the Minorities Commission, grants of money, plots of land, and other facilities and benefits to scheduled castes, identification with the scheduled castes and landless laborers who have been victimized by the landowning castes, promises to recognize Urdu as a second official language in states where Urdu-speaking Muslims are in a large minority, the establishment of the Small Farmers Development Agency and the Marginal Farmers and Agricultural Labourers Agency, and the nationalization of the banks and the establishment of regional and district banks explicitly designed to provide credit to the small and marginal farmers left out of local systems of power, patronage, and credit. It is noteworthy also that the Congress Manifesto for the 1980 elections specifically stressed that 'the planning process' would 'once again' be used 'to reorganize the national economy' and that the state governments would be persuaded to implement national, uniform policies on 'subjects included in the "State List" under the Constitution.'[78]

Despite Mrs. Gandhi's attempts to transcend regional issues and forces, however, they remain dominant in Indian society, in the economy, and in electoral politics. Every state in India has a distinctive group of landowning castes who continue to control the countryside. Where the Congress has lost support among such groups, as in north India, it is weak and vulnerable electorally. Such groups remain available to be organized by state-level politicians and regional parties. The interests of these groups also are best served by state governments and district institutions that they can control, by programs designed to satisfy local agricultural needs, and by taxation and price policies that favor the farmers. Linguistic and cultural differences also continue to provide strong support for regional political parties, persistent pressures for cultural pluralism, and demands for regional autonomy in states such as Tamil Nadu, Punjab, West Bengal, Kashmir, and Andhra. West Bengal and Kerala also have maintained persistently distinctive leftist political traditions that serve to differentiate those states politically from other states and from national political patterns. However, it is not only these states that are different. In fact, all states are politically distinctive in a more than superficial way on one measure or another.

Moreover, all the states have a common interest in relation to the center in extracting as many resources as possible for their own financial and developmental needs and goals. Had the center followed a consistent policy of either promoting the interests of the advanced or most 'progressive' states or alternatively had it pursued consistently a policy of interstate equalization with significant redistributive effects, it might have divided the states into supporters and opponents of a strong center with discretionary powers in resource transfers. However, the pursuit of either of these alternative strategies would divide the country and threaten its unity. Since the center cannot or will not follow either strategy consistently and rigorously, the optimal strategy for all the states is simply to demand an increasing share of revenues collected by the center. The main differences among the states are in how strongly they wish to push for such increased shares and in whether or not they prefer to control the entire tax collection process themselves. Clearly, only the better-off states with greater resources than the rest can sensibly prefer the latter strategy. Most of the states, however, can be satisfied indefinitely by tax and resource distribution policies that give them access to a substantial share of centrally collected resources while not requiring them to tax politically sensitive sectors, particularly the prosperous peasantry.

The great dilemma for a centralizing leader or party in India is that stable power at the center can be built up only through control over the states and districts of the country. That kind of power, however, is inherently regional and local in character. Control over the states by the Congress in the Nehru days made it possible for the national leadership to pursue its fancy and attempt through capital-intensive industrialization policies to transform India into a major power with a modern industrial economy. However, in the process, most of the state governments, whose primary political constituencies were the landowning peasantry, became largely patronage-oriented rather than policy-oriented. They were also frequently castigated for failing to implement cherished policies of the national leadership, such as land reform, or for failing to mobilize resources from the agricultural sector to pay for the large-scale industrialization of the country in which they often had little interest.

However, as it became clear in the late 1960s that the Nehru industrialization policy was faltering and that it was failing to solve problems of poverty and employment and to promote equality, that inflation was becoming a major concern in the cities, and that agriculture was being neglected and when Nehru himself passed from the scene, the hold of the Congress over the country, particularly in the north, began to weaken. When the prospect of a Green Revolution also began to materialize, pressures for policies more oriented to the needs of agriculture also began to develop. Since agricultural resource requirements are highly variable and regional and local in nature and since rural power structures are also, by definition, local and regional, the pressure for a shift in economic policy orientations towards agriculture is also pressure in the direction of decentralization of both the economy and politics.

Thus, there is a logic in both the political economy of India and in center–state relations that explains Mrs. Gandhi's methods of consolidating power, the social bases of her support and that of opposition forces, and the reasons for her defeat and subsequent return to power. The logic is as follows. Since the states could not be controlled by her when Mrs. Gandhi first came to power and since the agricultural constituency is not a national one, Mrs. Gandhi broke the power of the state bosses and sought a national constituency to free her to pursue the old policies of her father. However, since the landowning communities remain the principal political and economic forces in the countryside, Mrs. Gandhi and the Congress everywhere have had to maintain some support among some of the landed castes as well as the poor and disadvantaged groups in order to win power in the country. Moreover, the destruction of the power of the state bosses produced less a stable centralization of power than its fragmentation. The stability of few of the states could be counted upon. Consequently, it is ever more necessary for the center to intervene in the state legislatures for the sake of its own power at the center. The decline of the Congress party organization also, of course, meant its decline as an effective electoral machine. Success in national elections increasingly depended not upon the ability of the party organization to build and maintain alliances and get its supporters to the polls, but on the ability of Mrs. Gandhi to form alliances with leaders with influence over widespread voting blocs and on her personal ability to appeal to categories of voters.

Thus, the logic of India's political economy and center–state relations led to contradictions in the Congress' support base and in Mrs. Gandhi's methods of centralizing power. Mrs. Gandhi sought a national constituency, but she could not free herself from the need for support from the regionally powerful rural landowning castes. She sought to centralize power, but she continued to be dependent on control over the states, whose instability, which she had herself 'helped to create,'[79] had always to be watched for fear that the Congress would lose power in the legislatures through defection or through unfavorable electoral outcomes.

At the same time, the opposition of the bulk of the middle peasantry, particularly in the north, to Mrs. Gandhi and the Congress, provided a persistent base of support for opposition parties. Other bases of support for opposition parties also continued to come from the regionally dominant language, ethnic, and religious communities. Since both types of support are inherently regional and local in character, any opposition to the Congress at the national level must be an unstable coalition of parties and leaders with largely regional followings. It was such a coalition, whose central core was the north Indian middle peasantry and regional caste groups, supplemented by defections from Mrs. Gandhi's support bases amongst the minorities and the poor, that defeated the Congress in 1977. However, that coalition, by its very diversity and lack of any genuine common interests beyond opposition to Mrs. Gandhi, was difficult to put together, inherently unstable, and began to fall apart as soon as it was formed. When the coalition split and, at the same time, Mrs. Gandhi rebuilt her coalition of minorities and the poor, supplemented by some of the landowning groups, her victory at the national level was assured. The National Front coalition which defeated the Congress in 1989 was even more difficult to construct and comprised a range of north Indian caste and communal groups with regional political forces in the non-Hindi-speaking states.

The conclusion is inescapable, therefore, that centralization and consolidation of power in India's federal parliamentary system are bound to be ephemeral unless either authoritarian measures are taken to prevent the inevitable movement of the cycle towards disintegration and fragmentation of power or unless the institutional form of the system is changed to a presidential type. Both options hold great potential dangers for the future stability and integrity of India. The first option, already attempted once, would most likely culminate a second time, if pursued more single-mindedly, in a more violent way. The consequences of exercising the second option are more problematic, especially since there are several possible forms that a presidential pattern itself may take. The adoption of a presidential form that freed the center from dependence on state politics would probably enhance the stability of both. A presidential system of the French pattern, adopted with a view toward centralizing power and control over resources by the center, would probably be resisted strongly in those states with the most distinctive and 'deviant' political traditions, with the most divergent cultural traditions, and with the greatest internal resources, and might therefore ultimately also prove unworkable.

Thus, there is no 'solution' to the conflicting drives towards centralization and decentralization in the Indian polity, only alternatives that might moderate or intensify their destabilizing effects. Centralization and authoritarian rule ultimately promise a violent breakdown. Maintaining the present system requires a willingness on the part of state and central political leaders with conflicting goals to tolerate the continuance of the laborious and frustrating cycle of consolidation–disintegration. Adoption of a presidential system of the American type might free the system from the uncertainties and instabilities associated with that cycle, but, if American history is any guide, it will not eliminate the struggles between centralizers and decentralizers which, like party competition itself, must be recognized as a persisting element in any healthy and viable federal republican system of government.[80]

NOTES

1. Marcus F. Franda, 'Federalising India: Attitudes, Capacities and Constraints,' *South Asian Review*, Vol. III, No. 3 (April, 1970), pp. 199–213. Nor has there been any major study of the interactions between the central and state governments based on detailed examination of specific instances of decision-making since Franda's *West Bengal and the Federalizing Process in India* (Princeton, NJ: Princeton University Press, 1968). Aside from Dua's excellent and comprehensive work on President's Rule, cited subsequently, most books bearing a title relating to center–state relations focus on resource transfers, the decisions taken by the Finance and Planning Commissions with little attention to the political dynamics involved in their decisions, relations between central and state units of the Indian National Congress, studies of regional political forces and separatist movements, and broad assessments of general tendencies towards or away from centralization.
2. W.H. Morris-Jones, *The Government and Politics of India*, 3rd ed. (London: Hutchinson University Library, 1971), pp. 150–56.

3. S.A.H. Haqqi and A.P. Sharma, 'Centre–State Relations: A Study of Structural and Processual Determinants,' in K.A. Bombwall (ed.), *National Power and State Autonomy* (Meerut: Meenakshi Prakasan, 1977), pp. 42–47.

4. Morris-Jones, *Government and Politics of India*, op. cit., p. 152.

5. Myron Weiner, 'Political Development in the Indian States,' in Myron Weiner (ed.), *State Politics in India* (Princeton, NJ: Princeton University Press, 1968), p. 58.

6. Bhagwan D. Dua, 'Presidential Rule in India: A Study in Crisis Politics,' *Asian Survey*, Vol. XIX, No. 6 (June, 1979), p. 626.

7. B.D. Dua, *Presidential Rule in India, 1950–1984: A Study in Crisis Politics*, 2nd ed. (New Delhi: S. Chand, 1985), p. 396.

8. M. Venkatarangaiya and M. Shiviah, 'The Working of Indian Federalism,' in Bombwall, *National Power and State Autonomy*, op. cit., p. 63.

9. K.R. Bombwall, 'National Power and State Autonomy: A Note on the Socio-Political Dynamics of Indian Federalism,' in Bombwall, *National Power and State Autonomy*, op. cit., p. 211.

10. By pluralism, I mean a system that contains a multiplicity of social, cultural, economic, and political groups and that does not permit the imposition of the ideas, values, culture, or language of a single group to be imposed upon the others. By regionalism, in the political sense, I mean patterns of politics in the states that are best explained primarily in terms of conflicts and issues that arise within the states rather than in the national political arena and that deviate in easily discernible ways, such as in political party formations and voting patterns, from national trends. By decentralization, I refer to a process in which economic resources are controlled and spent locally, however they are collected, in which the important decisions affecting economic and political life in a federal system are made by political leaders at the state level, in which power is built from the bottom up, and in which power at the federal or central level depends upon the support of state political forces rather than the reverse. The argument of this chapter is not that India is a full-fledged pluralist, regionalist, and decentralized system but that tendencies and forces moving the country towards pluralism, regionalism, and decentralization are inherently stronger than those favoring homogeneity, nationalization, and centralization.

11. Cf. Rajni Kothari, who argued in 'Delivering the Goods,' *Seminar*, No. 242 (October, 1979), pp. 12–17 that the Indian political system was in crisis, but that 'no centralized solution can work in solving the basic crisis in the system.'

12. The policy and institutional areas selected for discussion in this paper were chosen partly on the basis of my own expertise, partly on the consideration of availability of information, and partly because of their evident importance for center–state relations. Obviously, many other institutions and policy areas might have been selected, perhaps with different results. For example, in a personal communication, Myron Weiner suggested that centralizing tendencies are more evident in 'the police services and [in] the use of paramilitary institutions' and that particular ministries such as Home have 'more control' than earlier. A complete account of the current balance in and future prospects for center–state relations clearly would have to cover such areas, in addition to those discussed below.

13. Selig S. Harrison, *India: The Most Dangerous Decades* (Princeton, NJ: Princeton University Press, 1960).

14. Harrison, *India*, op. cit., p. 305.
15. See esp. Paul R. Brass, *Language, Religion, and Politics in North India* (New York: Cambridge University Press, 1974), Jyotirindra Das Gupta, *Language Conflict and National Development: Group Politics and National Language Policy in India* (Berkeley: University of California Press, 1970), and T.N. Madan, 'Linguistic Diversity and National Unity: Dimensions of a Debate,' in A.H. Hanumantha Rao and P.C. Joshi (eds.), *Reflections on Economic Development and Social Change: Essays in Honour of Professor V.K.R.V. Rao* (New Delhi: Allied, 1980), pp. 393–410.
16. Sudhakar Dwivedi, 'Official Language Policy of the Union,' in Government of India, Ministry of Home Affairs, Department of Official Language, *All India Official Languages Conference Souvenir* (New Delhi, 1978), pp. 11–12 and 21.
17. A.P. Kamat, 'Ethno-Linguistic Issues in Indian Federal Context,' *Economic and Political Weekly* [hereafter referred to as *EPW*], Vol. XV, Nos. 24 and 25 (14–21 June 1980), p. 1063.
18. Government of India, Union Public Service Commission, *Civil Services Examination: Report of the Committee on Recruitment Policy and Selection Methods* (New Delhi: Government of India Press, 1976), pp. 19–21.
19. Brass, *Language, Religion, and Politics*, op. cit. Departures from the protecting role of the center towards minorities and the adoption of more interventionist and manipulative roles in relation to minorities in state politics have, however, been a major factor in the rise and intensification of ethnic conflicts in Punjab, Kashmir, and Assam in the 1980s. The rise of separatism in Punjab is discussed in chapters 5 and 6.
20. See, for example, Government of India, Ministry of Home Affairs, *The Twenty-Third Report by the Deputy Commissioner for Linguistic Minorities in India* (For the Period July 1982 to June 1983) (Delhi: Controller of Publications, 1985), *passim*.
21. V.O. Key, Jr., *American State Politics: An Introduction* (New York: Knopf, 1956), p. 7.
22. Key, *American State Politics*, op. cit., p. 8.
23. Government of India, Ministry of Planning, Department of Statistics, Central Statistical Organisation, *Monthly Abstract of Statistics*, December, 1978, Vol. XXI, No. 12, p. 3.
24. Government of India, Ministry of Planning, Department of Statistics, Central Statistical Organisation, *Monthly Abstract of Statistics*, June 1989, Vol. XLII, No. 6, p. 4.
25. S. Venu, *The Finance Commissions of India* (Madras: Institute for Financial Management and Research, 1978), pp. 104–5.
26. B.S. Grewal, *Centre–State Financial Relations in India* (Patiala: Punjabi University, 1975), pp. 85–86.
27. Birla Institute of Scientific Research, *Centre–State Financial Relations in India* (New Delhi: Abhinav, 1979), p. 127.
28. I.S. Gulati and K.K. George, *Essays in Federal Financial Relations* (New Delhi: Oxford & IBH, 1988), p. 14.
29. Gulati and George, *Essays in Federal Financial Relations*, op. cit., p. 9.
30. Government of India, *Report of the Finance Commission, 1973*, op. cit., p. 8.
31. Birla Institute, *Centre–State Financial Relations*, op. cit., p. 21.

32. Grewal, *Centre–State Financial Relations*, op. cit., pp. 104–8 and Gulati and George, *Essays in Federal Financial Relations*, op. cit., p. 25.
33. Grewal, *Centre–State Financial Relations*, op. cit., pp. 129–30.
34. Venu, *The Finance Commissions*, op. cit., p. 119; also Gulati and George, *Essays in Federal Financial Relations*, op. cit., pp. 24–29, whose data show that gross budgetary transfers over the entire period from 1956 to 1981 under all heads—statutory (Finance Commission), plan, and discretionary—have favored the high and middle income states over the low income states (UP, Rajasthan, MP, and Bihar).
35. L.S. Bhat, *et al.*, *Regional Inequalities in India: An Inter-State and Intra-State Analysis*, paper presented at an all-India conference on Centre–State Relations and Regional Disparities in India at New Delhi in August, 1980 (New Delhi: Society for the Study of Regional Disparities, 1982), p. 105.
36. Gulati and George, *Essays in Federal Financial Relations*, op. cit., p. 42; J.L. Bajaj, *et al.*, *Finance Commission and Backward States* (Lucknow: Print House, 1985), pp. 177–78.
37. Gulati and George, *Essays in Federal Financial Relations*, op. cit., pp. 76–77.
38. Grewal, *Centre–State Financial Relations*, op. cit., pp. 55–61 and H.K. Paranjpe, 'Centre–State Relations in Planning,' in S.N. Jain, *et al.*, *The Union and the States* (Delhi: National, 1972), p. 218.
39. Government of India, Planning Commission, *Draft Five Year Plan, 1978–83* (Delhi: Controller of Publications, 1978), p. 110.
40. *Asian Recorder*, 1979, p. 14816.
41. D.V.S. Sastry and A.K. Nag, 'Transfer of Resources from Centre and Growth in State Domestic Product,' *EPW*, Vol. XXV, No. 14 (7 April 1990), pp. 738–42.
42. M.M. Ansari, 'Financing of the States' Plans: A Perspective for Regional Development,' *EPW*, Vol. XVIII, No. 49 (3 December 1983), 2,077.
43. Sastry and Nag, 'Transfer of Resources from Centre and Growth in State Domestic Product,' op. cit.
44. Venu, *The Finance Commissions*, op. cit., pp. 76–77.
45. Venu, *The Finance Commissions*, op. cit., pp. 110–11.
46. India, *Report of the Finance Commission, 1973*, op. cit., p. 7.
47. V.K. Subramaniam, *The Indian Financial System* (New Delhi: Abhinav, 1979), p. 163.
48. S. Venu, *The Seventh Finance Commission's Report: A Critique* (Madras: Institute for Financial Management and Research, 1979), p. 14.
49. Birla Institute, *Centre–State Financial Relations*, op. cit., p. 5.
50. Paranjpe, 'Centre–State Relations in Planning,' op. cit., p. 212.
51. Paranjpe, 'Centre–State Relations in Planning,' op. cit., p. 216 and Grewal, *Centre–State Financial Relations*, op. cit., p. 61. However, see the contrary arguments noted in fn. 54.
52. Paranjpe, 'Centre–State Relations in Planning,' op. cit., pp. 222 and 235.
53. R.K. Sinha, *Fiscal Federalism in India* (Madras: South Asian Publishers, 1980), p. 91.
54. A contrary view emphasizes the point that statutory transfers still constitute only 40 per cent of total transfers and that the bulk of center–state transfers continue to be subject to the direct control of the central government through the Planning Commission or through discretionary transfers. It is also pointed

out that 'the importance of the Gadgil formula [used by the Planning Commission] itself has been progressively whittled down and now almost 50 per cent of the Central plan assistance to the States is given outside the formula'; Gulati and George, *Essays in Federal Financial Relations*, op. cit., pp. 14–15. The figures are clearly subject to different interpretations. Mine overall is that there is a struggle between the center and the states on financial transfers, as on other matters, in which the direction is either in favor of the states or the states have managed to hold their own in one way or another against the centralizing drives of the leadership in New Delhi.

55. B.M., 'Arithmetic is All,' *EPW*, Vol. XV, No. 52 (27 December 1980), p. 2169.
56. See esp. James Manor, 'Indira and After: The Decay of Party Organisation in India,' *Round Table*, No. 272 (October, 1978), pp. 315–24.
57. It may help to interpret the significance of the increased dispersion of the Congress vote by comparing it with similar figures for the United States. In the United States, it is generally agreed that nationalizing tendencies have been at work since the end of World War II that have resulted in an increasingly even spread of the vote for president and increasing competitiveness in the fifty states in contrast to pre-World War II patterns when sectionalism was greater. In pre-World War II elections, some states would be carried by a presidential candidate by large margins while others would be lost by similarly large margins. The standard deviation for the votes by state for the successful presidential candidate between 1896 and 1944 ranged between a high of 17.5 in the former year to a low of 12.3 in the latter year. From 1948 to 1976, in contrast, the range has been between 5.8 in 1960 and 10.3 in 1964. Thus, the dispersion of the Congress vote in India since 1971 has been more in conformity with pre-World War II patterns of presidential voting, whereas the pre-1971 standard deviations were similar to post-World War II American patterns. See Frank J. Sorauf, *Party Politics in America*, 4th ed. (Boston: Little, Brown, 1972), p. 53.
58. From 1967 to 1971, the swing in Tamil Nadu went down 29.2 percentage points from 41.7 to 12.5 and up 21.9 points in Karnataka from 49.0 to 70.9, the range being 51.1. From 1980 to 1984, the swing in Assam went down 27.4 percentage points from 51.0 to 23.6 and up 22.4 points in Haryana from 32.6 to 55.0, giving a range of 49.8.
59. Myron Weiner, *India at the Polls: The Parliamentary Elections of 1977* (Washington, D.C.: American Enterprise Institute, 1978), p. 97.
60. The parties are: Bharatiya Jan Sangh, Bharatiya Lok Dal, Bolshevik Party, Communist Party of India, Communist Party of India (Marxist), Forward Bloc (M), Forward Bloc (R), Hindu Mahasabha, Indian National Congress, Indian National Congress (O), Indian National Congress (S), Indian National Congres (U), Janata, Janata (S), Kisan Mazdur Praja Party, Krishikar-Lok Party, Praja Socialist Party, Ram Rajya Parishad, Republican Party of India, Revolutionary Communist Party, Samyukta Socialist Party, Socialist Party, and Swatantra.
61. The discussion in the above paragraph is based upon the statistical spread of the vote for the so-called 'national' non-Congress parties. There is, of course, a deeper question that requires a different kind of analysis, namely, whether or not the 'national' parties that exist in more than one state share much beyond a

common name and a national executive committee. It can be argued that the Congress itself is a 'national' party only in limited respects. James Manor has remarked that 'the Congress organizations' in states he analyzed during the 1977 elections—Maharashtra, Gujarat, Karnataka, Andhra Pradesh, and Kerala—'could be regarded primarily as regional parties alongside the regional parties ruling in Tamil Nadu, Kashmir, and West Bengal.' See his 'Where Congress Survived: Five States in the Indian General Election of 1977,' *Asian Survey*, Vol. XVIII, No. 8 (August, 1978), p. 803. Manor's argument is based partly on differences in the support bases of the Congress in these states and partly on the limited effectiveness of the central leadership in controlling the Congress governments and Congress organizations in them even during the Emergency.

62. The index is constructed on a scale of 0 to 1, with values closest to 1 representing the greatest fragmentation. See Douglas Rae, *The Political Consequences of Electoral Laws* (New Haven: Yale University Press, 1967), pp. 53–58.

63. Compare the figure in Key, *American State Politics*, op. cit., p. 27, which uses the states of Vermont and Florida to show an opposite trend of 'erosion of sectionalism' in the United States between 1896 and 1952.

64. The facts and figures in this paragraph come from Dua, 'Presidential Rule in India'; Shriram Maheshwari, *President's Rule in India* (Columbia, MO: South Asia Books, 1977), pp. 166 *ff.*; *Asian Recorder*; and India, Parliament, *President's Rule in the States and Union Territories* (New Delhi: Lok Sabha Secretariat, 1989).

65. Dua, 'Presidential Rule in India,' op. cit., p. 614.

66. I owe this point to a personal communication from Myron Weiner.

67. Although the state assembly elections have been 'nationalized' in the sense that their timing has now come to depend upon the outcome of the Lok Sabha elections and struggle for power at the center, the actual results in the several states do not in fact show as close a correlation with the nearest Lok Sabha election as when the elections at the two levels were linked, as indicated in the foregoing.

68. See Manor, 'Indira and After,' and James Manor, 'Party Decay and Political Crisis in India,' *The Washington Quarterly* (Summer, 1981), pp. 27–29. Manor argues in the latter article that Mrs. Gandhi's efforts to centralize power in her own hands have not only hastened 'the demise of the Congress machine' (p. 27), but have 'increased rather than reduced the disparities between national and lower levels' and have deprived 'the national level of reliable information from below' (p. 32). Another factor, therefore, in the decreased effective control by the center over state politics is lack of information about what is actually happening in the regions and localities and about the strength and reliability of local leaders and groups.

69. Dua, *Presidential Rule in India*, op. cit., pp. x, 1, 4, 21–22. In his revised edition of the original book, Dua comments on my own interpretation of his and Maheshwari Prasad's data and takes an even stronger position, arguing that the abuse of PR has gone beyond even 'the pathology of a federal system' and reflects rather the fact that India has become a 'corrupt state'. I do not wish to argue against this characterization of the contemporary Indian state, only to suggest that the center's efforts have failed to achieve the desired results.

70. Dua, 'Presidential Rule in India,' op. cit., pp. 612, 615–19, 622–26.
71. Maheshwari, *President's Rule*, op. cit., p. 173.
72. Maheshwari, *President's Rule*, op. cit., p. 174.
73. See also Manor, 'Where Congress Survived,' op. cit., p. 800, where he argues that Mrs. Gandhi's 'centralizing efforts did not produce tighter integration of the national organization of the Congress.'
74. Parliament played no role in the selection process under Nehru either, as James Manor points out in a personal communication. In fact, the only occasion on which Parliament played a role at this stage was during the second selection of Mrs. Gandhi in her contest with Morarji Desai after the 1967 elections. Cultivation of support in Parliament was also critical for the maintenance of Mrs. Gandhi in power from 1967 to 1971 and in the defeat of Morarji Desai and the selection of Charan Singh in 1979. However, the second stage referred to in the text concerns the period just after an election.
75. I believe control of district political and economic resources remains very important, but the old Congress system which involved constant struggle among groups at the state level for control over a majority of districts, which then provided the victors with the chance to take power at the state level in the party and in the government, is gone, at least in the north Indian states.
76. In a personal communication, Myron Weiner suggested that the central cabinet also became a weaker institution than it was under Nehru and that central coordination of programs became less effective than formerly.
77. Manor, 'Where Congress Survived,' op. cit., p. 802.
78. Indian National Congress (I), *Election Manifesto, 1980* (New Delhi: All India Congress Committee (I), 1979).
79. I owe this formulation to a personal communication from Myron Weiner.
80. It is not being suggested here that Mrs. Gandhi was inclined to approve the adoption of an American type of presidential system. If anything, it is more likely that, given a choice between the American and French types, she would have preferred the latter. However, my points in this paragraph do not relate to the personal preferences of contemporary leaders but only to the possible consequences of the adoption of different types of systems.

The Punjab Crisis and the Unity of India

INTRODUCTION

In the early years after independence in India, as in other countries of Asia and Africa, it was common to view the maintenance of national unity, peace, and internal order as among the central, if not the central, political problems. There was also a shared view among the leaders of the new states that national unity could best be maintained by a process of national integration that involved the development of new loyalties to a centralizing, modernizing state. That view was also shared by virtually all Western scholars who wrote about these questions in the 1950s and 1960s.

In *Language, Religion, and Politics in North India*, written in the late 1960s and early 1970s and published in 1974,[1] I argued

Acknowledgments: I am grateful to Joyce Pettigrew for her critiques of two earlier versions of this essay. I am afraid I may not have satisfied her on all matters. A lively exchange with Baldev Raj Nayar also helped me to sharpen my thinking, though we disagree even more substantially. A very heated exchange in Delhi with Rashpal Malhotra and his colleagues from the Centre for Research in Rural and Industrial Development in Chandigarh caused me to rectify some imbalances in my treatment of Mrs. Gandhi's policies and decisions and of the opposed points of view on some matters. I doubt, however, that we are yet in agreement. I appreciate also the comments of Kenneth Jones, Atul Kohli, Christopher Shackle, Bhagwan D. Dua, and Mark Tully and have revised the manuscript in several places as a result of some of their comments. With regard to this essay, however, more than most, it is necessary to emphasize that I am solely responsible for the accuracy of the statements, for the interpretation, and for the opinions expressed.

against the shared view. My position was that India was not and could not be a nation-state, but was instead a developing multi-national state. The argument was based upon a distinction between political integration of diverse peoples through politics, policies, procedures, and institutions and national integration through assimilation of diverse peoples to a common national culture. My view was that Indian policymakers had themselves made such a distinction in practice if not in principle at the central level, though not in the states, and had consequently developed workable means of maintaining political unity in the world's most culturally diverse country. The center had been following pluralist policies in relation to the various linguistic, religious, and other minorities in the country. The conflicts between language and religious groups that were so common in India in the 1950s and 1960s had their origins in local and regional conditions and were influenced by specific patterns of intergroup political and economic competition and state government policies. Such conflicts often became intense, politically destabilizing, and sometimes violent. Moreover, state governments, in contrast to the central government, often pursued assimilative and discriminatory policies in relation to minority groups within their jurisdictions.

In the face of the turmoils that arose in the 1950s and 1960s in nearly all the regions of India, I argued that the central government had not acted in a vacillating and indecisive way that led to the intensification of such conflicts, which was the common view. On the contrary, my view was that the central government had developed a set of consistent rules that were not all written down or consciously pursued, but that guided its actions in all these different situations. Those four rules, stated concisely, were that no demand for political recognition of a religious group would be considered, that explicitly secessionist movements would not be tolerated and would be suppressed by force whenever necessary, that no capricious concessions would be made to the political demands of any linguistic, regional, or other culturally defined group, and that no political concessions to cultural groups in conflict would be made unless they had demonstrable support from both sides in the conflict.

These rules provided a broad context for specific policies pursued by the Government of India which made it possible for lasting, agreed solutions to be reached on some highly controversial cultural issues. The two great successes in this regard were the adoption of a multilingual policy at the center and the completion of the long process of linguistic reorganization of states. These policies also facilitated the consolidation of a process of dual nationalism, the comfortable accommodation of most Indians to a recognition of themselves as members of two nations: a Sikh, Bengali, or Tamil nation at one level of identity and an Indian nation at another. Since Sikhs, Bengalis, Tamils, and most other regional nationalities either never or, because of the policies settled upon during the 1950s and 1960s, no longer came into conflict with each other, there was no reason why such a duality of loyalties could not be maintained indefinitely.

Although the Government of India did preside successfully over the satisfactory resolution of complex and difficult linguistic, religious, and other minority conflicts, several others were left unresolved, of which some became worse, and one 'new' (but really old) problem cropped up. The problems left unresolved concerned the status of minorities in the linguistically reorganized states, Hindu–Muslim relations, migrant–native conflicts in some parts of the country, and the conclusion of the reorganization of the Punjab.

The new problem, that is in effect a very old problem, that has arisen in the last fifteen years or more concerns the movement for increased regional autonomy in several of the Indian states, including Punjab. Although the contemporary salience of this issue dates to the 1973 Anandpur Sahib Resolution of the Akali Dal in Punjab, it cannot fail to remind Indian leaders and historians of the controversies that arose in the subcontinent in the 1930s and 1940s concerning center–provincial relations in an independent India. Many historians are also likely to point out that issues of center–provincial relations go back to the Mughals and even earlier in Indian history. Moreover, in contemporary times, the demand for regional autonomy preceded the secession of Bangaladesh from Pakistan.

It appeared, in fact, during 1982–84 that the old problem of Indian unity was approaching a new period of crisis concerning these old and new unresolved problems. The flash-points were, of course, Assam and Punjab primarily, but there were indications of problems to come in Kashmir as well. The conflict between the Congress at the center and the Telugu Desam in Andhra is also, I believe, relevant in this context. Finally, of course, Hindu–Muslim riots are always there and a severe one occurred in Bombay in 1984.

What I propose to take up in this paper is whether this combination of unresolved problems in contemporary Indian politics in fact constitutes a new critical test of Indian unity. The issue will be approached by asking whether the old methods of handling separatist, communalist, and regional problems broke down during the Punjab crisis in the 1980s or whether the old rules are in place and need only specific policies to be devised to resolve the contemporary crises. I propose to look in detail at Punjab in the early 1960s and in the 1980s to compare the way Sikh political demands were handled by the central government in these two periods. In this way, it will be possible to reassess the relationships in contemporary India among separatist tendencies, political integration, and national integration as they have revealed themselves specifically in the recent Punjab crisis.[2]

THE CHANGED CONTEXT OF CENTER–STATE RELATIONS

Fundamental changes in center–state relations and in the general process by which power is aggregated in India occurred during Mrs. Gandhi's tenure as Prime Minister. Those changes occurred because, for the first time since the struggle for power at the center in 1950–51 was decided decisively for a generation in favor of both the Congress as the dominant party in the Indian political system and Pandit Nehru as its leader, the dominant position of the Congress and the authority of its new leader, Mrs. Gandhi, were challenged after 1966. Moreover, the struggle for power at the center this time was much more prolonged both within the party and in the relations between Congress and opposition parties.

The major turning-points in this prolonged struggle for power that have been widely commented upon were the 1967 elections, in which the Congress lost power in half the Indian states and had to depend on support from other parties to retain a comfortable majority in Parliament as well, and the 1969 split in the Congress occasioned by the presidential election of that year. In 1971–72 after the massive electoral victories of the Congress under Mrs. Gandhi's leadership at the center and in the states, it appeared that the struggle had ended decisively once again in favor of the Congress as the dominant party and Mrs. Gandhi as its unchallenged leader. However, in the process of consolidating her power, Mrs. Gandhi took several actions that led to important transformations in the character of center–state relations. These included a decisive intervention in UP politics in September 1970, the delinking of parliamentary from legislative assembly elections in 1971, and the establishment of a new pattern of selection of chief ministers for most of the Congress-ruled states by Mrs. Gandhi herself in consultation with or relying on the advice of her personal advisers in New Delhi.

When the Congress lost power in half the Indian states after the 1967 elections, including in Punjab, it became increasingly evident that the Congress as a party and Mrs. Gandhi as its unchallenged leader could not retain their dominance unless stability, Congress dominance, and the dominance of persons loyal to Mrs. Gandhi were established in most of the Indian states. A decisive moment that, I believe, began a major transformation in the character of center–state relations occurred in September 1970 when the BKD of Chaudhuri Charan Singh failed to deliver the three votes that Mrs. Gandhi needed, and expected, to pass the Twentyfourth Constitutional Amendment Bill in the Rajya Sabha, abolishing the privy purses of the princes. In retaliation, the Congress, which had been in a coalition government with the BKD under Charan Singh in UP, withdrew from the UP government and brought it down. The significance of this moment is that, for the first time in the history of postindependence India, the fate of the central government and that of a state government became interlinked. The Congress could not remain in power at the center, let alone pass desired legislation, without controlling UP. But the lesson that the Congress leadership learned from this experience extended far beyond relations between Delhi and Lucknow, encompassing the whole pattern of center–state relations in India.

It was not that Mrs. Gandhi learned for the first time what her father surely knew very well, namely, that one must control the states if one is to control Delhi. It was, rather, that the old boundaries between central and state politics had been decisively broken and that state politics no longer mattered in their own right. The old pattern of the center intervening as an impartial arbiter to resolve conflicts in a state political arena that was largely autonomous was replaced by one in which the center became a partial intervenor in state political arenas to select chief ministers whose principal qualification would be their personal loyalty to Mrs. Gandhi. The process, which was later applied by the Janata government as well, did not, however, free the center from dependence on the states. Instead, it became increasingly dependent for its own stability on controlling the states and state chief ministers in turn became increasingly dependent on the favor of the center. Center–state politics became increasingly interlinked and interdependent and the autonomy of state politics disappeared.[3]

Moreover, the whole process of aggregating power in India was reversed. During the 1950s and 1960s, no one seriously thought of replacing Pandit Nehru as Prime Minister and Congress rule in Delhi seemed unshakeable. Ambitious politicians who wanted substantial power and control of government resources had to build their influence from the districts to the state level. District and state politics were largely autonomous, but the center intervened whenever it felt it necessary to do so to ensure that the ability of the Congress to control a state and win elections was not threatened.

From the mid-1960s onwards, however, most roads to extra-local and even to much local power and resources had to pass through Delhi. Ambitious politicians in both the districts and the states had to please the party leadership at the center to gain power and resources in the states. The center, for its part, had to be perpetually watchful to ensure that reliable persons were in power in the state capitals and even in the districts and that useful and reliable MPs were elected to Parliament.

In order to maintain power at the center, Mrs. Gandhi and the Congress felt obliged to centralize power, nationalize issues, and intervene increasingly in state and even district politics. Centralization of power occurred in the nomination process for selecting party candidates to contest elections, in the direct selection of chief ministers by the Prime Minister and her advisers, in the direct distribution of patronage from the central government to district politicians, bypassing the state government, and in the ruthless application of President's Rule at the whim of the central government. Nationalization of issues was facilitated by the delinking of parliamentary from legislative assembly elections, by the increasing use of slogans and symbols to appeal to broad categories of voters such as the poor and the minorities, by the dramatization and distortion of local issues involving violence, and by other means that placed a high premium on demagogic skills. However, intervention in state politics became increasingly necessary despite these tendencies because they both undercut the very bases of stable politics in the states, namely, autonomous leadership and strong local party organization. Finally, because of the very absence of autonomous state leadership and strong local party organizations, the interventions of the center increasingly became misguided, misinformed, and even desperate.

The Congress also faced a new challenge in the 1970s that it had not faced before, namely, the use of agitational tactics by opposition leaders to bring down Congress-dominated state governments and to threaten the central government as well. Two major agitations in 1974 led to the fall of a state government in Gujarat and the near-collapse of the Bihar government in the same year.[4] The following year, in June 1975, when a successful election petition threatened Mrs. Gandhi with the loss of her seat in Parliament and hence the prime ministership as well, she clearly also feared that a mass, nation-wide opposition agitation was in the offing that would make it impossible for her to survive politically. The Emergency regime from 1975 to 1977 was imposed in order to prevent that eventuality.

The Emergency, the massive defeat of the Congress after its withdrawal and the holding of parliamentary elections in January 1977, and the harassment of Mrs. Gandhi and her son, Sanjay, by the Janata regime between 1977 and 1980 added two further dimensions to the new context of center–state relations. One was the realization that, to maintain power at the center, one could not ignore state politics and one could certainly not permit state politicians to act autonomously even when massive and apparently secure majorities seemed to offer a respite in the perpetual struggle to retain power at the center. Second, the events between 1973 and 1980 brought a new ruthlessness into interparty and interpersonal leadership rivalries in Indian politics from the center down to the local level. When Mrs. Gandhi returned to power, opposition politicians had to be alert to the possibility that an attempt might be made to impose a new Emergency regime. Mrs. Gandhi in turn clearly harbored deep personal resentments over the treatment meted out to her and her son by opposition politicians between 1977 and 1980. At the state and local level also, especially in the north, politics was becoming increasingly ruthless and violent, the police were becoming more and more corrupt, criminalized, and lawless, and hooligans and ruffians were inducted into the Congress by Sanjay Gandhi personally.[5] Not only in Punjab, therefore, but everywhere in north India, most important politicians travelled with guns or bodyguards or both.

Punjab is not a critical state from the point of view of parliamentary seats in the new context of center–state relations. It has a critical importance in other respects, however. First of all, events in Punjab are linked to events in Haryana, which was formerly a part of the old Punjab province, and are thereby connected to events in the rest of north India. The course of Hindu–Sikh relations in Punjab, for example, may affect the attitudes and voting behavior of Hindus in north India and, thereby, the ultimate fate of the contest for power in Delhi. Second, agitational politics are endemic in Punjab, used by the leading non-Congress party there, the Akali Dal, to mobilize support when it is out of power. It is especially significant to note in this context that the *only* sustained agitational movement against the Emergency regime was carried out by the Akali Dal during those years. Third, as the home of a minority religious group in a border state, Punjab has always been of special concern to the government in Delhi. In the past, those concerns centered around the dangers of Pakistani involvement in and exploitation of potential secessionist feelings in Punjab, especially in the event of war. More recently, however, as demands for regional autonomy have been made by non-Congress parties in other peripheral, border, and non-Hindi-speaking states, such as West Bengal, Tamil Nadu, Andhra, Kashmir, and Assam, the center has felt obliged, since the Anandpur Sahib Resolution of 1973 demanding regional autonomy for Punjab, to be sensitive to the implications of such a demand for the whole pattern of center–state relations in the Indian union.

CENTER–STATE RELATIONS AND SEPARATIST POLITICS IN PUNJAB IN THE 1960s

The course of Sikh politics in Punjab and the relations among the

Akali Dal, the state Congress, and the central Congress leadership in the years between 1960–61 and 1966 illustrate clearly the application of the four rules as well as the general character of center–state relations during the period of Nehru's dominance in the Indian political system. In 1960–61, a major turning-point occurred in the history of Sikh politics and in the movement to gain control of a territory in which the Sikhs would be the dominant people and the Akali Dal the dominant party. Two of the leading figures in the Sikh movement, Master Tara Singh and Sant Fateh Singh, alternately attempted to coerce the Government of India to concede the Akali demands by going on fasts-unto-death, on the one hand, and to settle the dispute through negotiations with Pandit Nehru, on the other hand. The two leaders, though sharing the same objective of creating a Sikh-majority state in the Punjab, presented the demands somewhat differently. Sant Fateh Singh insisted that the Sikh political demand for a Punjabi Suba was not a religious communal one for a Sikh majority state, but simply a linguistic demand, no different from others conceded to numerous linguistic groups in India, for the creation of a Punjabi-speaking province within the Indian Union. Master Tara Singh, however, had always been associated with the idea that the Sikhs were entitled to determine their own future in 1947, but had been deprived of it by the Congress. He also never hesitated to declare that the Punjabi Suba he envisioned was to be a Sikh-majority province.

The Congress leadership, with Nehru at the center and Pratap Singh Kairon in Chandigarh acting in a united and coordinated way, refused to make any concessions to Master Tara Singh, whom they considered a communalist and potential secessionist politician. Moreover, according to an account by Pettigrew,[6] the Congress leaders went further and set out by outright bribery, use of liaison persons, and duplicity to divide the Akali Dal, discredit Master Tara Singh and replace him with Sant Fateh Singh. It chose to discredit and displace the more extremist, communalist, potentially secessionist leader and replace him with a no-less militant, but non-communalist, non-secessionist leader. Ultimately, when both Nehru and Kairon had passed from the scene and Sant Fateh Singh was firmly in place as leader of Akali Dal, the Congress under Lal Bahadur Shastri and then finally under Mrs. Gandhi moved to settle the dispute by agreeing in 1966 to create a Punjabi Suba defined as a Punjabi-speaking state. By its handling of the agitations and negotiations, however, the Government of India had made it clear that it would not consider demands made on the basis of religious communal identity by leaders whom it believed had secessionist inclinations.[7]

Several aspects of center–state relations in this period also should be noted here. First, the center was reluctant to take an action that could be seen as favoring one side over another in a regional conflict. The center was unwilling to divide the old Punjab province as long as both the Punjabi-speaking Hindus and the Hindi-speaking Hindus in Haryana were opposed. Only when the Haryana Hindu politicians agreed to accept the reorganization of the state and the creation of a Punjabi Suba was the Akali demand conceded. Second, the central and state Congress leadership took united and concerted action throughout every phase of the crises and negotiations. Third, the principal stage throughout the Punjabi Suba crisis was the state capital of Chandigarh and the principal actor was Pratap Singh Kairon. Nehru and the central Congress leaders played supporting, not directing roles. All the hatreds of the discontented politicians in both the Congress and the Akali Dal were directed against Kairon while the central leadership adopted a pose of benevolent willingness to facilitate compromise solutions.

THE CONTEXT OF PARTY POLITICS IN PUNJAB

Interparty Relations

Since independence, and most especialy since the creation of the Punjabi Suba, a persistent dualism has characterized party politics and interparty relations in Punjab in which the Congress and the Akali Dal have been the principal contenders for power.[8] That dualism, however, has been qualified in several important respects. It has been, first of all, unbalanced because the Congress has been generally the far stronger of the two parties. Second, the imbalance between the two main forces has required the weaker opponent, the Akali Dal, to seek interparty alliances in order to defeat the Congress and win power in the province. The Akalis' principal alliance partner since 1967 has been the Jan Sangh/Bharatiya Janata Party (BJP). Third, because the alliance with the Jan

Sangh/BJP makes the Akali Dal a genuine threat to the Congress' ability to win and maintain power in Punjab, the Congress has always included in its political tactics to defeat the Akali Dal efforts to divide it. The Congress has thus promoted defections and splits within Akali ranks in order to weaken its prospects for gaining an electoral victory or to bring down an Akali-led government on those occasions when the Akali Dal has defeated the Congress in legislative assembly elections.

Between 1967 and 1972, two Akali–Jan Sangh coalition governments were formed and both were brought down by factional quarrels within the Akali Dal. The fall of the first coalition was engineered directly by the Congress. In the case of the second, the Congress threw its support, ineffectually as it turned out, to the Gurnam Singh group that was toppled by the dominant group in the Akali Dal. Thus, the dualism between the Congress and the Akali Dal is qualified both by the necessity for interparty alliances with a third party (and with other parties as well) and by interparty communication and penetration across the divide between the two main contenders. Not only has the Congress penetrated the Akali Dal by dividing it and giving support to dissident factions within it, but often it has also recruited its own leaders from Akali ranks, including such prominent persons as Pratap Singh Kairon, Swaran Singh, Giani Zail Singh, and many others. In the past, the Akali Dal has also twice entered the Congress in a body, between 1947 and 1951, and again in 1957. Each time, the Akali Dal lost some of its members to the Congress when its leadership decided to withdraw and revert to an opposition role. In the period of unstable coalition politics between 1967 and 1971, there was a two-way flow of defections from the Akali Dal to the Congress and vice-versa.

It should be obvious from this description of the basic features of interparty competition and collaboration in Punjab that, until recently, party divisions did not reflect or promote a polarization between Hindus and Sikhs. Although Sikhs are a majority in the state and the Akali Dal is overwhelmingly a Sikh party, the Akali Dal is also a minority party. The Congress, as a majority party, has drawn support from both Hindus and Sikhs. The Akali Dal, in order to match the Congress, has had to seek political alliances with the Hindu-based Jan Sangh/BJP. Party politics, therefore, have normally tended to moderate Hindu–Sikh political polarization and to work against the entrenchment of communal divisions.

Two factors noted above, however, were at work in the 1970s and 1980s to alter this basic pattern. One was the increased interdependence after 1971 of central and state politics and the necessity for the Congress to control most of the states in the Indian Union, particularly the north Indian states, to maintain itself in power at the center. The second was the increased ruthlessness of interparty conflict in the country after the Emergency, manifested most strikingly in the induction into the Congress by Sanjay Gandhi of young men who did not follow the conventional rules of political behavior and of outright *goondas* (toughs), hooligans, and criminals.

In Punjab, these two factors merged in preparation for and after the 1980 elections. The 1977 parliamentary and legislative assembly elections in Punjab had made the Akali Dal appear a much more formidable rival than ever before. Previously, the Akali Dal had only once, in 1969, won more seats in the legislature than the Congress, and then only because of its alliance with the Jan Sangh and other parties, which made possible its better showing than the Congress despite a much smaller popular vote percentage. In the 1977 parliamentary elections, however, the Akali Dal polled a higher vote percentage than the Congress and won all nine Lok Sabha seats. In the legislative assembly elections that followed, the Akali Dal polled a slightly smaller vote share than the Congress but won, in alliance with Janata and the Communist Party (Marxist) (CPM), fiftyeight seats compared to only seventeen for the Congress. The previous electoral dominance of the Congress in Punjab, therefore, seemed less secure. Moreover, the former tactics used by the Congress when in opposition of engineering defections from the Akali Dal to bring down the government could not be effectual when the Congress was reduced to such a minority status in the legislature.

The strengthened position of the Akali Dal and the much weakened position of the Congress required, therefore, a different set of political tactics from before, namely, an attack on the support base of the Akali Dal in its core support areas and among its core support groups: the rural Jat Sikh peasantry under the political influence of the Akali Dal and under the religious influence of the Sants and preachers in the gurudwaras and missionary organizations in the Sikh-majority districts of the province. Sant Jarnail Singh Bhindranwale was used for that purpose and was supported by the Congress, most particularly by Sanjay Gandhi and Giani

Zail Singh from 1977 onwards, after the massive defeat of the Congress.[9] The involvement of Sanjay Gandhi in the recruitment of Bhindranwale also meant that criminal actions, manipulation of the police and the judiciary, and the use of violence were considered acceptable tactics by Congressmen, by the police, and by its allies to defeat and discredit the Akali Dal.

Bhindranwale did not prove to be especially effective in weakening the Akali Dal by conventional political means. Although his men contested against the Akali Dal candidates in the 1979 elections to the Shiromani Gurudwara Prabandhak Committee (SGPC), the body which manages all the Sikh shrines in Punjab and provides the main resources for the Akali Dal itself, they won only four seats. Nor did his support for a few Congress candidates have a significant effect in Punjab during the 1980 general elections.

However, Bhindranwale's violent confrontation methods did prove useful to the Congress at first. The Akali Dal leaders in the Akali–Janata government were divided and embarrassed by a violent clash between militant Sikhs and the heterodox Nirankari sect in April 1978, in which Bhindranwale played a prominent role. The Tohra–Talwandi faction in the Akali Dal used the Sikh–Nirankari clash against the dominant Badal–Longowal faction, which it accused of not acting firmly enough against the Nirankaris. The factional divisions within the Akali Dal in turn contributed to its defeat and the victory of the Congress in the 1980 elections.

When the Darbara Singh government came to power in Punjab in 1980, the time was ripe to put an end to Bhindranwale's activities, which, if they were not themselves murderous, included praise for those who killed Nirankaris.[10] Bhindranwale, however, was too useful in factional conflicts *both* in the Akali Dal and the Congress to be dealt with easily, though he had by no means yet become the pivotal figure in Punjab politics. Giani Zail Singh continued to find Bhindranwale a useful ally, now for two purposes: to use as a foil against his factional rival in the Congress, Darbara Singh, and simultaneously to keep the Akali Dal on the defensive. So, when Darbara Singh tried to arrest Bhindranwale for the murder of Lala Jagat Narain in 1981, Giani Zail Singh protected him.[11] From the viewpoint of Gurcharan Singh Tohra, the president of the SGPC and leader of one faction in the Akali Dal, Bhindranwale was useful as an ally in his struggles with the

Longowal–Badal faction. Consequently, Tohra permitted Bhindranwale to move into the Golden Temple complex with his men and arms. From September 1981 on, therefore, after his arrest and release in connection with the murder of Lala Jagat Narain, Bhindranwale alternated between the sanctuary of the Golden Temple and, when he wished to roam about, the protection of the Home Minister, which kept him safe until terrorists began murdering innocent Hindus in the Punjab. After a particularly vicious set of murders of innocent Hindus during September–October 1983, Mrs. Gandhi finally imposed President's Rule in Punjab and sent one of her most trusted police officers to Punjab to take firm action against all suspected terrorists, including Bhindranwale, who now took sanctuary in the Akal Takht within the Golden Temple complex itself.[12]

For its part, the Akali Dal, ousted from power by the Congress and placed on the defensive by Bhindranwale and other leaders and groups suspected of terrorist activities, who were placing themselves in the forefront as defenders of Sikh interests against the Congress, the central government, and the Hindu community, opted for the adoption of aggressive but non-violent confrontational tactics in pursuit of Sikh and Punjabi regional interests. It was in this context that the Anandpur Sahib Resolution of 1973 was reactivated and placed in the forefront of Akali demands. For, if the Akali Dal could achieve significant political concessions through a direct, but non-violent challenge to the Congress, it would strengthen its position in relation to non-Akali Sikh militants in Punjab. And, if center–state relations were readjusted in such a way as to reduce significantly the ability of the center to intervene in state politics, then the Akali Dal and other similarly placed regional parties in India would be strengthened and the regional Congress parties weakened.

Akali Factions during the 1960s and 1980s

Superficially, there would seem to be no substantial differences in the internal dynamics of Akali politics in the 1960s and 1980s. Rather, there would appear to be an uninterrupted tradition of internal factional conflict stretching back .o the 1920s, to the earliest days of the Akali Dal, up to the present. Before the 1960s, there were always at least two groups in the Akali Dal, who struggled for control both over the party organization itself and over the SGPC, which provided the bulk of the resources for the former. It was always the case, moreover, that no group could retain dominant leadership of the Akali Dal without also controlling the SGPC. Consequently, there was a compulsion to exert dual control of these two bodies by a single leadership, which was certainly the case in Master Tara Singh's heyday and then again under Sant Fateh Singh, when the latter wrested control of both bodies from the Master.

In the 1960s or, rather, from 1967, when the Akali Dal became a governing party in Punjab, a third source of factional power within the Akali Dal became available, namely, control over the chief ministership and the government of the state. Such control clearly offered enormous patronage power to whichever faction became dominant in government, but it was also inherently unstable in contrast to the resources of the SGPC, which were always available to the group in control. Consequently, control over the SGPC has remained the key to dominance in the Akali Dal up to the present. Until Sant Fateh Singh's death in 1972, his dual control over the Akali Dal and the SGPC made it possible for his faction to remain dominant in relation to the ministerial groups in control of government and even to replace a recalcitrant chief minister such as Gurnam Singh in 1970.[13]

After the death of Sant Fateh Singh, no single leader was able to unify the Akali Dal or even to gain decisive dominance in both the party organization and the SGPC. Instead, a three-way split developed in which the leaders of each wing sought the support of the others for their own purposes. Tohra, as SGPC chief, sought the support of the other groups to retain both the presidentship of the SGPC and a seat in the Rajya Sabha. Jagdev Singh Talwandi, as president of the Akali Dal, sought the support of Tohra in his struggles with Prakash Singh Badal, who controlled the ministerial wing of the party. In 1980, the Badal group successfully supported Sant Harchand Singh Longowal for president of the Akali Dal. The two then formed an alliance with Tohra to isolate Talwandi, who left the Akali Dal (Sant) to form a rival Akali Dal.

By the early 1980s, therefore, it appeared once again that a single group now controlled the Akali Dal and the SGPC. In fact, however, there were two distinct differences in the Akali Dal between the situation in the 1980s and that in the 1960s. One was that there was in fact no dominant group in the Akali Dal, but three groups forming alliances of mutual convenience: the group of Tohra (SGPC), of Longowal (Akali Dal), and of Badal (ministerial). Second, the terms of the factional quarrel were fundamentally changed *within* the Akali Dal by Congress actions outside it and by the rise of Bhindranwale.

In the 1960s, there were three principal resources in Akali factional struggles: the SGPC, government patronage, and agitational leadership in struggles against the Congress. Sant Fateh Singh, as leader of the Akali Dal, established his dominance in the party organization through his agitational skills and his ability to lead the Sikh community in its struggles *against* the Congress on, first, the Punjabi Suba issue, then the status of the city of Chandigarh. He was careful to let no one usurp his symbolic role as principal defender of Sikh interests as he himself had usurped the role of Master Tara Singh. That position in turn gave him the support necessary to gain control of the resources of the SGPC. Dual control of the Akali Dal and SGPC then made it possible for him to control the ministerial wing of the party.

The rise of Bhindranwale and other extremist and terrorist groups and leaders[14] made it impossible in the 1980s for any single leader within the Akali Dal to repeat the feat of Sant Fateh Singh, though Longowal tried very hard to do so through the revival of the Anandpur Sahib Resolution and through his various *roko* (stop or block) movements and the *Dharamyudha Morcha* in the period between 1981 and 1984. The shift in Congress tactics also made the repetition of Sant Fateh Singh's feat impossible. The Congress in the 1960s had, after all, materially helped Sant Fateh Singh to establish his dominance first by supporting him against Master Tara Singh, then by conceding his principal demand for Punjabi Suba. In sharp contrast in the 1980s, the Congress refused to accede to the major political and economic demands of Longowal and thus contribute once again to the establishment of a moderate leadership group in firm control of the Akali Dal. Since the government also was not only unable to control Bhindranwale, but had helped to launch him, the Akali leaders were forced to compete with an extremist, non-Akali leader to maintain agitational and symbolic leadership of the Sikh community. In turn, factional groups inside the Akali Dal which, in the 1960s, might have defected to the Congress or otherwise sought Congress support in their internal struggles with each other, now sought to use Bhindranwale and his demands, slogans, and *goondas* against each other. In particular, Tohra found his Sant in Bhindranwale to counter the alliance of Badal with Sant Longowal. In effect, therefore, the Congress itself through its drive to weaken its principal opponent in Punjab politics and through its initial support for Bhindranwale and its refusal to control his activities, terminated the old pattern of alternation between interparty conflict and interparty, intercommunal penetration and forced the moderate Akali Dal leaders into a competition with the extremist Bhindranwale and into a consequently inevitably escalating confrontation with the central government.

In the 1960s, Pandit Nehru and the central government made it clear to the Akalis that they would not bow to any pressure for creation of a Sikh-majority state defined in relation to religion. They, therefore, compelled the Akalis to moderate their principal demands to one consistent with the structure of the Indian federal system, which encompassed linguistic but not religious states. In contrast, in the 1980s, the central government supported, or at least failed to control, the most extreme proponents of Sikh hegemony, Hindu–Sikh confrontation, and explicit or implicit supporters of Khalistan while refusing to accede to the moderate, legitimately presented demands of the Akali Dal in pursuit of regionally defined interests and a reconsideration of the structure of center–state relations. Consequently, the Akali Dal's demands in its various agitations had to be framed with one eye on Bhindranwale. In particular terms, this meant that the Akali Dal had now and then to add to its long-established list of regional, political, and economic demands other demands of a specifically religious nature and demands to free Bhindranwale when he was arrested (since he was certain anyway to be freed by a government clearly not serious about restraining him). It was also compelled to use language that emphasized the nationhood and sovereignty of the Sikh people in presenting its demands, which the central government in turn used to argue that the Akalis too were supporters of Khalistan. It will be shown below, moreover, that when the Government of India did make concessions, again in utter contrast to its position in the 1960s, it conceded the religious demands of the Akalis and not its political and economic demands.

Congress and Congress Factions during the 1960s and 1980s

There were several critical differences in the character, functioning, leadership, and recruitment strategies of the Congress during the 1960s and 1980s as well that help to explain the containment of communal demands and conflicts in the earlier period and the fact that they went completely out of control in the 1980s. First, in the 1960s, as already noted, the Congress was dominated by a single leader and a single faction, with the solid backing of the central government. The situation that prevailed in the Punjab Congress and in relations between the state and national leadership of the Congress in those days conformed to the ideal pattern that Nehru favored: strong state leadership pursuing the secular, economic goals of planned development in close cooperation with the central government. A similar pattern existed in state politics and center–state relations in Bengal under B.C. Roy, for example, and in several other states from time to time.

Nehru hated and fought against factionalization in state politics and politicians who were not committed to his goals of economic development planning. He preferred 'bossism' in state politics for the sake of stability and electoral predominance and leaders who spoke the language of secularism and economic development. He detested politicians who did not at least pay lip service to socialism, planning, and industrialization as the methods and goals of Indian policy and who spoke instead a language of Hindu or minority communalism, casteism, linguism, and provincialism. Although Kairon was himself a former Akali politician, he conformed to Nehru's image of the ideal state boss politician when he established his dominance in the Punjab Congress. Under his leadership, minority communalism was controlled, the economic basis was laid in agriculture for the Green Revolution that began after his death and for the boom in small-scale industry in Ludhiana and Jullundur that provided off-farm employment for those displaced from the land.

After Kairon's and Nehru's deaths, Punjabi Suba was conceded, the Congress was factionalized, and the party was faced with much stronger opposition from its main rival, the Akali Dal, in the smaller Punjab state. After 1971, when Mrs. Gandhi reconsolidated Congress power in the country and, perforce, in Punjab as well, she did so on an entirely new basis and with the support of a different type of leadership and Congress organization in the states of the Union. She preferred sycophants to bosses and a factionalized Congress led by persons selected by her or her clique of advisers in Delhi. Like Nehru, she too preferred leaders who spoke the language of socialism, development planning, and industrialization. However, since the persons she selected were generally unable to or were not permitted to establish dominant groups of their own in state politics, they could not be effective and could not guarantee stability and electoral dominance. The lack was made up by the personal appeal of Mrs. Gandhi herself to large categories of voters, by the liberal use of money to buy and control politicians and, particularly after the Emergency, by the 'lumpenization'[15] and criminalization of the Congress organization at the local level.

From among the various Congress faction leaders who were contesting for dominance in the Punjab Congress after the death of Pratap Singh Kairon, Mrs. Gandhi selected Giani Zail Singh to be chief minister after the Congress achieved its huge electoral victories in Punjab, as elsewhere in the country, in 1971 and 1972. Although Zail Singh was a major contender in the factional politics of the Punjab Congress in those days and not a mere puppet of the center, it is generally acknowledged that his 'rapport' established with Mrs. Gandhi,[16] which his detractors have characterized as outright sycophancy, was the decisive factor in his selection as chief minister.

Zail Singh's tenure as chief minister is notable for the following features. Although the 'Green Revolution' continued its progress and the government provided support for tubewells, rural electrification, and rural link roads to facilitate transport of the agricultural surplus to markets, the ministry also emphasized, in conformity with Mrs. Gandhi's policies, programs in support of the scheduled castes and backward classes. Some of these programs, such as lowering land ceilings, antagonized the more prosperous rural Jat Sikh farmers. Although Zail Singh attempted to compete with the Akali Dal by appealing to the religious sentiments of rural Sikhs through such gestures as leading the great march in celebration of the completion of Guru Gobind Singh Marg, linking all the important religious sites of Punjab, and other similar acts, the ministry as a whole was identified more with the interests of Harijans, Mazhabi (lower caste) Sikhs, and the poor and smaller farmers than with the middle and upper segments of the Jat Sikh peasantry. Zail Singh himself was, aside from Giani Gurmukh Singh Musafir who had a brief tenure as chief minister in 1966–67, the first non-Jat Sikh chief minister in Punjab. He had no base among rural Jat Sikhs and was engaged in continuous factional rivalry with his own Jat Sikh ministers during his tenure as chief minister.[17] The 20-point program implemented during the Emergency also was aimed more at the poor, the landless, and the marginal farmers than at the middle Jat Sikh peasantry, who were effectively mobilized by the Akali Dal in a *morcha* that was sustained successfully throughout most of the Emergency period.

The most notable feature of the Zail Singh period, however, from the point of view of Punjab politics is what was not done. No efforts whatsoever were made to undercut the Akali Dal by resolving in a way acceptable to Punjab regional interests the major outstanding issues left unresolved at the creation of the Punjabi Suba in 1966, namely, the disposition of the city of Chandigarh, of the Hindu Punjabi-speaking tahsils of Abohar and Fazilka, and of the distribution of Ravi–Beas river waters.

During Mrs. Gandhi's darkest hours in the Janata period from 1977 to 1980, both Giani Zail Singh and Sardar Darbara Singh, his chief rival for power in Punjab Congress politics, each in his own way demonstrated steadfast loyalty to Mrs. Gandhi. Both remained with her when the Congress split in Punjab, as elsewhere in the country, in 1978. Both were relatively evenly balanced in their support among Punjab Congress legislators elected in the Congress victory of 1980. Consequently, Mrs. Gandhi, who rewarded those who had remained personally loyal to her during the Janata period, rewarded both men: Giani Zail Singh was made home minister in the Government of India and Darbara Singh the chief minister of Punjab.

Zail Singh, however, could not countenance the selection of Darbara Singh as Punjab chief minister, for he would certainly use his position to eliminate Zail Singh's supporters from power in the Punjab. Consequently, Giani Zail Singh used his personal influence with Mrs. Gandhi and his powers as home minister to undercut Darbara Singh throughout his tenure as chief minister. In this conflict with Darbara Singh, Bhindranwale again proved useful. He and other extremist elements had been found useful for embarrassing the Akali Dal–Janata government during the Sikh–Nirankari confrontations. He could now be used for the dual purpose of continuing to undermine the Akali Dal and to demonstrate the inability of Darbara Singh to govern Punjab effectively. For her part, Mrs. Gandhi, in sharp contrast to the relationship established by her father with Pratap Singh Kairon, allowed Zail Singh to continue to meddle in Punjab politics, consulted him for advice in handling the disintegrating political situation in Punjab, and failed to provide full backing to Darbara Singh's efforts to root out the terrorists by arresting Bhindranwale and other extremist leaders and clearing them out of the Golden Temple complex before they had taken sanctuary in the Akal Takht itself and had fortified the entire complex.[18]

The difference between Mrs. Gandhi's handling of the Punjab situation in the Congress in the 1980s and her father's in the 1960s is of a piece with the change in center–state relations in this period that Mrs. Gandhi herself brought about. Nehru often brought powerful and influential politicians, including ex-chief ministers, into his central cabinet from the states. He did not usually do so, however, as a device for solving factional conflicts in a state. Moreover, once at the center, such persons were expected either to use their provincial influence over their followers to maintain stability in their home states or they were expected to remain aloof from state-level conflicts so that they could be used as impartial arbiters to resolve crisis situations among contending state-level groups. The idea that a central minister would be used or even allowed to function in a manner that would undermine the stability of a province was entirely foreign to Nehru's method except on the rare occasions when Nehru himself deliberately set out to remove a chief minister whose policies or methods he disliked. Mrs. Gandhi, however, preferred weak chief ministers dependent on her, direct control from Delhi, and provincial instability, which she found useful in maintaining central control and ensuring the loyalty of all groups, whose leaders might be made or broken at her whim. Mrs. Gandhi's methods proved entirely unsuited to the escalating situation in Punjab which required decisive action and united leadership in Delhi and Chandigarh.

BHINDRANWALE AND THE SIKH COMMUNITY

Sant Jarnail Singh Bhindranwale emerged as the central figure in

discussions and analysis of the violent confrontations and terrorist
actions that occurred with increasing frequency in the period from
1981 until his death during the Indian army's storming of the
Golden Temple in June 1984. Bhindranwale's actual role in the
increasing violence of those days, his own purposes, and the extent
and sources of his support in the Sikh community remain highly
controversial matters. Many observers consider that Bhindranwale
was the actual source of the worst terrorist actions in the 1981–84
period and some also feel that he was in favor of Khalistan secretly
if not openly. Among such persons, Bhindranwale's vocation as a
preacher is either not considered relevant to the political issues or
is treated as a separate and secondary matter. For such persons,
Bhindranwale is considered to be merely one among many itinerant
preachers of Punjab, who happened to be picked up by prominent
Congress leaders of Punjab and brought into politics in order to
divide the Akali Dal and, thereby, ensure the persistence of
Congress rule in and political control over the state. Once brought
into politics, however, and built up in this way, he developed his
own line, his own methods, and increasing support that, according
to this view, made him an independent political force feared by all
politicians in Punjab, who ultimately reached such a pass that they
were willing to take no action that Bhindranwale might oppose
and became incapable of participating effectively in a political
process gone completely out of control and dominated by violence.[19]

An alternative view emphasizes Bhindranwale's role and background as a preacher, treats his political activities as incidental
thereto, and blames the violence primarily on other groups in the
Punjab, including extremist political groups, religious sects, and
the police.[20] In one account, Bhindranwale was an authentic saint,
with a 'charismatic appeal,' who was giving 'religious expression'
to 'broadbased rural discontent and anger' over the recent history
of alleged discrimination against Sikhs in the Punjab, including
police harassment and violence, in response to the Akali political
movements. To volunteers who came to see Bhindranwale before
courting arrest in Akali political campaigns, 'he gave a purely
religious message'.[21] In another view, his primary political role was
as a 'scapegoat'[22] used by the Congress government to displace all
the blame for its own disastrous policies in Punjab that were the
true source of its recent disorders.

The bulk of scholarly and journalistic writing on Bhindranwale favors the first view, though there are some elements of truth in the second. What is most important, however, is to assess his significance in relation to the perceptions of the Sikhs of themselves as a community and Bhindranwale's place in the Sikh sense of communal identity. It is known that Bhindranwale was, in fact, an itinerant preacher who, in 1977, at the age of 30, was chosen to become the head of a Sikh mission known as the Dam Dami Taksal. He was chosen in preference to the son of the previous head, Amrik Singh,[23] who nevertheless remained close to him in his religious and then in his political activities until they were both killed inside the Golden Temple. He is best described in origins as a Sikh preacher, who saw his mission in part as spreading Sikhism to non-Sikhs, to Sikh–Hindu groups such as Sahajdharis and Nirankaris, and to the untouchables in Punjab, whose uncertain religious identity as Sikhs or Hindus and political identity as Congress or Akali supporters has for decades been a major source of religious and political controversy in the Punjab.

Bhindranwale was also a 'revivalist,' that is, a 'religious puritan' who followed strictly and literally what he perceived to be the basic tenets of the Sikh faith transmitted by the Gurus, enshrined in the Guru Granth Sahib, and embedded in the rituals and outward markers of the Keshadhari Sikhs. Sikh students and 'rural Sikh youth' were the special targets of the mission of Bhindranwale and his closest companion, Amrik Singh, who became head of the All India Sikh Students Federation (AISSF). In their mission to the Sikh youth of Punjab, their design was certainly to get the young men of Punjab to take Amrit, to wear the outward signs and carry the markers of Keshadhari Sikhs, and to avoid the corrupting secular and Marxist ideologies to which they were otherwise susceptible in Punjab, where the Left was traditionally dominant among students.[24]

In these respects, Bhindranwale was hardly a new phenomenon in Punjab, which has been the scene of countless local and regional revivalist movements among Hindus, Sikhs, and Muslims during the past century. If there is anything new in this, it is not the doctrine or the message, but the use of contemporary methods of transmission, notably the distribution of taped messages, to the faithful, a practice lately used widely round the world from Rajneeshpuram to Iran. Such a movement among the Sikhs in the

Punjab inevitably has political implications, for one of its principal goals is to create solidarity and uniformity among practising Sikhs, to turn non-Keshadhari Sikhs, low caste Sikhs, and students attracted by secular ideologies into practising Sikhs, and to wean both these categories of practising and non-Keshadhari Sikhs from competing practices and ideologies, religious and political, which might dilute their identity as Keshadhari Sikhs or prevent them from embracing it fully.

Soon after his assumption of the headship, Bhindranwale's 'mission' brought him and his followers into a violent confrontation at Amritsar on 13 April 1978, with the Sant Nirankaris, a sect considered heretical by Keshadharis.[25] At the confrontation in Amritsar, thirteen people were killed from Bhindranwale's group and from another militant missionary group known as the Akhand Kirtani Jatha. From this point on, a bloody vendetta was launched among the followers of these three groups, during which the Nirankaris were paid back for the debacle of 13 April by the killing of forty of their leading persons, including their head, Gurbachan Singh. Although it appears that the principal anti-Nirankari terrorist group was an organization called the 'Babbar Khalsa,' led by the widow of Fauja Singh who, as head of the Akhand Kirtani Jatha, was killed in the 13 April massacre, Bhindranwale and his followers were widely blamed for the killings, possibly because he more openly expressed his satisfaction at the results than because he was responsible for them. In any case, from 13 April onward, Punjab became the scene of warfare among heavily armed terrorist groups bent on exterminating each other for the glory and purity of the Sikh faith. At first, it should be stressed, this conflict was confined to Sikhs, it was primarily Sikhs who were killed, and the issues concerned the solidarity of the Sikh community and the purity of the faith of those who claimed to be Sikhs.[26]

Congress Support for Bhindranwale

Congress leaders initially saw this sectarian conflict among Sikhs, which arose independently of party political calculations, as an opportunity to divide the Akali Dal and to weaken its control over the SGPC, a tactic which Congress leaders have followed repeatedly without success for decades. The Congress also intervened in the

Delhi Gurudwara Prabandhak Committee (DGPC), where the
Akali Dal has never had the same control as in the SGPC, in
support of its opponents. Congress leaders and the state administration and judicial system began to act in ways that implied
support for Bhindranwale. Bhindranwale and his followers were
released from prison and cleared of charges for the murders of the
Nirankaris in April 1978. Congress (I) leaders, including Giani
Zail Singh's and Sanjay Gandhi's emissaries, supported Bhindranwale and his followers in the 1979 elections to the SGPC in
which, however, they won only four seats out of 106. The Congress
also aided in the formation of the Dal Khalsa. Bhindranwale and
his men allegedly reciprocated by supporting the Congress in the
1980 Punjab general elections.[27]

Congress efforts to divide the Akali Dal and to draw rural Sikh
support away from it continued after the party's return to power in
Punjab and intensified when the Akali Dal resorted to agitational
tactics to achieve longstanding Akali demands pertaining to
Chandigarh, disputed territories between Punjab and Haryana,
division of river waters, and other demands contained in the
Anandpur Sahib Resolution of 1973. Moreover, throughout the
increasingly bitter and violent confrontations between the government and the Akali Dal, and among the extremist and terrorist
groups, and despite their spillover into the broader population,
leading to deaths of innocent people and Hindu–Sikh clashes in
the towns of Punjab and Haryana, the government was unable or
unwilling to reach a political accommodation with the moderate
Akalis on the outstanding issues. It will be argued below that the
failure of the government to reach such an accommodation was
partly because the Congress priority given to political control,
including division of the opposition to achieve it, remained till the
end of Mrs. Gandhi's life the guiding principle of the party's
political strategy to which the goal of a final settlement of the
issues in dispute in the Punjab remained secondary. The extent to
which this strategy remained primary was indicated by the remarks
of Rajiv Gandhi only weeks before Bhindranwale and his men
were killed by the Indian army in which he referred to Bhindranwale
as 'a religious leader' and declared his belief that the latter was not
responsible for the terrorism and 'extremist politics' prevailing in
Punjab.[28]

It is possible that the involvement of the Congress and the

government in Bhindranwale's rise has been exaggerated in the above account. In fact, it seems to me that Bhindranwale's goals and those of the Congress were ultimately incompatible, though they may have coincided temporarily. As already indicated above, Bhindranwale was operating within the hallowed Sikh ideal of Panthic unity, identity, and solidarity against all elements who would divide the Sikhs in their religious practices or in their political goals. The Congress was playing the opposite game, using whatever political divisions among the Sikhs it could to gain and maintain advantage over its main political rival, the Akali Dal.[29] Since their goals were fundamentally incompatible, it was inevitable that they would ultimately clash directly.

It was, however, only when Sikh terrorists began to kill Hindus, and when Hindu–Sikh communal clashes began to occur that the Congress political strategy began to change. The Congress had lost any influence it might have had over Bhindranwale and other extremist Sikh groups, the Akali Dal remained committed to an agitational strategy until the Congress conceded its demands, and the Congress hold over the Punjab Hindus now appeared threatened by the government's inability to protect innocent Hindu bystanders from random massacres. Most important, the government's inability to control the situation in Punjab, following its mishandling of the Assam situation in 1983, gave the opposition a stick that it thought might be powerful enough to bring down the Congress in the imminent parliamentary elections.

The Congress, therefore, began to use the government machinery to attempt to crack down on the terrorist groups. The AISSF was banned in March 1984.[30] However, the police were by now hopelessly divided themselves along communal lines and also feared direct confrontations with the extremist and terrorist groups. It is otherwise difficult to explain the fact that 150 companies of constabulary forces posted around the Punjab, including ninety around the Golden Temple itself, 'failed to check the massive induction of arms into the Golden Temple or the apparently free movement of people suspected to be terrorists.'[31] A serious crackdown would also have meant entering the gurudwaras, which were being captured by the AISSF on behalf of Bhindranwale and used as storehouses for arms and sanctuaries for terrorists. Government action in such circumstances, therefore, did nothing but increase the general level of terrorist violence and implicate the police

more deeply in it themselves. False encounters, used so effectively
to destroy the Naxalites in West Bengal in the 1970s and somewhat
less effectively against dacoits and others in UP in the 1980s, were
now used by the police in Punjab to kill suspected Sikh terrorists.
Congressmen in Haryana, allegedly supported by chief minister
Bhajan Lal, also 'organised mob violence' against Sikhs in the
towns of Haryana.[32]

Thus, as in the past, the Government of India responded to
lawlessness and violence with violence and lawlessness. What had
begun as an internecine sectarian conflict among Sikhs, and then
had become intertwined with the struggle for political control
among competing groups within Punjab in which the central
government backed one side, now became a direct confrontation
between the extremist, terrorist Sikh groups in Punjab, on the one
hand, and the central government, on the other hand. In this new
confrontation, the Punjab Congress was no force at all and the
Akali Dal became helpless. The Akali leaders would not condemn
Bhindranwale, who continued to speak in the language of Panthic
unity and solidarity, and it could not permit Bhindranwale to
emerge as the only prominent Sikh personality willing to confront
the central government in defense now not only of the political
demands of the Sikhs but of the lives and honor of Sikh youth.

Bhindranwale, Sikh Unity, and Akali Factions

One of the striking features of the dynamics of Sikh politics is the
remarkable degree of internal political fragmentation that occurs
under the cover of the ideal goal of communal solidarity. Any
amount of internal political factionalism appears to be tolerable,
but no faction will survive whose leaders are maneuvered into a
position of perceived betrayal of legitimate Sikh political demands.
Moreover, no leader who is seen to be sincerely pursuing Sikh
political goals can be criticized in public. Consequently, the frequent charges made in the press that the moderate Akali leaders
were cowards because they did not condemn Bhindranwale and
other militant and terrorist groups and their actions in Punjab,
while they make good rhetoric, are politically naive and meaning-
less.

The more Bhindranwale became the center of public and media

attention and the more his actions and speeches placed him in the
role of defending the Panth against an unjust central government
and its police, the less the so-called moderate Akalis could criticize
him and the more, in fact, they had to come closer to him in public
perception. Thus, SGPC president Tohra, who had other reasons
as well for supporting Bhindranwale, in December 1983 praised
him for having 'revolutionised' Sikhism.[33] The minority Akali Dal
led by Talwandi also moved towards Bhindranwale in March 1984
to gain advantage in its struggle with the dominant Akali Dal led
by Longowal. As for the Longowal forces themselves, while
differences between them and Bhindranwale's forces allegedly
became murderous in 1984, efforts were continuously made 'to
patch up differences' and to make a show of Panthic solidarity in
public.[34]

In fact, however, the main effort of the Longowal Akali Dal was
devoted to maintaining its political leadership of the Sikh community by pressing the longstanding Akali demands in non-violent
agitational movements. Thus, in the midst of the terrorist violence
extending its grip over Punjab, the Akali Dal launched its
Dharamyudha Morcha in September 1981, with a comprehensive
list of fortyfive demands encompassing every major and minor
grievance of the Sikh community, including several of the 'religious'
demands of the Bhindranwale group.[35] The moderate Akali
leadership, therefore, caught between the intransigence of the
center, the terrorist violence practiced, incited, or condoned by
the Bhindranwale–AISSF forces, and the demands of opposition
parties and the media for them to condemn 'the violent activities
of the Bhindranwale group and to distance itself from them,'[36] took
the bold, if not brave, risky, but the only politically feasible course
open to them of pursuing vigorously non-violent agitational
movements, including road and rail stoppages, constitution-burning,
and other symbolic devices. It was for the center to respond if it
wished to preserve the longstanding, competitive non-violent
relationship between the Punjab Congress and the moderate Akali
Dal by making the maximal concessions. Instead, the center chose
procrastination and countered violence with violence.

The failure of the Akali Dal to weaken the intransigence of the
central government, the failure of its movements to achieve any
significant concessions, meant inevitably its own decreasing
credibility and the increasing transfer of political initiative in the

Sikh community to Bhindranwale. The next *Dharamyudha Morcha*, therefore, in 1984, was launched by Bhindranwale around a demand for release of two of his arrested 'confidants'.[37] The Longowal Akali Dal this time had to join the Bhindranwale-declared *morcha*, but still managed to turn it into a broader political movement by linking it with the demand for acceptance of the Anandpur Sahib Resolution. Throughout, therefore, whether attempting to take the initiative or following Bhindranwale's lead, the moderate Akali leadership placed political demands in the forefront, demands which belong to the conventional discourse of Punjab politics. The center's response was again intransigent, including the declaration that the Anandpur Sahib resolution was secessionist and could not, therefore, even be considered.

Bhindranwale, the Akali Dal, the Sikh Community, and the Problem of Achieving a Political Majority in Punjab

Until the rise of Bhindranwale, the political struggle in Punjab between the Congress and the Akali Dal revolved around a few sociocultural realities that set the terms of the struggle and determined its outcome. These were the following:[38] the dominance of the Akali Dal among rural Jat Sikh farmers; the broad-based support of the Congress among Hindus, rural scheduled castes, and even some Sikhs; the confinement of the Communist Party of India (CPI) to rural Jat Sikh and scheduled caste support in some pockets of Punjab; and the confinement of the Jan Sangh/BJP to caste Hindu, particularly urban Hindu support. The most unambiguous features of the party struggle in relation to social, cultural, and religious groups in Punjab since independence have been the dominance of the Akalis among rural Jat Sikhs and the strong, but limited base of the Jan Sangh among urban Hindus. The Congress, though always the strongest force in Punjab, has also always depended upon an uncertain coalition of Hindus, Sikhs, and scheduled castes. The Akalis, the second strongest force, but the most narrowly based party in Punjab, have always required an alliance with the Jan Sangh to achieve a political majority in the state. In this struggle, as in the historic conflict over religious allegiances in Punjab as well, the large population of scheduled castes is a critical 'floating' element. It is here that the revivalist movement of Bhindranwale and the political struggle for votes and a governing majority in the Punjab link up.

A scheduled caste population confirmed in or converted to Sikhism is a great danger to the Congress political base in Punjab and a potential asset to the Akali Dal that could expand its voting base into one potentially larger than that of the Congress. In this respect, therefore, Bhindranwale and his followers posed a threat to the long-term political balance in Punjab. If he were to draw some Jat Sikh support away from the Akali Dal and gather support as well among rural scheduled castes, an alliance with him would benefit the Congress enormously and weaken the Akali Dal significantly. On the other hand, if he could develop his influence among rural scheduled castes to draw them away from the Congress politically, then the political majority of the Congress in Punjab would be endangered. The link-up between Sikh revivalism and the political struggle became clear in the 1983 panchayat elections when the Akali Dal and the Bhindranwale forces both sought to draw scheduled caste support away from the Congress, while the Congress struggled to maintain its base among the scheduled castes in preparation for the next round of parliamentary and legislative assembly elections.[39]

During his brief heyday, it was never certain how much support Bhindranwale in fact had. The only clear test of his rural influence, in the 1979 SGPC elections, came before his elevation to the center of Punjab politics. Panchayat elections never provide conclusive evidence of rural support one way or another since local factors are primary and alliances with outside party political forces are *ad hoc* and ephemeral. Bhindranwale in death and martyrdom, however, may have succeeded in altering the political balance in Punjab in just the ways most feared by the Congress. In the 1985 legislative assembly elections, it appears that the vast majority of Sikhs, rural and urban, Jat Sikh and lower caste, supported the Akali Dal, which won a large majority of seventythree out of 117 seats.[40]

Much has been made of whether or not Bhindranwale was loved by the Sikh masses, whether or not he is now perceived as a martyr and has thus become in death a more dangerous political foe even than he was in life, whether or not the Sikh peasantry and army mutineers were rushing to fight alongside Bhindranwale in June 1984, and the like.[41] In fact, too much attention has been given to

Bhindranwale personally and too little to his symbolic relationship to the Sikh community. I believe it does not matter to most Sikhs precisely what Bhindranwale did and what methods he used. He was seen as a sincere defender of Sikh values, Panthic unity, and communal identity. He was probably not himself as central a figure in the minds and hearts of the Sikh masses as he was made to be by the press. He may very well become forever enshrined among the long list of Sikh martyrs who gave their lives in an heroic struggle with external enemies against hopeless odds for the sake of the Panth. But, the Sikh peasants who attempted to rush to Amritsar and the Sikh soldiers who mutinied, in the worst such affair faced by the Indian government since 1857, were rushing to defend the greatest symbol of their faith and solidarity as a community and not in support of either Bhindranwale or any of his presumed political goals. Through their own involvement in and mismanagement of the crisis created by Bhindranwale in Punjab, the Congress created the very conditions it hoped to use Bhindranwale to prevent: an alteration in the political balance in Punjab produced by a greatly increased solidarity of the Jat Sikhs and a movement of the scheduled caste, so-called Mazhabi Sikhs, to the Akali Dal in the 1985 elections in Punjab.

Bhindranwale and Khalistan

If the Congress elevated Bhindranwale far beyond his likely fate unaided, the Congress, the government, and the press even more created the great Khalistan scare and Bhindranwale's association with that idea. The only outspoken proponents of the Khalistan idea were Sikh expatriates living abroad and a few extremists in Punjab itself. As for Dr. Jagjit Singh Chauhan of the Dal Khalsa, he was an opportunist politician, who moved from party to party in the unstable coalition politics of 1967–69. He was supported by the Congress in a contest for the speakership of the Punjab legislative assembly in March 1967. In November 1967, along with sixteen other independents and defectors, he was used by the Congress to bring down the first Akali Dal government in Punjab.[42] That this man of no political weight in or out of Punjab could have become the center of the great Khalistan scare to the extent of damaging Indo–British and Indo–US relations testifies to two things only:

the miraculous powers of the press even in a developing country where the media are less dominant in public opinion manufacture than they are in the West and the fears and insecurities of some Government of India leaders, who came to believe that the unity of the country was endangered by expatriate politicians in alliance with foreign governments and intelligence agencies.

It is not certain that Bhindranwale himself was bent upon achieving a separate, sovereign Khalistan in Punjab.[43] On the other hand, it is certain that the separateness and sovereignty of the Sikh people were integral to his beliefs and that those beliefs are widely shared among Sikhs in and out of Punjab. Such Sikhs demand an acknowledgment that they are a separate people, religion, and nation with the ultimate right, as of any sovereign people, to determine their own future and their relations with other peoples. Acknowledgment of that 'right' does not, however, necessarily imply a separate sovereign state. Some Sikhs would argue that the right has been exercised since independence through political accommodation within the Indian Union, but Akali political leaders and rural religious personalities such as Bhindranwale are extraordinarily sensitive to any perceived infringement on the ultimate sovereignty, equality, and separateness of the Sikh people.

It is often noted, and correctly so, that the Sikh perception that they are discriminated against in India is, if not false, a distortion of the actual position of the Sikhs as a whole in comparison with other groups, especially other minority groups. Sikh farmers are, on the whole, the most prosperous in the country, Sikh entrepreneurs have become wealthy not only in Punjab, but in major cities and towns across north India, and Sikhs are still heavily represented in the Indian armed forces far beyond their proportion in the population of the country. Yet, Sikh perceptions of discrimination are not without foundation. It continues to rankle that Punjabi Suba was the last linguistic state to be conceded in India, and only after two decades of agitation; that many Punjabi-speaking Hindus lied about their mother tongue to prevent it; and that the provincial capital, Chandigarh, has till now still not been formally handed over to Punjab and the other outstanding issues remaining from the decision to trifurcate the old Punjab province have yet to be satisfactorily resolved. It is also obvious that the Government of India has been following a determined policy to reduce the Sikh proportion in the army to one closer to the actual proportion to the Sikh population of the country. It also rankles that demands made in other parts of the country, whether it be for a linguistic state or for regional autonomy, are treated differently when made in Punjab, as more of an immediate threat to the unity of the country and as posing a secessionist danger. The Akali political position is that, as a sovereign people, the Sikhs chose to join with India in 1947 in the belief that their separate political status would be recognized, but that they were instead betrayed, tricked, and manipulated so that they have had constantly to fight even to have their separate identity acknowledged. Many Sikhs also feel that they have given far more than their proportionate share of blood for the country during the nationalist movement and in foreign wars, but still their loyalty is questioned and they are not trusted.

In this context, therefore, the demand for Khalistan is more significant as a reflection of Government of India fears than of any reality in the form of a broadly supported demand arising from the Sikh community, the Akali Dal, or Bhindranwale. It is perceived by the most important political forces in Punjab, associated with the Akali Dal, as a slander arising out of the deep prejudices among Indian political leaders and Hindus generally against the Akalis and the Sikhs as a community.[44]

CENTER–STATE RELATIONS AND SEPARATIST POLITICS IN PUNJAB DURING THE 1980s

There are similarities and continuities as well as differences and discontinuities in Sikh politics, Congress policies, and center–state relations between the 1960s and 1980s. In fact, a case can be made that all the old rules were followed in the 1980s and that Congress strategy and tactics were not substantially different in the 1980s as compared to the 1960s. I believe the differences are, in fact, critical and that they explain the utterly disastrous and extremely violent course of events in the 1980s. However, in order to provide a balanced perspective, I will consider first the similarities and continuities.

Similarities and Continuities

On the face of it. the Congress government at the center demonstrated once again by the sternest possible measures that it will not
tolerate secessionist movements anywhere in the country, including
especially Punjab. It has castigated the Khalistan demand and its
leaders and has protested against the governments of the US and
UK for their alleged support and tolerance of the Khalistan
leaders and movement. The White Paper justifying the assault in
the Golden Temple precincts on 6 June 1984 asserted that the
action was undertaken to eliminate terrorist and secessionist
groups who were using it as a base for their activities.[45] During the
action itself, the alleged secessionist leaders, Sant Jarnail Singh
Bhindranwale and Bhai Amrik Singh, were killed while the
moderate Akali Dal leaders were spared. And, until his dramatic
reversal of policy in July 1985, Rajiv Gandhi had refused to
negotiate with even the moderate Akali Dal leaders until they
disavowed the Anandpur Sahib Resolution, which he considered
separatist, and stopped using 'secessionist language'.[46]

The second principle of refusing to entertain any demands for
political recognition of a religious community has also been reasserted by the Government of India in relation to recent events in
Punjab. *The White Paper on the Punjab Agitation* claims that 'the
authenticated version' of the Anandpur Sahib Resolution, 'issued
in November 1982,' called for 'the constitution of "a single administrative unit where the interests of Sikhs and Sikhism are specially
protected".' Such a provision, if present (and there are several
'authenticated' versions of this Resolution), would provide further
justification for the Government of India's insistence that the
Anandpur Sahib Resolution could not 'be accepted as a basis for
discussion.'[47] The Government of India also has resisted the Akali
Dal demand in the Anandpur Sahib resolutions for granting of
'holy city' status to Amritsar as 'not in consonance with the secular
nature of our Constitution.'[48]

The principle of refusing to grant concessions to ethnic groups
capriciously is not especially relevant to Sikh demands of the 1980s
since the main demands of the Anandpur Sahib Resolution clearly
have the support of a major political party and a significant section
of the Sikh population. On the other hand, if we consider the
demand for a restructuring of center–state relations as a 'new'

political demand in India (leaving aside the previously noted fact
that it is a very old demand), then the Government of India has
been applying this rule in relation to this demand. It responded
initially by rejecting the Anandpur Sahib Resolution outright as
inconsistent with the 'concept of the unity and integrity of the
nation,' but also by acknowledging, through the appointment of
the Sarkaria Commission on Center–State Relations, the more
widespread existence in the country of a demand for restructuring
center–state relations. Then in July 1985, as part of the accord
between Rajiv Gandhi and Longowal, the Government of India
agreed to refer the Anandpur Sahib Resolution to the Sarkaria
Commission.

The fourth rule that even broad-based ethnic group demands
will not be accepted unless they have support on both sides of a
conflict has been very much upheld throughout the history of
postindependence Punjab politics, in which Haryana remains a
significant actor, up to the present. In fact, this principle has been
a major stumbling block to the settlement of the most important
outstanding issues between Punjab and Haryana since 1966, which
include the status of the city of Chandigarh, the transfer to Haryana
or the retention in Punjab of some disputed rural areas near the
borders of the two provinces, and the allocation of Ravi-Beas river
waters.

Differences and Discontinuities: The Failure to Reach a Political Settlement in Punjab

A brief review of the substance and course of the negotiations
between the central government and the Akali Dal leaders between
1980 and 1984 will bring out clearly the differences between Mrs.
Gandhi's approach and those of her father and her son. It needs to
be noted, first of all, that it was not until September 1981 that
Bhindranwale emerged as a central figure in Punjab politics. Until
that time, he and his activities had been largely a diversion from
conventional politics in Punjab, which centered as always around
the struggle for power between the Congress and the Akali Dal.
Moreover, until September 1981, the wrath of Bhindranwale and
his followers was directed mostly at Nirankaris and at other Sikhs;
it was primarily an internal affair among Sikhs and Nirankaris that

concerned issues of religious belief and practice. Bhindranwale
and his followers had not presented a coherent political program
of their own. Their principal demands of government until then
had been one articulated by the AISSF in May 1981 for the
banning of cigarettes in the area surrounding the Golden Temple
and the declaration of Amritsar as a 'Holy City'.

Until September 1981, therefore, the struggle between the
Congress and the Akali Dal was within the bounds of conventional
politics, which included the launching of agitations or *morchas* led
by the Akali Dal in pursuit of its demands against the state and
central governments. On 26 July 1981, the Akalis announced their
intention to launch a major *morcha* under the leadership of
Longowal in pursuit of a list of fortyfive demands, which contained
a combination of religious, political, economic, and social grievances. Some were trivial, some merely expressed resentment over
past wrongs, some were vaguely worded, and the major outstanding issues concerning Chandigarh, the status of Punjabi-speaking
areas left out of Punjabi Suba, and the river waters dispute were
consolidated in only one of the fortyfive points.[49] Such a diffuse list
of grievances and demands could only have mixed purposes: to
provide a basis for political mobilization to maintain the enthusiasm
of the workers in a party out of power, to assert the agitational
leadership of Longowal within the party, and to provide a list of
demands long enough to ensure agreement on some of them that
would avoid loss of face on the part of either the Akalis or the
government.

The entire situation changed dramatically, however, in September 1981, with the murder of the Hindu newspaper owner,
Lala Jagat Narain, the implication of Bhindranwale in the murder,
his arrest on the orders of the chief minister of Punjab, and his
release on the orders of the home minister of the Government of
India. This grand 'arrest-and release drama,'[50] followed by a
dramatic increase in incidents of terrorist violence in which
innocent Hindus were killed, brought Bhindranwale to centerstage
in Punjab politics. With Bhindranwale and the terrorists now
playing leading roles, the pressure on both the central government
and the Akali Dal for a face-saving conclusion of the Akali Dal
morcha increased significantly.

It has been charged that the central government responded with
procrastination, partial concessions on minor issues, and refusal to

concede the major Akali demands.[51] There were three major series
of protracted negotiations between the central government and
the Akalis between September 1982 (a year after the murder of
Lala Jagat Narain) and June 1983. On all three occasions, it has
been reported that agreement was reached between negotiators on
both sides on the major outstanding issues, but that the agreements were finally scuttled each time by reversals of position by
Mrs. Gandhi herself.[52] These reversals allegedly were made in
response to protests from Congress chief ministers in Haryana and
Rajasthan who argued that they would have difficulty in explaining
to the people of their states the granting of Chandigarh to Punjab
without any concession of territory to Haryana and the loss of river
waters to Punjab that were also needed in Haryana and Rajasthan.[53]
The official position of spokesmen of the Government of India
involved in these negotiations, however, is that government could
not negotiate on the basis of the Anandpur Sahib Resolution,
parts of which negated the unity of India and that the Akali
negotiators could never get the Akali Dal itself to accept any
agreement.[54] It remains in dispute, therefore, whether or not Akali
disunity or Government of India intransigence on the Anandpur
Sahib Resolution stood in the way of resolving the principal issues
concerning Chandigarh, the status of Abohar–Fazilka and of the
Punjabi-speaking areas left out of Punjabi Suba, and the distribution of Ravi–Beas waters. All three of these issues were
regional, secular matters having nothing to do with secessionism or
separatism.

Another noteworthy feature of the negotiations is that the only
agreement announced by the government during these three years
concerned some minor religious issues: banning of cigarette sales
near the Golden Temple, relay of Gurbani broadcasts from the
Golden Temple abroad, amendment of Article 25 of the constitution
to make clear that the Sikhs were not Hindus, and recognition of
the Personal Law of the Sikhs. Agreement on these issues was
announced unilaterally by Mrs. Gandhi in a Delhi gurudwara.
Mrs. Gandhi's supporters consider this move a generous gesture
on her part, while others argue that her unilateral announcement
failed to help the moderate Akalis who could not claim even these
concessions as a victory.[55] It has also been noted that the gurudwara at which Mrs. Gandhi made her announcement was controlled by her allies among the Sikhs, who were opponents of the Akali

Dal (Sant Longowal group).[56] Moreover, in the view of her critics, Mrs. Gandhi refused to reach agreement concerning regional, secular political and economic demands while conceding religion-based demands in a pattern opposite to the stance taken by her father.

The prolongation of the talks and negotiations between the government and the Akalis without any significant agreement placed the Akali leaders in an impossible situation between the government and Bhindranwale. If they accepted an unsatisfactory agreement, they would be condemned by Bhindranwale and his ally in the Akali leadership, Tohra. Consequently, their only recourse was to return to agitational politics after each breakdown in negotiations. In the meantime, the government's failure to act against Bhindranwale made the moderate Akali position increasingly vulnerable and also made it increasingly difficult for them to come to an agreement without taking Bhindranwale into account. Consequently, the Akalis would add to their list of grievances and demands some that arose out of Bhindranwale's confrontations with the police: concerning police repression, false encounters by police with killing of Sikhs alleged to be terrorists, release of alleged terrorists, and the like.

The stance taken by the central government in negotiations with the Akalis between 1981 and 1984 stands in sharp contrast to the negotiations between Nehru and later Lal Bahadur Shastri, on the one hand, and Sant Fateh Singh, on the other hand. Longowal, like Sant Fateh Singh before him, but much more so, needed a face-saving political settlement against Bhindranwale which would secure his leadership in the Akali Dal against Tohra. It was in the long-term interest of the government as well to bring about such a result if it wished to preserve a secular non-violent political process in Punjab. Mrs. Gandhi, however, never felt that she could make political concessions that would undermine the position of the Congress in the vast north Indian Hindi-speaking regions of the country. It was not simply a case of concern that a settlement favorable to the Akali Dal would help that party in Punjab and harm the Congress in the neighboring states of Haryana and Rajasthan, but that the Hindu reaction in the latter two states would spread to the huge states of UP, Bihar, and Madhya Pradesh, where widespread discontent over concessions to the Sikh minority could threaten the Congress with defeat in the next parliamentary elections.

Mrs. Gandhi's policies differed sharply from those of her father and her immediate predecessor Lal Bahadur Shastri as well. Nehru refused to concede a Sikh majority state to a movement led by a man he considered an extremist, a secessionist, and a fraud. Lal Bahadur Shastri laid the basis for the concession of Punjabi Suba to an Akali leadership helped to power by Congress policies. Mrs. Gandhi implemented the reorganization of Punjab and the creation of Punjabi Suba, which brought peace to Punjab for fifteen years, but she then failed to take advantage of the peaceful atmosphere and her own predominant power in the country to settle the outstanding issues.

The failure to complete the Punjabi Suba settlement was one objective basis for the often-repeated claims of the Akalis that the Sikhs were discriminated against in India. Before the Punjabi Suba was conceded, Punjabi-speaking Hindus had conspired to deny their mother tongue in order to prevent the concession of a Punjabi Suba as a Punjabi-speaking state. When a Punjabi-speaking state was at last conceded, the central government then refused to transfer to the new state its capital, initially created out of a Punjabi-speaking area, unless two tahsils of Punjab containing numerous Punjabi-speaking villages were simultaneously transferred to Haryana. In effect, therefore, the central government first appeared to be denying to Punjabi-speaking Sikhs the right to have a linguistic state of their own on the grounds that it was a cover for a Sikh-majority state and then, having conceded the demand, wished to take away some of the rural Hindu Punjabi-speaking areas which would, in effect, reinforce the Sikh-majority character of the Punjabi Suba. The Akalis also argued that the central government was favoring the states of Haryana and Rajasthan in the solution of the third major unresolved issue, namely, the disposition of Ravi–Beas river waters by allowing them to take a substantial share of the waters from rivers that flow only through Punjab. To accommodate the Akalis on this issue, however, the central government would have had to withdraw waters already flowing to these states and halt construction on a major canal project. Such actions would naturally arouse the anger of the affected population and their legislative representatives, with the potential loss of both states in the next election in consequence.[57]

Most political observers have thought that Chandigarh was the

principal issue. Moreover, all political parties in Punjab, including
the Jan Sangh/BJP, were in favor of retaining Chandigarh as the
state capital. Its symbolic importance to the people of Punjab was
well-known. Mrs. Gandhi's original decision in January 1970 to
award Chandigarh to Punjab was consistent with the linguistic
character of the original site, was politically sound, and recognized
the symbolic importance of Chandigarh to Punjab. Unfortunately,
that decision, which was to be implemented in five years, was
never implemented. Worse, implementation of the decision was
later linked to the disposition of the more controversial and
dubious decision to transfer the Abohar–Fazilka belt to Haryana,
which was both unprecedented in involving a corridor to link these
interior areas with Haryana and appeared discriminatory in award-
ing some Punjabi-speaking areas to Haryana. It needs to be noted
here also, however, that the Akalis themselves failed to demand
the separation of the Chandigarh and Abohar–Fazilka issues when
they were in power from 1977 to 1980 in coalition with the Janata
party, which was in power at the center.[58] Moreover, it needs also
to be acknowledged that Haryana has a claim to Chandigarh as
well since it is presently a bilingual, Hindu-majority city.

By itself, leaving aside the question of Chandigarh, the Abohar–
Fazilka question raises issues of principle that would be difficult to
resolve under any circumstances. This belt is a mixed Hindi- and
Punjabi-speaking area inhabited mostly by Hindus. In the 1961
census, which provided the basis for demarcating Hindi- and
Punjabi-speaking areas, many Hindus whose mother tongue was
Punjabi falsely declared their mother tongue to be Hindi, in these
areas and elsewhere in the pre-1966 Punjab province. The result
was that the Punjabi Suba was not, in fact, demarcated strictly on a
linguistic basis in the first place.

The issue of principle raised by this situation is whether or not
objective or subjective criteria should be used to demarcate linguistic boundaries. Mrs. Gandhi, however, never even considered
the issue in those terms. Until the very end of her life, in two
speeches before Parliament justifying the army assault on the
Golden Temple and blaming the Akalis for the failure to reach a
political accommodation on these issues, Mrs. Gandhi made it
clear that her decision on Abohar–Fazilka was entirely political in
the narrowest sense of the term. She said that Chandigarh 'could
not go (to Punjab) unless Haryana got something in its place.'[59]

Moreover, 'if Abohar and Fazilka were also to go to Punjab, then Haryana had to be compensated not just in money for their new capital, but with some territory.[60] Repeatedly, Mrs. Gandhi gave as her *only* criterion for this trade-off the prediction 'that there would have been trouble in Haryana'[61] if Haryana did not get some territory in exchange for Chandigarh. Naturally, the answer to such a politically-motivated response was another politically-inspired one. The Akalis countered that Haryana had been dominated mostly by Congressmen personally loyal to Mrs. Gandhi who, as her stooges, would do whatever she wished.

In fact, however, there was a much larger political issue behind this political trade-off, namely, the sentiment of many Hindi-speaking Hindus in the vast northern and central regions of the country without whose political support the Congress could not prevail in a general election. The principal opposition party in Haryana, the Lok Dal, was the leading opposition party in north India. The other important non-Congress party in Haryana and the rest of the northern and central region was the Jan Sangh/BJP, whose primary ideological stand centered around symbols of militant Hindu nationalism and whose strength, like that of the Lok Dal, was centered in the Hindi-speaking regions. Both these parties were prepared to exploit any political settlement that appeared to give in to the Akalis at the expense of Hindi-speaking Hindus in Haryana.

Moreover, despite the overwhelming majorities that Mrs. Gandhi obtained several times during her political heyday and despite her exercise of authoritarian rule for two years during the Emergency, there was never a time when Mrs. Gandhi felt politically safe enough to take a decision that would have appeared to favor Punjab. The initial decision to award Chandigarh to Punjab was taken in 1970, when Mrs. Gandhi and the Congress were extremely vulnerable. The time was only a year after the Congress split and before the 1971 and 1972 elections in which Mrs. Gandhi was returned with a massive majority in Parliament and in most of the states, including Punjab and Haryana. The year 1972 was a time when Mrs. Gandhi might have acted decisively to settle all outstanding Punjab issues, but she did not.[62]

During the Emergency, from 1975 to 1977, the Akalis were the only major political force in India brave enough to sustain agitations against the government. Mrs. Gandhi could hardly reward them for their defiance of her regime then.[63] After her and the Congress' victory in 1980 was another occasion for decisive action but, as has been shown, an entirely different game was being played. When the situation went completely out of control in Punjab, the 1984–85 elections were in the offing and, once again, the time was wrong for a decision that would antagonize the Hindi-speaking Hindus in north and central India.

In the end, in a curious paradox, it was Mrs. Gandhi's rigid stand in Punjab, including the assault on the Golden Temple, followed by her assassination, that released an enormous wave of Hindi–Hindu nationalism that swept her son and the Congress back to power in 1984 and 1985 and made politically possible the concession to the Akalis that Mrs. Gandhi had never been willing to make. Rajiv Gandhi and the Congress first exploited to the maximum this Hindu nationalism by stealing both the old Jan Sangh slogan of One United India and more than half of the old Jan Sangh voting base in north and central India[64] and then, with an unprecedentedly large and secure majority in Parliament and in most states, conceded everything to the Akalis that Mrs. Gandhi had refused. In the Rajiv Gandhi–Longowal Accord of July 1985, the central government agreed to hand over Chandigarh to Punjab on 26 January 1986, to appoint a commission to determine the Hindi-speaking areas to be transferred to Haryana, to refer the river waters dispute to a judicial tribunal, and to refer the Anandpur Sahib Resolution to the Sarkaria Commission on Center–State Relations.

CONCLUSION

There are several possible explanations for the tragic failure of the central government under Mrs. Gandhi's leadership and the moderate Akali leaders to resolve the Punjab issues. One is that the problems themselves are intractable because all solutions give zero-sum results: Punjab's gain is Haryana's and/or Rajasthan's loss. This argument cannot, however, be sustained for trade-offs have always been available. Funds can be provided to Haryana for another capital, canals can be built from other rivers to supply some of the needs of Haryana and Rajasthan, and consistent principles can be applied concerning the transfer of disputed territory. It is not, therefore, that solutions to the problems were not available; there were many possible solutions.

The failure to select a package to resolve the issues and to adhere to the chosen solutions was rather a consequence of the unwillingness of either Mrs. Gandhi or the moderate Akali leaders to adopt a solution that did not provide them with a political advantage or that threatened political damage. Moreover, both sides lost precious time when compromise solutions might have been reached and the political damage limited: the central government between 1972 and 1977, the Akalis when they themselves were in power in Punjab from 1978 to 1980. The Akalis had less time in power, however, than the Congress and it is doubtful that the Janata government in Delhi, with its Jan Sangh and Lok Dal components would have accepted a solution that conformed to Akali wishes. Moreover, because the implementation of a solution of the outstanding issues depended upon the initiative of the central government since its initial decision to create the Punjabi Suba in 1966, greater attention needs to be paid to the failure of the central government to move resolutely to resolve the issue.

One explanation, consistent with Tully and Jacob's analysis, would emphasize Mrs. Gandhi's alleged indecisiveness.[65] On this reckoning, Mrs. Gandhi, who clearly did show the ability to act decisively on many occasions, did so, however, only when pushed to the wall. This explanation, however, will not do to explain the *type* of response Mrs. Gandhi ultimately resorted to when forced finally to act. Why could it *not* have been political accommodation with the Akalis instead of an army assault on the Golden Temple?

The answer is too obvious and places her actions within both the changed (by her) context of center–state relations and the political bases of her own decisionmaking. Mrs. Gandhi altered the Indian political system in the 1970s in such a way that her power at the center depended on two things: (a) her ability to control most of the Indian states, which, however, remained always problematic because of the absence of strong state leaders; and (b) her ability to sway large categories of voters by creating a 'wave' on an emotive issue or set of issues. A wrong move on an issue such as Chandigarh and Abohar–Fazilka could have lost power for her in two states: in Punjab to an Akali Dal waxing victorious over her concessions and in Haryana to the Lok Dal, exploiting negative reactions to her concessions. More important, such a wrong move might have then precipitated a 'wave' in the wrong direction and her loss of power in Delhi and the country as a whole.

The second part of the answer is that Mrs. Gandhi failed to articulate the issues in terms of principle and to attempt thereby to contain their negative political consequences. She presented the issues herself largely in terms of political gains and losses and the need to make political trade-offs between one state and another, while insisting she was only protecting national unity and the interests of other parties than herself and while blaming the deterioration of the situation in Punjab upon the malevolent influence of 'foreign' hands, rather than her own government's failures.

EPILOGUE

The principal argument of this essay has been that relentless centralization and ruthless, unprincipled intervention by the center in state politics have been the primary causes of the troubles in Punjab and elsewhere in India since Mrs. Gandhi's rise to power. Rajiv Gandhi came to power in 1985 on a wave of Hindu militant nationalist sentiment that supported centralization, national unity, and intolerance towards aggressive minority demands. He then moved away from that sentiment in search of political solutions in Punjab and Assam and displayed a willingness to give up power in these small states for the sake of restoring peace and normalcy.

The Rajiv–Longowal accord of 24 July 1985 and the restoration of civil government in Punjab through the September 1985 elections, which brought a moderate Akali Dal government to power, were the principal manifestations of a serious effort on the part of the central government under Rajiv Gandhi to find a permanent solution to the Punjab crisis. The Accord provided a basis for a settlement consistent with the traditional rules followed by the central government in dealing with minority demands in the 1960s. However, that accord was never implemented. The commission appointed to adjudicate the Abohar–Fazilka dispute failed to reach a decision on the areas to be transferred to Chandigarh. Another commission called for Punjab to transfer 70,000 acres of land to Haryana in exchange for Chandigarh, which the Punjab government refused to accept. The central government failed to hand Chandigarh over to Punjab on the appointed date of 26 January 1986 without a general agreement. The Akalis on their part failed to work unitedly to demand implementation of the accord. The major responsibility for failing to implement this accord, however, rests with former Prime Minister Rajiv Gandhi, who alone could have made the decisions on the conflicting claims, restrain Congressmen in Haryana, and accept the political damage while the Congress' majority in the country was secure and time remained to repair the damage. It is regrettable, therefore, that the political will to implement the Punjab accord was lacking and that the opportunity to enforce a just solution while the Congress held an unshakeable position of political dominance in the country for five years was allowed to slip by.

On the contrary, the inability of the Punjab government to end terrorist actions and the killing of innocent Hindus in Punjab led the central government to impose President's Rule once again in the state in May 1987. The following year, the center went further and imposed an Emergency in Punjab under the terms of the newly passed 59th Constitution Amendment Bill, 1988, which authorized the central government in effect to eliminate the civil liberties of the people of the state.

New hopes for a Punjab settlement were again aroused by the defeat of the Congress in the parliamentary elections of 1989 and the installation of a National Front government under Prime Minister V.P. Singh. The latter immediately took a number of symbolic and concrete measures, which had a favorable impact among most political elements in Punjab. These included a personal visit in an open car to the Golden Temple, the repeal of the 59th Amendment, the replacement of the discredited Punjab Governor, Siddhartha Shankar Ray by Nirmal Mukarji, the holding of an all-party meeting in Ludhiana, the release of many detenus from Punjab jails, and the establishment of special courts to institute criminal proceedings against those suspected of instigating the pogrom against the Sikhs in 1984, among other measures.

By April 1990, however, V.P. Singh also had reached a stalemate in his efforts to find a solution to the Punjab problem. On the one hand, the Akalis again were disunited and divided into numerous extremist, militant, and moderate groups. The principal

potential negotiating partners for the central government were the
Akali group led by Simranjit Singh Mann, whose forces had won
six of the thirteen Punjab parliamentary seats with huge margins,
with the support of militant groups associated with Bhindranwale
and the AISSF, on the one hand, and the more traditional Akali
elements under the leadership of former chief minister Prakash
Singh Badal, on the other hand. However, these two forces were
unable to come together; Simranjit Singh Mann refused to enter
into negotiations with the central government, demanding instead
the holding of state assembly elections in which his group would be
expected to win a majority and emerge as the dominant political
force in Punjab and in control of the Punjab government. The
central government, faced with its own constraints presented by its
dependence upon the BJP to remain in power in New Delhi and by
a far more serious insurrection in Kashmir, in May opted to pass a
constitutional amendment permitting the extension of President's
Rule once again in Punjab for six months beyond the previous
constitutional limit. Once again, therefore, in mid-1990, the
Punjab crisis remained unresolved with no evident solution in
view.

Given the failure of two different central governments under
Rajiv Gandhi and V.P. Singh, which began with bold and constructive initiatives, to succeed in reaching a settlement, it would
be easy to conclude that the Punjab crisis is simply intractable, the
pressure of the extremists too great, the divisions among the
Akalis too evident, and the future options limited to military ones.
That is not, however, the conclusion of this essay which is rather
that these repeated failures to resolve the Punjab crisis reflect the
existence of a major structural problem in the Indian political
system that requires a broader political solution. That structural
problem arises from the tensions produced by the centralizing
drives of the Indian state in a society where, as I have argued in the
previous chapter, the predominant long-term social, economic,
and political tendencies are towards pluralism, regionalism, and
decentralization. Mrs. Gandhi fought those tendencies by centralizing power and decisionmaking in Delhi, nationalizing issues, and
intervening incessantly in the politics of every state. A more stable
political solution will require just the opposite: willingness to
accommodate regional political demands and to grant greater
powers to the states.

What is special about the Punjab crisis is not the fact that militant demands are coming from a minority religious group. Rather, it is that the tension between centralizing and decentralizing tendencies, between proponents of 'national integration' and pluralism can find no stable equilibrium in this state because the political dynamics prevent it. The demand for regional autonomy in other states in India has been subdued because regional political forces at least have achieved power in the states where important regional forces are most favorable towards a restructuring of center–state relations. What has made the Punjab crisis so intractable is that the Akali Dal has never been able to establish its political dominance in this state, with the consequence that the frustration of its efforts to do so have encouraged militant elements among the Sikhs within and outside of the 'Akali Dal to raise ever more vigorously complaints that Sikhs are discriminated against and demands for regional autonomy. The response of the central government, whether under a centralizing Congress government such as that of Indira or Rajiv Gandhi or under a National Front government beholden to the centralizing BJP for its majority in Parliament, has been to resist facing the deeper structural problems of the Indian Union. It should be clear after a decade of violence in Punjab and the rise of an even more serious separatist movement in Kashmir that the consequences of such continued resistance to the natural tendencies towards regionalism on the subcontinent are more dangerous for the future of Indian unity than facing up to the need to decentralize the Indian state.

NOTES

1. Paul R. Brass, *Language, Religion, and Politics in North India* (New York: Cambridge University Press, 1974).
2. My focus in this paper, therefore, is deliberately restricted to the political context of Punjab politics and center–state relations to the neglect of the socioeconomic background to the Punjab crisis of the 1980s. The explanations to be offered subsequently, therefore, for the disastrous course of events in Punjab between 1980 and 1984 are proximate rather than remote explanations. By remote explanations, I mean those that would draw our attention to changes in class relations in Punjab during the past two decades arising out of the Green Revolution and other economic developments in the province or to

increases in university enrollments and in the numbers of the idle educated classes at a time when military recruitment of Sikhs that previously had offered desirable careers for many educated youth in Punjab had declined.

It is possible, however, that the remote causes of Punjab events in the 1980s may be of equal or greater importance than the proximate causes in the sense that, without them, the situation would never have reached such drastic proportions. In other words, it may be that the decisive differences between the 1980s and the 1960s lie in the changed socioeconomic context rather than in the changed political context. To deal adequately with changes in both contexts, however, would require a book not a chapter. My view is that there are sufficient differences in the political context between the 1960s and 1980s to warrant specific attention to the changed political context as a causal factor, but that changes in the socioeconomic context provided additional stimulus and a recruiting basis for terrorist violence among Sikh youth in Punjab.

For some explanations that emphasize the socioeconomic context, see especially: Sucha Singh Gill and K.C. Singhal, 'The Punjab Problem: Its Historical Roots,' *Economic and Political Weekly* [hereafter referred to as *EPW*] Vol. XIX, No. 14 (7 April 1984), pp. 603–8 and Prakash Tandon, 'Another Angle,' *Seminar*, 294 (February 1984), pp. 35–37. See also the next chapter in this volume.

3. See Paul R. Brass, 'Pluralism, Regionalism, and Decentralizing Tendencies in Contemporary Indian Politics,' in A.J. Wilson and Dennis Dalton (eds.), *The States of South Asia: Problems of National Integration* (London: C. Hurst, 1982), pp. 246–55.

4. John R. Wood, 'Extra-Parliamentary Opposition in India: An Analysis of Populist Agitations in Gujarat and Bihar,' *Pacific Affairs*, Vol. XLVIII, No. 3 (Fall, 1975), pp. 313–34.

5. On the increasing importance of violence and the threat, manipulation, and control of violence at the local level in north India, see my 'National Power and Local Politics in India: A Twenty-Year Perspective,' in Paul R. Brass, *Caste, Faction, and Party in Indian Politics*, Vol. I: *Faction and Party* (New Delhi: Chanakya Publications, 1984), pp. 196 and 210–20.

6. Joyce Pettigrew, 'A Description of the Discrepancy between Sikh Political Ideals and Sikh Political Practice,' in Myron J. Aronoff (ed.), *Ideology and Interest: The Dialectics of Politics*, Political Anthropology Yearbook I (New Brunswick, NJ: Transaction Books, 1980), pp. 151–92.

7. This is not to say, however, that the mere change in the rhetoric used to formulate the Punjabi Suba demand explains its acceptance by the Government of India. The latter may have had as much to do with the Indian government's desire to recognize the critical military role played by Sikh forces in the armed services and the strategic importance of a stable Punjab in general in the aftermath of the 1965 Indo-Pakistan war, on the one hand, and the fact that, with the death of Pratap Singh Kairon in 1964, there was no Congress leader in the Punjab strong enough to stand up to the Akalis, on the other hand. The change in rhetoric was a precondition for acceptance of the demand, which required other conditions for its success. I am indebted to Bhagwan D. Dua whose comments in a personal communication stimulated this clarification.

8. See Paul R. Brass, 'Ethnic Cleavages and the Punjab Party System, 1952–1972,' in

Myron Weiner (ed.), *Studies in the Electoral Politics of Indian States*, Vol. IV: *Party Systems and Cleavages* (Delhi: Manohar Book Service, 1975), pp. 7–69.

9. The involvement of Sanjay Gandhi and Giani Zail Singh in the building up of Bhindranwale was widely reported in some sections of the press in India and among opposition parties. The most recent support for this analysis comes from Mark Tully and Satish Jacob, *Amritsar: Mrs. Gandhi's Last Battle* (London: Jonathan Cape, 1985), pp. 57–62. See the section below on Bhindranwale and the Sikh community for further details on the rise and significance of Bhindranwale.

10. Tully and Jacob, *Amritsar*, op. cit., pp. 65–66.

11. The position of Congress leaders close to Mrs. Gandhi on this matter of arresting Bhindranwale was stated by one of them in the following way: 'The point is you have all kinds of people floating around. You don't go about grabbing them and putting them in jail. . . . Bhindranwale was one of the Sants. Now, how do you proceed against a Sant until he does something? And if he is a Sant, if he is a saint, then you give him a longer rope, if at all. So, how does anyone expect us to go and grab Bhindranwale and put him in a jail? . . . For instance, Zail Singh was Home Minister here. Now, they [critics of the government] say you should have put him behind bars in Delhi [after the murder of Lala Jagat Narain]. He's on his way to Punjab. It is for the state government of Punjab to grab him or do whatever it is, whatever they want to do *if* he has done anything wrong, if he has really been guilty of something. It's not in transit that you do this. This is just hindsight. You avoid bloodshed, you avoid going into a temple, you avoid laying your hands on a person who is a saint, who has his own school . . . in the hierarchy of saints. . . . So how can you simply grab him and put him behind bars?' Interview in New Delhi on 22 August 1986.

One response to these comments is that the Government of India, using various preventive detention laws, often puts people behind bars to prevent violence or even lesser alleged threats to civil order. Bhindranwale was placed in a special category, even though there were obviously grounds for his arrest and trial, let alone detention. The account of whose responsibility it was to arrest him, the Government of India or the Punjab government, supports very strongly one of the main themes of this chapter, namely, that the central and state governments did not act in unison as they did under Nehru and Kairon.

12. Up to this point, Bhindranwale and his men had been taking refuge in the hostel complex adjacent to the Golden Temple, but not in the areas of the Golden Temple complex considered sacrosanct.

13. Dalip Singh, *Dynamics of Punjab Politics* (New Delhi: Macmillan India, 1981), pp. 104–7.

14. Bhindranwale, of course, was never convicted in a court of law of murder or of supporting terrorist activities. However, the term 'extremist' may be applied to him and his followers in the way he defined it, namely, Sikhs who have taken Amrit, who keep weapons, who obey any orders 'given by the Panth,' 'who seek justice for the martyrs,' especially for those who suffered at the hands of police officials whose names and locations were given during his public addresses at the Golden Temple. It is difficult to imagine a clearer form of incitement to violent, revengeful, murderous activities than this combination in

the circumstances of the time. Citations and references are from Sant Jarnail Singh Bhindranwale's Address to the Sikh Congregation (November 1983?), translated from the original in Punjabi by Ranbir Singh Sandhu (Columbus, Ohio: Sikh Religious and Educational Trust, 1985). For a different view, see the reference in fn. 20.

15. Pritam Singh, 'Punjab: Lessons of Panchayat Elections,' *EPW*, Vol. XVIII, No. 43 (22 October 1983), pp. 1822–23.

16. Singh, *Dynamics of Punjab Politics*, op. cit., p. 221.

17. Singh, *Dynamics of Punjab Politics*, op. cit., pp. 75–76 and 87.

18. For details, see Tully and Jacob, *Amritsar*, op. cit., pp. 66–70, and below.

19. This is a composite view of Bhindranwale, various elements of which can be found in Khushwant Singh, 'Genesis of the Hindu-Sikh Divide,' in Amarjit Kaur, *et al.*, *The Punjab Story* (New Delhi: Roli Books, 1984), pp. 9–11; Avtar Singh Malhotra, *Save Punjab, Save India* (New Delhi: Communist Party of India [CPI], 1984), pp. 11, 12, 19; *EPW*, Vol. XVIII, No. 41 (8 October 1983), p. 1725; Vol. XVIII, No. 44 (29 October 1983), p. 1858; Vol. XIX, No. 12 (24 March 1984), p. 482; Vol. XIX, Nos. 22 & 23 (2–9 June 1984), p. 865; Vol. XIX, No. 26 (30 June 1984), p. 965; Vol. XIX, No. 28 (14 July 1984), p. 1076; Gill and Singhal, p. 607; Kuldip Nayar and Khushwant Singh, *Tragedy of Punjab: Operation Bluestar & After* (New Delhi: Vision Books, 1984), pp. 30*ff*; Tully and Jacob, chs. iv & v.

20. The Sikh English-language weekly newspaper, the *Spokesman*, generally subscribed to several aspects of this alternative view. See, for example, the issues of 10 January 1983 and 14 January 1985.

21. Joyce Pettigrew, 'Take Not Arms Against Thy Sovereign,' *South Asia Research*, Vol. IX, No. 2 (November 1984).

22. Letter of Ranjit Singh Sandhu (a Sikh living in America), 25 April 1985.

23. See Pettigrew, 'Take Not Arms,' Tully and Jacob, *Amritsar*, op. cit., pp. 52–54, and Kuldip Nayar and Khushwant Singh, *Tragedy of Punjab*, op. cit., pp. 24–25.

24. Pritam Singh, 'Akali Agitation: Growing Separatist Trend,' *EPW*, Vol. XIX, No. 5 (4 February 1984), p. 196; Pritam Singh, 'Punjab: AIR and Doordarshan Coverage of Punjab after Army Action,' *EPW*, Vol. XIX, No. 36 (8 September 1984), 1571; *Spokesman*, 10 January 1983.

25. There are two heterodox groups which carry the Nirankari name. One, the older of the two, is referred to by Khushwant Singh as a Sikh–Hindu group which is considered heretical because of its 'worship of gurus other than the ten recognised by [orthodox] Sikhs,' *A History of the Sikhs*, Vol. II (Princeton: Princeton University Press, 1966), p. 125; John C.B. Webster, however, points out that this group was not involved in the 13 April clash, which took place between the followers of another group known as the Sant Nirankaris and the followers of Bhindranwale; see his *The Nirankari Sikhs* (Delhi: Macmillan, 1979), pp. 32–35 and 58–60, on this point and on the relationships between the two Nirankari sects.

26. Khushwant Singh, 'Genesis of the Hindu–Sikh Divide,' op. cit., pp. 9–10; Gill and Singhal, *EPW*, Vol. XIX, No. 14 (7 April 1984), p. 602; Malhotra, *Save Punjab*, op. cit., pp. 5–7.

27. Arun Kumar, 'Punjab: Wages of Past Sins,' *EPW*, Vol. XIX, No. 28 (14 July 1984), p. 1076. According to Tully and Jacob, *Amritsar*, op. cit., p. 61, Bhindranwale 'campaigned actively for the Congress in three constituencies.' It should be kept in mind that Bhindranwale was not yet a major political force in

Punjab. Involvement in three out of 117 legislative assembly constituencies does not constitute a major intervention on Bhindranwale's part.

28. *EPW*, Vol. XVIII, No. 41 (8 October 1983), p. 1725; Gill and Singhal, 'The Punjab Problem,' op. cit., p. 607; *EPW*, Vol. XIX, Nos. 22 & 23 (2–9 June 1984), p. 865; Malhotra, *Save Punjab*, op. cit., p. 12; *EPW*, Vol. XIX, No. 26 (30 June 1984), p. 965.

29. One leading Congressman close to Mrs. Gandhi and the Punjab situation denied that Bhindranwale was a Congress creation, insisting that he came up on his own with his own ambition, but admitted that local Congressmen may have decided to support or ally with him. However, he justified the general practice of dividing one's rivals and its application to Bhindranwale in the following words: 'Now, if I have somebody who is my own opponent in another party and if I find that that party has two factions, one is a more powerful faction who is fighting me and whom I'm fighting and there is another faction, what do I do? Do I ask them to unite? What is politics? Is it not dividing . . . opponents and uniting friends? What are they [opposition party leaders] talking about? Are they not doing the same thing among Congressmen? . . . There is always this effort to drive a wedge.' Personal interview in New Delhi on 22 August 1986.

The Congressman's response here is certainly a valid description of Indian—perhaps all—political behavior. However, it raises two questions. One concerns the suitability of the allies chosen for the purposes of dividing the opposition. Bhindranwale clearly did not serve Congress purposes as well as did Sant Fateh Singh against Master Tara Singh in the 1960s. The second question is at what point statesmanship enters into situations such as that in Punjab and responsible leaders decide that routine politics no longer apply.

30. *EPW*, Vol. XIX, No. 12 (24 March 1984), p. 482.
31. *EPW*, Vol. XIX, Nos. 22 & 23 (2–9 June 1984), p. 865.
32. Malhotra, *Save Punjab*, op. cit., p. 17.
33. *Spokesman*, 2 January 1984.
34. *EPW*, Vol. XIX, No. 17 (28 April 1984), pp. 694–95 and Malhotra, *Save Punjab*, op. cit., p. 12.
35. This *Dharamyudha Morcha* went on fitfully and intermittently over the next two years, interspersed with periods of negotiations between the Akalis and the central government when *morcha* activities were halted.
36. *EPW*, Vol. XIX, No. 17 (28 April 1984).
37. Gill and Singhal, 'The Punjab Problem,' op. cit., p. 608.
38. For details on the support bases of political parties in Punjab, see Brass, 'Ethnic Cleavages in the Punjab Party System, 1952–1972', op. cit., M.S. Dhami, 'Caste, Class and Politics in the Rural Punjab: A Study of Two Villages in Sangrur District,' in Paul Wallace and Surendra Chopra, *Political Dynamics of Punjab* (Amritsar: Guru Nanak Dev University, 1981), pp. 292–317; Pramod Kumar, *et al.*, *Punjab Crisis: Context and Trends* (Chandigarh: Centre for Research in Rural and Industrial Development, 1984), pp. 63–72; and Dalip Singh, *Dynamics of Punjab Politics*, op. cit., pp. 252–60.
39. Pritam Singh, 'Punjab: Lessons of Panchayat Elections,' op. cit.
40. See esp. the article by Janardan Thakur in *The Times of India Sunday Review*, 13 October 1985. It is probable that the Akali Dal also won the votes of many Hindus who saw a greater possibility of peace in Punjab under an Akali than under a Congress government.

41. See, for example, Khushwant Singh, 'Genesis of the Hindu–Sikh Divide,' op. cit., p. 11; Arun Kumar, 'Punjab: Wages of Past Sins,' p. 1077; and Pritam Singh, 'Punjab: Lessons of Panchayat Elections,' p. 1570.

42. Dalip Singh, *Dynamics of Punjab Politics*, op. cit., p. 96 and personal interview in Chandigarh on 27 May 1967.

43. In a translation of a taped address given by Bhindranwale at the Golden Temple, thought to have been given in November 1983, Bhindranwale is quoted as having said: 'We are not in favor of Khalistan nor are we against it . . . . If the Center gives us Khalistan, this time we shall not say no. We shall take it. We shall not repeat the mistake of 1947.' Sant Jarnail Singh Bhindranwale's Address to the Sikh Congregation.

44. *Spokesman*, 14 January 1985.

45. Government of India, 'White Paper on the Punjab Agitation: A Summary,' in Kaur, *The Punjab Story*, op. cit., pp. 184–99. [Hereafter referred to as *WP*.]

46. *Overseas Hindustan Times*, 2 March 1985.

47. *WP*, op. cit., p. 188.

48. *WP*, op. cit., p. 186.

49. The fortyfive points are contained in Kuldip Nayar and Khushwant Singh, *Tragedy of Punjab*, op. cit.. pp. 138–39.

50. *EPW*, Vol. XIX, Nos. 22 & 23 (2–9 June 1984), p. 865.

51. See particularly the issues of the *Spokesman* from September 1982 through June 1983, which reflect moderate Akali attitudes towards the progress of the negotiations and blame the central government for their failure.

52. On these negotiations, see, among other sources, Kuldip Nayar and Khushwant Singh, *Tragedy of Punjab*, op. cit., pp. 60–63; Harkishan Singh Surjeet, *Developments in Punjab* (New Delhi: CPM, 1984), pp. 3–6; Avtar Singh Malhotra, *The Punjab Crisis and the Way Out* (New Delhi: CPI, 1984), pp. 18–21; Tully and Jacob, *Amritsar*, op. cit., ch. vi; and, for a government view, *The Situation in Punjab*, Statement of Home Minister in Parliament on 28 February 1984 (New Delhi: Government of India, Ministry of Information and Broadcasting, 1984).

53. Tully and Jacob, *Amritsar*, op. cit., pp. 78–79.

54. Personal interview in New Delhi on 22 August 1986.

55. Tully and Jacob, *Amritsar*, op. cit., pp. 90–91.

56. Malhotra, *Save Punjab*, op. cit., p. 5.

57. It is not necessary for purposes of this paper to go into the details of this issue. See fn. 52 for some references on this, as well as other issues in dispute.

58. I discovered in a visit to Punjab in January 1990 that there is a great difference between urban and rural Sikh attitudes towards the Chandigarh and Abohar–Fazilka issues. Rural Sikhs whom I interviewed in Amritsar and Tarn Taran cared far more for Abohar–Fazilka than for Chandigarh. The former was considered valuable because it was agricultural land, whereas Chandigarh was described as merely concrete! This attitude would also explain why the Akali Dal cannot trade Abohar–Fazilka for Chandigarh.

59. Indira Gandhi, *Punjab and National Unity*, Speeches of the Prime Minister during the discussions on the White Paper on Punjab in the Lok Sabha on 25 July 1984 and in the Rajya Sabha on 24 July 1984 (New Delhi: Government of India, Ministry of Information and Broadcasting, 1984), p. 8.

60. Indira Gandhi, *Punjab and National Unity*, op. cit., p. 28.
61. Indira Gandhi, *Punjab and National Unity*, op. cit., pp. 9 and 29.
62 Dua argues that Mrs. Gandhi's initial decision on Chandigarh was motivated completely by political considerations and was tied into her broader struggle in the country as a whole to consolidate her power and defeat the state party leaders in the Congress (O). For this purpose, she needed the support of Akali MPs in Parliament who might otherwise have joined forces with the Congress (O). After her massive victory in the 1971 elections, Dua argues, she no longer needed the support of the Akali MPs and, therefore, had no further incentive to implement the award. Bhagwan D. Dua, 'India: A Study in the Pathology of a Federal System,' *Journal of Commonwealth & Comparative Politics*, Vol. XIX, No. 3 (November 1981), pp. 269–70 and personal communication.
63. Some Sikhs believe that Mrs. Gandhi's alleged unwillingness to satisfy the demands of the Akali Dal in the 1980s related to her annoyance over the Akali agitation against the Emergency; for example, *Spokesman*, 1 September 1986, p. 6. In this connection, it is sometimes also noted that it was Longowal who led the agitation against the Emergency regime. Such an interpretation of Mrs. Gandhi's motivations, though consistent with her actions in other matters in rewarding those who were loyal to her and punishing those who opposed her during and after the Emergency, would suggest a pettiness on her part in the face of a grave crisis that goes beyond the argument of this paper concerning her political actions.
64. See the 'Postscript: The 1984 Parliamentary Elections in Uttar Pradesh,' in Paul R. Brass, *Caste, Faction and Party in Indian Politics*, Vol. II: *Election Studies* (New Delhi: Chanakya Publications, 1985).
65. Tully and Jacob, *Amritsar*, op. cit., pp. 13–14.

6

Socioeconomic Aspects of
the Punjab Crisis

The Punjab crisis is generally acknowledged to have had its religious roots in a violent clash between a heterodox sect, the Nirankaris, and militant orthodox Sikhs in April 1978 in the Sikh religious capital city of Amritsar in which thirteen people were killed. The merging of this religious sectarian strife with the principal political conflicts in Punjab is traced to the period between the April 1978 clash and the general elections of 1980. During that time, as indicated in the previous chapter, Congress leaders in and out of the state, including persons close to the then Prime Minister, Indira Gandhi, sought to make use of Sikh militants involved in these incidents to create a divisive force within the principal opposition to the Congress, the Sikh political party, the Akali Dal. The Sikh militants, however, under the leadership of Sant Jarnail Singh Bhindranwale, had their own goals which were not entirely consistent with those of the Congress, especially after the victory of the latter in the Punjab state elections of 1980.

Although, as noted before, Congress support for the Sikh militants caused great strains both between the latter and the moderate Akali Dal politicians as well as within the ranks of the Akali Dal itself, the divisions increasingly took the form of a competition concerning which party, faction, or leader was most militant and determined to protect and promote the interests of the Sikh Panth (community). These interests were expressed especially at first in the revival of demands to settle the outstanding issues left over since the creation of the Punjab state in 1966. The most important issues were the undecided status of Chandigarh (the former capital city of undivided Punjab), the disposition of other disputed territory on and near the borders of the predominantly Hindu, Hindi-speaking state of Haryana, and the division of river waters among the states in the region.

Violence, not uncommon even in the everyday life of the peopie of Punjab, began to spread widely in the state. At first confined to Sikh religious and political sectarians in their struggles with each other, it later spread to attacks on Hindu newspaper owners and politicians considered unsympathetic to Sikh interests and to terrorist attacks on innocent Hindu civilians. When the state and central authorities finally decided to take stronger measures against alleged extremists and terrorists, the violence escalated still further as the police engaged in their own forms of terrorist actions against Sikh young men. In effect, therefore, by the time of the assault on the Golden Temple by the Indian army in June 1984, the state of Punjab was in a condition of anarchy and war, in which no life or property was secure.

Although there is a considerable scholarly consensus on this general description of the origins and course of the Punjab crisis, it is sometimes supplemented by accounts which introduce economic factors into it more centrally or reduce the political struggles to merely 'contributory' status.[1] In the first category are interpretations which urge us to pay more attention to economic and social factors, which are often bracketed at the same time with other root factors such as the 'communal ethos' or attacks on civil liberties. The stronger, usually Marxist, arguments go further and insist that economic and class forces are primary and the political–communal factors merely reflections of the underlying class forces, whose leading segments operate to manipulate the political–communal situation.

Before one can assess the relative weights to be assigned to political, cultural, and economic factors in the Punjab situation, one must be clear about what aspect of the crisis is to be explained. This chapter will deal with the extraordinary levels of violence which have been associated with the current Punjab crisis, in contrast especially to the last major series of political movements in behalf of Sikh political demands which occurred in the early 1960s and which remained mostly non-violent. I have already discussed these two sets of movements in the previous chapter, focusing on the political differences in leadership and in the context of center–state relations. The focus here will be primarily on the extent to which social and economic factors must be included in a complete explanation of the degeneration of the Punjab crisis of the 1980s into terrorist actions and violent confrontations between militant Sikh youths and the Indian army and various other military, para-military, and police forces.

CASTE, CLASS, AND ECONOMIC CONFLICTS IN PUNJAB

A by-product of the current situation has been to increase tendencies towards consolidation of the two communities of Hindus and Sikhs into separate, unitary blocks, but that consolidation is far from complete. Such consolidation has been prevented especially by continuing internal divisions among the Sikhs. There has been a decline in interelite cooperation and communication across the Hindu and Sikh boundaries, but there are good grounds to doubt the permanence of that change in the situation.

Internal Division among Sikhs and Hindus in the Punjab

Caste composition of the Sikhs

Sikhism does not recognize caste. Nevertheless, commensal and marriage restrictions have persisted within Sikhism.[2] Today, nearly two-thirds of the Sikhs come from 'the peasant castes,'[3] who are mostly Jats and who comprise 39 per cent of the total population of the state (Table 6.1).

The rest of the Sikh population is usually divided into three broad sets of castes: the scheduled castes (untouchables), 'rural artisan' and service castes, and the urban trading castes (mostly Khatris and Aroras). The 'rural artisan' and service castes, sometimes called 'lower backward' castes, comprise those somewhat above the scheduled castes in ritual status and in economic well-being whose traditional occupations have been as blacksmiths, barbers, carpenters, and the like.[4]

The third important grouping of non-peasant Sikh castes are the

TABLE 6.1: Percentage Distribution of the Total Population in Punjab by Religion and Four Caste Groups in 1971

Caste group/ other religions	Percentage-wise break-up of each caste group among Hindus and Sikhs in the total population*		Percentage distribution of total Hindu and Sikh population among four caste groups
	Hindu	Sikh	Total
1. Higher castes	15.4 (86)	2.5 (14)	17.9
2. Peasant castes	4.4 (10)	39.3 (90)	43.7
3. Servicing and artisan castes	4.1 (35.5)	7.5 (64.5)	11.6
4. Scheduled castes	13.8	10.9	24.7
Total of four caste groups	37.7	60.2	97.9
Other religions			2.1
Grand total			100.0

Source: M.S. Dhami, 'Communalism in Punjab: A Socio-Historical Analysis,' Punjab Journal of Politics, Vol. IX, No. 1 (January–June 1985), 26.
* Percentage distribution within each caste group by religion (for Hindus and Sikhs) is given in parentheses.

Khatri and Arora Sikhs, mostly refugees from Pakistan, now living in 'urban areas' and 'by and large, highly successful businessmen and entrepreneurs.' They 'provided political and cultural leadership to the community' in the late nineteenth century, especially through the revivalist Singh Sabha movement[5] and also in the leadership of the Akali Dal up to the 1960s.

Hindus comprise 38 per cent of the total population of the state, but are heavily concentrated in the major cities and towns of the province where they outnumber the Sikhs. Among Hindus, there are two numerically large groups: the 'higher caste' Hindus, mostly the urban trading castes of Khatris and Aroras, who comprise above 15 per cent of the total population of the state, and the scheduled castes who comprise nearly 14 per cent of the state population (Table 6.1). There are small numbers of non-agricultural high castes and artisan and service castes among the Hindus as well, but the bulk of the rural Hindu population comes from the scheduled castes.[6]

The scheduled caste population of Punjab, though often divided into Sikh and Hindu sections, requires separate treatment because of the fluid religious identities of these castes, their subordinate economic status, and their swing political role. Altogether, the scheduled castes comprised 26.87 per cent of the total population in the 1981 census. There was 'an influx' of persons from such castes to Sikhism in the late nineteenth century as a consequence of the proselytizing activities of the Singh Sabha movement.[7] However, many have become involved in other religious movements and sects in the space between Hindu and Sikh orthodoxies, such as 'the Sant Nirankari, the Radha Soami [sic.] and the Adi Dharam movements.'[8] Although no studies are available on the social composition of the contemporary Nirankari sect, its appeal to both Hindu and Sikh lower castes (including scheduled castes) would add a socioeconomic basis to the religious conflict between orthodox Sikh revivalists and this heterodox sect despised by orthodox Sikhs.

Economically, the scheduled castes, both Sikh and Hindu, stand in subordinate relationships with the Jat Sikh peasantry, for whom they work as agricultural laborers. Economic conflicts over wages with the dominant Sikh peasantry, therefore, is a further factor which has contributed to the weakness of the religious and cultural ties of the lower castes to Sikhism which, however casteless, has historically been associated with the culture of the Jat Sikh peasants and the urban Sikh trading castes.[9]

Party leadership and support bases

There is no question that the main political parties in Punjab, especially the Congress and the Akali Dal, the two leading contenders for power, draw differential support from the two religious communities and from their internal segments. Since the creation of the Punjabi Suba in 1966 until the recent crisis, the Congress has been the most broadly-based of the two main parties. Its strongest support has tended to come from the Hindu and scheduled caste populations, but there have been elections in which it has won considerable support from rural non-scheduled caste Sikhs as well.

In the 1970s, during the chief ministership of Giani Zail Singh, himself a non-Jat Sikh from one of the backward castes, the

Congress in Punjab sought to identify with and build a stronger base of support among all non-Jat Sikhs from both the scheduled and 'lower backward' castes and from the urban Sikh trading castes. The policy was largely successful. However, as everywhere in north India, Congress lost support even among the scheduled and backward caste groups in the post-Emergency 1977 election and was defeated in Punjab by a coalition of the Akali Dal and the Janata party. During the period of the Akali–Janata coalition government the Congress sought to restore its base among non-scheduled caste Sikhs and also to divide the Akali Dal itself by supporting Bhindranwale and other militant Sikh groups. It succeeded for the most part in doing so and won support in 1980 especially from Hindus, from both Hindu and Sikh scheduled castes, and even from 'a small section of the Sikh peasantry.'[10]

However, the escalating conflict increasingly became focused upon the alleged discrimination of the Congress government at the center against the Sikhs generally in Punjab, especially after the June 1984 assault on the Golden Temple and the mass murders of Sikhs in Delhi and elsewhere in November 1984. In these circumstances, the Congress was unable to maintain the broad-based coalition of the 1970s. Nevertheless, even in the 1985 election, the Congress polled 37.9 per cent of the vote, virtually the same vote share as the Akali Dal (Table 6.2). The Congress retained its base among the Hindus and the scheduled castes, including most Sikh scheduled castes.[11] The most striking fact about Congress electoral support in the Punjab assembly, therefore, is that it has retained an irreducible minimum vote share of above one-third, that it retained an ability also even in the most extreme circumstances of Hindu–Sikh communal division to draw support from some sections of the Sikh community, and that in normal times the addition to its basic coalition of support from other non-Jat Sikh castes and from a small percentage of the Sikh peasant castes as well has ensured its electoral victory in the state.

The Akali Dal, no less than the Congress, must engage in intercommunal coalition building. The problem for the Akali Dal, however, is that its electoral support is based overwhelmingly on the Jat Sikh peasantry and secondarily on the urban Sikh trading castes. In the early 1960s, there was a change in the leadership of the Akali Dal from the former 'urban higher caste leadership' to a 'new rural Jat peasant leadership'.[12] Sant Fateh Singh, the new

TABLE 6.2: Percentage of Votes Polled by Leading Political Parties in Punjab Legislative Assembly Elections, 1967–85

Party	Elections					
	1967	1969	1972	1977	1980	1985
Congress (I)	37.7	39.2	42.8	33.6	45.2	37.9
Akali Dal (Sant)	20.5	29.4	27.6	31.4	26.9	38.0
Jan Sangh/Janata/						
BJP	9.8	9.0	5.0	15.0	6.5	5.0
CPI	5.3	4.8	6.5	6.6	6.5	4.3
CPM	3.2	3.1	3.3	3.5	4.1	1.9
Other parties	7.7	5.6	2.5	0.4	4.4	1.1
Independents	15.8	8.9	12.3	9.6	6.5	11.9
Total	100.0	100.0	100.0	100.1	100.1	100.1

Source: V.B. Singh and Shankar Bose, *State Elections in India: Data Handbook on Vidhan Sabha Elections, 1952–85* (Vol. 1), *The North* (Part 1) (New Delhi: Sage, 1987).

leader of the party, was the first rural preacher to become the predominant leader of the Akali Dal and his rise consolidated the hold of the party on its rural Jat Sikh base.

The shift in Akali leadership and in its support base and the establishment of the new Punjabi Suba came on the eve of the Green Revolution. The Jat Sikh farmers of Punjab responded eagerly and dramatically to the new opportunities in agriculture and soon required and demanded increasing quantities of the new inputs at minimal prices as well as maximum prices for their produce, demands which were also reflected in Akali party manifestoes and in government policies when the party came to power.

The economic requirements of the Jat Sikh peasantry and dependence of the Akali Dal on their support in elections, however, confronted the Akali leaders with a political dilemma. The more they identified with the economic needs of the peasantry, the more they risked further alienating the rural scheduled castes and losing the support of the urban Sikh classes as well.[13] On the other hand, the support of the rural Jat Sikh peasantry was not at all sufficient to win a majority and rule the state.

The third important political party in Punjab is the Bharatiya Janata Party (BJP), formerly the Janata party and originally called the Jan Sangh. The BJP is a party of militant Hindu nationalism.

In Punjab, it is based overwhelmingly upon the urban Hindu trading and professional classes. In the period since the formation of the Punjabi Suba in 1966, there have been four Akali Dal–Jan Sangh/Janata coalition governments. Except, therefore, for the unusual 1985 elections with its victory for the Akali Dal and the formation, thereafter, of a one-party Akali government, an intercommunal alliance between the Akali Dal and the Jan Sangh/Janata has been necessary to displace the Congress from power in the state.

The fourth important political party in Punjab is the Communist Party of India (CPI). It has some support among the Jat Sikh peasantry in two rural districts and has also drawn consistent support from Hindu and Sikh scheduled castes in both the rural areas and the cities and towns of Punjab.

Off and on since independence, political parties with various names have sought to represent specifically and exclusively the scheduled caste population of the state. These parties have included the Scheduled Caste Federation, which contested the 1952 and 1957 elections, the Republican Party which replaced it between 1962 and 1972, and the Dalit Soshit Samaj Sangharsh Samiti, which contested the 1985 state legislative assembly elections. Since the formation of the Punjabi Suba, however, no such party has been able to win above 2 per cent of the popular vote.

The electoral arena and coalition politics in Punjab, therefore, have been dominated by four political parties since 1966, each of which has a distinctive social base. From the point of view of voting patterns within the electorate, the Jat Sikhs and urban Sikh trading castes vote primarily for the Akali Dal, urban Hindus for the Congress and the BJP, scheduled castes for the Congress or the Communist parties. It is evident from both the relative population proportions of the two religious communities and from the internal social and political divisions among them that intercommunal electoral or post-electoral alliances are necessary to gain political power in this state.

The caste basis of communal conflict

Few scholars of Punjab politics would dispute the outlines given above of the socioeconomic distribution of support bases by caste for the main political parties of the Punjab. However, those who favor socioeconomic explanations for the current situation take the analysis two steps further by merging caste and economic differences with the broader communal differences in the state and then using the latter as an explanation for the crisis of the 1980s. In this approach, the internal differences *within* the two communities are subordinated to the allegedly more decisive differences *between* the leading elements of the two religious populations.

The basic argument begins by noting that the Jat Sikhs dominate agricultural production, while the Hindu trading castes dominate the urban sector, including the marketing of agricultural produce. These dominant castes, it is claimed, are naturally in economic conflict with each other. In order to gain advantage against their economic enemies, they 'invoke the solidarity of their religious group in safeguarding their economic interests from the encroachment of the dominant castes of the opposite religious group.'[14]

In this explanation, the Sikh 'trading castes' are relegated to a secondary role economically but a major role politically. 'Clashes of interests' occur between Hindu and Sikh traders in urban areas.[15] However, the natural economic resentments of the Sikh peasantry against the Sikh traders is overcome through the use by the Sikh trading castes of 'religious symbols' to defend 'their trade interests'.[16] These 'Sikh traders' also 'invoke religious fundamentalism to wean away the Sikh agriculturists from Hindu traders.'[17]

A sketch of the complete set of caste/economic alignments posited by proponents of this type of explanation of the Punjab crisis is given below.[18]

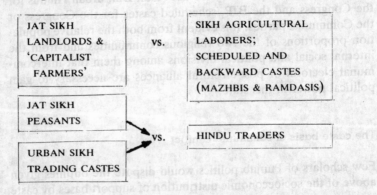

These arguments for a clear caste/economic polarization as an explanation for the Punjab crisis, however, have been criticized by Gurharpal Singh who argues that they ignore 'the persistence of cross-cutting and overlapping economic, social, cultural, caste, and political interests of Sikhs and Hindus' even in the face of 'the tragic events of 1984.'[19] Moreover, Marxist analysts of the Punjab crisis tend to switch ground from the argument that communal divisions *reflect* the basic, underlying caste/economic cleavages to the position that communal divisions *supersede* them through the exercise of class hegemony or through diversionary tactics which, in effect, produce a 'false consciousness'.[20]

ECONOMIC FACTORS IN THE PUNJAB CRISIS

Among the problems in finding a satisfactory economic explanation for the Punjab crisis is the fact that, on the great majority of aggregate economic indicators, Punjab is at the top or very close to the top in comparison with all other Indian states.[21] Moreover, per capita plan expenditures have been consistently higher in Punjab than in every other major Indian state for the past twenty years.[22]

Explanations for the development of the Punjab crisis in the 1980s nevertheless sometimes refer to specific economic factors which preceded it and which allegedly provided the catalyst for it. One view places the source of the discontent and disturbances of the 1980s in the frustrations of the Jat Sikh peasants. A levelling off in the Green Revolution, a declining ratio between farm produce prices and input costs, and a change to a Congress government in 1980 which reduced the availability of state patronage for agriculturists embittered the Jat Sikh peasants, especially the new class of 'Jat Sikh capitalist farmers'.[23]

In this explanation, the demands of the moderate Akali politicians for a change in center–state relations granting more autonomy to the states, including Punjab, and the demands of militant groups for the creation of a separate sovereign state of Khalistan are subsumed under the general economic demands of the Jat Sikh peasantry for political action to relieve their economic problems. One difficulty with this interpretation is that the regional autonomy demand in Punjab was framed as early as 1973 but was not pushed very strongly until after the crisis of the 1980s was in full swing and was presented primarily as a counter to the more extreme separatist demands of the Khalistan supporters. Moreover, there is absolutely no evidence that the Khalistan demand itself was supported by 'Jat Sikh capitalist farmers' at all.

A second major explanation for the Punjab crisis concerns the allegedly worsening employment situation in the state, to which the stalemate in agriculture also is said to have made a contribution. The case for unemployment as a major cause of the Punjab crisis has been presented by I.K. Gujral, who has argued that the crisis was preceded by 'severe unemployment . . . particularly amongst the educated' in excess of 'the all-India averages' in many categories of education graduates. Increasing numbers of young persons entered the cities and towns of Punjab looking for satisfying jobs at a time when the agricultural economy was tapering off, when alternative employment opportunities were not being created through 'industrial growth,'[24] and when previous alternative sources of employment were shrinking. Opportunities for migration abroad to both the United Kingdom and the Persian Gulf countries had declined and the Government of India had altered the pattern of recruitment into the Indian army in such a way as to threaten a reduction in recruitment of Sikhs.

There are several problems with the unemployment explanation. For one thing, all the evidence so far provided has been inferential, based on general economic and specific employment figures, but not on analyses of the social composition and employment status of Sikh militant political activists. Second, the reduction in recruitment of Sikhs into the armed forces has been, in fact, only proportionate. That is, recruitment has increased in other parts of the country, but it has not declined in Punjab. Third, even for the educated youth, no argument has been made or evidence provided that there is an imbalance in opportunities in this regard between aspiring Sikh and Hindu seekers of education and employment in the urban areas, which would inflame Hindu–Sikh relations.

On the other hand, general unemployment figures do show a sharp increase over the decade for Punjab in comparison with all-India averages and with other states.[25] The number of applicants for jobs on the live register of the employment exchanges in India in the decade from 1970 to 1980 increased by 3.89 times. The corresponding figure for Punjab was 4.66. However, several other states had even higher increases over the decade.

Unemployment figures from the Sixth Five Year Plan for Punjab also provide some support for the argument that there were unemployment problems among educated graduates on the eve of the beginning of the Punjab crisis in 1978. The deviations from the all-India averages, however, were not extreme in all cases and Punjab was better off than the rest of the country in some respects. The highest deviation was an unemployment rate of 26.4 per cent compared to the all-India average of 4.5 per cent for commerce graduates, but the unemployment rate among arts graduates was only 12.6 per cent compared to the all-India average of 15.7 per cent.[26]

On the whole, therefore, it is certainly the case that students and youth have provided the principal source of militant political activity in Punjab in the period from 1978 to the present. It is very likely that many young persons were unemployed and found their political activities a satisfying alternative outlet for their energies. It is, however, not clear that Punjab was significantly worse off with regard to its population of discontented unemployed youth, educated or otherwise, than most other states. What is most unclear is the extent to which economic discontents provided the motive for participation by Sikh youths in Punjab during the intensification of the crisis.

The Actual Economic Demands of the Akalis and of the Sikh Militants and the Class Character of Akali Leadership

There is not much evidence in the statements and speeches of Sant Jarnail Singh Bhindranwale to support the view that economic issues were at the forefront of his concerns and, by implication, of his followers. Reports and transcripts of his speeches refer primarily to religious, communal, political, and civil liberties issues.[27] He stressed over and over again the separateness of the Sikhs from Hindus and the distinctiveness of their religion and scripture and he protested against Hindu denials on these matters and against alleged efforts to absorb Sikhs into Hinduism. He demanded, therefore, that a constitutional amendment be passed recognizing the Sikhs explicitly as a separate religion in India. He urged Sikhs to carry arms and to be prepared to use them 'to protect' their faith. Reports of Bhindranwale's speeches, however, are virtually empty of references to economic issues.

The Akalis, on the other hand, did include economic demands, along with political and religious issues, in their statements, speeches, and manifestoes. Their famous Anandpur Sahib resolution of 1973 demanded an increase in the land ceiling from 17.5 to 30 standard acres, 'cheap inputs and abolition of excise duty on tractors, and remunerative agricultural prices.' It also demanded 'complete nationalisation of trade in foodgrains and unrestricted movement of foodgrains in India.' The latter demand has been seen as an expression of the 'opposition of the capitalist farmers to traders and monopolists.'[28] The demand for regional autonomy for Punjab, the most famous item in the Anandpur Sahib resolution, has also been interpreted as a demand for the more effective pursuit of the interests of 'capitalist farmers' in a political unit where 'their own political representatives' would be in power.[29] The Akalis responded to the government's shift in military recruitment policies by demanding 'restoration of the Sikhs' fair share in the three branches of India's armed forces.'[30]

While the Akali economic demands have been undeniably present—and before the beginning of the crisis of the late 1970s and early 1980s—it is noteworthy that the emphasis *shifted* during the crisis to political and religious issues. Moreover, there was a noticeable difference between the limited public response to economic protest movements and the more massive responses to movements based on religious/communal demands.[31]

Marxists argue that the dominant groups in the Akali Dal, who represent the 'rich farmers' especially, who in turn 'have hegemony over the whole of the peasantry,' use religious appeals to mobilize the broad mass of the peasantry for their own purposes and maintain their hegemony over them as well by making use of such appeals from time to time.[32] Such arguments assume there are major differences in the economic needs of the rich peasantry, on the one side, and the middle or small peasantry, on the other side, which are hidden by the religious appeal. While it would be wrong to deny the mobilizing potential of caste and religious identities as a basis for organizing groups around economic issues, it is another matter to argue that the bulk of the persons so mobilized are being manipulated towards ends which are against their economic interests.

It is preferable, rather, to make a distinction between the social bases and the economic demands of the Akalis and other parties in Punjab in normal times and the economic and social bases of movements involving the mobilization of the major part of the Sikh community. In times of crisis, broadly defined symbolic, cultural, and religious issues drawing on a broad sense among Sikhs of their separate identity provide the principal basis for mobilization of the Sikh community.[33] In normal times, however, the natural economic and political differentiation within the Sikh community expresses itself in internal political divisions among Sikhs, including Sikh scheduled castes, and external political alliances with Hindu and secular political parties.

CONCLUSION

It has been argued in the foregoing that the evidence for an economic explanation of the Punjab crisis of the 1980s is lacking. The Punjab crisis was precipitated by a religious conflict between militant orthodox and fundamentalist Sikh groups and a heterodox Sikh–Hindu sect.

Sikh fundamentalist appeals were then used by both the Congress—to divide the Akalis—and by Akali factions in their internal struggles for political dominance against each other. The broader political context of these conflicts was the continuing struggle for power between political groups in the state of Punjab, which was in turn integrated into the struggle for power in the country as a whole. The latter struggle had intensified and become increasingly bitter after the imposition of the Emergency regime of Mrs. Gandhi in 1975, its temporary replacement by a non-Congress coalition between 1977 and 1979, and the return of Mrs. Gandhi and the Congress to power in 1980. The subordination by the ruling Congress of local political considerations to national ones also involved a lessened sensitivity to local ethnic, regional, and religious sentiments and, in the case of the Punjab, a willingness to exploit religious fundamentalist appeals without regard for the broader consequences.

The principal grievances and demands of the Akalis and the Sikhs in Punjab now fall under three categories. At the forefront—in the aftermath of the assault on the Golden Temple, the massacre of Sikhs in Delhi and elsewhere in November 1984, and the deprivation of the civil liberties of the people in Punjab during the police and army operations of the past five years—is a set of demands which amount to restoration of Sikh self-respect. These include such demands as the trial and conviction of those responsible for the massacres, the release from prisons of all Sikh detenus, the rehabilitation of Sikh deserters from the Indian army, and the like. The second set of demands concern the unfinished character of the reorganization of Punjab, including the failure to transfer the city of Chandigarh to the Punjabi Suba.

Very few of the agreements contained in the Rajiv–Longowal Accord, which covered especially the first two sets of issues, were implemented by the Congress government of Rajiv Gandhi. Several measures were taken in its first days by the V.P. Singh government which were in line with the spirit of the Accord and the demand for symbolic and material gestures to restore Sikh self-respect. These measures, noted in the previous chapter, included V.P. Singh's visit to Amritsar, the release of many Sikh detenus, promises to release and rehabilitate Sikh army deserters, and the appointment of special courts to institute proceedings against persons considered responsible for the Sikh massacres of November 1984. The third set of issues concerns the demand for implementation of the provisions in the Anandpur Sahib resolution concerning regional autonomy. Most of the outstanding issues and demands are political ones or concern Sikh identity and self-respect. Only the issue concerning division of river waters is clearly economic, though the regional autonomy demand conveys to Sikh peasants a vision of higher prices for farm products.[34]

Underlying all other issues, however, is the question of the unstable political dynamics of Punjab, the absence of a stable governing coalition. Although I have argued that the communal division in Punjab is highly permeable, it has been great enough to prevent the development of a Punjab-wide regional consciousness such as exists in several other states of the Indian Union and which provides in those states the basis for political integration.

I believe that the resolution of the Punjab crisis, therefore, must move through three stages: restoration of the Sikh pride that they are a valued community in India, full implementation of the Accord, and the beginning of serious discussions on the whole matter of the future of center–state relations in India. It is likely that the resolution of the first two matters combined with an earnest new approach to center–state relations would even now bring the Punjab crisis to a resolution and that the secessionist demand and the terrorist actions would recede and normalcy be restored to the state. Such a resolution would then reveal once again the socioeconomic factors and forces which are prominent in Punjab politics in normal times, but which provide little help in understanding the sources of the current crisis. No permanent resolution to the problems of Punjab, however, can be attained until the political dynamics are altered in such a way as to produce either a stable governing coalition or alternative governing coalitions both of which draw support from Sikhs and Hindus united in a desire to promote the interests of the people of Punjab within a federal Union in which a high degree of political autonomy of all the states is respected.

NOTES

1. See esp. Sucha Singh Gill and K.C. Singhal, 'The Punjab Problem: Its Historical Roots,' *Economic and Political Weekly* [hereafter *EPW*], Vol. XIX, No. 14 (7 April 1984), pp. 603–8; Harish K. Puri, 'The Akali Agitation: An Analysis of Socio-Economic Bases of Protest,' *EPW*, Vol. XVIII, No. 4 (22 January 1983), pp. 113–18; Joyce Pettigrew, 'Take Not Arms Against Thy Sovereign,' *South Asia Research*, Vol. IX, No. 2 (November 1984), pp. 102–23; M.S. Dhami, 'Communalism in Punjab: A Socio-Historical Analysis,' *Punjab Journal of Politics*, Vol. IX, No. 1 (January–June 1985), pp. 1–30; and Gurharpal Singh, 'Understanding the "Punjab Problem",' *Asian Survey*, Vol. XXVII, No. 12 (December 1987), p. 1275.

2. W.H. McLeod, *The Evolution of the Sikh Community: Five Essays* (Oxford: Clarendon Press, 1976), pp. 84–88.

3. M.S. Dhami, 'Religio-Political Mobilisation and Shift in the Party Support Base in 1985 Punjab Assembly Election,' *Punjab Journal of Politics*, Vol. XI, No. 1–2 (1987), p. 21.

4. McLeod, *The Evolution of the Sikh Community*, op. cit., pp. 93–94 and 102; I.K. Gujral, 'The Economic Dimension,' in Amrik Singh (ed.), *Punjab in Indian Politics: Issues and Trends* (Delhi: Ajanta, 1985), p. 14; Gopal Singh, 'Socio-Economic Bases of the Punjab Crisis,' *EPW*, Vol. XIX, No. 1 (7 January 1984), p. 42; Amrik Singh, 'An Approach to the Problem,' in Amrik Singh (ed.), *Punjab in Indian Politics: Issues and Trends* (Delhi: Ajanta, 1985), p. 2.

5. Dhami, 'Religio-Political Mobilisation and Shift in the Party Support Base,' op. cit., pp. 10–11.

6. Dhami, 'Religio-Political Mobilisation and Shift in the Party Support Base,' op. cit., p. 21.
7. McLeod, *The Evolution of the Sikh Community*, op. cit., p. 55.
8. Puri, 'The Akali Agitation,' op. cit., p. 117.
9. Dhami, 'Religio-Political Mobilisation and Shift in the Party Support Base,' op. cit., pp. 22–23; Gill and Singhal, 'The Punjab Problem,' op. cit., p. 605.
10. Dhami, 'Religio-Political Mobilisation and Shift in the Party Support Base,' op. cit., p. 18; Dhami in 'Communalism in Punjab,' op. cit., p. 27, estimates that the Congress was 'able to secure around 14 per cent of the peasants' support' in 1980.
11. Dhami, 'Religio-Political Mobilisation and Shift in the Party Support Base,' op. cit., p. 35.
12. Puri, 'The Akali Agitation,' op. cit., p. 114.
13. Gopal Singh, 'Socio-Economic Bases of the Punjab Crisis,' op. cit., p. 43; Dhami, 'Communalism in Punjab,' op. cit., p. 27.
14. Victor S. D'Souza, 'Economy, Caste, Religion and Population Distribution: An Analysis of Communal Tension in Punjab,' *EPW*, Vol. XVII, No. 19 (8 May 1982), p. 783.
15. D'Souza, 'Economy, Caste, Religion and Population Distribution,' op. cit., p. 792.
16. Puri, 'The Akali Agitation,' op. cit., p. 116.
17. Gopal Singh, 'Socio-Economic Bases of the Punjab Crisis,' op. cit., p. 46.
18. Gopal Singh, 'Socio-Economic Bases of the Punjab Crisis,' op. cit., p. 42; Gurharpal Singh, 'Understanding the "Punjab Problem",' op. cit., p. 1275; also Iqbal Singh, *Punjab Under Siege: A Critical Analysis* (New York: Allen, McMillan and Enderson, 1986), p. 125.
19. Gurharpal Singh, 'Understanding the "Punjab Problem",' op. cit., p. 1276.
20. E.g., see Gill and Singhal, 'The Punjab Problem,' op. cit., p. 603.
21. John R. Westley, *Agriculture and Equitable Growth: The Case of Punjab-Haryana* (Boulder: Westview Press, 1986), pp. 298–319.
22. Amaresh Bagchi, 'First Award of the Ninth Finance Commission: An Appraisal,' *EPW*, Vol. XXIII, No. 49 (3 December 1988), p. 2597.
23. Pramod Kumar, *et al., Punjab Crisis: Context and Trends* (Chandigarh: Center for Research in Rural and Industrial Development, 1984), p. 62.
24. Gujral, 'The Economic Dimension,' op. cit., pp. 48–49.
25. Calculated from Government of India, Ministry of Labour, *Annual Report of the Department of Labour & Employment, 1970–71*, Vol. II (New Delhi: Government of India Press, 1972 [?], pp. 56–57 and *Report, 1980–81*, Vol. II, pp. 55–57.
26. Gujral, 'The Economic Dimension,' op. cit., p. 48.
27. E.g., Sant Jarnail Singh Bhindranwale, Address to the Sikh Congregation, translation of address thought to have been given at the Golden Temple, Amritsar in November 1983.
28. Gill and Singhal, 'The Punjab Problem,' op. cit., pp. 606–7.
29. Gopal Singh, 'Socio-Economic Bases of the Punjab Crisis,' op. cit., p. 44.
30. Yogendra Malik, 'The Akali Party and Sikh Militancy: Move for Greater Autonomy or Secessionism in Punjab?' *Asian Survey*, Vol. XXVI, No. 3 (March 1986), pp. 352–53.

31. Puri, 'The Akali Agitation,' op. cit., p. 113; Gopal Singh, 'Socio-Economic Bases of the Punjab Crisis,' op. cit., p. 43.

32. Gopal Singh, 'Socio-Economic Bases of the Punjab Crisis,' op. cit., p. 43.

33. Puri, 'The Akali Agitation,' op. cit., p. 114.

34. The few peasants I was able to interview in a tour of Amritsar and Tarn Taran in January 1990 all saw regional autonomy as a slogan meaning higher prices!

III

Ethnic Groups and the State

Introduction

The focus of the three papers in this part is on the role of the state and of government policy in the formation and/or decline of ethnic identities in multiethnic societies. Chapter 7 provides a discussion of the existing theoretical literature on these issues and presents an alternative approach which emphasizes the active role of the state and the interaction between the state and elites within ethnic groups in the process of ethnic identity formation and decline. Chapter 8 applies the theoretical framework to the two largest and most diverse multiethnic societies in the world, India and the Soviet Union. The concluding chapter 9 is a critique of the influential consociational approach to conflict resolution in deeply divided societies.

These chapters emphasize the overall importance of centralizing state policies and their consequences for patterns of elite competition within and between ethnic groups. Chapter 7 elaborates and provides further examples of the basic patterns of elite interaction identified in chapter 2 and specifies also the consequences for processes of ethnic community-building and nationality-formation of the roles played by the centralizing state in these interactions. Attention is also paid to the kinds of state strategies, institutional mechanisms, and specific policies that governments have used to control processes of ethnic identity formation and ethnic group conflict.

The arguments made in these chapters draw upon and are meant to apply to the experiences of both postindustrial and contemporary developing societies, although it is also argued that patterns of elite competition tend to change as state activities expand with the drive to industrialize. At the same time, it is also the case that the kinds of ethnic group relations and conflicts discussed in these chapters are especially relevant to contemporary developing societies and to the more diverse multiethnic states such as the Soviet Union. I believe the reasons for this special relevance arise not from the nature of ethnicity but from the nature of the modern centralizing European nation-state form, which since the end of World War II and of Western imperialism in Asia and Africa has been extended to every corner of the world. This extension has taken place despite the absence of 'nations' corresponding to the boundaries of most of the new states and despite the rise of new movements of ethnic separatism among minorities in the older European states and the Soviet Union.

During the period of Western colonial dominance in Asia and Africa, the colonial powers sought to justify their rule by demonstrating that the territories over which they ruled were unfit for independent statehood because of the cultural diversities of these societies and the antagonisms which allegedly existed among the various peoples within them. They made great efforts to count and classify the peoples within the boundaries of the territories they ruled, fitting them into 'discrete, bounded groups' where before, as Southall has noted, there were often only 'interlocking, overlapping, multiple identities.'[1] The state authorities and Christian missionaries also sometimes created entirely new categories, some of which ultimately took hold in the form of new identities, others of which did not. The European colonial state also tended to make differentiations among various categories of people, favoring some groups and ignoring others.

Simultaneously with the imposition upon the peoples of Asia and Africa of these processes of identifying, counting, classifying, and defining the boundaries of groups there developed a body of 'knowledge' about them and a theory, known as the theory of the plural society, which supported the colonial argument that such societies could not be viable independent states. The new elites who led the nationalist movements in the former colonial societies and took control of them after independence sought to counter the colonial myth with myths of their own concerning the ancient lineages of their new states and to create nations to conform to the boundaries of the new states, adopting the slogan of 'national integration'. That slogan, however, flew in the face of the existing cultural diversities and the classifications and differentiations added to them by the colonial powers, who often also attempted to manipulate ethnic differences in their struggles against the nationalist forces. Consequently, after independence, ethnic movements, parties, and leaders arose to take advantage of the greatly increased opportunities made available by the expansion of state activities that increased 'the stakes of cultural competition'.[2]

Close scrutiny of the methods used by the colonial state to identify, describe, and virtually 'charter' ethnic groups supports the idea argued in chapter 1 and again in chapter 7 that it is often a mistake to think of cultural categories in multiethnic societies as 'givens'. Moreover, the use of such methods indicates clearly the differentiating role of the modern state which divides some ethnic groups and seeks to unify others, allying now with one elite group, now with another in the process simplified and reviled by nationalist leaders as the policy of 'divide and rule.'

In the process of consolidation of colonial rule and in the transition to independence, the activities of the state increase, precipitating a change in the nature of ethnic relations. In the early stages of colonial rule, the main issues are local control and the search by the authorities for favored collaborators. Elite competition and the state's search for collaborators tend at this stage to focus primarily on local aristocracies and religious elites. In the later stages and in the postindependence period, issues of differential access by ethnic groups to new economic opportunities made available by an expanding state become increasingly prominent. At this point, issues concerning the language of education and the official state language become particularly important.

Issues of ethnic group competition for economic resources and struggles for recognition of a group's language are, however, by no means confined to postcolonial developing states. Such issues have arisen even in the postindustrial societies of the West and in the late 1980s most evidently in the Soviet Union. Chapter 8 in this part compares and contrasts these issues in India and the Soviet Union and relates the development of ethnic group competition and language conflicts to centralizing state policies and patterns of elite competition.

It is argued in chapter 8 that ethnic group conflicts in these two states have not affected all groups equally and at all times. There is nothing given, natural, or inevitable about the rise of ethnic group conflicts in either the Soviet Union or India. Like ethnic conflicts everywhere, their prominence at particular times among specific groups requires contextual rather than teleological explanations. The factors emphasized in chapter 8 are the relations between the centralizing state and regional ethnic elites, whether or not one ethnic group and one language are perceived to be dominant and to stand in the way of the advancement of other ethnic groups, and the extent to which the state leadership recognizes the cultural, linguistic, and religious rights of minority ethnic groups or seeks to deny such rights or intervene in local ethnic group conflicts for its own political advantage.

Of particular importance in the rise of ethnic group conflicts in multiethnic states are changes in the political context and in the balance of center–periphery relations which arise especially under three types of circumstances: during transfers of power from colonial to postcolonial states, during succession struggles, and at times when central power appears to be weakening or the balance in center–periphery relations appears to be changing. At such points, the relationships between the center and particular regions of the country may be renegotiated and new alliances may be formed with particular elites within ethnic groups or with spokesmen for segments of ethnic groups (such as caste or dialect groups within a speech community or sectarian groups within a religious community), precipitating new ethnic movements.

It follows from the explanations for ethnic mobilization and conflict given in this section and throughout the book, which emphasize state policies and elite competition, that conflict resolution in multiethnic states must focus on center–regional relations and elite group interactions. Policies of state centralization which at the same time select regional collaborators in their policies from among particular ethnic group elites will ultimately produce counterelites within the regions to challenge their regional rivals and the centralizing state allied with them. Under some circumstances such countermovements may turn secessionist. Consequently, state leaders who wish to avoid such movements will have to consider decentralization of power and economic decisionmaking and de-centering of ethnic group relations by playing the role of mediator in regional conflicts rather than intervening directly in them except as protector of those without power.

It is here that the link between assumptions about the nature of ethnicity and nationalism, explanations for ethnic group mobilization and interethnic group conflict, and modes of ethnic conflict resolution become clear. Those who begin with assumptions concerning the naturalness of ethnicity and the inevitability of ethnic group demands for political recognition and of ethnic group conflict in multiethnic societies will naturally reach different conclusions concerning their resolution. This is most evident in the school of conflict resolution for deeply divided societies, which goes by the name of consociationalism. This school of thought, criticized in the concluding chapter, proposes a new principle of representation for such societies as an alternative to the predominant liberal, adversarial system of representation based on the principle of open competition of individual interests. The consociational principle, in contrast, is based on the idea that identity, not interest, is the mainspring of political behavior, that conflict of identities is dangerous, and that, therefore, it is better to freeze and accommodate differences between groups than to permit their resolution through competition.

The model for consociationalism was built from the experiences of the Netherlands and Belgium where, it is argued, ethnic conflicts have been settled through various devices of group representation. Covell, however, has shown that ethnic conflicts in Belgium–like those in contemporary developing countries or in the Soviet Union in the 1980s and 1990s—have been primarily about access to resources for groups.[3] The consociational devices in Belgium were not developed to resolve 'violent societal conflicts,' but were rather mechanisms by which elites 'defend[ed] their own position and that of their following.'[4] In fact, elites have used these mechanisms for conflict purposes, when necessary, to pursue their interests, with the result that conflict has increased rather than declined as a consequence of their adoption. In other words, the group representation and consociational devices adopted in Belgium were not designed to resolve conflict but to pursue interest and gain control over resources.

Consociationalism, therefore, like the theory of the plural society from which it derives as a 'solution' to the allegedly otherwise insoluble problems of conflict-ridden societies, suffers from the deficiencies of its own assumptions. It reifies ethnicity, treats it as a 'given,' assumes the solidarity of group identities, and therefore arrives at the conclusion that ethnic conflicts cannot be resolved except in a political order based on group representation. If, however, one takes the view that the assumptions are wrong, then consociationalism appears as a mystification of ethnicity and

ethnic group conflicts which accepts at face value the justifications
used for its adoption by those who stand to benefit from it.

NOTES

1. Crawford Young, 'Ethnicity and the Colonial and Post-Colonial State in Africa,'
   in Paul R. Brass (ed.), *Ethnic Groups and the State* (London: Croom Helm,
   1985), p. 74, citing Aidan Southall, 'The Illusion of Tribe,' *Journal of Asian and
   African Studies*, Vol. V, Nos. 1–2 (January–April 1970), p. 36.
2. Young, 'Ethnicity and the Colonial and Post-Colonial State in Africa,' op. cit.,
   p. 85.
3. Maureen Covell, 'Ethnic Conflict, Representation and the State in Belgium,' in
   Brass, *Ethnic Groups and the State*, op. cit., pp. 228–61.
4. Covell, 'Ethnic Conflict, Representation and the State in Belgium,' op. cit.,
   p. 255.

7

Ethnic Groups and the State

INTRODUCTION

The theme of this chapter is the effects of the state, its official ideologies, its structural forms, its alliance strategies, and its specific policies upon ethnic identity formation. Ethnic identity formation is viewed as a process that involves three sets of struggles. One takes place within the ethnic group itself for control over its material and symbolic resources, which in turn involves defining the group's boundaries and its rules for inclusion and exclusion.[1] The second takes place between ethnic groups as a competition for rights, privileges, and available resources. The third takes place between the state and the groups that dominate it, on the one hand, and the populations that inhabit its territory on the other. Its focus is on the maintenance and extension of its control over local territories and populations and the provision of qualified manpower to administer its institutions, implement its policies, and create wealth, power, and safety for itself and its inhabitants. These three sets of struggle intersect in different ways at different times, but it is possible to specify particular patterns of elite competition within and between ethnic groups, the role of the state in each pattern, and the potential consequences of each pattern for ethnic identity formation and political mobilization.

Most available theories that touch directly or indirectly on the issue of the relationship between ethnic groups and the state are deficient in one or more respects to deal adequately with the issues raised in this chapter. Several problems recur in the literature on ethnic groups and the state that prevent a proper appreciation of the role of the latter in relation to internal struggles for control of ethnic communities and competition between ethnic groups. One concerns the treatment of the state, that is, whether it is to be seen as an instrument of a class or an ethnic group or as a relatively autonomous force, as a distributor of privileges or a promoter of justice and equality among groups, as an impartial arena for conflict resolution or a partial intervenor in societal conflicts.

A second set of problems concerns the categories to be used in the analysis of society and how they are to be defined. Is the study of ethnicity a sub-branch of interest group politics or of class analysis or a separate subject in its own right? Or, to put it another way, are interest groups, classes and ethnic groups to be treated as analytically separable and coequivalent or is one or another category primary?

A third set of problems concerns the level of analysis and the central theoretical issue or issues. Most sociological theories that are relevant to a discussion of ethnic groups and the state focus on society as a whole and take as their main theoretical issue the conditions for conflict or cohesion, national integration or internal war and treat the societal units—interest groups, classes, or ethnic groups—as givens rather than as objects for examination themselves. Too often neglected is the issue of how identity and cohesion within groups are formed and maintained in the first place, how political mobilization of groups occurs, and how and why both group cohesion and mobilization often decline. It is not that there is no literature on the latter question but that its insights tend to be neglected when scholars move to the societal level.

The discussion in this chapter on these matters will be divided into five sections. The next section will take up the issue of the role of the state in relation to social conflicts. It will be argued that the state inevitably plays a differentiating role as a distributor of privileges among groups. The following section will take up the issue of the relevant units of analysis—interest groups, classes, and ethnic groups—and how they should be defined and analyzed. It will be argued in this section that the tendency to reification and objectification of categories, particularly those of class and ethnic group, class, and ethnic group—must be treated as analytically distinct. The next section will take up issues of conflict, integration, and identity. The dangers of treating social groups, particularly ethnic identity. The dangers of treating social groups, particularly ethnic groups, as givens and of assuming the inevitability of disintegrative conflict among them will be discussed. It will be argued that, although conflict between ethnic groups is endemic in multiethnic societies, neglect of the internal conflicts within them distorts both history and attitudes toward the future of such societies.

The last section presents an alternative perspective on ethnicity and the state that focuses on identity formation and elite competition within and between ethnic groups. It will be asserted in this section that, although the state inevitably plays a critical role in conflicts within and between ethnic groups and that its role is always in some sense partial, its policies can be assessed and evaluated as more or less conducive to political integration and more or less favorable to particular ethnic groups. However, the ethnic groups favored by state policies are not necessarily the dominant groups.

THE STATE AS A DIFFERENTIATING FORCE

Recent revivals of discussion on the origins, composition, and character of the modern state have focused primarily on two sets of issues. One concerns the question of the relative independence or dependence of the modern state upon the units which it encompasses, the units being individuals and interest groups for some theorists, classes or ethnic groups for others. The second set of issues focuses on whether the modern state is to be seen as a promoter of equality and distributive justice or as a promoter of uneven development among regions, classes, and ethnic groups and a distributor of privilege.

Most contemporary theories of the modern state can be broadly distinguished in terms of whether or not they see the state as an arena, as an instrument of group domination, or as a relatively autonomous entity with interests and strategies of its own. The first view arises out of the group pluralist perspective. The second is held in common by both classical Marxists and by theorists of the plural society. The third point of view has been developed most systematically by a number of contemporary neo-Marxist theoreticians.

The Group Pluralist Perspective

In the group pluralist or interest group perspective, the state is seen as a largely neutral arena of interest group conflict. The results of such conflict may be that the state adopts policies, distributes resources, or creates agencies specifically of relevance to particular categories of the population. Those policies, resources, and agencies themselves may then become catalysts for further interest group organization. The state then in the group pluralist approach is seen as both a responder to the demands of organized groups in the society and as a precipitator in the formation of new groups, including ethnic groups. However, the state is not in this perspective a force that acts independently to prevent the organization of particular groups or to facilitate the organization of others.[2] The state is viewed neither as dominated by the groups that contest in its arena nor as an autonomous force in relation to them. Rather, it is seen as a more or less neutral agency whose policies are the products of the encounters of groups in conflict.

The ethnocentrism of this view of the state will be evident to many specialists in comparative politics and history. It derives from observation of American politics primarily, though it has been extended to western democratic societies generally. Obviously, it is not of much relevance to absolutist states, to contemporary authoritarian states, and to other societies where groups are not permitted to organize freely or are 'chartered by the state in accordance with the state's and not the groups' ' own interests.[3] A more serious criticism of the group pluralist conception of the state as a neutral arena arises from the fact that, even in the liberal democratic states, access of groups to policy making is often selectively controlled.[4] In many cases, particular interest organizations succeed, with the help of the state, in capturing virtually monopolistic control over some policy areas for long periods of time, a point to which I will return below.

Neo-Marxist, Core–periphery, and Internal Colonial Theories

At the other extreme from the group pluralist view of the state as a neutral arena are the formulations of some Marxists and neo-Marxists who view the state as an instrument of domination. In the classical Marxist view, the state is not only partial rather than neutral, it is the instrument of one class, the bourgeoisie, in its struggles with the proletariat. It is 'an organ of class domination, an organ of oppression of one class by another.'[5] This classical Marxist view of the state has been modified considerably in recent years by two groups of theorists working in the Marxist frame of reference. One group of neo-Marxists, including such writers as Althusser, Habermas, Poulantzas, and O'Connor, has moved to the view that the modern industrial non-Communist state is not simply a product of the class struggle but is a relatively autonomous force.[6] In this view, the managers of the state apparatus develop interests of their own, particularly an interest in maintaining their power and control, which may lead them to act independently of or even against the wishes of the dominant bourgeois groups. Some neo-Marxists even approach the group pluralist school in seeing the modern industrial and post-industrial state 'as a field of power balance and conflict resolution,'[7] although one that is not neutral with respect to maintaining the existing capitalist order as a whole.

A second group of neo-Marxist theorists, those associated with the core–periphery and internal colonial perspectives particularly, have modified the classical Marxist position in another direction by bringing ethnic struggles to the forefront. The first group of neo-Marxists have noted that the modern capitalist state has played a protective and even an emancipatory role in relation to some minority and disadvantaged groups, but their spokesmen have ignored or treated only in the most peripheral way the roles of ethnic groups generally in the modern state. The second group of neo-Marxist theorists, however, have gone much further and have argued in fact that, under present conditions, ethnic struggles are more pervasive and salient than class struggles. The reason for this state of affairs is that the capitalist world economy and imperialist state expansion have led to a differential distribution of state resources and valued employment opportunities among ethnic groups.[8]

Although the core–periphery and internal colonial theorists do not directly take up the issue of the relative autonomy of the modern capitalist state, the implications of their position can only be that its autonomy is restricted in two ways. It is embedded externally in a world economic system in relation to which it cannot act independently.[9] Internally, it is dominated by minority or plurality ethnic groups engaged in the differential distribution of privilege. For Wallerstein, the essence of the modern state is not its relative autonomy but its role as a distributor of privileges and a differentiator among ethnic groups. In another formulation by Hechter, the modern capitalist state is an upholder of a 'cultural division of labor' that distributes valued jobs and economic development unevenly, in such a way that the core region of the country controls the best jobs while the peripheral regions are dependent upon the core and ethnic groups that inhabit those regions are confined to the least skilled and prestigious jobs.[10]

The State in the Plural Society

The neo-Marxist view of the state as an instrument of domination by privileged ethnic groups is one which is shared with the school of pluralist thought associated with Furnivall and M.G. Smith. In their conceptions of the plural society, defined as a social order consisting of institutionally segmented cultural groups living 'side by side, yet without mingling, in one political unit,' one cultural section monopolizes power,[11] controls the state apparatus, and dominates over other cultural groups who are admitted to participation in their own governance in a limited way, if at all. Furnivall, of course, had in mind colonial societies created by conquest and regulated in the interests of colonial capitalists, which were sharply distinguished from Western democratic societies. Smith, however, who extended the definition of plural societies to both postcolonial and to some contemporary industrial societies, saw the form of the state arising not out of conquest but out of the 'cultural incompatibility' of its plural parts, which made it impossible for the members of different cultural groups to act as citizens in a common political enterprise and, therefore, inevitable that the stronger group would use the state as an instrument of domination over the others.[12] In fact, the society could be maintained at all only by domination. In short, the political form of the plural society was a 'despotism' of one cultural group, usually a minority, over others.[13]

The Differentiating Role of the State

It is apparent that most contemporary theories of the state, with the exception principally of the group pluralist theory, view the state as either always dominated by particular social forces, a particular class or ethnic group or combination of classes and/or ethnic groups, or as at most relatively autonomous from the dominant social, economic, or ethnic groups in society. Some theories of the state refer only to a particular type of society, such as the internal colonial type or the plural society, and allow for the existence of other types of states and societies and state–society relations. Such theories, however, tend at most to present dichotomous or trichotomous classifications of states.[14] All these theories, however, derive from more or less holistic models of state–society relationships that are convincing only if one accepts their underlying assumptions. Moreover, none of the theories provides an adequate basis for analyzing the state and its policies separately from the groups that compose society. Some of the neo-Marxists argue that the state is relatively autonomous from the dominant classes in society, but not from the capitalist economic order as a whole, which it acts to preserve.

If one is not willing to begin an analysis of ethnicity and the state with a set of assumptions derived from one of the prevailing models and one wishes to consider the specific relationships established between the state and social groups over time, how then is one to proceed? An analysis by Rae of the attempts by contemporary states to pursue egalitarian policies and the inevitable contradictions involved in their attempts to do so provides an alternative kind of beginning from prevailing theories that is free from their assumptions.[15] Rae's analysis shows that one does not have to accept the underlying ideological premises behind Wallerstein's description of the modern liberal state or that of anyone else to accept the argument that it, in common with all states, is always engaged in the differential distribution of resources among categories in the population. Even when the state sets out to be 'ostentatiously egalitarian,' it must choose, as Rae has pointed out, between types of 'equalitarian' policies that invariably favor some groups or categories in the population and discriminate against others.[16] Moreover, it often does so for reasons of its own convenience as well as to favor or protect particular groups against others.

Most modern states either select certain categories of the population for favored or protected treatment or select certain areas of life in which inequality will be prohibited, or establish rules that distribute inequalities in life impartially, or randomly. They do so for a variety of reasons. The state may be controlled by a class or ethnic group or some combination of classes and/or ethnic groups, whose members it chooses to favor. Or, the dominant groups may seek support among certain categories in the population and may adopt an 'equalitarian' policy for that purpose. Or the state may choose a particular equalitarian strategy for its own administrative convenience. Such choices may be faced both by postindustrial and contemporary developing societies.

It is sometimes assumed that the state, through such 'equalizing' policies as 'affirmative action' and 'protective discrimination,' actually creates or precipitates the formation of new identities among various categories of persons. In some cases, it may in fact do so, in other cases such new identities may be quite shallow and temporary. However, such policies never precipitate organization among all relevant categories of the population. Consequently, the identification of groups for whom claims are made in response to such state policies should be the beginning not the end of analysis.

Likely to be far more important in affecting the identity, cohesion, and mobilization of particular ethnic groups than specific govern-ment policies are the selection by governments of particular leaderships, elites, and organizations within an ethnic group as collaborators or channels for the transmission of government patronage. Sometimes, a government is more or less compelled to accept and collaborate with a leadership or elite group that arises independently, but government support may then reinforce and sustain a dominance achieved by the group's leadership. At other times, government's decision to collaborate with a particular leadership or elite may be made before any political mobilization takes place and may prevent it or channel it in ways that either preserve an existing sense of community among a group of people or forestall its development.

The main point to be noted here is that the government or the state is not simply an arena in which competing groups or interests work out their conflicts and shape policies that then precipitate the formation of new groups. Rather, the government or the state tends to work through specific leaderships and groups over long periods of time and to go for advice to selected leaders and elites in shaping its policies. Sometimes a particular leadership within a group may even gain control over an entire area of government policy and the institutions associated with it and use them as a means for consolidating their leadership of their own community. Many examples of this process have been documented for economic and professional interest groups in the US, such as the American Farm Bureau Federation's dominance in the agricultural community or the American Medical Association's dominance in the medical community, both made possible not only by persistent government patronage and support but by the control over government policy and institutions maintained by these organizations themselves. Research on ethnic groups and the state must explore these kinds of relationships and their effects on ethnic identity, mobilization, and control.

The view of the state that is being proposed to facilitate this kind of analysis is more in accord with the relative autonomy neo-Marxist perspective than with the classical Marxist or group pluralist perspective. That is, the state is not simply an arena for group conflict nor an instrument for class domination but a relatively autonomous entity that tends, however, both to favor some classes and ethnic groups at particular points in time and also to develop relationships with elites within selected communities to serve its own interests. Those interests include local control, administrative convenience, and the gathering of popular support. Even when the state attempts to adopt an equalitarian set of policies, it cannot usually succeed for reasons pointed out by Rae. However, the state is not simply a policy-producing mechanism balancing different notions of equality against each other. Every state, rather, tends to support particular groups, to distribute privileges unequally, and to differentiate among various categories in the population.

The above argument does not imply that the state always and inevitably takes a stand on the side of one group or another in conflict situations. Often it does. However, the state may choose to remain 'neutral' at times when groups are in conflict. Neutrality, however, like egalitarianism, is a difficult strategy to pursue and not only because groups in conflict nearly always seek the support of the state. It is diffcult also because a neutral policy often means, in effect, support for the status quo, a refusal to rectify an existing imbalance between groups.

Finally, although it seems most appropriate to begin with the notion that the state can be and is most often a relatively independent, if not a dominant, actor this is not to deny that it can also

be captured by particular groups or segments of a society for long
periods of time. The main point here is that the state invariably
makes distinctions, classifies its populations and distributes resources differentially. It is a principal task of research on ethnic
groups and the state to determine how privileges are distributed
among different ethnic categories, with which elites within an
ethnic group state leaders tend to collaborate, and what the
consequences of both are for ethnic group identity formation and
political mobilization.

CLASS, ETHNICITY, AND INTEREST

Deciding how to analyze the role of the state obviously resolves
only half of the problem in the analysis of the relations between
ethnic groups and the state. Several issues recur in the literature
on ethnicity concerning the other half of the problem. They include:
how to treat ethnic groups on their own terms, how to treat them
in their relations with other social formations, and how to analyze
processes of ethnic identity formation within ethnic groups.

The first issue is the familiar one of whether or not ethnic groups
have a reality of their own or are better seen as subtypes of or
substitute formations for other forces, such as classes or interest
groups. Even in a study of ethnicity and the state, most Marxists
would argue either that classes remain the relevant units of analysis
or that ethnic groups can be properly understood only in relation
to class categories and formations. The group pluralists see neither
classes nor ethnic groups as the relevant units but individuals and
concrete, membership groups. Classes and ethnic groups are artificial categories for the group pluralists whose focus is on explicitly
organized groups and their relations to individuals, to each other,
and to the state. Ethnic groups or classes become relevant only
insofar as they establish concrete membership organizations that
pursue their interests. At that point, the principal question
becomes how effectively or genuinely the group does in fact
'represent'—in all the meanings of the term—its 'constituency'.
The cultural pluralists, that is, the school founded by Furnivall and
Boeke and continued by Smith, Schermerhorn, Kuper, and van
den Berghe has tended either to see ethnic groups and cultural

communities as the principal social formation in contemporary states, or as at least coequivalent with and not reducible to any other kind of formation, such as class or interest.

Many difficult analytical issues could be avoided if it were possible to accept the view that ethnic groups are simply a type of interest group seeking resources in and from the modern state. However, it is not possible to adopt such a view for three reasons. First, ethnic groups are centrally concerned with cultural matters, symbols, and values and with issues of self-definition that distinguish them from other types of interest associations. Second, the interest group approach pays attention only to groups formally organized to press demands upon the state, whereas the organizations of many ethnic groups are internal to the community. Many ethnic groups of potential political significance would thus be ignored in a strict interest group analysis. Third, interest group analysis pays no attention at all to potential groups, to categories of people that may or' may not develop internal organization and/or enter the political arena as interest groups in the future. For the latter two reasons, scholars who rely on interest group analysis are nearly always taken by surprise when class or ethnic movements suddenly burst forth in a political arena previously dominated by conventional interest associations.

At the other extreme from the interest group approach that seriously considers only concrete membership groups are those types of sociological and political analyses that focus on classes and ethnic categories, but reify or objectify them or treat them as 'givens'. By reification, I mean the tendency to attribute to mere categories a reality that they may not have or that may be merely temporary. By objectification, I mean the assumption that one or another category, class or ethnic group, represents a primal reality or has a greater significance or is more 'fundamental' than others. Objectification is, of course, common among Marxists who assign an objective reality and primacy to class and class conflict. Objectification is to a large extent built into Marxist analyses of whole societies, though not necessarily into the analyses of processes of class formation. Objectification is also a feature of the work of many specialists in ethnicity, particularly those who emphasize the 'primordial' character of ethnic groups and nations. If interest group analysts tend to be caught unawares by the sudden florescence of new political movements, class and ethnic group analysts tend to be surprised by the waning of revolutionary movements or the ebb and flow of ethnic movements or the rise of ethnic movements where class movements were anticipated.[17]

Of course, these choices regarding the appropriate stance to be taken with regard to the categories we use as social scientists raise fundamental epistemological issues.[18] One concerns how we can talk about groups at all rather than individuals, which is a subject that cannot be addressed here. Another is whether or not some ways of talking about groups are closer to reality than others. Many social scientists avoid such issues entirely by arguing that all analytical and conceptual choices in the social sciences involve arbitrariness and that it is a form of crude empiricism to insist that our concepts mirror 'reality'. All that matters is how well the concepts succeed in predicting the outcomes of social processes.

My own view on these matters is that there is no group that has a concrete reality that can be successfully captured, whether through membership lists, studies of socioeconomic composition, or public opinion polls. If such a reality could be captured, it would constitute no more than a snapshot in time in which we arbitrarily get our subjects to hold still for the camera, as in an election or in a Gallup poll. Since all group and even individual realities, for that matter, are merely moments in time, we are forced to use categories that we think reflect underlying realities or that we anticipate may acquire meaning for numbers of people in future.[19]

My point here is not that it is a mistake either to be too concrete or too arbitrary in our selection of categories of analysis, but that concreteness is momentary and categoric groups are arbitrary constructions that are useful as ways of bringing into focus long-term processes of change. If we want to study variations and be prepared for change, we need to focus on categoric groups, while avoiding reification and objectification of them. One method of avoiding or minimizing the consequences of reification and objectification is to bring in a distinction between subjective and objective social formations. A second is to make use of sub-units of analysis that are not merely concrete in the sense of voting or membership units, but are identifiable on-going elements and potential building blocks in the construction, in reality, of the categories in question. In this chapter, those elements are elites, defined as leadership segments with concrete characteristics and statuses, whose actions are critical in determining whether or not such categoric groups as classes and ethnic communities will be mobilized for political purposes or not. The importance of the subjective–objective distinction is what is primarily at issue in this section. The question of subgroup analysis will be discussed in the next section.

Most Marxists and some specialists in ethnicity make a distinction between objective and subjective formations that at least avoids problems of reification if not of objectification. For Marxists, whose focus is on the conditions for revolutionary change, the important question is not one of membership in concrete groups but of consciousness. What matters is not whether or not members of different ethnic groups, for example, belong to the same trade union, but whether they perceive their unity and separateness as a class from the owners and managers of the means of production and the fact that their interests are fundamentally opposed to those of the owners. If they do not, it is either because their class consciousness has not yet developed because of failures of class leadership or because of some form of false consciousness.

Among some specialists in ethnicity, a distinction is made between objectively distinct cultural categories and subjectively conscious communities that corresponds to the Marxist class-in-itself and class-for-itself distinction. For such scholars, the study of ethnic groups in society must be preceded or informed by an analysis of the conditions that lead to the creation of ethnic communities from ethnic categories in the first place and of an appreciation of the degree of selfconsciousness that exists among ethnic groups in the society in question. Not all scholars of ethnicity, however, accept this distinction. For many, the array of ethnic groups in a society at a particular point in time is a given. What matters for ethnic group relations and societal order is the degree of differentiation among the groups on various measures and their extent of isolation, compartmentalization, and autonomy.

The distinction between objective and subjective formations is, therefore, much better accepted among Marxists than among specialists in ethnicity. On the other hand, problems of objectification are more common among the former than the latter. The tendency among Marxists to read class interest behind ethnic movements is far more common than any tendency among ethnic analysts to read ethnic sentiment behind class movements.

When it comes to analyzing the processes of movement from

objective to subjective formations and the interrelations between classes and ethnic groups, ethnic group analysts tend to be more attentive to questions of class than class analysts to questions of ethnicity. Marxists who analyze the movement of a class-in-itself to a class-for-itself or who are concerned with the relations between the state and the dominant social class use concepts such as degree of differentiation among classes or that of class fraction. These concepts, however, all focus on the relationship between classes or segments of classes to the mode of production and/or to the mode of appropriation of surplus value. They do not usually discuss the differentiation of classes in terms of ethnicity because economic interest is generally considered pre-emptive. A major exception to this general trend among Marxists, however, is the school of neo-Marxists that adopt the core–periphery and internal colonial perspectives.

Although I have said that contemporary specialists in ethnicity are likely to be more attentive to questions of class, this has not always been so. M.G. Smith analyzed the divisions of the plural society nearly exclusively in terms of its cultural segments and did not bother to differentiate those segments in terms of class. Other contemporary proponents of the cultural pluralist school, including Kuper and especially van den Berghe have, however, rectified this neglect of class among theorists of the plural society and have developed complex and sophisticated analyses of the interrelations between class and ethnicity in the plural society. It has even been argued that the neo-Marxist internal colonial school and the theory of the plural society have, in effect, merged.[20]

The significance of the theoretical problems just discussed and the consequences of different approaches to them for understanding the relationships between ethnic groups and the state can best be illustrated by contrasting the approaches of the core–periphery and internal colonial schools, on the one hand, and that of the theorists of the plural society, on the other hand.

The Core–Periphery and Internal Colonial Approaches

With regard to the core–periphery and internal colonial approaches, four points are especially relevant to this discussion. The first is that Wallerstein and Hechter each assert the analytical distinctiveness of both class and status or ethnic group.[21] Second, Wallerstein takes the position that both ethnicity and class boundaries are fluid.[22] Third classes have, however, an underlying objective reality that ethnic groups do not. Moreover, despite his explicit rejection of the idea that ethnic group consciousness is a form of 'false consciousness,' Wallerstein brings the notion of 'false consciousness' back in when he defines 'status groups' as 'blurred collective representations of classes,'[23] which will emerge once again when ethnic conflicts recede. For, the 'fundamental political reality' of the contemporary world is the existence of a capitalist world economy and of 'class struggle' within it. The form that the class struggle takes, however, changes constantly, sometimes taking the 'overt' (true?) form of 'class consciousness,' sometimes taking the (false?) form of 'ethno-national consciousness'.[24]

It should be evident that it only confuses matters to insist, as Wallerstein does, that the class struggle is the underlying reality and class consciousness and ethnic group consciousness the two forms that it takes. Nothing but ideology or a reified construct such as the capitalist world system can justify attributing to class any greater reality than status group. Both need to be defined in both objective and subjective terms. The issue before the social scientist is to specify the conditions under which any set of objective criteria in a social order, whether they be the common economic circumstances in which different individuals are placed or the cultural markers shared by people, become transformed into subjectively felt bases for identification with a group and for common action to achieve group goals.

Class and Ethnicity in the Plural Society

In the view of the plural society articulated by Furnivall and Smith, the fundamental social reality was the existence of 'cultural sections,' each living 'its own life' separately from the others, meeting only in a very limited way outside the marketplace.[25] In Smith's view, these sections constituted corporate groups whose basic institutions were distinctive and intact. Insofar as these separate cultural groups interacted with each other in the political arena, their relations were marked by dominance and subordination or by conflict. The Furnivall–Smith pluralist view is very much the obverse, therefore, of the classical Marxist view.

Several adherents of the cultural pluralist school, particularly Kuper and van den Berghe, have moved away from the Furnivall–Smith model,[26] as have Wallerstein and Hechter from the classical Marxist model of society. Van den Berghe in particular has insisted that classes and ethnic groups must be treated as analytically distinct, open and fluid, and not reducible to each other.[27] What is missing from van den Berghe's work, as well as from that of other theorists of the plural society, is a dynamic schema that permits an analysis of the interrelationships among elites and leadership groups *within* ethnic groups and classes. It is not enough to say that ethnic groups and classes are fluid and permeable. One must also have a method of analyzing the fluidity and permeability.

Neither van den Berghe nor any of the other theorists of the plural society have provided any methods or approaches for analyzing the internal workings of the separate cultural groups and the types of differentiation that exist within them. The task they propose for the analyst is not to analyze the internal dynamic processes of change and interaction within the group, but is the static one of classifying the various institutions of each group,[28] comparing them to the institutions of other groups, and thereby judging the degree of incompatibility and the likely lines of conflict among them. One gets no sense from these theorists of the internal controversies over dogma, dialect, reform, and power that invariably take place within any large, sophisticated, and complex cultural group. Associated with this deficiency is another: the absence of any tools or methods to analyze processes of intergroup relations and communication.

Summary

In this section, I have attempted to clarify a few distinctions and to indicate some of my own assumptions. The first distinction is between interest groups, on the one hand, and social categories, on the other hand. Classes and ethnic groups are unlike concrete membership groups in that they have to be analyzed both as objective categories and as subjective communities. Nor is there any underlying objective reality for either class or ethnic group. Rather, there are a multiplicity of ways in which economic and cultural categories within these two sets will become subjective groups and/or concrete membership groups such as political parties, interest groups, or sovereign states. The specific theoretical problem raised in this volume is what role the state and its policies may play in this process.

The second important distinction is between classes and ethnic groups. Although they are both categoric groups and, therefore, both distinct from membership groups, they are also to be distinguished from each other. That is, ethnic groups are not to be seen either as merely interest groups or as 'blurred collective representations of classes'. My own definitional preference is for two definitions of ethnic groups, one for objective ethnic categories and the other for subjective ethnic communities. In chapter 1, I have defined an ethnic category as 'any group of people dissimilar from other peoples in terms of objective cultural criteria and that contains within its membership either in principle or in practice the elements for a complete division of labor and for reproduction.' An ethnic community is an ethnic category that 'has adopted one or more of its marks of cultural distinctness and used them as symbols both to create internal cohesion and to differentiate itself from other ethnic groups.'[29] In this way, one is provided with a set of definitions that corresponds to the subjective–objective distinction among Marxists between class-in-itself and class-for-itself. Ethnic groups are categories more variable than any other social formation because they can also sometimes be classes or interest groups, but what distinguishes ethnic groups clearly from both are that the former are defined in relation to cultural markers, practices, or behavior patterns and as potentially whole societies. Insofar as class is concerned, it is not necessary for my purposes to choose between competing definitions, Marxist or Weberian. The important consideration is to maintain the distinction shared by both Marxists and Weberians between classes defined objectively, whether in relation to the means of production, to the appropriation of surplus value, or to life chances in the market, and classes defined as selfconsciously organized groups ready for struggle with other classes.

The third major point of this section is to draw attention to the fact that even those theorists of class and ethnicity who have avoided reification and objectification of the categories, class and ethnic group, have not taken the next step of providing methods of analyzing the internal and external relations of class and ethnic group segments with each other and with the state. Rather, they have been concerned primarily with state–society relations as a whole, with the conflict potential of particular types of overlap or division between classes and ethnic groups, and with the issue of the relative dependence or independence of state and social structure upon each other. Insofar as Marxist class analysis is concerned, there is a tradition of analyzing internal class groupings or 'fractions' and interclass relations. There is not, however, a corresponding tradition for the analysis of intraethnic groupings.

It will be argued in the concluding section of this chapter that internal conflicts within ethnic categories for control over the material and symbolic resources of the group are of critical importance in its internal mobilization and its external relations with other groups. It will also be contended that, in this struggle for local and internal control over ethnic groups, the state and state policies also play important roles as they do in relations among ethnic groups. Before taking up the latter issues, however, I wish to pursue in the next section the consequences of more traditional forms of analysis for understanding problems of conflict and integration in multiethnic societies.

CONFLICT, INTEGRATION, AND THE STATE

The three principal types of analysis that have been discussed in this chapter, namely, the group pluralist, Marxist and neo-Marxist, and cultural pluralist modes are all essentially conflict theories. The Marxist and cultural pluralist schools in fact explicitly reject consensualist structural-functional and systems modes of analysis. The three modes differ primarily in whether or not and how they approach the question of integration at all. Most Marxists and neo-Marxists are concerned primarily with the conditions for conflict and revolution in societies and only secondarily with the methods of socialization and conflict reduction used by contemporary bourgeois states to maintain themselves. Both the group pluralist and cultural pluralist schools, in contrast, assume the existence of conflict in society, but they are ultimately concerned also very directly with the possibilities and conditions for integration of functionally and ethnically diverse societies. All three approaches, however, take a fundamentally negative view of the prospects for integration in most multiethnic and multinational societies, at least in 'the short term'.[30]

It has already been noted that the group pluralists begin with the evident functional and group diversity of modern industrial societies, from which they develop two theoretical arguments. One is that, such diversity being much less marked in totalitarian and pre-totalitarian than in democratic societies, the presence of diversity must be seen as a favorable factor in the preservation of democracy. However, diversity may or not be favorable to integration, which depends upon the cleavage structure of the society. The leading argument of this school on this matter was developed by Bentley as the theory of cross-cutting cleavages.[31] This well-known proposition states that the intensity and the disruptive consequences of conflict are reduced and cohesion enhanced in societies where individuals belong to a multiplicity of groups that criss-cross each other in such a way as to reduce the homogeneity of groups. On the other hand, where individuals belong to relatively homogeneous groups and where group membership in different types of functional and religious or ethnic groups are reenforcing, the potential for conflict is high. The theory of cross-cutting/overlapping cleavages as applied to ethnic interest groups then states that the conflict potential between ethnic groups is reduced if the members of different groups find themselves in the same functional membership groups and is enhanced if they do not. That is, if members of ethnic groups A and B belong to different churches, have different occupational spreads, read different newspapers, and belong to different social and recreational clubs, then communication between them is reduced and the potential for conflict is increased. The latter type of situation of overlapping cultural cleavages is what the cultural pluralists consider the prototypical situation of the plural society. Insofar as the group pluralists assume that such a situation is inherently conflictual in nature, their approach is similar on this issue to that of the cultural pluralists.

Most Marxists obviously see conflict arising not from overlapping cleavages, but from class struggle between selfconscious classes. Moreover, the notion of cross-cutting cleavages as an inhibitor of consciousness and conflict would most likely fall under the heading of 'false consciousness' to the extent that members of a social class see any other ties than that to class as politically significant. Most forms of ethnic identity, of course, also come under the heading of false consciousness for most Marxists and neo-Marxists.[32] However, for neo-Marxists such as Wallerstein and the internal colonial school, who treat ethnicity more centrally, ethnic conflict is considered to be endemic in multiethnic states. Wallerstein argues that it will also be the predominant form of social conflict until the class-based world-revolutionary upheaval overturns the entire world capitalist economy. Hechter argues that contemporary multiethnic industrial states contain internal colonies formed by 'imperial expansion' in which ethnicity persists and ethnic nationalism among peripheral peoples is a recurring threat to the existence of the state itself.

Two of the principal pluralists, Furnivall and Smith, were very strongly oriented towards the conflictual aspects of the plural society, which they saw arising inevitably out of the external relations of the cultural sections. Not only was conflict in the plural society endemic, it was more invasive and more intense than in other societies. Conflicts that in other societies would be considered normal, 'between town and country, industry and agriculture, capital and labour' were intensified in the plural society because the opposing sides were likely to belong to different racial or cultural groups.[33] Moreover, there is a greater tendency for conflicts 'over specific issues' between members of different groups to become 'generalized' in scope and to involve the entire group than is the case in other societies.[34] Nor did either Furnivall or Smith consider the possibility that intergroup associations and the creation of shared institutions in the modern state might 'modify the political consequences of cultural pluralism' and that it might be a matter of choice on the part of leaders in different cultural groups in plural societies to magnify or minimize cultural differences.[35]

Other exponents of the cultural pluralist school have modified the emphasis on the inevitability of conflict. Kuper, for example, argues that the relationship between pluralism and conflict is more problematic than Furnivall and Smith were prepared to concede. Such modifications notwithstanding, for all the cultural pluralists the social system of the plural society is characterized by the coexistence of culturally distinct segments whose relations with each other are potentially if not actually conflictual.[36]

Geertz's famous statement of the matter, which itself is an elaboration of an earlier statement of Shils,[37] is similar in some respects to that of the theorists of the plural society. For Geertz, the array of ethnic groups that exist in any society and the cultural baggage they carry with them are 'givens'. Ethnic identities are relatively fixed from birth or early life, are rooted in fact in the non-rational foundations of the human personality, and are, therefore, readily available for purposes of political mobilization by elites who wish to use or misuse them for political purposes. Such ethnic political mobilization brings different ethnic groups into conflict with each other and also creates a 'tension between primordial and civil politics' that can be resolved ultimately only through an 'integrative revolution'. How such an integrative revolution was to be brought about was never made clear by Geertz, but Shils, who initially formulated the problem, thought it would be brought about through the tutelage of the great liberal cosmopolitan leaders of the postcolonial developing countries: men such as Nehru, Bourguiba, and Nyerere, with whom, clearly, Shils and most other liberal intellectuals of that time felt an ideological kinship.[38]

It is remarkable to what extent the pessimism concerning the future of multiethnic states has cut across ideological and analytical boundaries. Non-national or multinational states in the developing world especially have been seen for the most part as either inherently unstable and non-viable in the long run or potentially viable only by means of an 'integrative revolution'. Existing Communist multinational states such as the Soviet Union and Yugoslavia are either considered viable only within the context of 'proletarian internationalism' or are considered multiethnic empires that will ultimately disintegrate, depending upon one's ideological perspective.

I believe that the reasons for the common negative evaluation of the viability of multiethnic societies is the tendency for nearly all analysts, when they move from the group to the societal level, to analyze societal cleavages in terms of encounters between solidary groups[39] and to be relatively inattentive to questions of identity formation and internal conflict within the groups they consider the fundamental units of society. Even where analysts are attentive to processes of identity formation, as in the case of some Marxists, they are attentive only to one type, whose beginning and end are known, that is, the formation of a class-for-itself from a class-in-itself. Absent from Marxist analyses of processes of class formation, however, is a recognition of alternative processes of identity formation with different beginnings and different end states, such as occur with ethnic formations. Most Marxists are also insufficiently attentive to specific formations or elites within particular classes, with interests of their own, whose actions may lead to other forms of social mobilization of peoples than the creation of selfconscious classes or to collaboration with other intraclass and intraethnic group formations that prevent or forestall any form of social mobilization for long periods. Moreover, when they move to societal-level analyses, most Marxists are less concerned with 'intra-grouping cleavage' than with 'conflict *between* major groupings (classes)'.[40]

Insofar as the theorists of the plural society are concerned, Furnivall and Smith saw no need to raise the issue of identity formation at all since the groups they spoke of were, in their eyes, already cohesive selfcontained entities. Van den Berghe has introduced a objective–subjective distinction into the analysis of the cultural sections of plural societies that is similar to the Marxist distinction between class category and selfconscious class. However, the cultural segments of the plural society are seen as constituting persistent objective categories in the population whose members may at any time arrive at a 'subjective perception' of the objective differences between their group and other groups[41] that may lead to intense conflict. In effect, the view presented by van den Berghe is of groups with two modes, 'objective' or inactive, and 'subjective' or active, the latter being the conflictual mode.

An alternative approach to the standard sociological model of solidary groups in conflict or evolving toward conflict is one that begins with a model of intergroup relations that assumes both the existence of subgroups within each class or ethnic category and of different relations between each subgroup within and across categorical boundaries.[42] While such an approach would maintain the objective–subjective distinction in analyzing the process of identity formation, thereby recognizing the possibility that objective categories may be selfconscious classes, ethnic communities, or nations, it would also remove the teleological assumptions from the analysis. The achievement of broad class or ethnic group consciousness would be recognized rather as a rare event, often conflictual and even pathological in its 'end state,' but usually partial and short-lived even when it seems to have reached such a state. The 'normal' reality, in contrast, would be recognized as one in which each subgroup has actual or potential relations of conflict or cooperation with every other subgroup that are *more* important or at least as important as the over-all relationship between the two groups.

It would be recognized also that, while ethnic mobilization that obliterates internal class distinctions and class mobilization that overrides ethnic distinctions may occur, it is also possible for ethnic elites from different ethnic groups to collaborate in relation to common class interests while retaining a strong sense of a separate ethnic identity. Such interethnic class collaboration may take two forms. It may be a limited, informal economic collaboration or identity of interests that does not extend to social and political relationships where ethnicity may remain primary. It may also involve more institutionalized relationships such as those that exist in 'consociational' regimes where elites from different ethnic groups collaborate on a regular basis to preserve both ethnic separateness and interethnic elite dominance in relation to subordinate classes.[43]

Such an approach would be attentive to patterns of intersectional communication and collaboration between segments of separate ethnic groups. It would also avoid the usually untenable assumption that particular states are creatures of particular classes or ethnic groups and be attentive to the more usual reality, which is one of alliance between the state and particular subgroups within a class or ethnic group. Finally, it would involve an awareness that processes of collaboration with or competition against other groups lead to new perceptions concerning one's own identity and sometimes even to new and broader or narrower identities. Thus, from this perspective, ethnic identities would not be seen as fixed for life, but as variable, subject to change according to context and circumstance. It would also involve a realization that even more variable than ethnic identities are their manifestations in political form. Finally, it would qualify the common pessimism concerning the future of multiethnic societies and lead to an appreciation of the multiple possibilities for alliance and collaboration, as well as conflict, across ethnic group boundaries and between ethnic groups and the state.

The analytical implications of the shift from focusing discussion on conflict and integration in whole societies to discussion of processes of identity formation and decline and of subgroup relationships are the subject of the next section.

ETHNICITY AND ELITE COMPETITION FOR STATE POWER, STATE RESOURCES, AND LOCAL CONTROL: AN ALTERNATIVE PERSPECTIVE

Prevailing theories of ethnic groups and the state all suffer from one or another of several problems that have been identified above: reification of either classes or ethnic groups or both; attempts to assert the primacy of one or another line of division, ethnicity or class, and to treat one as a mere representation of the other; inadequate treatment of internal divisions within classes and ethnic groups; an excessive concern with the issue of whether or not the state is an instrument of class or ethnic group domination and too little concern with specific state strategies and policies toward ethnic groups. In this section, I want to show how these problems can be avoided by adopting an alternative perspective from those discussed above.

The first step in any kind of social science analysis is to decide what the issues are and what units of analysis will be used to deal with them. In most of the literature discussed above, the issue is the possibilities of national integration in plural or multiethnic societies. The basic units of analysis are ethnic groups, generally treated as primordial groups or plural segments; classes, often presumed to have an 'objective' reality underlying social conflicts whether or not the principal cleavages are ethnic, religious, or social; and the state, defined as being more or less dominated by or autonomous in relation to classes and ethnic groups.

An alternative starting point is to raise the issue of the conditions for identity formation among different groups in society and to ask what are the consequences for group formation of different types of state strategies and policies, leaving aside for the moment the issue of the stability or permanence of the existing states. The units of analysis then become ethnic and class categories and state strategies and policies. No assumptions are made about whether or not the various ethnic and class categories are primordial, given, or 'objective' in the sense of one being more real than another. No assumptions are made about whether or not the state is an instrument of class domination or of ethnic 'parasitism'.[44]

The two intertwined issues then become: first, explaining how and why some ethnic categories and not others, in particular times and places, form themselves into selfconscious communities and take sometimes the further step of making demands for a greater share of state resources, for civil equality, for political recognition, or for sovereignty. On the other side, the issue is not, or at least not only, which groups dominate the state structure, but what specific alliance strategies and policies they follow in relation to ethnic and cultural groups. Which groups are recognized, which not recognized? How are they recognized? Many categories and groups are not even recognized by the census authorities, that is, they are not even counted in the literal sense of the term and, in such cases, do not 'count' politically in the figurative sense of the term. Some categories and groups are singled out for special protection or privilege by the state, given or denied citizenship, given or denied proportional or extra representation in electoral constituencies or government bodies or in government service. Some categories and groups are entitled to special protection of their language or religion or personal laws, some are not.

The view of the state that I wish to propose here is not that of an impartial arena in which organized interests compete and resolve their conflicts or of a relatively autonomous entity operating partly independently of the dominant classes or ethnic groups but acting to maintain a particular economic or racial order. Rather, I propose a view of the state as comprising a complex set of persisting institutions over which elites in conflict are engaged in a struggle for control. For this array of institutions, we conventionally use the shorthand term, 'the state,' which contributes to the tendency to reify this set of institutions. However, in this case, reification is not something that can be corrected by careful social science analysis. On the contrary, reification of the state is part of the process by which dominant groups in society establish either their right to rule or their right to compete for power and control over the institutions of 'legitimate authority'. The state is said to express the persisting interests, goals, and values of the 'nation'. Groups in conflict that confine their struggles to control over the existing institutions rather than to their overthrow and replacement compete for the right to carry forward those interests, goals, and values or to articulate new ones, but always for the benefit of the nation as a whole and in the interests of the state as the political form of the nation.

The state then becomes, especially in societies undergoing secularization, modernization, and industrialization both a resource and a distributor of resources, on the one hand, and a promoter of new values, on the other hand. Consequently, the state is also not simply an agency pursuing equality or distributive justice. The state and its policies are a potential benefit to some groups and communities, but they are also a threat to others, particularly to local elites and communities and to groups whose values differ from those of the secular, modernizing, industrializing state.

State strategies and policies change over time as different elites gain control over its commanding institutions, but dominant elites in society often remain in control for long periods during which they establish alliances and coalitions with other elites who control significant material or symbolic resources. In advanced industrial societies and in the larger and more complex multiethnic developing countries, one is not likely to find a small and easily identifiable 'power elite' with interlocking connections. But, it is usually possible even in such societies to identify those groups that are disproportionately represented and favored in and by state institutions and state policies and with whom they ally in the broader society.

The state is itself both a resource and a distributor of resources. It is not an abstraction, but a set of repressive, allocative, and distributive institutions and decisionmaking bodies. Its functioning is facilitated and the potential for violent conflict in the struggle for control over it is reduced if the state operates behind a veil of legitimacy and if contestants in the struggle for control operate according to widely accepted rules. Therefore, all states have a legitimating ideology or 'political formula' that provides a minimum basis of popular support for its actions irrespective of their content. The more stable regimes also have well-established procedures and conventions for securing influence or control over decisionmaking bodies that determine the content of state actions.

The state is also a threat, especially in developing or centralizing countries. Particularly in such countries, it threatens the power and authority of local elites who have previously maintained control over local populations relatively independently of or as locally autonomous agents of a central authority. It does so by the extension of its own bureaucratic apparatus for extracting resources, allocating benefits, and settling disputes. It does so also by attempting to instill loyalty to itself and its legitimating ideology in a direct relationship with the local population. Such a direct relationship is usually established by two methods: the establishment of government schools that socialize the population with a new set of values and the solicitation of popular support for new state projects and programs by leaders and political parties. Such projects and programs are usually justified by the promise of a different and better life for the people or their children and one also that will free them from the limitations and repressions of the life they have previously led under the control of locally dominant elites.

Since the state requires a legitimating ideology, it also poses a threat to the traditional controllers of symbols and values in society—the priests, *ulema*, rabbis, monks, and others—insofar as its premises are different, as they often are, from those held and taught by the latter. They tend to be different because most modern states seek to establish the bases for their authority in sources other than a deity, because they pursue secular goals, and because they arrogate to themselves the right to establish laws of behavior even in those areas such as the regulation of personal and family life that have traditionally been considered the prerogatives of the clerics or of sanctified customs and traditions interpreted by clerics.

The 'development' process in centralizing, modernizing, industrializing states is usually accompanied by struggles for control at the center over the state as resource and distributor of resources and the state as a source and promoter of new values. It also often involves struggles for control between central authorities and local elites. At the center in such societies, the struggle tends to be dominated by elites in control of bureaucratic organizations such as the military, the civilian bureaucracy, and political parties. The struggle between the center and the localities may take the form of conflict between elites at the center allying with forces in the localities opposed to the locally dominant elites or of conflict between the civilian bureaucratic apparatus or local political party organizations and local notables. The local elites are predominantly of two types: those who control the primary material resources, which is land for the most part in preindustrial societies, and those who control symbolic resources, the clerics.

Alternatively, elites at the center may choose to extend their influence at the local level by allying with the locally dominant elites or by adopting a policy of non-interference with respect to religious and cultural matters but not in economic matters. Alliances and various collaborative arrangements are commonly made between central elites and local landlords, chiefs, and feudal patrons. Decisions by the center not to interfere in local religious practices are designed to prevent opposition from local religious elites. For example, it may be decided to leave them in control of schools or to prohibit competitive proselytization by outside elements.

Clearly, both types of conflicts—for control at the center and for control over local territories and communities—take on an added significance when elites in competition are from different ethnic groups and/or use different languages. The ability to mobilize large numbers of people around symbols and values with a high emotional potential is a major, though ustable, resource that can be brought into the fray against the controllers of bureaucratic apparatuses, instruments of violence, and land. They are likely to be used most by elites who lack bureaucratic instrumentalities or instruments of violence that can be deployed at will in a struggle. That means primarily political party elites and religious elites.

Political parties that become institutionalized in the long run develop bureaucracies or extensive cadres of their own that can compete with those of the civilian and military bureaucracies. Religious elites also may control extensive networks of temples, shrines, endowments, and schools. However, in most developing countries, political party bureaucracies and cadres are not sufficiently well developed to compete effectively with or to maintain control over the civilian and military bureaucracies. The institutional resources that are controlled by religious elites, such as schools and shrines, also are usually no match for armies and state bureaucracies, though there have been notable exceptions both in Western history and in that of contemporary developing countries. For the most part, however, particularly in developing countries, political parties and religious elites are effective rivals with the civilian and military bureaucracies because of their ability to mobilize popular support and because of their control over symbolic resources and values that are needed to legitimize authority.

In industrial and postindustrial societies that have developed a consensus on fundamental values and agreement on procedures, a stable division of function develops in which mass political parties with their own bureaucracies and cadres exercise effective control over the civilian and military bureaucracies both because they have the organizational strength to do so and because they have established effective control over the deployment of the secular symbolic resources of the society. In such societies, the religious authorities either provide additional symbolic support for political authority or they remove themselves from the competitive political sphere altogether. Such societies are rare and the neat division of functions just described is fragile. Moreover, even in societies where a stable balance of this sort seems to be well-established, social and economic changes in a local community and new encroachments by already centralized states or expansions in their sphere of activities may precipitate new center–locality conflicts in which issues of language and religion come into play again and provide bases for ethnic political mobilization.[45]

The view of the state, then, that is being proposed here is not simply an arena or an instrument of a particular class or ethnic group, though it may sometimes be one or the other. More broadly, however, the state is itself the greatest prize and resource, over which groups engage in a continuing struggle in societies that have not developed stable relationships among the main institutions and centrally organized social forces. It is also a distributor of resources, which is nearly always done differentially. It is as well a threat to locally dominant landed elites and to religious leaders, particularly in developing countries. Elites who seek to gain control over the state or who have succeeded in doing so must either suppress and control central and local rivals or establish collaborative alliances with other elites. When elites in conflict lack the bureaucratic apparatus or the instruments of violence to compete effectively, they will use symbolic resources in the struggle. When elites in conflict come from different cultural, linguistic, or religious groups, the symbolic resources used will emphasize those differences.

It is not always necessary to answer the question of which groups

actually control the state apparatus and what purposes, revealed
or hidden, they hope to achieve by the policies they pursue to
assess the specific consequences for the formation, persistence, or
transformation of a group's identity and cohesion of particular
state alliance strategies and policies. The questions I propose,
rather, are how particular strategies and policies affect the formation of groups in the first place or the persistence of particular
groups already formed.

One initial aspect of state policy that has been given considerable
attention in the literature on ethnicity is the differential allocation
of state resources, particularly government jobs, among different
ethnic groups. In fact, there is a school of ethnicity or an approach
to ethnicity that takes the position that ethnic competition for state
power and state resources is the heart of the matter of ethnic group
formation.[46] Ethnic categories develop selfconsciousness and
identity when persons of that category perceive that persons from
another category are getting a disproportionate share of government jobs. Or, alternatively, it is argued that the state, by deliberately pursuing quota policies or policies of 'affirmative action,'
precipitates the formation of new ethnic groups or new identities
among previously dormant ethnic groups who wish to take advantage
of the opportunities made available by the state or resent the
benefits provided to other groups than their own, as a consequence of which they may develop a sense of being discriminated
against. In some formulations of this approach, contemporary
ethnic groups, far from being seen as primordial groups, are
viewed as merely another type of interest group among other
groups competing for scarce resources in the modern state.

The 'resource competition' approach to ethnicity has much to
recommend it because, clearly, this is a primary form in which
ethnic group relations are conducted. Treating ethnic groups as
just another type of interest group, however, is an analytical error,
for it ignores the cultural matters that are important to all ethnic
groups and that distinguish such groups from other types of interest
associations. Ethnic groups, by definition, like the state itself, are
concerned not only with material interests but with symbolic interests. Moreover, no matter how old or new, 'genuine' or 'artificial,'
rich or superficial the culture of a particular ethnic group may be,
its culture and the definition of its boundaries are critical matters
that do not arise in the same way for other interest groups. The

culture and the boundaries of an ethnic group are nearly always problematic in one sense or another. Most important, the definition and articulation of the central values of the group and, consequently; decisions concerning which persons are rightfully members of the group are matters of frequent concern within it. That means that issues of control over the community and its central values and symbolic expressions are also a matter of recurring concern.[47]

It is this dimension of group dynamics that both the plural society and the interest group schools of ethnicity overlook. The plural society theorists—and the primordialists—treat ethnic groups as unitary and given. They consider their work of characterizing these groups as done when they have specified the extent of institutional separateness of one group from another and/or the type of cross-cutting cleavages that exist between two groups. The internal struggles within the group on these very matters are ignored. The interest group theorists who concentrate only on the material demands of ethnic groups are even less concerned with these matters.

The neglect in most of the sociological and political science literature on ethnicity of matters of internal definition and control and the focus on so-called 'objective' factors has meant also an exclusive focus on ethnic group relations, which in turn are not fully understood because half the important matters are left out of account. One consequence of the attention to 'objective' factors and intergroup relations is an inability to deal with or even comprehend, let alone predict, the ebb and flow of ethnicity and nationalism among particular peoples at different times and the sometimes dramatic shifts in ethnic group identifications. Theories of the plural society, for example, cannot begin to explain why most Muslims in south India with similar Islamic values and institutions to those of Muslims in the north have had more peaceful relations with Hindus on the whole than Muslims in the north and did not support the Pakistan movement until its closing stages, why the Pakistan movement could not provide a sustaining ideology for the Pakistan state after independence, why that state ultimately disintegrated in 1971, and why its future remains still uncertain. For the theorists of the plural society, the Muslims of India would be simply a plural segment, rather than a category containing a multiplicity of different ethnic groups, ideological tendencies, and religious sects. If they were to probe deeper, they might argue that there were plural segments within the broader Muslim plural segment, they might also argue consistently with their theoretical position that differences in intergroup relations with Hindus—an even more dubious plural segment—explain the differential orientations of Muslims in north and south India. However, they would still not be in a position to understand or predict the course of identity formation, intergroup relations, and political demands because their theory does not direct them to the intergroup conflict within the various Muslim communities for self-definition and for control that are indispensable to a full understanding of the rise, decline, and resurgence of Muslim separatism in South Asia.

Nor can the interest group theorists provide any help on these matters, for their theory offers no basis for distinguishing one ethnic group from another. They are all treated as if they were creatures of the opportunities made available by the state. They come and go as the opportunities come and go. But the facts are otherwise: some come and go, but some remain to fight another day, often in different clothes. Those that do remain are the ones that are engaged in internal struggles as well as making external demands. In fact, it can be asserted that *only* those ethnic groups that do engage in recurring internal argument and struggles for control over the meanings of the values and symbols of the group and over its boundaries are likely to have sufficient dynamism to persist through time.

A recognition of the critical importance of intragroup struggles for control and of the right to speak on behalf of the group also helps to resolve the persisting difficulties in the literature on ethnicity that arise from reification and objectification of the categories, ethnic group and class, and that have made most treatments of the relations between class and ethnicity deficient in one way or another. For, once it is recognized that the processes of ethnic—and class—identity formation and of intergroup relations always have a dual dimension, of interaction/competition with external groups and of an internal struggle for control of the group, then the direction for research on ethnicity and on the relationships between ethnic groups and the state are clear. It becomes critical to have analytical categories that can be used to analyze both the internal conflicts and the external relations of the group and the points of intersection between the two.

Without such categories, it is not possible to analyze with any precision the relations between the state and ethnic groups. For, state authorities do not deal with abstractions and with solidary groups, but with particular leaders and elites. At times, they hope that the leaders and elites with whom they choose to deal can carry their group with them solidly as a support for the legitimacy of the state or as a bank of votes for the ruling party. At other times, they hope that the leaders with whom they ally have sufficient influence to divide a group that has opposed the state or the ruling party.

In chapter 1, I have shown that it is possible to specify the major lines of division within and between ethnic groups both in pre-industrial and in industrializing societies, the possible conflicts and alignments that may develop between elites, and the consequences of particular conflicts and alliances for ethnic group identity and politicization.[48] In preindustrial societies, the primary issues are not, in fact, allocation of state resources, but control of local communities, which is an issue both within ethnic groups and between ethnic groups and external forces, including other ethnic groups and the state. Since in preindustrial societies, the principal source of political and economic power is control over the land and the principal source of social control is religion, the main lines of conflict involve the local landowning and religious elites in conflict with each other or with alien elements.

In the struggle for control over local communities, three characteristic lines of conflict may develop with different consequences for identity formation and for state control (see Figure 7.1). One potential line of conflict is between a local aristocracy attempting to maintain its privileges against an alien conquering group or against centralizing state power. In that struggle, the local aristocracy may choose to fight and to mobilize the community by an appeal to ethnic or religious values or it may choose to collaborate, thereby postponing or preventing ethnic mobilization and nationalism. Most native aristocracies choose the second path when it is left open to them. A second line of conflict is between competing religious elites from different ethnic groups: between external missionaries and native religious elites or between competing local religious elites for control over the allegiances of marginal groups. In either case, ethnic or ethnoreligious mobilization is very likely to take place. If the state is seen as supporting an external force, then that ethnoreligious mobilization may be directed against the state and its authority

FIGURE 7.1: Patterns of Elite Competition/Collaboration, State Action, and Ethnic Mobilization/Assimilation in Preindustrial Societies

	Pattern		Role of State	Likely Consequences	Examples
LA	Local aristocracy	vs. Alien conqueror or centralizing state	Antagonistic	Rebellion or defeat/displacement of local aristocracy, sometimes involving local ethnic separatism	Imposition of non-Czech, Catholic landlord class in Czech lands by Habsburgs in 17th C.[a] Indian Mutiny of 1857 Magyar 'aristocratic nationalism' of 18th C.[a]
B	Local aristocracy	collaborates with Alien conquerors or centralizing state	Collaborationist (indirect rule)	Ethnic dormancy ('Clientelistic Loyalties')	Anglicized Welsh aristocracy in Wales in 19th C. Malay Sultans during British rule Indian princes, Talukdars and Zamindars during British rule Sub-Saharan African Chiefs during colonial rule Southern feudal patrons in Italy after 1860[b]
II	Local Religious elite 'A'	vs. Local religious elite 'B' / External missionaries or dominant religiously distinct external group	Neutral or supports one side	Ethnoreligious mobilization	Competitive Hindu-Muslim-Sikh-English missionary proselytization in Punjab in 19th C. Competitive proselytization in Eastern Europe in 18th-19th C.[a]
III	Local religious elite	vs. Local collaborationist aristocracy	Supports aristocracy	Ethnoreligious mobilization	Nonconformist ministers leading nonconformist tenantry in Wales against Anglican, Anglicized Welsh landlord class Split in north India between 'traditionalist' ulema of Deoband and aristocratic modernists of Aligarh Muslim University
IV	Local religious elite	vs. Local, but alien aristocracy	Supports aristocracy	Ethnoreligious mobilization	Buddhist monks against Christian missionary schools and Europeanized collaborationist aristocratic elite in Sri Lanka Parish priests and lower clergy against Magyar nobility in Slovakia and Transylvania; against Turks in Serbia and Bulgaria; against Magyar and Magyarized Romanian aristocracy (Catholic and Calvinist) in Romania[a]

[a] These examples come from chapter 1 of this volume where the sources also are given.
[b] See Alberto Palloni, 'Internal Colonialism or Clientelistic Politics? The Case of Southern Italy,' *Ethnic and Racial Studies*, Vol. II, No. 3 (July, 1979), pp. 360-77.

A third type of elite conflict in preindustrial societies is predominantly intraethnic in form. It occurs when a local, indigenous aristocracy collaborates with external authority, typically the colonial state. The local aristocracy may or may not convert to the religion of the dominant authorities, but its members generally adopt some aspects of their culture and behavior. For example, in the typical Western colonial setting, they may or may not become Christian, but they usually adopt Western values. If the local religious elites feel that their authority is being threatened or the values that sustain their relationship with their followers are being undermined, they may promote the mobilization of their followers in ethnoreligious terms. A fourth type of elite conflict is a variation on the third that was common in Eastern Europe in the eighteenth and nineteenth centuries, in which the local aristocracy is not only collaborationist but alien.

While these four types of elite conflict in preindustrial societies, especially the first three, are simple in form, there are complexities that are not so easily reduced to a two-dimensional chart. Even so, however, the basic patterns may be recognizable within the complexities. For example, David Laitin, in his work on internal divisions among the Yoruba people,[49] has attempted to explain the greater salience and persistence into contemporary times of 'ancestral city' in contrast to religion as a form of identification in the face of the greater sociocultural significance of religion than place of origin in contemporary Yoruba relations. His explanation is provided in terms that fit well into the basic patterns of Figure 7.1. In his explanation, the British policy of indirect rule in Yorubaland involved not only collaboration with local chiefs, but the selection of some chiefs for special status. In Yorubaland, the King of Oyo and his city were singled out for special favor, especially in relation to the modernizing, more cosmopolitan city of Ibadan, but also in relation to other, more traditional cities such as Ife, Ijebu, and Ekiti. Insofar as religion was concerned, however, the British, who originally supported Christian missionary activity, reversed that policy to one of neutrality and occasionally even support for Muslim religious institutions. The primary route to political favor, however, was through identification with one's ancestral city and the primary form of political competition was between persons from different cities. That competition intensified as modernization proceeded and the people of Ibadan moved ahead of those of Oyo despite British protection—in fact, because of British protection—of traditional Oyo political authority and social structure.

In terms of the typical conflict patterns identified in Figure 7.1, therefore, what we have in Yorubaland is a variation that has developed as follows. There were two principal forms of local conflict: between local chiefs from different cities and between Muslim and Christian missionaries. The state supported the local chiefs in general, but favored some chiefs over others and some cities over others. The state remained neutral with regard to religion. The consequence was the politicization of sub-group identities along the lines of ancestral origin and the depoliticization of religious identities.

The Yoruba case of depoliticization of religious cleavages, of course, contrasts quite sharply with the situations that developed in India under British rule, particularly in Punjab (Figure 7.1, example II) and Bengal. In those two regions, religious cleavages between Hindus and Muslims (and Sikhs as well in Punjab) were the fundamental politicized cleavages. In contrast to the situation in Nigeria, religious divisions were recognized by the British and religious competition was encouraged by the creation of separate electorates for the main religious communities and by other forms of direct political acknowledgment by the British of the significance the colonial regime attached to religious differences.

In modernizing and in postindustrial societies, when new opportunities arise, most of them created by the state, for educational advancement and for new kinds of employment, other kinds of conflicts develop (see Figure 7.2). They arise because of two processes often precipitated by state action. One is the almost invariably uneven spread of education, industrialization, and employment opportunities across regions, communities, castes, and classes. The second is the creation of new elite groups out of processes of social change, particularly educated elites in search of government employment and professional groups in private practice operating in relative freedom from old forms of social control and creating new types of community networks through their own professional activities. The spread of non-religious education, including exposure to Marxist, nationalist, and other contemporary political ideologies also promotes tendencies toward secularization

FIGURE 7.2: Patterns of Elite Competition/Collaboration, State Action, and Ethnic Mobilization/Assimilation in Modernizing and Postindustrial Societies

Pattern	Role of State	Likely Consequences	Examples
1. Ethnic educated elite 'A' vs. Ethnic educated elite 'B' / Ethnic educated elite 'C'	Neutral or supports one side	Ethnocultural, ethnolinguistic or caste mobilization	Blacks vs. other minorities vs. privileged white ethnic groups in U.S. Brahman/non-Brahman conflict in Madras. Malay vs. Chinese and Indian educated commercial elites
II. Local religious elite vs. Local secular educated elite vs. External ethnic elite	Neutral or supports one side	Competing religious and secular nationalisms or only secular nationalism	Mid-20th century Quebec[a]
III. Local ethnic educated elite assimilates Dominant ethnic group	Supports assimilation	Assimilation (may or may not be permanent)	Jews in Hungary during mid-19th century[b]

[a]See, for example, Kenneth McRoberts, 'Internal Colonialism: The Case of Quebec,' Ethnic and Racial Studies, Vol. II, No. 3 (July 1979), pp 293-318.

[b]See George Barany, '"Magyar Jew or: Jewish Magyar"? (To the Question of Jewish Assimilation in Hungary),' Canadian-American Slavic Studies, Vol. VIII, No. 1 (Spring, 1974).

and leads to the rise of new secular elites, oriented toward achieving political power in institutions and arenas created by the
modern state.

These two types of processes in turn precipitate two characteristic and well-known forms of competition that affect the formation
or transformation of ethnic group identities and the relationships
between ethnic groups and the state. One is competition between
persons from different ethnic categories or regions for government
jobs, for places in educational institutions, and for representation
in elected and appointed government bodies. Sometimes such
competition occurs initially between ethnic categories that have
very little subjective selfconsciousness as communities.

For example, in late nineteenth and early twentieth century
Madras province in India (Figure 7.2, example I), disappointed
job applicants from the more advanced of the non-Brahman castes
and fathers who wished to see their sons advance in government
service discovered that Brahmans occupied an overwhelmingly
disproportionate share of government jobs. Neither non-Brahmans,
who formed 97 per cent of the population nor Brahmans, who
formed 3 per cent, were anything but ethnic categories without an
underlying social reality and solidarity. However, the non-Brahman
movement merged with a cultural movement that asserted the
distinctiveness of Dravidian south Indian culture, of which Tamil
culture was a part, identified that culture with non-Brahmans as a
whole, branded Brahmans as historic invaders from the north, and
used these new symbolic constructions to provide a stronger social
basis for their economic demands.[50] The movement ultimately did
not lead to the creation of a non-Brahman ethnic community as
such, but rather, through a larger process of change, became
transformed into a movement of Tamil regional nationalism with
the Tamil language as its central symbol. The political spokesmen
for Tamil nationalism claimed to represent the culture and interests of the Tamil-speaking people as a whole against alleged
dangers from New Delhi and north India. The symbols of Tamil
regional nationalism ultimately came to provide a new context in
which elites struggled for control over the government administration of a Tamil-speaking province.

The point here is that resource competition by itself does not
produce ethnic political cohesion. It must be associated with
groups that have a common pool of symbols to draw upon and an

elite or elites capable of transmitting to the ethnic groups a sense of increasing attachment to those symbols as a basis for social and political mobilization. In Tamil Nadu, transcendent symbols of Tamil regional nationalism ultimately prevailed over the symbols of social protest associated with intercaste relations in a long historical process of identity transformation in which both the elites in conflict and the broader political context of struggle also changed dramatically. The relationship between elite competition and ethnic identity formation, therefore, is not to be seen as either wholly material in character or as producing instant ethnic communities.

The role that the state plays in such situations is often to support the non-dominant groups. It may do so for several different reasons. In the case of Brahman–non-Brahman conflict in late nineteenth and early twentieth century Madras, the British supported the non-Brahmans in part because they themselves feared the disproportionate dominance of Brahmans in the administrative service and because they resented Brahman participation in the developing nationalist movement. They therefore supported non-Brahmans with a view toward creating a counterweight against Brahman dominance in public life.

In the United States after World War II, the federal government has consistently and increasingly intervened on the side of the Black middle class with legislation and programs to eliminate discrimination, to provide employment in government and higher levels of industry, and to provide higher educational opportunities. It has done so largely because the social and ideological climate changed in such a way as to make it politically necessary for political parties to compete for the support both of a liberal white middle class in sympathy with Black aspirations and for the support of the increasing Black population in the northern cities. Government support for Black middle class aspirations then led to the so-called 'backlash' and countermobilization of white ethnic groups.

Whether or not one wishes to characterize state policy in these two instances as 'divide and rule' tactics or a search for collaborators or an opportunistic desire for electoral support, the two situations illustrate the point that state policy is not a simple reflection of the 'interests' of a dominant class or ethnic group in maintaining its dominance. At the same time, they also illustrate how state policy may lead to long-term collaboration with particular segments of an ethnic group, which in turn influences processes of ethnic mobilization and countermobilization. Finally, however, while the state's action may precipitate new forms of ethnic mobilization, it does not determine the outcome, that is, the ultimate extent of internal solidarity achieved by ethnic groups. That result is likely to be more influenced ultimately by internal changes and conflicts among segments within the group and external relations between elites and segments of other ethnic groups.

The second type of conflict in modernizing and postindustrial societies is between old religious elites and new secular elites which, in turn, may take two forms: a struggle for a redefinition of the central values and purposes of the group and/or a struggle between the two for support within the community and the right to represent the community in relations with outside forces, particularly the state authorities, and in new state institutions. In either case, the state authorities often choose to intervene since they too have an interest in control over local communities and in who comes forth to represent them. The state, for example, may choose to support the religious elites by agreeing to leave either personal law or education in their hands or it may promote civil law and secular education. When the state supports religious elites, secular elites from different ethnoreligious groups may join hands and form alliances against the state authorities.

Sometimes, the two types of conflicts—external competition for jobs with other ethnic groups and internal struggles for control—may become intertwined. For example, the secular elites from one religious group may try to mobilize the group as a whole to assist them in the scramble for jobs and political advancement by claiming that the disadvantages of its elites are a threat or insult to the group as a whole. The secular elites may then find they need the support of the religious elites in order to mobilize the community effectively.

A few further examples will help in illustrating the consequences for ethnic identity formation and mobilization of interelite competition and the specific role of the state. They are illustrated in Figure 7.3. The first concerns Basque nationalism in Spain. In his analysis of this case, Greenwood has shown the importance of conflicts of interest between industrial/commercial elites and a working class divided between native and immigrant segments,

FIGURE 7.3: Patterns of Elite Competition/Collaboration, State Action, and Ethnic Mobilization/Assimilation: Variants

	Pattern		Role of State	Likely Consequences	Examples
I.	Native industrial commercial elite **vs.**	Native urban middle class elites — Working class (Native | Immigrant)	Supports industrial/ commercial elites	Ethnic mobilization led by urban middle class elites supported by native working class	Basque nationalism in Spain[a]
II.	Regional/ local ethnic bourgeoisie **vs.**	Dominant ethnic or interethnic bourgeoisie	Supports dominant bourgeoisie and clergy	Regional ethnoreligious mobilization	Slovakia in late 19th and 20th C.
	Regional/ local ethnic lower clergy **vs.**	Dominant ethnic clerical hierarchy			
III.A.	French Catholic clergy **vs.**	English-speaking Irish church hierarchy	Neutral	Limited ethnoreligious ('French Catholic') mobilization	French Acadians, 1860-1960
B.	French Catholic clergy ↑ New secular political elite **vs.**	Dominant English community	Federal government supports new secular political elite	Ethnolinguistic mobilization	French Acadians, 1960-present
IV	Urban refugee Sikh leadership ↑ Rural Jat Akali Sikh leadership ↑ Secular Congress Sikh leaders **vs.**	Rural Hindi-speaking Hindu elites — Urban Punjabi-speaking Hindu elites	Supports secular Congress Sikhs	Competitive ethnoreligious and ethnolinguistic mobilization	Punjabi Suba movement in 1960s

[a]See Davydd J. Greenwood, 'Castilians, Basques, and Andalusians: An Historical Comparison of Nationalism, "True" Ethnicity, and "False" Ethnicity,' in Paul R. Brass, *Ethnic Groups and the State* (London, Croom Helm, 1985), ch. vi.

with the urban middle classes in the middle. In these conflicts, the state has allied with the industrial/commercial oligarchy. The consequence has been ethnic mobilization led by the urban middle class elites supported by the native working class.[51]

The second example in Figure 7.3 comes from the history of Slovak nationalism in the Hungarian state in the period between 1870–1910.[52] At the end of the nineteenth century, the expansion of the Hungarian state and school system into the Slovak territories was accompanied by a policy of assimilation to Magyar language and culture. The effect of this state expansion was to place Slovak-speaking peoples increasingly in contact with Magyar-speaking bureaucrats and teachers, thus leading Slovaks to perceive the state as alien. The industrial elite in the Slovak areas was Magyar–German–Jewish. Although some Magyarone Slovaks collaborated with this industrial elite, a local-regional Slovak bourgeoisie also developed that promoted Slovak nationalism.

Ultimately, two lines of elite competition developed within Slovakia. One was between the local Slovak and the Hungarian–German bourgeoisie. The second was between the Slovak lower clergy and the Magyar hierarchy in the Roman Catholic church. In both cases, the Slovak elites turned inward to the opportunities available in their region, toward contact with the peasantry, and toward the use of Slovak nationalist sentiment as an entry into politics. At the same time, the state's policies of assimilation and Magyarization aligned the state with the Hungarian–German bourgeoisie and the Magyar church hierarchy and, thereby, provided obvious targets for Slovak nationalism.

The third example concerns Acadian nationalism in the Canadian province of New Brunswick from 1860 to the 1970s and is drawn from the work of Fox, Aull, and Cimino.[53] According to Fox and his co-authors, Acadian nationalism has passed through several stages in the past century. Between 1860 and 1960, when it moved through its formative phases, there were two important developments. The first was the creation of 'an Acadian elite consisting mainly of clerics, but including lay professionals, lawyers, doctors, and teachers,' produced from College St. Joseph founded in 1864.[54] The second was the development of conflict between the French Catholic clergy and the English-speaking Irish church hierarchy. These two developments led to the formation of a 'French Catholic' Acadian ethnic identity.

The recent phase, which began in the 1960s, developed out of intraethnic elite conflict between the older church-dominated Acadian elite and a new secular political leadership. The latter, led by Louis J. Robichaud, the first Acadian premier of the province, promoted new secular programs, including secular schools, that threatened church control and authority. Out of this conflict, in which the state supported the new secular political elite, a new Acadian nationalist organization led by the new elite was created that displaced the older Acadian nationalist organization. After the replacement of the Robichaud government in 1970 by a provincial government less favorable to French Acadian interests, the new secular Acadian elite became involved in confrontation with the provincial government over enforcement of the federal government's bilingual policies in the province.

The French Acadian example illustrates several features of the process of identity formation. First, it demonstrates that ethnic mobilization is promoted or limited by specific elites. Second, it shows that intraethnic elite conflict can be as important in ethnic mobilization as interethnic conflict. Third, it indicates how boundary definition also may change when the dominant elite in control of the movement changes, in this case moving from a French Catholic religious identification to a French Acadian identity in which the religious aspect is far less prominent than the linguistic. Finally, it demonstrates the critical role that the state may play in shifting the balance of power within an ethnic group by allying with one subgroup rather than another.

A particularly interesting and complex example from the post-independence Indian Punjab, discussed in detail in chapters 5 and 6,[55] brings out clearly the critical importance in the course of ethnic group relations of intragroup conflicts, of relations between subgroups across communal boundaries, and of the role of the state (see Figure 7.3, pattern IV). It also illustrates how the political definition and boundaries of an ethnic group may change in the course of political conflict and negotiation.

In the aftermath of the partition of the Indian Punjab in 1947 and the integration of the semi-autonomous Sikh princely states into the province of east Punjab, a new Punjab province came into existence in India. In the conventional classificatory terms of the census and common opinion, the new Punjab contained two religious communities, Hindus and Sikhs, two principal languages,

Hindi and Punjabi, and two geographical regions, Punjab proper and Haryana. In the province as a whole, Punjabi-speaking Sikhs were in a minority and Hindi-speaking Hindus in a majority. In Punjab proper, however, the position was reversed.

After partition in 1947 and for the next two decades, a long-established Sikh political party, the Akali Dal, demanded the creation of a separate Sikh state within the Indian Union to be created out of the Sikh-majority areas of the province. Agitations, negotiations, struggles, and compromises occurred off and on between 1947 until the creation of a Punjabi Suba in 1966, defined not as a Sikh province but as a Punjabi-speaking province, though it was also a Sikh majority province in fact. A dramatic turning-point in the conflict occurred in 1960–61 when two of the leading personalities in the Sikh movement went on fasts-unto-death on behalf of the Sikh demand. A change in the leadership of the movement occurred at that time that led finally to the agreement between the Akali Dal and the Government of India by which the Punjabi Suba was created.

During the course of the conflict, it often appeared to be and occasionally was in fact true that there were two relatively solidary communities locked in a struggle with each other that often threatened to turn violent. The militant spokesmen of the two sides defined the two sides as Punjabi-speaking Sikhs and Hindi-speaking Hindus. One subgroup, Punjabi-speaking Hindus, believed so strongly in the opposition between the two blocs that many disavowed their own mother tongue in the census declarations and sent their children to Hindi-medium schools.

Insiders, however, especially Congress leaders in the province, knew better. In fact, there were five significant subgroups and several others of importance as well. However, for purposes of this analysis, it will be sufficient to discuss the conflict in relation to these five groups only. Within the Akali Sikh community, there were two leadership groups with different social bases: urban refugee Sikhs from the Pakistan Punjab led by Master Tara Singh and rural Jat Sikhs, whose principal symbolic leader became Sant Fateh Singh. There was also a leadership group of 'secular' Sikhs in the Congress, whose most important leader in the late 1950s and early 1960s was the state's chief minister, Pratap Singh Kairon. Among Hindus, there were two principal subgroups: rural Hindi-speaking Hindus concentrated in Haryana, whose political spokesmen were predominantly in the Congress, and urban Punjabi-speaking Hindus, whose leaders were either in the Congress or in the Hindu communal party, the Jan Sangh.

On the face of it, the conflict was an intractable struggle between two solidary groups defined in religious communal terms over the demand for a state in which the Sikh religious group would be a majority and the Hindus a minority. It conjured up prospects of violence in an area that had emerged from catastrophic religious communal violence within the living memory of all participants in the struggle. Yet a compromise ultimately was reached by which the Sikh demand was conceded, but its terms redefined. The compromise was also facilitated by a change in the leadership group of the Akali Dal.

In order for the Punjabi Suba compromise of 1966 to be worked out, however, the various divisions within the two communities had to be exploited and made manifest. Pettigrew describes the intricate maneuvers by which the secular Congress Sikh leaders exploited the divisions between the followers of Master Tara Singh and Sant Fateh Singh in such a way that the latter emerged as the preeminent leader of the Akali Dal.[56] Sant Fateh Singh was an acceptable leader of the Sikh community in the eyes of the Congress, largely because his definition of the Sikh demand as one for a Punjabi-speaking state rather than a Sikh religious state was considered negotiable whereas the demand for a Sikh state was not.

On the other side, the Hindus too had to be divided. Specifically, the rural Hindi-speaking Hindus had to be separated from the urban Punjabi-speaking Hindus, who were the principal social subgroup opposed to the demand. This split ultimately developed for two principal reasons: the Congress Hindu political leaders of Haryana would acquire power in the new province of Haryana to be separated from Punjab and they would avoid the unpopular imposition on the population of Hindi-speakers of the province of the burden of having their children learn Punjabi in school, which was becoming a political liability for them.

In these conflicts and compromises among subgroups, the state—both the provincial and union government—played an active and partial role. It did not, however, act as an instrument of domination of one group, class or ideological tendency over another. It was not an instrument of Hindus or of intercommunal secularists promoting an 'integrative revolution'. Rather, it was a powerful skillful external force operating within, and on behalf of, one subgroup in the politics of the province, working for a political bargain consistent on the face of it with its political principles and one that would also permit the ruling party to emerge from the struggle without losing its base of support in the region.

Nor is there anything unique about the Punjab situation described previously. Although it was more complex than most ethnic group conflicts, the situation has a very close parallel in Belgian ethnic group relations.[57]

It should be evident from this brief survey of some of the principal lines of intergroup and intragroup conflict that it is a great fallacy and an analytical distortion of very serious proportions to continue to use the term 'plural segments' to refer to the divisions and cleavages in multiethnic societies. It should also be clear why the interest group theory of ethnicity is extremely superficial and takes us nowhere in understanding the issues of identity formation and, therefore, of ethnic persistence in contemporary industrial societies. It provides no basis whatsoever for analyzing the internal processes by which group cohesion is created.

Thus, the two types of theories are, in a sense, opposite sides of the same coin. Theorists of the plural society objectify ethnic groups and, therefore, ignore the internal conflicts within groups and the possibilities for change and for alliances between elites of different ethnic groups as well. Interest group theorists ignore the internal processes of consolidation within ethnic groups by which solidarity may (or may not) be achieved for a time and, therefore, cannot distinguish an ethnic category from an ethnic community or the latter from any other type of interest association.

Finally, two points need to be emphasized about the elite competition theory of ethnic group formation and ethnic group conflict. The first is that it is not an 'elitist' theory. It is not assumed that elites can do whatever they wish with the cultures and symbols of the groups they seek to represent. It is, rather, assumed that some elites can sometimes get away with representing their groups to the state authorities even without a popular base, especially when the state authorities for their own purposes wish to recognize them as the group's sole representative. However, in a free competition with other elites from their own groups or with elites from other ethnic groups, it matters a great deal how effective competing elites are in interpreting, reinterpreting, and manipulating the symbols of the group for purposes of political mobilization. The availability of the group for a political movement in turn depends upon such factors as the existence of a socially mobilized population, in Deutsch's sense of the term, and the existence of historical and/or contemporary grievances and hostilities in relation to other groups or to the state.[58]

However, it is central to the argument here that elites and interelite competition of specific types and alliance patterns with the state are the critical precipitants in ethnic group conflict and political mobilization. All other factors, including the richness or paucity of available cultural symbols, regional economic inequalities, patterns of differential social mobilization, and the like are but backdrops and resources for elites to draw upon for the purpose. Without elite entry into such situations, injustices and inequalities may be accepted, cultural decline or assimilation may occur, and grievances may be expressed in isolated, anomic, or sporadic forms of conflict and disorder. Moreover, skillful elites who lack such 'objective' bases for mobilization as, say, systematic discrimination or evident regional inequalities will often create images or perceptions of them by magnifying minor cases of discrimination or specific instances of regional inequality.

The second point is that the term elite is not meant to be used as a substitute for class, but is meant to refer to formations within ethnic groups and classes that often play critical roles in ethnic mobilization. Thus, aristocratic elites clearly belong to a specific class within an ethnic group; religious elites refer to the clerics, priests, *ulema*, rabbis, whose class origins may or may not be relevant, and often are not relevant, to their ability to control or mobilize their communities; secular elites may come from many different classes. Each of these elite groups may choose to act in terms of ethnic appeals or in terms of class appeals. Neither their ethnicity nor their class predetermines their action. Rather, their specific relationship to competing elites in struggles for control over their ethnic group or in competition with persons from other ethnic categories and groups for scarce political and economic benefits and resources are the critical factors.

NOTES

1. The term 'ethnic group' in this chapter, as in the volume as a whole, is used in the most general and generic sense, rather than in the specific sense of a concrete, corporately organized entity. I view the process of ethnic identity formation as a movement from an ethnic category to an ethnic community, from a merely objectively distinct cultural cluster of people to a subjectively conscious social formation. The term 'ethnic group' will be used simply for generalized references encompassing ethnic formations at any point along that continuum. For a more extended discussion of the definitional issue, see chapter 1.
2. Alfred Stepan, *The State and Society: Peru in Comparative Perspective* (Princeton, NJ: Princeton University Press, 1978), pp. 11–14.
3. Stepan, *The State and Society*, op. cit., p. 15.
4. Stepan, *The State and Society*, op. cit., p. 16.
5. V.I. Lenin, *State and Revolution* (New York: International Publishers, 1932), p. 9.
6. For useful analyses of the views of this group of Marxist theorists, see Robert Solo, 'The Neo-Marxist Theory of the State,' *Journal of Economic Issues*, Vol. XII, No. 4 (December 1978), pp. 829–42 and Boris Frankel, 'On the State of the State: Marxist Theories of the State after Leninism,' *Theory and Society*, Vol. VII (1979), pp. 199–242. The idea of the relative autonomy of the state was, in fact, present in Marx's work in Karl Marx, *The Eighteenth Brumaire of Louis Bonaparte* (New York: International Publishers, 1963), esp. pp. 122–23.
7. Solo, 'The Neo-Marxist Theory of the State,' op. cit., p. 841.
8. Immanuel Wallerstein, *The Capitalist World-Economy* (Cambridge: Cambridge University Press, 1979), esp. p. 187.
9. See, for example, Immanuel Wallerstein, 'The World System: The States in the Institutional Vortex of the Capitalist World-Economy,' *International Social Science Journal*, Vol. XXXII, No. 4 (1980), pp. 747–48.
10. Michael Hechter, *Internal Colonialism: The Celtic Fringe in British National Development* (London: Routledge & Kegan Paul, 1975).
11. M.G. Smith, *The Plural Society in the British West Indies* (Berkeley: University of California Press, 1974), pp. 86–88 and Leo Kuper, 'Plural Societies: Perspectives and Problems,' in Leo Kuper and M.G. Smith (eds.), *Pluralism in Africa* (Berkeley: University of California Press, 1969), p. 13.
12. Smith, *The Plural Society in the British West Indies*, op. cit., pp. 13–14.
13. Pierre L. van den Berghe, 'Pluralism and the Polity: A Theoretical Exploration,' in Kuper and Smith, *Pluralism in Africa*, op. cit., p. 67.
14. Hechter, for example, allows for the existence of nation-states and segmentary states as well as internal colonial states. They are hardly discussed, however. See Hechter, *Internal Colonialism*, op. cit., p. 48 and Michael Hechter and Margaret Levi, 'The Comparative Analysis of Ethnoregional Movements,' *Ethnic and Racial Studies*, Vol. II, No. 3 (July 1979), p. 264. Van den Berghe and other theorists of the plural society have tended toward trichotomous classifications of states according to whether or not they are plural societies and, if they are plural, whether or not they are dominated by a minority ethnic

group. See, for example, Pierre L. van den Berghe, *The Ethnic Phenomenon* (New York: Elsevier, 1981), pp. 78–82.

15. Douglas Rae, 'The Egalitarian State: Notes on a System of Contradictory Ideals,' *Daedalus*, Vol. CVIII, No. 4 (Fall, 1979), pp. 37–54. I do not believe that Rae's analysis is meant as an argument against egalitarian policies. It is certainly not my point here, which is meant only to demonstrate the difficulties faced even by states that deliberately pursue equalitarian policies in achieving equalitarian results. The inability to achieve ideals in an imperfect world is never an argument against their pursuit. D. John Grove, in his cross-national quantitative studies of the effects of public policies in promoting ethnic equality, has argued that such 'policies are an important mechanism in promoting greater ethnic equality,' but that they also 'often create new disparities'; see his 'Does Economic Development Create a More Equitable Ethnic Distribution,' unpublished paper prepared for the International Political Science Association's round table on 'Politics and Ethnicity,' St. Anthony's College, Oxford, 26–28 March 1979, pp. 15–16. Rae's point is that a close examination of all equalizing policies will reveal contradictions of one sort or another. Obviously, however, some inequalities may be considered more or less acceptable in different societies at different times.

For a careful assessment of preferential policies designed to promote equality among ethnic groups in India with explicit comparisons to similar policies in the US, see Myron Weiner and Mary F. Katzenstein, *India's Preferential Policies: Migrants, the Middle Classes, and Ethnic Equality* (Chicago: University of Chicago Press, 1981). See also the rather more polemical than logical updating of Nathan Glazer's views on these issues for the US in his 'Affirmative Discrimination: Where Is It Going?' *International Journal of Comparative Sociology*, Vol. XX, Nos. 1–2 (1978), pp. 14–30.

16. Rae, 'The Egalitarian State,' op. cit., pp. 37–38.

17. For an interesting and exceptional neo-Marxist comparative analysis of South Africa, Alabama, Northern Ireland, and Israel that places the persistence of 'racial conflict and domination' at the center of discussion and attempts to explain it without resort to notions of false consciousness and without objectifying class and class conflict, see Stanley B. Greenberg, *Race and State in Capitalist Development: Comparative Perspectives* (New Haven: Yale University Press, 1980).

18. My comments here were stimulated by suggestions from Davydd Greenwood.

19. Another way of presenting the general mode of analysis that I am proposing here is as a merging of the methods of comparative history and social science. I agree with the comparative historian who argues that 'the kind of flux, contingency, and temporality' that he confronts in analyzing historical 'change and development' 'cannot be adequately subsumed under rigid structural categories or incorporated into simplified and static models'; George M. Fredrickson, *White Supremacy: A Comparative Study in American and South African History* (New York: Oxford University Press, 1981), p. xvi. On the other hand, meaningful comparison is not possible unless we approach comparative studies with categories of analysis that can be used cross-culturally. My proposal is to use categories of analysis that are defined in the same way for different societies, but that can be used for dynamic comparisons over time as well as across space.

The questions I am raising here are, given an array of possible forms of class
and ethnic consciousness that might develop (on the basis of specified theoretical assumptions) in societies whose people are differentiated objectively in
terms of particular relationships to the means of production and to the market
and in terms of cultural characteristics and markers, how do we explain the
development of class consciousness or ethnic consciousness as political force
among particular categories of people and not others in different societies at
different times?

20. Harold Wolpe, 'The theory of Internal Colonialism: The South African Case,'
    in Ivar Oxaal (ed.), *Beyond the Sociology of Development: Economy and
    Society in Latin America and Africa* (London: Routledge & Kegan Paul, 1975),
    pp. 229–54. On the general question of 'convergences' in approaches to class
    and ethnic groups among Marxists and theorists of the plural society, see also
    John Rex, 'Race Relations and Minority Groups: Some Convergences,' *Inter-
    national Social Science Journal*, Vol. XXXIII, No. 2 (1981), pp. 351–73 and
    Pierre L. van den Berghe, 'Nigeria and Peru: Two Contrasting Cases in Ethnic
    Pluralism,' *International Journal of Comparative Sociology*, Vol. XX, Nos. 1–2
    (1978), p. 162.
21. Hechter, *Internal Colonialism*, op. cit., and Wallerstein, *The Capitalist World-
    Economy*, op. cit., p. 230.
22. Wallerstein, *The Capitalist World-Economy*, op. cit., pp. 184–85 and 224.
23. Wallerstein, *The Capitalist World-Economy*, op. cit., p. 181. See also Waller-
    stein, 'The World System: The States in the Institutional Vortex of the Capitalist
    World-Economy,' p. 750, where he says that 'status-group solidarities' may
    'obfuscate the class struggle'.
24. Wallerstein, *The Capitalist World-Economy*, op. cit., p. 230.
25. J.S. Furnivall, *Netherlands India: A Study of Plural Economy* (Cambridge:
    Cambridge University Press, 1939), p. 447 and Smith, *The Plural Society*, op.
    cit., p. 81.
26. For a contrast between early and contemporary theorists of the plural society,
    see Sammy Smooha, 'Pluralism and Conflict: A Theoretical Explanation,'
    Plural Societies, Vol. VI, No. 3 (1975), pp. 69–89. For van den Berghe s own
    statement of the differences between his approach and that of Furnivall and
    Smith, see Pierre L. van den Berghe, 'Pluralism,' in John J. Honigmann (ed.),
    Handbook of Social and Cultural Anthropology (New York: Rand McNally,
    1974), ch. xxii.
27. See especially Pierre L. van den Berghe, 'Nigeria and Peru: Two Contrasting
    Cases in Ethnic Pluralism,' op. cit., pp. 162–63.
28. Van den Berghe has insisted that 'the main contribution of the pluralist
    orientation is not the classification of societies into yet another taxonomy,' but
    the reorientation of anthropology and sociology away from its previous
    primary focus on processes of consensus and integration. He argues for greater
    attention to 'the interplay' between corporate groups and 'the movement of
    individuals' between them; van den Berghe, 'Pluralism,' p. 966. My point here
    is that this is not what the theorists of the plural society do in practice and that
    their concepts do not lead beyond taxonomy.
29. Paul R. Brass, 'Ethnicity and Nationality Formation,' *Ethnicity*, Vol. III, No.
    3 (1976), p. 226.

30. In the long term, as Greenberg and many other students of ethnicity and nationalism have pointed out, there is surprising agreement among modernization, integration, and nation-building theorists such as Deutsch, and classical Marxist writers that ethnicity and ethnic conflict will be transcended in favor of 'new forms of community and new forms of conflict'; Greenberg, *Race and State*, op. cit., pp. 8–12, citation from p. 8. Greenberg does not agree with the shared perspective nor do I, but it is not an issue that I am taking up in this chapter.

31. The classic statement is in Arthur F. Bentley, *The Process of Government* (Cambridge, Mass.: Harvard University Press, 1967).

32. However, see Greenberg, *Race and State in Capitalist Development*, op. cit., esp. p. 406.

33. Furnivall, *Netherlands India*, op. cit., p. 451.

34. M.G. Smith, 'Some Developments in the Analytical Framework of Pluralism,' in Kuper and Smith, *Pluralism in Africa*, op. cit., pp. 438–39.

35. Kuper, 'Plural Societies,' op. cit., p. 15.

36. Smooha, 'Pluralism and Conflict,' op. cit., esp. p. 80.

37. Clifford Geertz, 'The Integrative Revolution: Primordial Sentiments and Civil Politics in the New States,' in Clifford Geertz (ed.), *Old Societies and New States: The Quest for Modernity in Asia and Africa* (New York: Free Press, 1963), pp. 105–57 and Edward Shils, 'Primordial, Personal, Sacred and Civil Ties: Some Particular Observations on the Relationships of Sociological Research and Theory,' *British Journal of Sociology*, Vol. VIII, No. 2 (June 1957), pp. 130–45.

38. See Edward Shils, *Political Development in the New States* (The Hague: Mouton, 1966) for the idea of tutelage and the specific notion of 'tutelary democracy' in the developing countries.

39. Cf. J.H. Robb, 'A Theoretical Note on the Sociology of Inter-Group Relations,' *Ethnic and Racial Studies*, Vol. I, No. 4 (October 1978), pp. 465–73.

40. Robb, 'A Theoretical Note on the Sociology of Inter-Group Relations,' op. cit., p. 471.

41. Van den Berghe, 'Pluralism and the Polity,' op. cit., p. 70.

42. Robb, 'A Theoretical Note on the Sociology of Inter-Group Relations,' op. cit., p. 468.

43. For one of Lijphart's many statements on this type of regime, see especially his *Democracy in Plural Societies: A Comparative Exploration* (New Haven: Yale University Press, 1977). See also chapter 9 of this volume for a critique of the consociational proposals for conflict resolution in deeply divided societies.

44. Van den Berghe, *The Ethnic Phenomenon*, op. cit., p. 56.

45. Cf. Anthony Smith, who argues that the 'genesis' of ethnic nationalism in modernizing societies is from the penetration of centralizing bureaucratic authority and institutions into outlying areas, which precipitates the revival of 'ancient and declining ethnic ties' among secular urban intelligentsia denied entry into the privileged cadres of the bureaucracy and in conflict also with traditional religious elites in their own local communities; 'The Diffusion of Nationalism: Some Historical and Sociological Perspectives,' *British Journal of Sociology*, Vol. XXIX, No. 2 (June 1978), esp. p. 246. There are several points of contact between my approach and that of Smith. However, he emphasizes

the admittedly important role of the urban secular intelligentsia more than I do. There is an emphasis on ideology as a motivating and emotionally satisfying force for participants in ethnic movements in his work that goes beyond what I find necessary to the sociological explanation of such movements. Smith also de-emphasizes religion and elevates 'language and history' as the preeminent modern 'routes' to ethnic nationalism (p. 245), whereas I consider religion to be a persisting force in the development of many nationalist movements up to contemporary times. His model is a diffusionist one which, despite his efforts to universalize it, is excessively tied to the historical experience of eighteenth and nineteenth century Europe. Finally, Smith discusses only cases where ethnic mobilization has occurred whereas I believe it is essential for socio-logical theory to consider also often comparable situations where ethnic mobilization and nationalism have *not* occurred. Nevertheless, some of Smith's illustrative examples in both the above-cited article and in his *The Ethnic Revival* (Cambridge: Cambridge University Press, 1981), esp. pp. 128–32, would fit into my schema in Figures 1.1 to 1.3.

46. See Leo A. Despres (ed.), *Ethnicity and Resource Competition in Plural Societies* (The Hague: Mouton, 1975).

47. Perhaps the best balanced statement of the issues in this paragraph may be found in Abner Cohen, *Custom and Politics in Urban Africa: A Study of Hausa Migrants in Yoruba Towns* (London: Routledge & Kegan Paul, 1969), esp. pp. 183–214.

48. See also Brass, 'Ethnicity and Nationality Formation,' op. cit.

49. David D. Laitin, 'Hegemony and Religious Conflict: British Imperial Control and Political Cleavages in Yorubaland,' in Theda Skocpol, *et al.* (eds.), *Bringing the State Back In* (Cambridge: Cambridge University Press, 1985), pp. 285–316.

50. See Eugene F. Irschick, *Politics and Social Conflict in South India: The Non-Brahman Movement and Tamil Separatism, 1916–1929* (Berkeley: University of California Press, 1969) and Marguerite R. Barnett, *The Politics of Cultural Nationalism in South India* (Princeton, NJ: Princeton University Press, 1976).

51. See Davydd J. Greenwood, 'Castilians, Basques, and Andalusians: An Historical Comparison of Nationalism, "True" Ethnicity, and "False" Ethnicity,' in Paul R. Brass, *Ethnic Groups and the State* (London: Croom Helm, 1985), ch. vi.

52. David Paul, 'Slovak Nationalism and the Hungarian State, 1870–1910,' in Brass, *Ethnic Groups and the State*, op. cit., ch. iv.

53. See Richard G. Fox, Charlotte Aull, and Louis Cimino, 'Ethnic Nationalism and Political Mobilization in Industrial Societies,' in Lamar Ross (ed.), *Inter-ethnic Communication* (Athens, GA: University of Georgia Press, 1978), pp. 113–33 and 'Ethnic Nationalism and the Welfare State,' in Charles F. Keyes (ed.), *Ethnic Change* (Seattle: University of Washington Press, 1981), pp. 221–32.

54. Fox, *et al.*, 'Ethnic Nationalism and Political Mobilization,' op. cit., p. 122.

55. See also Baldev Raj Nayar, *Minority Politics in the Punjab* (Princeton, NJ: Princeton University Press, 1966); Paul R. Brass, *Language, Religion, and Politics in North India* (Cambridge: Cambridge University Press, 1974); and Joyce Pettigrew, 'A Description of the Discrepancy between Sikh Political

Ideals and Sikh Political Practice,' in Myron J. Aronoff (ed.), *Ideology and Interest: The Dialectics of Politics*, Political Anthropology Yearbook I (New Brunswick, NJ: Transaction Books, 1980), pp. 151–92.

56. Pettigrew, 'A Description of the Discrepancy between Sikh Political Ideals and Sikh Political Practice,' op. cit.

57. See, for example, Maureen Covell, 'Ethnic Conflict, Representation and the State in Belgium,' in Paul R. Brass, *Ethnic Groups and the State* (London: Croom Helm, 1985), pp. 230–61.

58. On the interrelationship among these several sets of variables in the process of ethnic nationality formation, see Brass, *Language, Religions, and Politics*, op. cit., esp. pp. 43–45.

8

Language and National Identity in the Soviet Union and India

INTRODUCTION

Much of the Western literature on Soviet ethnic and nationality problems does away at the start with the questions of greatest theoretical interest in the comparative study of processes of ethnic identity formation and their expression in nationalist political activity. The existence of more or less clearly defined and bounded nationalities based primarily on language is too often assumed rather than proven. It is also assumed that their 'natural' instincts for cultural and political self-expression were long suppressed by the totalitarian state. This assumption is especially pronounced in relation to the formerly independent Baltic states absorbed into the Soviet Union during World War II.

Although disagreements exist among social scientists and historians of India regarding the conditions for the origin and political expression of ethnic and nationality differences, there is much greater sensitivity to questions concerning the identification and demarcation of distinct ethnic and national groups and to explaining the differential existence and strength of regional nationalist loyalties and their political expression. Rather than seeing the state and nationalities as inevitably opposed to each other, much scholarship on India has noted the decisive role of the state itself in creating many of the identities which now seem to have 'inevitably' come into existence.

Acknowledgements: This chapter has benefited from the critical comments and suggestions of Daniel Chirot, Alexander J. Motyl, Myron Weiner, and T.N. Madan.

Yet, both the USSR and India today seem to be confronted by crises of national unity, including the expression of explicit secessionist demands from several ethnic and nationality groups in different parts of these two countries. There is, of course, another way of viewing the relationship between the Soviet state and the nationalities within it, namely, as a colonial empire comprising a number of subjugated nations. From this perspective, it is a misnomer to refer to movements among these nations as secessionist, which should instead be seen as anti-colonial movements for the restoration of their independent statehood. This claim would apply especially to the Baltic states.

It is less clear, however, that there is a substantial difference between the status of other nationalities in the Soviet Union and the principal nationalities in India. In other words, it is at least arguable that the Azerbaijanis or the Georgians have no greater or lesser claim to independence arising out of their previous legal status than, say, Kashmiris or Punjabi Sikhs in India. Moreover, even among those nationalities in the Soviet Union which have experienced a separate political/legal existence in the past, the intensity of the demand for separation from the Soviet Union and the extent of support for it are not uniform. The argument of this essay is simply that, whether forcibly integrated into the Soviet Union or not, other factors than the previous legal status of the Soviet nationalities must be considered in explaining the differential timing, breadth of support, and intensity of the expressions of nationalist and separatist sentiment and demands. From this point of view, it might be more useful to put aside the usual view of the Soviet Union as either a modern industrial superpower or as the last colonial empire and think of it instead as the most advanced of the developing countries. That, at any rate, is what is proposed in this paper, which will focus on the roles of state policies and elite competition in explaining the differential expression of linguistic nationalism among distinct cultural groups in these two multiethnic states.

Comparative analyses of processes of ethnic identity formation suggest that cohesive ethnic groups arise not out of their inevitable march toward their historical destiny, but out of un-predetermined struggles, which take three forms: within the group; between ethnic groups; and between the state and its dominant groups, on the one hand, and local elite groups and populations in its outlying territories, on the other hand. Struggles within the group take place over control of resources—material and symbolic—and over definition of the group's boundaries. Struggles between groups focus on privileged access to scarce resources. Struggles between state authorities and non-dominant groups focus on issues of local control in general, but especially in relation to 'peripheral' regions of a country, and on the recruitment of skilled manpower to maintain, expand, defend, aggrandize, and industrialize the state and its territory.

In this perspective, as discussed in the previous chapter, the state—and most especially the modernizing, industrializing state— is viewed as itself both a resource and a distributor of resources and a promoter of new values. In most developing countries, elites in control of state institutions form alliances and coalitions with other elites who control significant material or symbolic resources. In extreme circumstances, of which the Stalinist developing state was probably the most extreme, the state may forcibly repress or even physically eliminate entire or virtually entire elite groups and impose new ones from the center. Ultimately, however, the modernization process itself leads to the development from within the local societies of new elites with whom the necessity for alliance and coalition will again emerge.

The legitimating ideologies of twentieth century developing states also promote new values which normally include, more or less strongly, elements of secularization, democratization, uniform legal codes, egalitarianism, the creation of disciplined workforces, and the very idea that the state itself deserves man's highest loyalty. For these reasons also, the modernizing state is a threat to local elites through the spread of its bureaucratic apparatuses into new areas of social life and to peripheral regions and through the inculcation by these means of the state ideology.

The 'development process,' therefore, involves a dual struggle for control of resources and values between bureaucratic groups and political organizations at the center and between elites at the center and in the localities. Local elites are of two types: controllers of material resources, particularly land in preindustrializing societies and other forms of wealth and property in all societies, and controllers of symbolic resources, particularly clerics and controllers of communication—writers, academics, journalists, and the avid consumers of their productions in the middle and professional classes generally.

Both sets of struggles—for influence at the center and for control over localities—take on added significance when competitive elites are ethnically or linguistically different. The ability to mobilize large numbers of people around symbols and values with a high emotional potential is a major resource for political parties and religious elites in their struggles with controllers of bureaucratic apparatuses, instruments of violence, land, and wealth. When elites in conflict come from different cultural, linguistic, or religious groups, the symbolic resources used to mobilize people will emphasize those differences.

In modernizing societies, new opportunities are created for educational advancement and employment, which are nearly always unevenly spread. New elite groups are created out of processes of social change, some of them privileged, others disadvantaged by the unevenness. Most of the new elite groups, however, tend to be secularized.

Two characteristic types of conflicts, therefore, flow naturally from this new situation. One arises out of competition between persons from different ethnic categories or regions for government jobs, for places in educational institutions, and for representation in elected and appointed government bodies. The second involves old religious elites against the new secular elites in a struggle for a redefinition of the central values and purposes of particular ethnic groups, on the one hand, and for support within the community and the right to represent the community in relations with outside forces. In countries where the centralized state is the principal creator of new opportunities, conflicts which focus on issues of unevenness, privilege, and perceived disadvantage naturally involve the state directly as a perceived—and actual—force distributing privileges and advantages partially, not as an impartial arena of conflict resolution as in the liberal democratic model of the modern state.

These arguments can be illustrated through detailed comparisons of particular cases in the Soviet Union and India, but my purpose in this chapter is rather to compare the broad structures of federalism and center–state relations in which the types of conflicts outlined above have taken place and the consequences of different kinds of state policies for the ebb and flow of language-based ethnic and nationality conflicts in the two states. The main points which will be emphasized in the comparisons below can be summarized briefly.

Both Soviet and Indian leaders have had to confront the problems associated with building a modern, industrialized, centralized state in societies marked by enormous cultural diversities in which some of the cultural groups have resisted the authority of the state. State power, including enormous military establishments, were considered essential in the two states to preserve socialism in the Soviet case and national unity in both cases in a world considered dangerous to both. The leaders of each state also propounded a 'political formula' to justify state goals, summarized in the slogans of 'proletarian internationalism' and 'building Socialism/Communism' in the Soviet Union and nationalism, anti-colonialism, and 'national integration' to preserve and strengthen the independence of India. Under the rubric of these state ideologies, both states also pursued specific policies to accommodate persisting language and other cultural differences within their societies. Their leaders had to decide especially issues concerning the official or dominant language of the Union and the extent of linguistic and cultural autonomy to be permitted within the republics and states of their respective Unions.

State power and the degree of centralization were, of course, enormously greater in the Soviet Union under Stalin than in any comparable period in postindependence Indian history. Moreover, the regime structures of the two states have been fundamentally different, the one often designated totalitarian, the other a highly competitive democratic republic in which, however, one party was dominant at the center throughout most of the postindependence period. It should be admitted at the outset, therefore, that such profound differences as have existed between the Soviet Stalinist and the liberal democratic Indian regime under Nehru restrict the possibilities for some kinds of comparisons. It would not, for example, be a sensible question to ask why regional linguistic movements developed in India under Nehru but not in the Soviet Union under Stalin.

At the same time, both the Soviet Union and India have undergone considerable changes in the character of their leaderships and the types of policies pursued by them on matters of state centralization and recognition of linguistic and cultural differences. Moreover, the differences between the political structures of the two states have lessened considerably since the rise of Gorbachev in the Soviet Union. The strains facing the two states from regional nationalist movements and their abilities to cope with them seem far more comparable now than ever before. In fact, in a strange reversal of political borrowing, the Soviet Union has gone to India for some of its new constitutional provisions, including the adoption of the Indian system of President's Rule as a device for imposing central rule in states undergoing social and political turmoil. It is, therefore, possible to compare the consequences of different language policies under different regimes within each state—differing in the degree of state centralization and authoritarianism—as well as to make comparisons between the two states at different periods. Such at least is the purpose of this paper.

Centralizing state policies, as noted above, require local collaborators among elites in peripheral regions. Except under a ruthless regime such as Stalin's, elites in the regions who collaborate with central state leaders will face opposition from counterelites within their region. In a competitive political regime, such opposition will tend to emphasize regional language and cultural issues and will demand greater regional political autonomy. In such a regime, the struggle will take place in the party-electoral arena. In a more authoritarian regime such as the Soviet Union's under Stalin or Brezhnev, such struggle may lie dormant, but will come to the surface when the political context changes through a change in leadership or in the structure of the regime, as in the Soviet Union today.

Tensions between centralizing and decentralizing policies and elite groups are not sufficient by themselves, however, to explain the differential expression of linguistic nationalism. It is when competition for scarce resources such as jobs or housing is linked to these different policies and when blame for scarcities can be attached to centralizers or decentralizers that linguistic nationalism is most likely to appear. Tendencies for linguistic nationalism to be directed against the centralizing leaders are especially likely to develop when the central elite is perceived to come from a dominant ethnic group, to favor centralization, and to hold predominant control over scarce resources, as in the case of Russians in the Soviet Union. However, even in a state such as India, where there has been no comparable dominant ethnic elite, centralizing policies which involve also central intervention in regional politics may precipitate strong regional reactions from language communities and demands for regional autonomy and even secession.

EXTENT OF DIVERSITY IN THE TWO STATES

There are some broad similarities in the extent and limits of diversity in the two states, but the differences between them are more significant. There are practical implications and lessons to be learned from both the similarities and the differences.

Although there is a huge array of languages and tribal and other small ethnic communities in each country, complexity ultimately gets reduced to the rather more analytically controllable figure of fourteen or fifteen major language groups or nationalities, comprising the vast majority of the population. Moreover, in each country, the major nationalities are for the most part concentrated in compact geographical units where they also dominate numerically.

Fifteen languages have official recognition as national languages in the Eighth Schedule of the Constitution of India, including fourteen major vernacular languages encompassing 95 per cent of the total population. Of the major recognized languages, eleven are dominant in a single state comparable to the position of the republic languages in the Soviet Union. There is no single state, however, like the RSFSR, comprising all the speakers of Hindi, the largest of the vernacular languages, which instead is the official language in six separate states. Nor does the total population of Hindi-speakers comprise a majority of the population of the country, as does Russian in the Soviet Union. The total population of Hindi-speakers is itself a matter of dispute. Figures range between a third and two-fifths depending upon which mother tongues are classified as belonging to the Hindi or some other speech community.

Each Indian state now has a dominant language group, but issues of language conflict persist, arising from the existence of linguistic minorities in linguistically reorganized states. The regional dominance of the major nationalities in India and the Soviet Union also produces comparable problems of actual or alleged discrimination against minorities within the states and republics.

Bilingualism is much more widespread in the Soviet Union than in India, but it has produced contradictory tendencies in different parts of the country: assimilative tendencies in the Slavic regions and resistances to assimilation in other parts. Bilingualism is mainly in Russian, there being no 'neutral' *lingua franca* as is English in India. Bilingualism in Russian is extensive and increasing, having gone from 49 to 62 percent between 1970 and 1979.[1]

Though extensive, bilingualism has not increased integration in the Soviet Union. On the contrary, it has increased the potential for job competition and, therefore, of ethnic conflict between native and non-native Russian speakers.[2] Increasing levels of education, especially at the secondary stage and above, among the non-Slavic nationalities especially have produced increasing job competition between indigenous nationalities and Russians. Measures to alleviate this type of job competition were taken during the 1970s by using political–administrative positions in the republics to satisfy the demands of indigenous job-seekers who were in a less competitive position than Russians for jobs in the economy, thereby creating 'bloated bureaucracies'. On the other hand, the 'general economic slowdown' in the Soviet Union, while differential growth rates between and within regions have continued, has intensified ethnic competition.[3]

Only 8.3 percent of the total population of India is bilingual (1961), but 43.7 percent of persons living outside their linguistic state are bilingual.[4] Bilingualism is not primarily in a single direction, as in the USSR. Rather, these figures include bilingualism in English, Hindi, and other regional languages. Bilingualism at the elite level, with English the second language for most such people, has equalized the competition between vernacular language speakers rather than producing the conditions for job competition between Hindi-speakers and non-Hindi-speakers.

There are differences in migration patterns in the two countries also: the universality of the Russian presence in the non-Russian republics contrasting with the greater diversity of migration patterns in India. Migration has become an important demographic phenomenon and a political issue in a variety of contexts in India. There has, however, been no overall pattern of migration by one dominant linguistic/cultural group into regions inhabited principally by speakers of a non-dominant language.

Increasing educational levels among newly-mobilized linguistic and caste groups lead to job competition between persons from different ethnic groups, providing the major source of ethnic conflict in India. However, these conflicts have tended to be intraregional rather than between local groups and outsiders (except in the cases of migrants). There is no general pattern, as in the USSR, of conflict between regional groups and a dominant all-India nationality.

The relative absence of sufficient job opportunities in the private sector in India has led the government to allow the number of government and public-sector jobs to expand incessantly to satisfy increasing numbers of educated job-seekers. The term 'bloated bureaucracies' would apply as well to the Indian states as to the Soviet republics. The focus of most ethnic conflicts has been on gaining privileged access to these jobs which, no matter how rapidly they increase, cannot increase fast enough to keep pace with the demand.

All these differences revolve ultimately around what appears to be a single decisive one in the overall pattern of diversity between the two countries, namely, the existence of a dominant nation in the Soviet Union and the absence or more problematic existence of a dominant nation in India.

THE QUESTION OF A DOMINANT NATION

USSR

Soviet specialists agree that the Great Russian people have occupied a dominant position historically in both the Tsarist Empire and the present Soviet Union. The Russian language, in addition to historical and numerical dominance, has added further weight to ethnic Russian predominance in the Soviet state. Russian remains both the *lingua franca* of the Soviet Union and the 'language of success,'[5] providing the prospect for entry into privileged positions of power and economic security. Russian is also the most highly developed language in the Soviet Union, into which there has been considerable historic assimilation on the part of non-Russian, especially Slavic groups.

The most rapid linguistic assimilation has occurred among Byelorussians, where the figures for those who do not declare Byelorussian as their native language went from 19.4 to 25.8 per cent between 1970 and 1979. In the Ukraine, a similar but smaller decline of 2.9 per cent also occurred in the declaration of Ukrainian as the native language.[6] Bilingualism in Russian and a non-Russian language as well as assimilation of ethnic non-Russians to the Russian language has been much less pronounced among most other republic nationalities. Moreover, it has been repeatedly noted by Soviet specialists that neither bilingualism nor linguistic assimilation necessarily implies subjective incorporation into the Great Russian nation.

The argument for the existence of a politically dominant Great Russian nation in the present-day Soviet Union, however, depends upon whether or not their historical preeminence, numerical and linguistic dominance, and other aspects of Russian nationality have also placed ethnic Russians in a privileged position. Motyl argues that the Bolshevik party was 'institutionally Russian' and identified as Russian from the beginning 'with territorial subunits of the party' viewed 'as regional parts of the Russian whole.'[7] Moreover, Slavic dominance of the CPSU was maintained under Stalin at both the center and in the republics. A change occurred, however, under Brezhnev, involving increased control of republic party machines by non-Russians (barring the 'second-secretary position') and increased 'non-Russian representation' at the center itself, including the Politburo.[8] Motyl, nevertheless, argues that all 'strategic elite' institutions in the CPSU in particular and in the state in general have been not only Slavic but Russian-dominated, that they were, in effect, Russian institutions and that the Soviet state has been, therefore, a Russian 'national state'[9]

India

Although there have been many writers and political activists who have argued that there is also a dominant nation in India, its existence is far more problematic, its definition more unclear, and its potential boundaries more indefinite than those of the Great Russian nation. Historically, north India, like Muscovy, has been the center of all empires which have come close to extending their

sway over the subcontinent as a whole. However, in contrast to
Russia, there have always been linguistic and religious divisions
within the potential core culture group.

The most recent pre-British empires, for example, were north
Indian, but Muslim. The struggle for independence from the British
was led mostly by Hindus. Muslim political elites withdrew from it
and ultimately fought against the Hindu-dominated Indian National Congress. The division of the country into two sovereign states,
one predominantly Hindu the other overwhelmingly Muslim, was
the result. The division, however, still left the north Indian core of
the independent Indian state divided religiously between Hindus
and Muslims and the rest of the country divided between north-
Indian Hindi-speakers and speakers of other vernacular languages.

There is, therefore, no Hindi-speaking dominant ethnic group
or nation in India. On the other hand, the idea has for long existed
among segments of the Hindu population of the country, especially
in north India, that there is or ought to be a Hindu community and
nation in India and that the country rightfully belongs to it. Since
this type of nationalism has been expressed particularly among the
Hindi-speaking elites of north India, regional elites in other parts
of the country, especially in the southern states, have sometimes
perceived the country as being dominated by north Indian Hindi-
speakers favoring centralized rule from New Delhi. Such regional
elites have from time to time argued that the Union and their
regional cultures can only be safe if the states are granted greater
regional political autonomy.

The Bharatiya Janata Party (Indian Peoples Party) [BJP], a
militant Hindu nationalist party, acquired increased strength in the
1989 parliamentary elections and subsequent state legislative
assembly elections and has been broadening its support base among
the Hindu population in northern and western India. The BJP
view is that minorities, especially Muslims, are welcome in the
country and are free to practice their religion, but that they must
acknowledge the centrality of Hindu culture and civilization to the
political definition of the Indian nation.

Nevertheless, there remains in India today considerable ambi-
guity concerning the use of the word 'Hindus' to define any clearly
demarcated group of people in the subcontinent and considerable
doubt about the existence of a Hindu political community.
Revivalist or militant Hinduism is a pervasive and politically

important presence in contemporary Indian politics. The tendency among militant nationalist organizations such as the Rashtrya Swayamsevak Sangh (RSS)[10] and the BJP to insist that Hindu and India are virtually interchangeable categories also has spread beyond the organizational confines of these two organizations. On the other hand, the very identification of Hindu nationalism with north Indian Hindi-speakers has divided south Indian and Bengali Hindus politically from the north Indian Hindu community and prevented the emergence of such a dominant all-India communal group.

USSR: LENINIST NATIONALITY POLICY IN THEORY AND PRACTICE

The official Soviet view is that Lenin's formulation of a nationality policy and a federal structure for the Soviet Union in which to contain it were sound and that deviations from them have produced the current discontents. The argument runs as follows. Lenin opted for a federation that combined 'the right to self determination' for each nationality with joint Soviet efforts to create socialism. The Leninist aim was to preserve and develop the 'national individuality' of the various peoples of the USSR while at the same time promoting the 'formation of a new social community—the Soviet people.'[11] However, Lenin also expected that 'national distinctions would be present well into the future' and saw fusion as a distant goal.[12]

After Lenin's death, however, and a period in the 1920s when national languages and cultures were not only encouraged but even forcibly promoted in some cases, a policy reversal occurred. In the face of increasing orientations among the various peoples of the USSR towards national histories, culture, and traditions, the Soviet leadership sought to ignore these developments and Lenin's caution and instead to accelerate processes of assimilation. During the Stalinist heyday and under Brezhnev's leadership as well, assimilation meant Russification, which was in turn accompanied by political and economic centralization.[13]

Having identified the causes of the current crisis of national unity in the Soviet Union in this way, the solution proposed by the present leadership is consistent with the analysis, namely, to restore 'the Leninist principle of national self-determination in its true sense' (FBIS, 17 Aug 89, p.42). The proposed restorations include redressal of the imbalance in union–republic relations by transferring greater powers to the republics, establishing their capacity to become 'self-financing,'[14] recognizing their rights to choose their official state languages and languages of instruction in the schools, and providing adequate representation of all peoples in institutions and agencies of power and state authority at the center itself.[15]

This official view of the causes of the current crisis of national unity in the Soviet Union is only partly accepted by most Soviet scholars, who tend instead to see amid the shifts in policy on nationality issues and center–republic relations some unshakeable consistencies. The latter consist, it is argued, in the maintenance from the beginning, or at least since Stalin, of an essentially unitary state and party apparatus, dominated by ethnic Russians, whose unchanging goal has been the elimination of national differences in the USSR through the 'fusion' of nations, which could only mean their ultimate Russification in practice.[16] Since Stalin's death, it is argued, there has been only a loosening of the concentration of political power in Moscow and its domination by Russians.[17]

It is argued further that some of the recent manifestations of discontent in the republics of Central Asia especially and in some of the other republics in the Transcaucasus and the Baltics as well can be traced to the entrenchment of local elites in republic party apparatuses which occurred during Brezhnev's rule in the face— and despite the maintenance—of the practice of appointing Russian second secretaries. Specifically, Gorbachev's attempts to remove indigenous corrupt party officials in the Central Asian republics precipitated ostensibly 'nationalist' reactions, notably in Alma Ata in 1986.[18] In effect, therefore, despite his opening up of the Soviet system in so many respects, Gorbachev has attempted to increase the authority of the central party over local organizations.[19] He has so far refused to entertain any change in the policy of 'inter-republic exchange of cadre.'[20]

Language Issues

The Soviet 'solution' to the language issues in this vast multilingual state has sought to balance the need for a single language for interethnic and inter-provincial communication with the acknowledged rights of all peoples to be educated in, and to use in official dealings, their own language. The Soviet Union formally has no official language, but the language of interethnic and inter-provincial communication obviously has been Russian.

A common criticism of the Soviet multilingual solution has been that, in practice, a policy of Russification has been followed since the 1930s which has involved the neglect of native languages in education and publishing and has also attempted to introduce Russian in the republics to 'the lower grades of all elementary schools.'[21] The dominance of the Russian language as the sole or primary language through which advancement is possible in the central party apparatus, in higher education, in science and technology, and in management positions in industry makes moot the Leninist distinction between avoiding coercion, but permitting 'persuasion' in language choice.[22] Russian language—and ethnic—dominance has also been evident in the past absence of any requirement for Russians living in non-Russian republics to learn the language of the republic in which they live.

Evidence of discontent in the republics with Soviet language policies which favor Russian appeared in the 1978 agitations in Georgia, resisting efforts from the center to remove the official status of the Georgian language from the new republic constitution.[23] The agitations led to the insertion in the Georgian and in the new Armenian and Azerbaijanian republic constitutions of provisions continuing the recognition of the republic languages as official state languages.[24]

New state language laws also contain requirements, as in Estonia, that persons recruited into public service positions learn and use the official language of the state. These requirements are directed primarily at the Russian migrant population, but, in several republics, would involve Non-Russian language groups as well: Abkhazians and Georgians, Armenians and Azerbaijanis.[25] The establishment of a single language as the sole official republic language also raises important questions concerning the rights of minorities to be instructed in schools through the medium of their mother tongue.[26]

INDIA: NATIONALITY POLICY UNDER NEHRU

The principal contention of this paper is that the most successful and balanced nationality policy which has been pursued in either India or the Soviet Union—and that closest to the Leninist ideal— was the set of policies pursued by the Indian state in the period of Nehru's leadership from 1947 to 1964. After independence, the two most divisive nationality issues concerned the official language(s) of the Union and the reorganization of the multilingual British-created provinces and former princely states to conform to the linguistic boundaries of the major language groups in the country.

As in all postcolonial developing countries, the ultimate goal was declared to be 'national integration'. 'National integration' is a rather more vague term than 'assimilation' or 'fusion' of nationalities, which have been described as the ultimate goals of the Soviet state. In practice, a distinction was evolved under Nehru between 'national integration' and mere political integration, which recognized in fact that India was a developing multinational state in which the various major peoples of India held dual loyalties—to their regional national group and to the Indian 'nation' or state as a whole. Evidence of the practical recognition of the multinational character of India is provided by the resolutions which were arrived at in relation to the major divisive issues of official language and linguistic reorganization of states.

Insofar as the question of official language is concerned, the principal issue in the Constituent Assembly, and for two decades thereafter until the passage of the Official Languages (Amendment) Act, 1967, was whether or not Hindi was to be imposed upon the entire country as its sole official language. The official compromise, which was ultimately reached and formalized in the Official Languages Act, 1963, and its amendment in 1967, was to retain both Hindi and English, with the former the 'sole official language' of the country and English as an 'associate additional official language'. In practice, the solution was not just bilingual but multilingual, for all the fourteen major regional languages of India were also recognized as legitimate media of examination for entry into the highest ranks of the administrative service of the country. The major contrast here between India and the Soviet

Union—and one which perhaps holds lessons for the Soviet future—is that the Indian solution to the official language question in practice has been both multilingual and permissive *at the center* itself.

The process of linguistic reorganization of states in India under Nehru also bears comparison—in some ways quite closely, in other ways paradoxically—with the creation of nationality-based republics in the Soviet Union. Ultimately, after prolonged struggles, in some cases involving violence, all the non-Hindi-speaking multilingual provinces of the country were, in stages, reorganized into states in which a single regional language was dominant and was generally adopted also as the sole official language of each such state. In the course of these struggles over reorganization, four rules were applied in relation to them in practice. One was that secession would not be entertained and that any explicitly secessionist movement would be suppressed by whatever force was required. The second was that no demand for the creation of a state based on the principle of dominance by a single religious community would be accepted. The third was that demands for reorganization of multilingual, multicultural provinces would not be accepted unless all major groups were in agreement on its desirability. The last rule was that no reorganization would be carried out on the basis of a demand which lacked demonstrable popular support even if the language group spoken for was clearly a distinct and separate language from others in a multilingual province.

In principle, the Soviet constitution recognizes the right of self-determination of all peoples in the Soviet Union, including the right of secession. The right has been honored in the past in relation to Finland and cannot be ruled out in future in relation to the Baltic states. In practice, however, until the formulation in 1991 of a new treaty union and the resistance of six republics to entering into it, the actual rule had been the same as in India: no tolerance for secession and suppression by force or coercion of any overt expressions of secessionist sentiment.

The second principle of opposition to the creation of federal units based on religion has been rigorously followed in the Soviet Union as well, most notably in the Central Asian republics where special efforts were in fact made to divide up the Muslim Turkic-speaking peoples into a number of different republics based upon language/dialect differences.

The third rule of consent by all major parties to a linguistic reorganization has, for the most part, not been relevant. The republic system was imposed from above with some concern for local interethnic relations, no doubt, but the decisions were made at the center on behalf of the peoples concerned.

The fourth rule has no counterpart in the Soviet Union. In fact, exactly the contrary rule appears to have been followed, namely, the creation of federal units on 'objective' grounds of linguistic differences irrespective of whether or not a strong subjective consciousness had developed among the peoples concerned.

Although there are, therefore, some similarities between Soviet and Indian nationality policies in principle and practice, the differences between the Stalinist and Nehruvian policies are, of course, stark and can be summed up briefly. The Stalinist and neo-Stalinist (Brezhnev) program was one of coerced imposition of a nationality policy from above in which finally no political expressions of nationalism were tolerated and even cultural expressions in practice also were allowed only limited expression. In the Nehru era in India, in contrast, a nationality policy emerged out of struggles and movements from below in which both cultural and political expressions of regional nationalist sentiment were tolerated within a set of formal and informal guidelines or rules.

POLITICAL CENTRALIZATION AND THE DECLINE OF PLURALISM UNDER MRS. GANDHI

India at independence, like the Soviet Union after the Bolshevik revolution, discarded proposals for confederal solutions to issues connected with language, religion, and nationality differences. Once partition of the country was decided upon, the leadership in the Constituent Assembly moved decisively towards the writing of a Constitution which would provide India with a strong state—federal, but with many unitary features.

Despite the massive powers retained by the center and the high degree of economic centralization during the Nehru period, the dynamics of the system were pluralist not only with respect to cultural issues but with respect also to political policies, particularly center–state relations. On cultural issues, the center not only pursued the pluralist language policies discussed above, but also took upon itself the role of protector of minorities, notably the large Muslim minorities spread throughout the country, and other minorities who remained within the linguistically reorganized states. With regard to center–state relations, although the constitutional balance favored the center, the political practices which emerged in the Nehru period were summarized in the terms 'bargaining federalism' and 'cooperative federalism,' which implied not only the absence of dictation from the center, but the existence of a bargaining relationship in which the states—those with strong leaders better than others—were able to extract resources and favors from the center. In a word, the Nehru period of center–state relations was characterized by a balance between a strong centralized state and pluralist practices, between a strong center and strong states, exactly the balance which has become the favored current slogan in the USSR, where the phrase is the virtually identical 'strong republics and a strong union.'

A prolonged struggle for succession ensued after Nehru's death and the interregnum prime ministership of Lal Bahadur Shastri (1964–66), which culminated in the decisive victory of Mrs. Gandhi in the 1971–72 elections and the reassertion of the hegemony of the Indian National Congress throughout the country. Mrs. Gandhi, however, never felt secure and adopted measures to gain and maintain power which used and abused all the constitutional powers available to her to control politics throughout the country. These measures included extensive use of emergency powers, notably in the period 1975–77 when an authoritarian system known as 'The Emergency' was in place, and widespread use of President's Rule to take over the direct administration of any states of the Union where the ruling party might gain some political advantage by doing so on one pretext or another.

The interests of the country also came to be identified with the person of Mrs. Gandhi and that of the Nehru family in general, including her two sons. The boundaries between central and state politics were eroded. The state leaderships of the Indian National Congress lost their autonomy as party and government leaders were chosen directly from the center and replaced at will.

These measures of centralization and concentration of power in New Delhi, however, had quite the opposite results of those intended and of those which prevailed during the Nehru period.

Instability and weak leadership prevailed in the states ruled by the Congress, an increasing number of the non-Hindi-speaking states came under the rule of non-Congress parties, several of them standing for regional nationalism and regional autonomy in opposition to centralized control from New Delhi. Since it is not possible to retain power in New Delhi for long without firm political control in most of the states in India's federal parliamentary system, the overall political result was just the opposite of what prevailed in the Nehru period: a weak center and weak states. Although continuing efforts were made to maintain centralization of economic decisionmaking—even intensified through the proliferation of centrally-sponsored schemes and projects throughout the country—in practice, the economic planning process disintegrated.

The consequences for ethnic group relations and national unity of all these political changes were disastrous. Instead of keeping a step removed from regional and local conflicts and adopting a mediating posture, as was the practice under Nehru, the central leadership under Mrs. Gandhi became directly involved in these conflicts and took sides in them. Inevitably, these interventionist policies turned local and regional conflicts into confrontations between local and regional groups, on the one hand, and the center.

The center's interventionist policies contributed markedly, some would argue even that they virtually created, the Punjab crisis of the 1980s. In an effort to reestablish power in this state which had been lost to the opposition between 1977 and 1980, central government leaders close to Mrs. Gandhi worked to divide the leading opposition party by supporting directly and indirectly the militant, extremist, and allegedly murderous activities of a religious preacher, Sant Jarnail Singh Bhindranwale. Within a few years, Bhindranwale became the central political figure in Punjab, surrounded and supported by groups of militant youth, including many accused of terrorist and other forms of murderous activity. In the process, not only the Congress, but all moderate political groups lost credibility in the politics of the state and explicitly secessionist demands were increasingly heard from the militants.

The center's interventionist policies in the northeastern states of Assam, Nagaland, and Mizoram, and in the northwestern state of Jammu and Kashmir also contributed to, if they did not directly cause, the intensification of violence in those areas and the rise of a secessionist movement in Kashmir.

In these various interventionist moves during Mrs. Gandhi's tenure in power, two other shifts in state policy—towards minorities and towards the Hindu 'majority'—of the country also occurred. The guiding principle of the center's interventions in the states was often nothing more than the maintenance or restoration of the Congress as the ruling party wherever its position was threatened. If that strategy meant breaking an old alliance with a minority group or appealing directly to the religious sentiments of Hindus, it was done. Increasing appeals also to the religious and nationalist sentiments of segments of the Hindu population, particularly in north India, also represented a shift in state policy away from the dominant secular orientation of the Indian state under Nehru.

SYSTEMS OF REGIONAL PARTY AND ADMINISTRATIVE CONTROL IN THE SOVIET UNION AND INDIA

Party Cadre Policy in the Soviet Republics

Connor has argued that Leninist nationality policy was vitiated in practice by the CPSU party cadre policy, that is, the policy of using 'nonindigenous cadre' in the republics to act as a check upon indigenous party personnel.[27] This policy, whose central feature was the appointment of Russians as second secretaries 'in charge of cadres' was not a creation of the Stalinist era, but rather was regularized during the middle of Khrushchev's tenure.[28]

The effectiveness of this policy as a system both of party and ethnic political control over non-Russian republics and nationalities was, however, itself vitiated by Brezhnev's cadre policy. Although the device of appointing Russians as second secretaries continued, Brezhnev instituted a policy of 'stability of cadres' with regard to the first secretary and other party positions in the republics, which led to the dominance of republic bureaucracies by indigenous nationalities and the creation of 'entrenched political machines'.[29]

Some of the widely publicized nationality problems faced by Gorbachev since 1985 in turn have arisen out of his efforts to reverse Brezhnev's cadre policy, which he perceived as having led to 'the spread of corrupt economic and political practices throughout the national regions.'[30] The five Central Asian Republics of Uzbekistan, Kazakhstan, Kirgizia, Tajikhistan, and Turkmenistan were the principal targets of this new policy. Local elites in those republics, faced with dismissal, succeeded in portraying the policy as an insult to local national pride, notably in Alma-Ata, where a Russian was appointed as first secretary in place of the dismissed Kunaev in December 1986.[31]

It is noteworthy, however, that Gorbachev has continued to adhere to the principle of interrepublic exchange of cadre, which he evidently considers to be indispensable to the pursuit of his policies of economic and political reform and which he may also now consider to be important as well for the future of the Union itself.

Center–State Party Relations in India

While, therefore, the Soviet party retained its unitary form even after the establishment of the system of nationality-based republics, the Indian National Congress reorganized the party along linguistic lines long before the postindependence linguistic reorganization of states. The inevitable consequence was the regionalization of the Congress organizations and their social bases, though the central leadership of the party, known as the 'High Command,' retained throughout the independence period the ability to impose its will over the regional party organizations at all decisive moments.

Regionalization of the Congress party organization became ever more pronounced after independence and especially after linguistic reorganization of states. The central party leadership retained considerable influence and final authority in practice on many important matters, including the selection of candidates to contest elections for both the national parliament and the state legislative assemblies. Inner party factionalism was rampant in the states and followed no principles even approximating the Soviet principle of 'democratic centralism'. When it became necessary for the center to intervene, the High Command would send emissaries to the states to mediate between contending factions. At no time and in none of the states, however, were any party positions held by party cadres from the center or from other states of the Union.

The center–state party balance changed completely in the era of Mrs. Gandhi's leadership. Mrs. Gandhi faced a long struggle with state party bosses before establishing her decisive dominance in the Indian political system during 1971–72. In achieving dominance, however, the state party bosses and their independent bases of support were smashed by using a number of personal, party, and governmental devices and mechanisms. Neither under Nehru nor Mrs. Gandhi, however, did anything comparable to the Soviet party cadre problem arise. Wherever and whenever changes in party leadership in the states are made, they are always made from among persons indigenous to the region.

More comparable issues arise when the Soviet party cadre system of control is compared with the system of elite administration in India through the Indian Administrative Service (IAS). The IAS, successor to the British system of administrative control of India through the Indian Civil Service (ICS), is an elite service of approximately 4,000 officers, recruited through uniform competitive examinations from all regions of the country. All officers selected for entry into the IAS are deputed to state cadres, but movement back and forth from state to center and vice versa is permitted and the ultimate authority for such movement is in the hands of the home ministry of the Government of India, including the appointment of the highest ranking secretary in state administration, the chief secretary to the government.

Demands have come from the leaders of regional nationalist and regional autonomy movements in some states of India for greater state control over the selection and posting of IAS officers from the center or for the elimination of the practice altogether. Chief ministers from some states have seen the IAS officers sent from New Delhi as instruments of central control and surveillance even though the officers are required to submit to the authority and control of the chief ministers once they are posted to a state.

With regard to the two preeminent all-India institutions, therefore, there is nothing comparable either to the important role played by the second secretaries in the Soviet party or to the system of ethnic Russian/Slavic administrative surveillance over minority republics. The Gorbachev slogan of 'inter-republic exchange of cadre' bears some comparison with the recruitment and disposition of IAS officers. However, there are also important differences here, notably that recruitment is truely from all regions,

persons from any region of the country may be deployed to any
other region, actual exchange of cadre is confined to movement
between the center and the states, and there is no pattern of
persons from the largest linguistic group, the Hindi-speakers,
being systematically distributed into important positions in all
regions of the country.

Contrasts and Comparisons

Comparison between the Soviet and Indian systems suggests that a
major factor influencing the ultimate course of center–state relations in such huge multiethnic states is the congruity or non-
congruity of nationality policy and systems of regional party and
administrative control. There have been several distinct patterns
in the two states. The predominant pattern in the Soviet Union has
involved a contradiction between the official, 'Leninist' nationality
policy and the high degree of central control and direction of the
political life of the republics. Under Stalin, this meant for some
time the encouragement of regional nationalism by regional elites
wholly tied to and dependent upon a ruthlessly authoritarian
centralizing dictator. Under Brezhnev, the contradiction continued,
but in a different form: the Soviet state persisted in centralized
economic planning and pursued assimilationist policies of Russification, but permitted at the same time the development of new
regional party elites in the republics. Gorbachev, in his early
years, sought to remove this contradiction and to make the system
of regional political control congruent with the pursuit of national
policy goals of continued centralized economic development planning—but more efficient and less corrupt—by displacing the very
regional elites installed under Brezhnev. The attempt to undo this
contradiction has contributed, in the changed and liberalized political context introduced by Gorbachev himself, to the rise of
regional nationlism in several of the republics.

The greatest degree of congruity between language and nationality policy and regional political control existed in India during
the period of Nehru's political dominance. Although Nehru's
governments pursued centralized economic development planning
modeled on the Soviet Union, nationality policy evolved in a
pluralist direction while a balance was maintained in center–state

relations in which state leaders operated with considerable political autonomy. Under Mrs. Gandhi, the balance was upset. Economic planning disintegrated and the struggle for political control became primary, involving increasing central intervention in the politics of the states. In this case, the contradiction was between a nationality policy established during the Nehru period which encouraged the development of strong regional linguistic communities and cultures, on the one hand, and a strategy of political dominance which involved the undermining of regional political autonomy. This latter contradiction contributed to the rise of militant ethnic separatist movements in the 1980s.

In both cases, therefore, i.e., in the Soviet Union under Gorbachev and India under Mrs. Gandhi, changes in the existing balance in center–state relations precipitated crises of national unity. The two patterns, however, are entirely different: in the Soviet case a failed effort to remove a contradiction to which regional elites had adjusted, in the Indian case the introduction of a contradiction which upset the previous balance in center–state relations. While the patterns are different, the common elements in both situations are the changed political context produced by a succession struggle in which the center–state balance itself was at stake and in which the changes introduced created the conditions for new regional elites to challenge the centralizing drives of the Soviet and Indian states.

In both the post-Stalinist Soviet Union and post-Nehru India, the maintenance of power at the center has depended upon maintaining political control in the republics and states, which in turn has involved dissolving former alliances between central and regional elites and creating new ones. Brezhnev's power rested in part on his links with republic elites. Gorbachev, in turn, felt that his control over the country and his ability to change economic policy directions could not be completed until the old linkages between central and regional party cadres established by Brezhnev had been broken. In the liberalized political environment which he also created partly to destroy the power of the neo-Stalinists, Gorbachev's efforts to dislodge regional elites forced him to confront party personnel who were ready to make use of regional linguistic and cultural symbols and demands to maintain themselves in power.

Similarly, when Mrs. Gandhi came to power in 1966, she found that the party organizations at the center and in most states of the country were under the control of a group of state party bosses who had become entrenched in power at the end of Nehru's life. To consolidate her power in a succession struggle which continued from 1966 to 1971–72, Mrs. Gandhi first split the party organization nationally and then proceeded to use her control of state power to destroy the party bosses in their home states. For a time, Mrs. Gandhi's strategy seemed to be remarkably successful, culminating in two massive election victories for her and her wing of the Indian National Congress in the parliamentary elections of 1971 and the state assembly elections of 1972. However, during the 1970s and 1980s, a strong counter-reaction set in as new regional elites in state after state arose in new political parties, articulating the demands of regional caste, language, and religious groups disgruntled over the support given by the central government to regional elite groups allied with her. In several states, as noted above, these new elite groups have supported militant, violent, and secessionist movements.

ELITE COMPETITION FOR JOBS
AND INTERETHNIC CONFLICT

USSR

The bursting forth of interethnic conflicts and nationalist sentiments in widely dispersed parts of the Soviet Union has been connected both with elite political conflict and job competition.[32] Sometimes, the two factors have been closely connected. Interethnic competition over jobs and other resources takes place within the Soviet Union in a context of ethnic Russian dominance of the Soviet state.

The sources of contemporary elite political conflict can be traced to the real 'devolution of power' to the republics which occurred under Brezhnev.[33] 'Republic elites' then took advantage of this political change in the Brezhnev period by packing 'universities with professors and students of the indigenous nationality' and by taking 'control of an ever greater number of levers of economic and political power.'[34]

The 'emergence of new, non-Russian elites' in 'the last generation'[35] has provided the principal basis for interethnic conflicts and increasing national consciousness. The expansion of 'university enrollments' 'in many republics,' for example, Estonia, has created a situation where there are not enough jobs for the more well educated persons from indigenous nationalities, who then find themselves in competition with Russians for inferior jobs,[36] thus creating a double resentment over the absence of the right types of jobs and the necessity to compete with Russians for the types of jobs that are available.

In a time of shrinking economic resources, needs for maximizing efficiency in the use of available resources have come into conflict with the interests of 'entrenched elites' in the republics wedded to 'ethnic favoritism' and 'affirmative action' policies and the expectations of 'many non-Russians' that jobs will be provided to them on the basis of 'nationality' rather than the strict application of merit criteria.[37] Wherever competition has developed between Russians and non-Russians for jobs in the republics, 'the situation [has been invested] with ethnic meaning' by both sides.[38]

Burg has provided an illuminating account with firm statistical evidence of the nature and political consequences of a three-way job competition among the 'scientific and technical cadres' in the Central Asian Republics in the 1960s and 1970s. In these republics, he noted, 'Russians comprised from 38 to 57 per cent of all scientific workers . . . in 1960 while the titular nationalities constituted from 22 to 34 per cent. Jews accounted for about 5 per cent of the scientific cadres in these republics at this time.'[39]

In the decade between 1950 and 1960, there was a dramatic increase in 'the number of scientific workers of Central Asian nationality,' which occurred at the same time that 'large numbers of skilled personnel from the European areas of the Soviet Union were entering the Central Asian labor force.'[40] The consequence was 'growing competition between native and Russian cadres for positions in the scientific elites of the non-Russian republics.'[41]

The issue had become a major concern for central leaders by 1965 and was especially important in the Central Asian Republics.[42] As increasing numbers of persons from indigenous nationalities in all Soviet republics began to enter the job market for scientific and technical personnel, 'the native cadres found a large proportion of desirable positions . . . already . . . occupied by non-native personnel.'[43] It was this situation which produced the 'affirmative action' policies of the Brezhnev era as demands were made for the 'creation or reservation of positions in the scientific elite for native (or "indigenous") cadres.'[44]

Gorbachev's new economic and political policies designed to

eliminate corruption in republic party organizations and introduce more stringent merit criteria into employment policies have clearly run afoul of the delicate balancing mechanisms introduced by his predecessors. The declining significance of the increasingly dispensable Jewish minority will also increase the likelihood of more direct job competition and ethnic conflicts between the immigrant Russian/Slavic populations and the indigenous nationalities in the Central Asian and other republics.

India[45]

Each region of India has a dominant language group and particúlar castes, usually of elite status, who have long held disproportionate shares of public employment and educational and political opportunities. Often, educated persons from different religious, language, caste, and other categories compete for the most prestigious and secure jobs in public service and for the educational opportunities to gain access to them.

Most 'nativist' or 'sons of the soil' movements in India, which have sought to restrict local job opportunities to the indigenous population of particular regions of the çountry, have their origins in the discontents arising from frustrated aspirations or perceived limited life-chances among groups whose members seek desirable positions in the modern, middle class sectors of the economy. These conflicts, though sometimes bitter and violent, normally do not threaten the political unity of the country because of the absence of a dominant ethnic group identified with the Indian state as a target for nativist ideologies.

Although the Soviet Union has avoided any declaration of an official language for the country as a whole, Russian has been the *de facto* official language, the principal vehicle for access to prestigious and powerful positions and for career advancement for educated elites. When job competition arises in such a situation, it easily becomes converted into ethnic hostility, into conflict between the dominant language speakers and the non-dominant ethnic groups. In India, in contrast, an official compromise was reached on the language issue and implemented in practice which avoided the same potential conflicts between speakers of a nearly dominant language, Hindi, and speakers of the other regional languages of the country.

CONCLUSION

This comparison of the relationships between state policies on language issues and the rise of ethnic and nationality movements in the two largest multiethnic states in the contemporary world demonstrates the cross-cultural, cross-political validity of several arguments in the theoretical literature on ethnicity and nationality. The first is the absence of any inevitable connection between language differences as such and ethnic and nationality movements. In fact, it appears that language differences themselves are almost never the basis for such movements, which require instead the presence of one or more other factors. The superimposition of another cultural difference, such as religion, upon the language demarcation is one, but even in such situations, it would be simplistic to resurrect the old argument in the social science literature that congruent cultural cleavages produce political conflicts.

On the contrary, the essential ingredients required to transform language—and other—cultural differences into political conflicts are struggles for political control between central and local elites and elite competition for jobs and other scarce resources, such as education, housing, and the like.

Specific evidence from both the Soviet Union and India supports this argument, but the general political context out of which contemporary political movements in these two countries have emerged must also be considered. Curiously enough, given the profound differences between these two political systems and their leaderships, there is a sense in which the two have moved in a parallel fashion with comparable results. Brezhnev was a neo-Stalinist and Nehru one of the great political liberals of the twentieth century. Yet, during both their rules, a balance in center–state relations was achieved under which regional elites in the republics/states acquired significant autonomy. Similarly, the contemporary world views Gorbachev as a liberalizer, while most India specialists consider Mrs. Gandhi to have moved India towards authoritarian practices. Yet, both leaders sought to break the power of locally entrenched elites, thereby precipitating local nationalist reactions. These comparisons do not argue for a revision of our views of these leaders. Rather, they suggest that there are inherent difficulties in maintaining political control in centralized multiethnic states in the twentieth century, whether democratic or authoritarian, which make inevitable under certain circumstances the expression of ethnic and nationality conflicts.

In order to maintain effective political control in such states, the leadership seeks a legitimating formula: 'proletarian internationalism' and the creation of a new 'Soviet man' or 'national integration'. It then seeks to form alliance patterns with local elites who will support the formula or to create new elites where no collaborators are forthcoming. Absent a Stalinist system where no effective local resistance is possible, elites left out of the new alliances will attempt to use ethnic differences such as language to mobilize local support against the center. In the Soviet case, such mobilization was prevented by Stalinism in the first instance and by Brezhnev's alliance strategies with local elites in the second instance. In the Indian case, under Nehru, where political mobilization was possible, regional elites organized effectively soon after independence. The balance in center–state relations achieved in the first two decades thereafter was arrived at through prolonged struggle.

Center–periphery balances, however, are difficult to maintain in large multiethnic countries when the political context changes or when large processes of social and economic change are in progress or reaching culmination. The opening up of the Soviet system under Gorbachev and his search for new allies in the republics has completely transformed the political context in the Soviet Union. The succession struggle which followed Nehru's death led Mrs. Gandhi also to seek new alliances. Where these two leaders faced entrenched elites and/or took steps which were insensitive to local nationalist sentiments, opposition developed and made use of such sentiments to gain or maintain local political control.

Economic changes have also contributed in both countries to the rise of ethnic and nationality conflicts. Vast processes of social and economic development in the Soviet peripheries have led to the creation of new elite groups, particularly among the potentially most volatile educated professional middle classes able to operate effectively in two cultures and in two languages. Similarly in India, enormous expansions in secondary and higher education and the entry of previously unrepresented or underrepresented language and other groups into educational institutions have produced millions of new graduates seeking employment in the government, public, and modern urban professional sectors of the economy. Wherever these new aspiring groups have perceived their life-chances blocked by ethnic groups whose social mobilization preceded theirs, economic competition has been sooner or later converted into ethnic competition.

Although both the Soviet Union and India now face serious secessionist movements in some parts of these two countries, the danger to the preservation of their unions seems greater in the former than in the latter country. There are two principal reasons. The first is the fact that several of the Soviet republics, notably the Baltic states, have had the experience of independent statehood recognized by the international community. The internal strength and international support for the demands coming from these republics, therefore, are enhanced because they are considered anticolonial rather than secessionist movements.

The second lies in the existence in the Soviet Union of the perception that the Russians constitute a dominant and privileged nation and the fact of their widespread dispersal throughout the minority republics. The latter fact precipitates fears and conflicts over both local political control and job competition. The Baltic republic peoples, for example, feel their political control in their own countries as well as their economic opportunities threatened by the presence of large Russian minorities. The presence of Russians, other Slavic groups, Jews, and Armenians occupying the most prestigious jobs in other republics, particularly in Central Asia, has also contributed to the articulation of regional national-ist sentiment in several republics.

In India, in contrast, where there is no dominant nation and no single large ethnic group dispersed throughout the country in privileged positions, the potential for a complete unravelling of the country's unity seems less great. If it is difficult for militant nationalist parties in north India to unite the Hindi-speaking region politically and still less the Hindu majority in the country as a whole, it is even more difficult to unite the non-Hindi-speaking areas politically against the center. Contemporary crisis areas in India, however militant, violent, and separatist, are confined to relatively small units: Punjab, Kashmir, and the northeastern tribal areas.

In neither India nor the Soviet Union can any single group

successfully challenge the center. Nor is it likely even in the Soviet Union that dissident nationalist movements in different parts of the country can unite against the center. However, even if the leadership of these two multinational states succeed in thwarting immediate threats to the maintenance of their unity and in preventing internal disintegration, the consequences of such dissidence for their effective functioning are severe. Dissident nationalist movements divert the attentions of national leaders in these vast centralized states ever more towards the unending task of consolidating their political control, distracting attention from the pursuit of policies for effective economic development. Yet, the predominant leadership in both countries persist in believing that strong centralized control remains essential for both national unity and economic development. As long as the leaderships of these two states persist in this delusion and resist genuine political and economic decentralization, it is certain that dissident ethnic and nationality movements will continue to assert themselves now in one region, now in another.

NOTES

1. Gertrude E. Schroeder, 'Social and Economic Aspects of the Nationality Problem,' in Robert Conquest (ed.), *The Last Empire: Nationality and the Soviet Future* (Stanford, CA: Hoover Institution Press, 1986), p. 295.
2. Paul A. Goble, 'Gorbachev and the Soviet Nationality Problem,' in Maurice Friedberg and Heyward Isham (eds.), *Soviet Society Under Gorbachev: Current Trends and the Prospects for Reform* (Stanford, CA: Hoover Institution Press, 1986), pp. 84–86.
3. Goble 'Gorbachev and the Soviet Nationality Problem,' op. cit., p. 89.
4. Myron Weiner, *Sons of the Soil: Migration and Ethnic Conflict in India* (Princeton: Princeton University Press, 1978), p. 57. [These are 1961 census figures; later figures are unfortunately not available.]
5. Walker Connor, *The National Question in Marxist-Leninist Theory and Strategy* (Princeton, NJ: Princeton University Press, 1984), p. 487.
6. John B. Dunlop, 'Language, Culture, Religion, and National Awareness,' in Conquest, op. cit., p. 270.
7. Alexander J. Motyl, *Will the Non-Russians Rebel? State, Ethnicity, and Stability in the USSR* (Ithaca: Cornell University Press, 1987), pp. 46–47.
8. Goble, 'Gorbachev and the Soviet Nationality Problem,' op. cit., p. 89.
9. Motyl, *Will the Non-Russians Rebel?* op. cit., p. 42.
10. The RSS is a Hindu revivalist organization which promotes Hindu solidarity and 'character building' through disciplined daily activity in 'rituals, physical

exercises and lessons'. Its members provide cadres for the BJP and many other organizations in India devoted to strengthening the Hindu community. See Walter K. Andersen and Shridhar D. Damle, *The Brotherhood in Saffron: The Rashtriya Swayamsevak Sangh and Hindu Revivalism* (New Delhi: Vistaar Publications, 1987), citation from p. 1.

11. FBIS, SOV-89-158, 17 August 1989, CPSU Releases 'Draft Nationalities Policy', PM1608141589 Moscow PRAVDA in Russian, 17 August 1989, p. 40.

12. Martha Olcott, 'Gorbachev's National Dilemma,' *Journal of International Affairs*, Vol. XLII, No. 2 (Spring 1989), p. 402.

13. FBIS, 17 August 1989, pp. 40–41.

14. FBIS, 17 August 1989, p. 42.

15. FBIS, 17 August 1989, p. 46.

16. For example, see especially Dunlop, 'Language, Culture, Religion, and National Awareness,' op. cit., and Motyl, *Will the Non-Russians Rebel?* op. cit.

17. Alexander J. Motyl, 'The Sobering of Gorbachev: Nationality, Restructuring, and the West,' in Seweryn Bialer, *Politics, Society, and Nationality Inside Gorbachev's Russia* (Boulder, CO: Westview, 1989) pp. 150–51.

18. Olcott, 'Gorbachev's National Dilemma,' op. cit., pp. 404–6.

19. Olcott, 'Gorbachev's National Dilemma,' op. cit., p. 400.

20. Olcott, 'Gorbachev's National Dilemma,' op. cit., p. 403.

21. Dunlop, 'Language, Culture, Religion, and National Awareness,' op. cit., p. 258.

22. Connor, *The National Question*, op. cit., pp. 480–81.

23. Motyl, 'The Sobering of Gorbachev,' op. cit., p. 162.

24. Dunlop, 'Language, Culture, Religion, and National Awareness,' op. cit., p. 265.

25. Dunlop, 'Language, Culture, Religion, and National Awareness,' op. cit., p. 285.

26. FBIS, 17 August 1989, p. 46.

27. Connor, *The National Question*, op. cit., pp. 479–80.

28. John H. Miller, 'Cadres Policy in Nationality Areas: Recruitment of CPSU First and Second Secretaries in non-Russian Republics of the USSR,' *Soviet Studies*, Vol. XXIX, No. 1 (January 1977), pp. 19–20.

29. Goble, 'Gorbachev and the Soviet Nationality Problem,' op. cit., p. 89.

30. Olcott, 'Gorbachev's National Dilemma,' op. cit., p. 403.

31. Olcott, 'Gorbachev's National Dilemma,' op. cit., pp. 405–6.

32. The weight to be attached to these two factors, however, certainly varies from republic to republic. While I think these factors would be relevant, for example, even in the Baltic republics, including Lithuania, the political history of these republics places them in a position intermediate between the countries of Eastern Europe always acknowledged to be independent and the other Soviet republics whose previous history provides a much less clear claim to independence. In the Baltics, therefore, even without the kinds of elite political conflict and job competition discussed in the text, demands for the restoration of independence might best be explained as a logical consequence of the collapse of the Soviet political order.

33. Goble, 'Gorbachev and the Soviet Nationality Problem,' op. cit., p. 97.

34. Goble, 'Gorbachev and the Soviet Nationality Problem,' op. cit., p. 80.

35. Goble, 'Gorbachev and the Soviet Nationality Problem,' op. cit., pp. 81–82.
36. Goble, 'Gorbachev and the Soviet Nationality Problem,' op. cit., p. 87.
37. Motyl, 'The Sobering of Gorbachev,' op. cit., p. 165.
38. Goble, 'Gorbachev and the Soviet Nationality Problem,' op. cit., p. 91.
39. Steven L. Burg, 'Russians, Natives and Jews in the Soviet Scientific Elite:
    Cadre Competition in Central Asia,' *Cahiers du Monde Russe et Sovietique*,
    Vol. XX, No. 1 (January–March 1979), p. 58*fn*.
40. Burg, 'Russians, Natives and Jews,' op. cit., pp. 46–47.
41. Burg, 'Russians, Natives and Jews,' op. cit., p. 43.
42. Burg, 'Russians, Natives and Jews,' op. cit., pp. 49–50.
43. Burg, 'Russians, Natives and Jews,' op. cit., p. 49.
44. Burg, 'Russians, Natives and Jews,' op. cit., p. 50.
45. For a more elaborate statement of the general argument presented in the first
    two paragraphs here, see Paul R. Brass, *The Politics of India Since Indepen-
    dence* (Cambridge: Cambridge University Press, 1990), pp. 132–33.

Ethnic Conflict in Multiethnic Societies: The Consociational Solution and Its Critics

In the face of increasing disenchantment and despair over the future of multiethnic states, a new school of thought founded by Arend Lijphart has argued that the consequences of ethnic conflicts in deeply divided societies may be avoided through political engineering of new state forms based on the consociational model. Lijphart argues that this model, neglected by theorists of the modern state, holds the possibility of both stability and democracy for plural societies in the West and in the developing countries. A considerable debate has developed concerning both the empirical validity of the consociational model in general and its relevance to ethnically-divided societies especially.

Indeed, the debate has been so extensive that one feels the need to justify yet another contribution to it. The justification for this one is the perception that all scholars involved in the debate have been caught in a discourse based on similar assumptions and premises that either objectify or reify ethnicity and ethnic conflict or are simply false. For, the arguments of both the proponents and critics of the consociational solution suffer from several common deficiencies: the mistaken assumption that cultural differences among ethnic groups are 'objective' factors; inadequate treatment of the relationships between class and ethnicity and of cross-cutting cleavages; and an assumption that either democracy does not exist or that all 'democracies' are more or less elitist and that, therefore, an elitist solution to ethnic conflict, such as consociationalism, is a viable and desirable 'democratic,' if not competitive, political form. A more appropriate set of assumptions would recognize the variability of ethnic identities, the pervasiveness of intraethnic, as well as intraclass cleavages in most societies, and would recognize also that a fully-developed consociational system is inherently undemocratic and violates both the rights of non-recognized groups and the rights of individuals.

The consociational model also deserves to be rejected on other grounds. First, it fails to recognize that political accommodation in democratic societies is an art not a system. Second, the recognition of group rights does not require consociational democracy. Third, it fails to give due recognition to the experience of India, the largest and most culturally diverse society in the world, whose successes and failures in resolving ethnic conflicts do not support the assumptions of either the consociationalists and their critics or the solutions offered by the consociationalists.

Finally, the model and the debate about it divert attention from the actual roles played by the state in ethnic conflicts, which has been the main purpose of Part III of this volume to demonstrate. The debate over the model frames the issues into a choice between consociational and adversarial approaches to political conflicts and conflict resolution. The whole point of the argument in Part III of this volume, in contrast, is that whatever system of conflict and conflict resolution prevails in a given state, the state itself is always involved in interventions in alliance patterns which occur between ethnic groups and within ethnic groups and often itself allies with particular elements within an ethnic group. The issue, therefore, with respect to the prevention of extreme forms of ethnic conflict is how well the state plays its role and chooses the groups with which it allies.

Originally developed by Lijphart in the 1960s as a term to describe the political regime created by the Dutch to accommodate differences among the segmented religio–political groupings in that society, the term 'consociational democracy' was soon extended to apply to several others of the smaller European democracies that had developed similar patterns of accommodation to overcome the potential conflicts in deeply divided societies. Included in this first extension of the net were Belgium, Austria, Switzerland, and Lebanon. Within a few years, the 'concept of consociationalism' was being presented by Lijphart and his followers as a prescriptive model applicable to plural societies in developing countries generally[1] and to other deeply divided societies in the West such as Canada and Northern Ireland.

The leading characteristics of the system of consociational democracy can be summarized briefly since they are by now fairly well-known. Its 'essential characteristic,' Lijphart has emphasized, 'is not so much any particular institutional arrangement as overarching cooperation at the elite level in a culturally fragmented system.'[2] However, the system is generally associated with four additional specific characteristics: (a) 'government by a grand coalition'; (b) 'the mutual veto or "concurrent majority" rule'; (c) proportionality in recruitment to decisionmaking bodies and the public services and in 'allocation of public funds'; and (d) 'a high degree of autonomy for each segment to run its own internal affairs.'[3] The idea 'is not to abolish or weaken segmental cleavages but to recognize them explicitly and to turn the segments into constructive elements of stable democracy.' In effect, 'plural societies' are to be made 'more thoroughly plural'.[4]

By the mid-1970s, the consociational idea was beginning to come under scrutiny as a contribution to political theory and to political engineering. It was welcomed as a valuable emendation to existing taxonomies of contemporary political systems and praised for its assertion of the autonomy of political leaders and groups over 'social forces' or 'political cleavages' and for its reestablishment of political action as an independent factor even in societies divided by deep social and ethnic cleavages. As a contribution to political theory and, more specifically, to democratic theory, however, it has been criticized for its elitist bias, on the one hand, and for its alleged overemphasis on the freedom of elites from social constraints, on the other hand.

However, the most telling criticisms against consociationalism have focused upon its empirical validity in relation to the cases upon which the model itself has been built and its consequent relevance for other societies, particularly ethnically-divided societies. Barry, one of the leading and most thoroughgoing critics of the whole consociational idea, has criticized the model from both points of view.[5] He has argued that Switzerland provides no support for consociationalism because its institutions and procedures do not, in fact, fit the consociational model. He considers Austria a doubtful case in the sense that it is not clear that its consociational institutions from 1945 to 1966 actually serve to explain that country's stability in that period in contrast to the period of elite conflict and political collapse during the 1918–34 period. As for the Netherlands and Belgium, although Barry has his doubts even about these two cases, he accepts for the sake of argument that they do fit the consociational model descriptively, that is, in the way decisions are made. However, he argues that it is dangerous to extend the relevance of this model based on a method of resolving church–state and working-class issues in these two countries to ethnically divided societies, including Belgium where, he insists, it has not in fact been used to deal with the conflicts between Flemings and Walloons.

Barry's arguments against the relevance of consociationalism to ethnically-divided societies are as follows. (a) Ethnic divisions are more inflammatory than church–state and working-class issues. (b) It is more difficult for ethnic group leaders to keep their followers in line than for leaders of religious and class groups. (c) The interests of ethnic groups are clearer than those of religious and class groups and, therefore, less negotiable. (d) Ethnic divisions raise secessionist issues that religion and class do not.[6] He argues especially that both the depth of ethnic feelings and the phenomenon of outbidding, amply demonstrated in countries 'with elections dominated by ethnically-based political parties' (such as Guyana, Sri Lanka, Northern Ireland, and Nigeria), and the occurrence of 'communal massacres' in the Indian subcontinent, Indonesia, Cyprus, and Northern Ireland both suggest the futility of consociationalism in such situations.[7]

In the face of such criticisms of his model, Lijphart has persisted in his insistence that consociational democracy is both an empirical model that explains the political stability of several smaller European democracies, namely, Austria, Belgium, the Netherlands, and Switzerland and a normative model for 'the plural societies of the Third World.'[8] He continues to argue even that Lebanon was not a failure: the system there broke down because of external intervention and imperfections in the consociational arrangements which needed to be repaired. He insists that it is still the only solution there.[9]

In his reply to the critique that consociationalism is not relevant to ethnically-divided societies, Lijphart argues that differences in the intensity of cleavages in ethnically-divided societies as compared to societies divided by religion and class are matters of degree, not of kind, and that even 'these differences in degree should not be exaggerated.'[10] In any case, Lijphart himself is rather modest in his claims for the relevance of consociational devices to plural societies. His argument is not that consociational democracy is a cure-all for the problems of such societies, only that it is a more sensible choice than the British style of adversarial democracy that is an inappropriate model for deeply-divided societies.[11]

In a chapter on 'consociationalism' in his book, *The Ethnic Phenomenon*, van den Berghe also considers whether 'consociational democracy' represents a possible alternative to conflict or assimilation in plural societies. The answer he gives 'is a highly qualified "yes",'[12] rather more qualified than that of Lijphart. Unlike Barry, he accepts the relevance of the consociational model for ethnically divided (but not racially divided) societies on the assumption that, in such societies, a class interest may develop among 'the ruling elite' to preserve a 'unitary multiethnic state' rather than permit the state to break 'down into its ethnic components.'[13] However, such an arrangement can easily break down 'when counterelites . . . arise' to challenge 'the status quo' and choose to do so by mobilizing ethnic sentiments that 'can easily be fanned into raging separatism, escalating to civil war.'[14] Moreover, consociational democracy is suited in the first place only to a limited range of plural societies, namely, those in which 'the ethnic collectivities are: (*a*) not too different to start with; (*b*) united by a multiple network of cross-cutting ties and affiliations'; and (*c*) 'somewhat territorially mixed.'[15] Van den Berghe's conclusions for the future of consociational democracy 'are definitely pessimistic.' It rarely succeeds and, when it does, it is questionable whether it is a 'success of democracy or simply a collusion of class interests between ethnic segments of an elite.'[16]

It should be apparent at this point that the debate on the issue of the relevance of consociational democracy to ethnically-divided societies has been taking place among scholars who share a number of assumptions about ethnicity and about plural societies and who also share a basically pessimistic outlook concerning the future stability of those societies. The range of attitudes is from the hopelessness of Barry to the pessimism of van den Berghe to the cautious hopes of Lijphart. It should also be clear that they share a common analytic focus on the stability and viability of the modern state, not simply or even primarily on the prospects for democracy in deeply divided societies. I propose to argue in the rest of this paper that the assumptions, the analytical focus, and the attitudes of all sides on this debate are distracting attention from other important issues concerning the relationships between ethnic groups and the state and that a different set of assumptions and a different analytical focus may also lead to quite different conclusions about the possible futures of such societies.

The first shared assumption among these authors is that cultural differences among ethnic groups are 'objective' factors or primordial sentiments or 'givens'.[17] Even van den Berghe, who is well aware of the subjective features of ethnic identity and of processes of assimilation between ethnic groups, tends to treat the array of ethnic groups in a plural society at any point in time as solidary entities. It follows from this first assumption that all three authors discussed above and most others who have involved themselves in this debate tend to overestimate the degree of segmentation among ethnic and communal groups in Asia and Africa. Insofar as these authors do recognize the possibility of intraethnic divisions in plural societies, it is to worry that such divisions will lead to outbidding, ethnic rampages, raging separatism, and civil war. This worry arises from another assumption, namely, that ethnic divisions are more inflammatory than other types. The latter assumption is not shared by Lijphart, but that is only because he thinks that all segmental cleavages are more or less equally dangerous and all require consociational solutions.

A second defect common to both Lijphart and van den Berghe is the inadequacies of their treatments of the relationships between class and ethnicity and of cross-cutting cleavages. It may seem strange to make such a criticism since both authors devote considerable space to both types of issues, often with considerable insight. Nevertheless, their analyses suffer from the same weakness of objectification of the categories of class and social cleavage.

Van den Berghe presents valuable and interesting typologies of the types of interrelationships between ethnicity and class and of their consequences for social mobility and ethnic conflict. Lijphart effectively challenges the prevailing notions in political science and sociology that coincident cleavages are conflict-producing and cross-cutting cleavages are conflict-moderating. However, both authors treat class, ethnicity, religion, and language as objective factors and largely as 'givens'. Lijphart goes to the extent of using and devising indexes and angles of cross-cutting social cleavages in different societies. Van den Berghe insists that it is mistake to reify class[18] and argues that class consciousness is more difficult to create out of a class category than ethnic identification out of an ethnic category, but his analysis of the relationship between class and ethnicity leads to nothing but a four-cell taxonomy of low/high ethnic mobility, stratification and low/high class stratification with one cell empty.[19] Missing from both Lijphart and van den Berghe are dynamic analyses of the relationships between ethnicity, class, and other social cleavages that would suggest the conditions under which political elites choose to make use of and can effectively make use of ethnic, class or other ties for purposes of political mobilization.

Lijphart and van den Berghe also arrive at a strangely similar attitude toward democracy despite some apparent differences. Insofar as van den Berghe is concerned, there is simply no such thing. There are only systems of domination. What is called 'liberal democracy' is simply the tyranny of a majority rather than of a minority.[20] Lijphart, who is willing to use the term 'democracy' for the system he proposes, has responded to the criticisms of it that it is in fact an elitist not a democractic solution by arguing that most other democracies are equally elitist. However, the point surely ought to be that, while conceding the relative lack of democracy and the prevailing elitist tendencies even in societies that consider themselves democratic, some types of institutional and political arrangements tend toward more and some toward less elitism.[21]

It is obvious that consociationalism by definition is elitist and postpones democratization of multiethnic societies. Lijphart is explicit that the principle of 'segmental isolation,' which is central to consociationalism, 'entails a strengthening of the political inertness of the non-elite public and of their deferential attitudes to the segmental leaders.'[22] Just how elitist and conservative it is should be clear from the fact that Lijphart even points to the Southern blockage of civil rights in the US for decades as an effective consociational arrangement.[23] It ought, therefore, to be a matter of some concern for those who favor democratization of such societies to be advised that consociationalism is the *only* possible 'democratic' solution to the dilemma of plural societies.[24] In giving such advice and in explicitly ruling out the possibility of adversarial politics for such societies, Lijphart ignores the fact that adversarial politics have in fact worked to an extent in non-homogeneous societies such as Great Britain, which is almost invariably, though falsely, considered to be homogeneous, and in the US, another decidedly non-homogeneous society. They have 'worked' in the sense that, historically, a considerable degree of assimilation of a multiplicity of ethnic groups has occurred in both societies despite the maintenance of systems of competitive politics and a fair amount of democratization.

The insistence upon consociationalism as the only democratic alternative and the rejection of competitive politics arise out of the two assumptions that ethnic groups are generally non-divisible, but that when they are divided it is only to become more extreme. Such assumptions lead to a failure to consider the alternative that ethnic communities may be divided internally in a system of open adversarial politics in ways that undermine the segmental cleavages of plural societies and permit inter-segmental alliances on other bases than interelite agreement. Lijphart is, for example, very clear about the limited practical choices that he thinks are available to such segmented societies as Canada. The future of Canada, he argued in the 1977 book, depends upon 'whether it moves in the direction of greater consociationalism and, as a result, greater stability and unity, or in the direction of a more centrifugal regime with a partition of the country as its most likely outcome.'[25] Nowhere in his analysis of Canada and Quebec separatism does he consider historic and contemporary political divisions within the French community and the possibility that those divisions might be great enough and persistent enough to prevent the secession of Quebec provided that the political parties do *not* opt for consociational devices that cause the French–English divide to become congealed. Since 1977, of course, the Quebecers have rejected a referendum in favor of independence, in which many French-speaking Quebecers must have voted for the maintenance of the Canadian union. In 1990, the Canadian Union remained intact, though still threatened, after the defeat of a constitutional formula which would have recognized French-speaking Canadians as '*une sociétée distincte*'. The Canadian case, therefore, would seem to confute 'the proposition that plural societies do not have two alternative democratic options and that consociationalism is their only democratic option.'[26]

In such a situation and in others like it, it is ridiculous to propose that the party system reflect the communal cleavages of the society when the party system may be the only mode of intercommunal communication available. The reenforcement of segmented autonomy by eliminating all political means of non-elite inter-communal communication and the creation instead of monoethnic political parties whose leaders have to do nothing more to gain access to state patronage than to agree not to press any extreme claims on behalf of their group clearly must lead to a self-sustaining system that can last only as long as the mass public remains politically inert and deferential.

That a consociational system itself may be defeated by 'out-bidding' is evident from the attempt of Malaysia at consociational democracy between 1955 and 1969. Although Lijphart argues that consociational democracy was working successfully until its breakdown in 1969, it is noteworthy that 'it broke down after the 1969 elections in which the Alliance parties lost much of their popular support . . . to a number of anti-Alliance communal parties,' after which there was a breakdown of civil order, the suspension of parliament, and the strengthening of the consocia-tional system by undemocratic means. Yet, somehow, Lijphart considers Malaysian democracy in the period before 1969 as 'an inspiring example' for the future of democracy in Asia and Africa.[27] On the contrary, the experience of Malaysia, Lebanon, Cyprus, and Algeria, all examples that Lijphart gives of attempts at con-sociational democracy, suggest that consociational democracy offers no better guarantee of democratic stability in plural societies than the systems of competitive politics that have persisted in such plural societies as Canada, India, and Sri Lanka.

Insofar as Lebanon is concerned, it is evident that the so-called plural segments of that society are internally divided—and very deeply—and not just into sub-segments of an ethnic sort, but into political factions, criminal gangs, and smugglers of all sorts. To propose consociationalism for this society means reifying some categories above others, investing these opportunists and criminal gangs with formally recognized leadership of their so-called segments, and retarding further the prospects of democratization, secularization, and intercommunal cooperation. Moreover, of the possible solutions that could be conceived for the restoration of civil society in Lebanon, consociational democracy in such a situation would appear to be the worst possible.

It is most unfortunate that Lijphart and his followers have transformed their insights concerning the autonomy of politics and the potential creativity of political elites into a prescriptive formula for developing countries, particularly in the light of the evident non-democratic features of the system they propose. Lijphart has performed a useful service in identifying the great variety of devices available to political elites who wish to attempt to accommodate ethnic conflicts in plural societies. However, it is not at all useful to elaborate all these devices into an ideal model to be emulated and to be used to judge the extent to which plural societies have followed the prescriptions of the consociational engineers.

It is not useful for the following reasons. First, political accommodation in democratic societies is an art not a system, and one that has to be pursued persistently in the face of changing circumstances. Consociationalism is a device for freezing existing divisions and conflicts and reducing the art of political accommodation to formulas that can work only as long as processes of social, economic, and political change do not upset them.

Second, if one is concerned with group rights and not with the maintenance of existing states, the recognition of group rights does not require consociational democracy. It requires only that the cultural rights of groups not be infringed and that those groups which wish to act as groups can do so in such matters, for example, as having government schools in which the language and culture of the group can be taught. On the other hand, consociational democracy inevitably violates the rights of some groups and the rights of individuals. It violates the rights of those groups in being and those that may develop in future whose existence is not recognized by the state. It also certainly fails to provide protection to and may lead to the oppression of individuals who wish not to be identified with or wish to free themselves from identification with particular cultural groups. The use of particular consociational devices does not necessarily have this effect, but the creation of a system based on rigid segmental autonomy and isolation certainly does.

For some reason, the consociationalists and the theorists of the plural society consistently ignore the experience of India, the largest, most culturally diverse society in the world that has, except for a period of two years, functioned with a highly competitive and distinctly adversarial system of politics. India is both a plural society[28] and a society that has experienced considerable conflict, sometimes violent, between various of its plural segments.[29] Yet, it is not a consociational democracy at all,[30] though it has adopted many consociational devices, some permanently, some temporarily, to deal with interethnic conflicts and center–state conflicts as they have arisen. In the country as a whole and in its federal segments, many of which are larger than most other countries in the world, the party system includes interethnic aggregative parties as well as ethnically exclusive or primarily monoethnic parties. Historically, politics at the center and in the several states have been dominated by intercommunal and interethnic parties which have persisted in the face of recurrent hostilites between communal and ethnic groups. Violence has threatened or has occurred mostly when some leader has driven hard to consolidate a particular community or ethnic group into a politically solidary force, as Jinnah did with the Muslim League in the pre-independence period when politics were more elitist than they are today.

However, in the postindependence period, it has sometimes proved possible for monoethnic and multiethnic political parties to cooperate, even form coalitions after elections and reach agreement on controversial matters affecting their cultural rights or the claims of different groups. In this big and bustling political system based on universal adult franchise and free-wheeling competition. it has, however, proven extremely difficult for any political party to capture the solidary support of a single ethnic group. Several parties have been overwhelmingly monoethnic in composition and in popular support, but few ethnic groups have been represented by or given their support to only one political party. Even in Punjab before the partition of 1947, as in America before the Civil War, the last intersegmental tie to break was the bond of party.

Even today, the crisis in Punjab discussed in chapters 5 and 6 of this volume does not support the arguments on behalf of consociationalism as preventive or solution.[31] The crisis there was precipitated by a disruptive adversarial strategy. Nor can it be solved by consociationalism. On the contrary, the elements required are a combination of political accommodation, division of the Sikh 'segment' in a way which isolates the violent elements, and suppression of terrorism.

The experience of India with regard to the relationship between competitive political parties and ethnic/communal cleavages has demonstrated the following characteristics. First, parties play independent roles in creating, shaping, and moderating ethnic group loyalties and antagonisms. They do not merely reflect the existing cleavages of the society. They may sometimes create new ones, shape old ones in new political directions, or moderate tensions.

Second, the striving for power in India—and I believe in other multiethnic societies with parliamentary systems—tends to promote intercommunal collaboration either before or after elections. Moreover, one does not need a theory of consociationalism to explain this. The natural tendency of politicians in pursuit of power is to search for new alignments or divisions that will provide them with a base to achieve it. The more open and competitive the political system, the more likely it is that, in the long run, political divisions will develop even within majority ethnic groups that dominate minorities. It is not, of course, an automatic process and is likely to be most difficult when the opportunities for domination of one ethnic group by another are great, as in many dual ethnic states such as Cyprus and Northern Ireland.

However, the real trade-offs are between competition with the possibility of ethnic conflict and consociationalism with the likelihood of domination of some ethnic groups and individuals by others or of the mass of the people by an elite and with the long-term likelihood of a violent breakdown. For example, consociationalism practised between the North and the South in the US for nearly a hundred years involved the oppression of blacks by whites and the retardation of the political and economic emancipation of the black people for the same period. It terminated only in the 1950s and 1960s, leaving in its wake the violent conflicts associated with race relations in the US for the next two decades.

Third, the principle dangers of violent conflict arise when all routes to power in an existing system seem closed to an organized force and when the possibility of changing the political arena is a real one. The existence of one of these conditions is often sufficient to be conducive to ethnic conflict. The existence of both is particularly dangerous. One or both of these conditions have existed in such far-flung places as India in 1947, Pakistan in 1971, Northern Ireland for quite some time, and the Soviet Union in the mid-

1980s. In Canada in the 1970s, however, only the second condition was present. Moreover, the central authorities did not rule out secession for the province of Quebec, which in turn moderated the seriousness of the potential conflict and lessened the likelihood of its occurrence.

In fact, secession is not an option which political elites with access to power in an existing system normally prefer. Political elites tend to seek maximal power at minimal risk. Secession usually promises maximal power but at great risk. It is when both options are closed, access to power and the right to self-determination, or when it is feared that they will be closed, that political elites are likely to raise secessionist demands. Recent secessionist demands from Lithuania and several other republics in the Soviet Union have been made possible by the changed political context in the Soviet Union. The course of events in 1989–90 made it clear to the Lithuanian leaders, however, that secessionism even in a liberalized Soviet state remained a high cost strategy better postponed at least for the time being.

Finally, some of the discussion of consociational arrangements focuses excessively on procedures for resolving or failing to resolve differences and too little on the results. When one ethnic group is blatantly discriminating against or oppressing another, it is nothing but an analytical distraction to propose a consociational remedy. The analytical issue then is whether or not the system of control being exercised can be maintained or not.[32] Also, it is nonsensical to present extensive discussions of angles of cross-cutting cleavages and predisposing and non-predisposing factors for consociationalism when the real issues are overt domination, repression, and discrimination perpetuated by one group over another over a long period, as in the case of Northern Ireland or South Africa. In other words, there is no substitute for looking at the actual issues and conflicts and the way they are dealt with by the dominant groups in a society. In some circumstances, it is simply futile to propose consociational solutions. In others, it is itself a form of repression. One thing, however, is certain. When well-entrenched ethnic elites see that their interests will be better served by dividing up state patronage proportionally, they do not require advice from political scientists to seize the opportunity.[33]

NOTES

1. Arend Lijphart, 'Cultural Diversity and Theories of Political Integration,' *Canadian Journal of Political Science*, Vol. IV, No. 1 (March 1971), p. 10.
2. Lijphart, 'Cultural Diversity and Theories of Political Integration,' op. cit.
3. Arend Lijphart, *Democracy in Plural Societies: A Comparative Exploration* (New Haven: Yale University Press, 1977), p. 25.
4. Lijphart, *Democracy in Plural Societies*, op. cit., p. 42. See also his solution to the ethnic problems of South Africa in Arend Lijphart, *Power-Sharing in South Africa* (Berkeley: Institute of International Studies, University of California, 1985), where he says: 'By explicitly recognizing the [plural] segments, by giving segmental organizations a vital formal function in the political system, by subsidizing them on a proportional basis, and by encouraging segmental political parties through proportional representation, consociational democracy increases the organizational strength of the segments. But instead of creating conflict, the strengthened segments now play a constructive role in conflict resolution'; pp. 106–7.
5. Brian Barry, 'Review Article: Political Accommodation and Consociational Democracy,' *British Journal of Political Science*, Vol. V (1975), pp. 477–505.
6. Barry, 'Review Article,' op. cit., pp. 502–3.
7. Barry, 'Review Article,' op. cit., pp. 504–5.
8. Lijphart, *Democracy in Plural Societies*, op. cit., p. 3.
9. Lijphart, *Power-Sharing in South Africa*, op. cit., pp. 12–13.
10. Lijphart, *Democracy in Plural Societies*, op. cit., p. 234.
11. Lijphart, *Democracy in Plural Societies*, op. cit., p. 238. See also *Power-Sharing in South Africa*, op. cit., p. 86, where he says: 'A majoritarian democracy in a plural society is likely to result in violence and democratic collapse.' Further, on p. 89, Lijphart makes the non-demonstrable argument that consociational democracy 'certainly has a much better chance than majoritarian democracy.' Lijphart also says (p. 100) that consociational democracy does not always work, but that when it fails it is a failure of management on the part of segmental leaders. This argument is a proverbial case of having and eating one's cake. In any case, the same argument can be made about majoritarian democracy. In fairness to Lijphart, however, it needs to be noted that his arguments are clearly stated in probabilistic terms: consociational democracy is *more likely* to succeed in plural societies than majoritarian democracy and majoritarian democracy is *more subject* to failure the more truly plural the society. My point, which will be developed further subsequently, is that the more plural the society the more important it is to keep some possibility for change, internal division, and secularization open for the sake of the ultimate integration of the people in a common political order and to preserve individual rights and the future prospect of individual autonomy.
12. Pierre L. van den Berghe, *The Ethnic Phenomenon* (New York: Elsevier, 1981), p. 185.
13. Van den Berghe, *The Ethnic Phenomenon*, op. cit., p. 188.
14. Van den Berghe, *The Ethnic Phenomenon*, op. cit., p. 191.
15. Van den Berghe, *The Ethnic Phenomenon*, op. cit., p. 193.

16. Van den Berghe, *The Ethnic Phenomenon*, op. cit., p. 213.
17. Both Lijphart and van den Berghe are intellectual descendants of the theorists of the plural society (see chapter 7), Lijphart perhaps even more than van den Berghe. Lijphart argues that his critics 'seriously underestimate the strength and persistence of segmental divisions. These are social facts'. (From *Power-Sharing in South Africa*, op. cit., p. 108). My point is there are no such things as 'social facts,' only social constructions with more or less short lives and always in flux.
18. Van den Berghe, *The Ethnic Phenomenon*, op. cit., p. 241.
19. Van den Berghe, *The Ethnic Phenomenon*, op. cit., p. 247.
20. Van den Berghe, *The Ethnic Phenomenon*, op. cit., p. 80.
21. Lijphart cites the authority of Robert Dahl (in *Power-Sharing in South Africa*, op. cit., p. 110) in support of his contention that consociational democracy is 'perfectly democratic' (p. 111) because half the democracies in Dahl's top eight are consociational democracies. However, Dahl's whole concept of democracy or 'polyarchy' is based on voting and choosing alternatives in a decision process, the sanctity and significance of which constitutes the central myth of the vitality of contemporary so-called mass democracies.
22. Lijphart, *Democracy in Plural Societies*, op. cit., p. 169.
23. Lijphart, *Democracy in Plural Societies*, op. cit., pp. 112–13.
24. Lijphart, *Democracy in Plural Societies*, op. cit., p. 109.
25. Lijphart, *Democracy in Plural Societies*, op. cit., p. 129.
26. Lijphart, *Power-Sharing in South Africa*, op. cit., p. 108
27. Lijphart, *Democracy in Plural Societies*, op. cit., p. 153.
28. It is not clear, however, if India is plural according to Lijphart's latest criteria: (*a*) can the plural segments be 'clearly identified'; (*b*) can the size of each be 'exactly determined'; (*c*) do segmented boundaries coincide with political, social, and economic; (*d*) do 'segmental parties receive the stable electoral support of their respective segments?' (*Power-Sharing in South Africa*, op. cit., p. 87). By these standards, India is not. My points, however, are that (*a*) the standards themselves are unrealistic or are artifacts or impositions on the normal complexities of plural societies and that (*b*) even where such plural segmentation exists, it is unwise to reenforce it.
29. For a full statement of the argument here, see Paul R. Brass, *Language, Religion, and Politics in North India* (Cambridge: Cambridge University Press, 1974).
30. Lijphart wants to make it not 'purely majoritarian' (*Power-Sharing in South Africa*, op. cit., p. 103) and, therefore, a case that does not contradict consociational theory. I give him an out in fn. 28 above by saying it is not completely plural either. However, if it is *not* completely plural, I do not know what societies are *more* plural.
31. Despite the sharpness of the critique of consociational theory in this chapter, I want to acknowledge that I have found much of Lijphart's work useful and relevant to my own work on India, particularly in my *Language, Religion, and Politics* and in some of my work on Punjab. I found especially useful *The Politics of Accommodation: Pluralism and Democracy in the Netherlands* (Berkeley: University of California Press, 1968) because of its recognition of the independent role of parties and leaders in social conflict situations, which I

extended to develop a further argument that political parties and leaders in modern times actually *reshape* the boundaries of the groups and communities they lead. I also argued that politics in Punjab has at times contained features of 'segmented pluralism,' consociational democracy, and politics of accommodation, but that segmentation was not complete and parties were not fully institutionalized. See Paul R. Brass, 'Ethnic Cleavages and the Punjab Party System, 1952–1972,' in Myron Weiner (ed.), *Studies in the Electoral Politics of Indian States*, Vol. IV: *Party Systems and Cleavages* (Delhi: Manohar, 1975), pp. 7–69). I also believe that Mrs. Gandhi's adversarial politics in Punjab in the late 1970s and early 1980s destroyed the peace of Punjab. However, while I have always favored pluralist solutions to ethnic–communal problems in India in general and in Punjab in particular, I depart from Lijphart in being unwilling to consider strengthening of segmentation as desirable and as the only solution for deeply divided societies such as Punjab.

32. Sammy Smooha, 'Control of Minorities in Israel and Northern Ireland,' *Comparative Studies in Society and History*, Vol. XXII, No. 2 (April 1980), pp. 256–80.

33. This closing sentence places me among those who hold 'the cynical view that segmented leaders promote both pluralism and consociationalism for their own selfish purposes.' (Lijphart, *Power-Sharing in South Africa*, p. 107). Skepticism would be a less pejorative and more acceptable term under the circumstances or, perhaps, realism.

Acknowledgments

All the essays in this volume except the last were originally published eleswhere. The original sources are given below in the order of their appearance as chapters in this volume.

Chapters 1 and 2: Originally published as a single introductory chapter, 'Ethnic Groups and Nationalities: The Formation, Persistence, and Transformation of Ethnic Identities over Time,' in Peter F. Sugar (ed.), *Ethnic Diversity and Conflict in Eastern Europe* (Santa Barbara: ABC Clio, 1980), pp. 1–68.

Chapter 3: 'Elite Groups, Symbol Manipulation, and Ethnic Identity Among the Muslims of South Asia,' in David Taylor and Malcolm Yapp (eds.), *Political Identity in South Asia* (London: Curzon Press, 1979), pp. 35–77.

Chapter 4: 'Pluralism, Regionalism, and Decentralizing Tendencies in Contemporary Indian Politics,' in A. Jeyaratnam Wilson and Deniis Dalton (eds.), *The States of South Asia: Problems of National Integration* (London: C. Hurst & Co. and Honolulu: University of Hawaii Press, 1982), pp. 223–64.

Chapter 5: 'The Punjab Crisis and the Unity of India,' in Atul Kohli (ed.), *India's Democracy: An Analysis of Changing State–Society Relations* (Princeton, NJ: Princeton University Press), pp. 169–213.

Chapter 6: 'Socio-Economic Aspects of the Punjab Crisis.' Not yet published.

Chapter 7: 'Ethnic Groups and the State,' in Paul R. Brass (ed.), *Ethnic Groups and the State* (London: Croom Helm, 1985), pp. 1–56.

Chapter 8: 'Language and National Identity in the Soviet Union and India,' in Alexander J. Motyl (ed.), *Thinking Theoretically About Soviet Nationalities* (New York: Columbia University Press, forthcoming).

Chapter 9: Not previously published.

Index

354

ETHNICITY AND NATIONALISM

Guru Gobind Singh Marg, 185

Habermas, 251
Habsburg Emperor, 60
Haqqi, S.A.H., 115
Hardy, P., 87
Harrison, Selig, 118
Haryana, 126, 174, 175, 201, 203–8,
    211, 221, 290
Hellenic civilization, 32
Hechter, M., 252, 260, 266
'High Command', 320
Hindi language, 77, 290, 306, 307, 314
Hindi movement, 118
Hindi-Urdu controversy, 83, 85, 98
Hindu(s), 195, 222, 223; elite, 30, 98;
    identity, 75–86; killing of, in
    Punjab, 202; -Muslim relations,
    79–80, 169, 282; -Muslim con-
    flicts, 78, 83; -Muslim riots,
    170; nationalism, 207, 208;
    revivalism, 79–80, 92; -Sikh
    relations, 174, 177, 225, 230,
    289
Hindu Code Acts 1955–56, 81
Hindu Mahasabha, 79
Hungary, 34, 35, 288

identity formation, 62, 101, 268–70, 278
INC(U), 140
India, 28, 49, 60, 61, 341, 344; language
    and national identity in, 300ff
India: The Most Dangerous Decades,
    118
Indian Administrative Service, 119,
    321–22
Indian Civil Service, 322
Indian National Congress, 78, 317; see
    also, Congress
Indonesia, 336
industrialization, 25, 34, 35, 131
interest group approach, 255, 257, 292
interethnic conflict, 57, 324–26
internal colonial theories, 250–52
Islamic beliefs, 88, 92
Islamic symbols, 102
Islamic values, 76
Israel, 49, 73

Jacob, S., 209
Jagat Narain, Lala, 179, 180, 202, 203
Jami'yat-al-ulama, 89, 90
Janata government, 126–29, 131, 147,
    172, 173, 209
Janata Party, 128, 138, 140, 153, 186,
    226
Jan Sangh, 79, 209, 291, see also
    Bharatiya Janata Party
Jat Sikh(s), 227–29; base for Akali
    Dal, 226; peasants, 178, 186,
    195–97, 224–26
Jews, 34, 35, 48, 49, 74; deportation
    of, 50, 51; ethnic separatism,
    25; minority in Russia, 325–26;
    traders in Eastern Europe, 43
Jinnah, M.A., 93, 94, 100, 343
job competition, 307–8

Kairon, Pratap Singh, 175, 176, 177,
    184, 185, 187, 290
Kamaraj Nadar, 143
Kamaraj Plan, 147, 152
Kashmir issue, 156, 169, 212, 213,
    318, 319, 329
Kashmiris, 301
Kazakhstan, 320
Kenya, 42, 43
Kerala, 133, 140, 141, 143, 156;
    Muslims in, 90; President's
    Rule in, 144–45
Keshadhari Sikhs, 189, 190
Key, V.O., Jr., 122, 123
Khalistan, demand for, 188, 200, 229;
    supporters of, 183, 230; Bhind-
    ranwale and, 197–99
Khatris, Punjabi, 222, 223
Khan, Ayub, 55
Khan, Sayyid Ahmad, 88, 90, 92
Khilafat movement, 93
Khrushchev, N., 319
King, Martin Luther, 49
kinship relationships, 71
Kirgizia, 320
Kuper, 256, 260, 262, 266

Labour Party, 56
Laitin, David, 281
Lal, Bhajan, 193